Ben-Gurion's Spy

The Story of the Political Scandal
That Shaped Modern Israel

Ben-Gurion's Spy

The Story of the Political Scandal
That Shaped Modern Israel

Shabtai Teveth

Columbia University Press
New York

New York   Chichester, West Sussex

Library of Congress Cataloging-in-Publication Data
Teveth, Shabtai,
    Ben-Gurion's spy : the story of the political scandal that shaped
  modern Israel / Shabtai Teveth.
        p.   cm.
    Includes bibliographical references and index.
    ISBN 0-231-10464-2
    1. Israel—Politics and government. 2. Givly, Benjamin, 1919–
  3. Lavon, Pinhas, 1904– . 4. Ben-Gurion, David, 1886–1973.
  5. Intelligence Service—Israel. 6. Israel. Tseva haganah le
  -Yiśra'el. Agaf modi' in. 7. Espionage, Israeli—Egypt.
  8. Operation Susannah. I. Title
  DS126.5.T48   1996
  956.9405'2—dc20   95-43068

Contents

vi   Contents

Preface
The Fissure and the Abyss

In 1955 Pinhas Lavon, Israel's defense minister, was forced to resign his office as a consequence of a series of disastrous sabotage operations carried out in Egypt the previous summer by Israeli undercover agents, for whose acts he was ultimately responsible. For five years he plotted a campaign to rehabilitate himself. Then, in 1960, Lavon charged that his fall from office was the result of a conspiracy hatched by Military Intelligence officers of the Israel Defense Force, acting in league with Chief of Staff General Moshe Dayan and Director General of the ministry of defense, Shimon Peres, the "whizz kids" of former Prime Minister and Minister of Defense David Ben-Gurion.

Lavon's charge triggered the virtual earthquake now known as the "Lavon Affair," which rocked Israel and set in action a chain of events that in 1963 brought down Ben-Gurion, the country's founding father. For nearly twelve years the Lavon Affair was a hotly debated issue, the details of whose inception, development, and conclusion became public property; there was not a child who did not know of the failed sabotage operations in Egypt (commonly referred to as the "Sad Mishap") and of Lavon's accusations and his demand for rehabilitation. Ultimately, the affair heralded the demise of Mapai, Ben-Gurion's Labor Party—that had governed the Jewish Community in Palestine, and later the state of Israel, since 1933—paving the way for the reign of Menahem Begin and his revisionist

Likud party, which came to power in 1977. Indeed, the Lavon Affair lies
at the root of Israeli politics and the position of Israel in the world today.

The origins of the Lavon Affair go back to the formative years of the
state, specifically to June 1948, at the height of the War of Independence, and the blood-curdling drumhead court-martial and execution
by a firing squad of Meir Tubiansky, an innocent army captain who had
been accused of treason—a scandal which only recently has received the
public attention and censure it deserves. It was Benyamin Givly, oppor-
tunistically seeking to further his career in Military Intelligence (MI) by
catching and trying the first Israeli traitor, who was largely responsible
for this miscarriage of justice. Givly's disrespect for the truth, revealed
during the subsequent inquiries, which cleared Tubiansky, and the later
trials of then-DMI Isser Be'eri, can be seen as a harbinger of his later
behavior at the inquiries into the "Sad Mishap."

The whole story is indeed a strange one. The episodes comprising
it—the Tubiansky execution and the Egyptian sabotage operations—
seem, at first sight, completely separate and unrelated. They resemble
pieces of a giant jigsaw puzzle scrambled and hidden away by history,
which had to be found, sorted out, and pieced together. Observing the
pattern thus revealed makes one wonder: was it the result of accident
and coincidence, a simple play of chance, or was it the product of conditions and circumstances unique to Israel? Here was a people with a historic past, a rich legacy and a common dream, but who were newcomers
to their old land, possessing hardly any experience of common national
life. Was history trying to teach us that it is impossible to go contrary to
its course—that a people who have spent two thousand years in exile
cannot become a nation and a state—and surely not at the expense of
another people?

Or, beyond its historical significance, and the insight it provides into
Israel's political life and issues of foreign affairs and defense, is this simply a human story: one might say, the story of the fall of the great?

It tells, first, of David Ben-Gurion, Israel's by now legendary founding
father, its visionary and first prime minister and minister of defense.
Ben-Gurion first became a national figure in 1935, when he was elected
chairman of the Jewish Agency Executive. In 1960 he was seventy-four,
and had been the leader of the Jewish community in Palestine for twen-
ty-five years. His is the story of a leader who stayed too long in power.

Second, it is the story of the fall of Israel's most brilliant diplomat and
first minister of foreign affairs, Moshe Sharett, a devout ally who in the

end turned against his idol. In the summer of 1956, Ben-Gurion forced Sharett to resign as foreign minister because their policies conflicted. Sharett thus lost not only the ministry he had founded, but also the practice of diplomacy, the love of his life, the field in which he had worked since 1932 and the only profession in which he was second to none. To add insult to injury, in 1957 Ben-Gurion accused him, falsely as it turned out, of not having done enough as foreign minister to secure for Israel the weapons it needed for the 1956 Sinai Campaign. Sharett never forgave him, and this, perhaps, was why he supported Lavon in 1960. He died a bitter man in 1965.

And third, it is the story of the fall of the enigmatic Lavon, arguably the most intellectually gifted of all Israeli statesmen. Once he was tapped by Ben-Gurion himself as his successor, there was nothing in the way of his ascendancy but his own peculiar personality: brave, independent, sharp, and unpredictably destructive. In his wrath he destroyed his admirer-turned-foe, Ben-Gurion, his party, and most of all himself.

Compromising links between obscure figures and prominent leaders have created scandals so unstoppable that they brought down a presidency or a government. In this respect the Lavon Affair ranks with the Watergate and Profumo scandals. It would never have assumed such proportions but for a series of unlikely connections. The first was that between Benyamin Givly, an intelligence officer destined to obscurity except for his misconduct in the willful execution of Tubiansky, and his role in bringing down the formidable Ben-Gurion. The second connection was between Levi Eshkol, the powerful minister of finance and Ben-Gurion's successor as prime minister, and his secretary Dalia Carmel. As a young conscript she had previously served as Givly's secretary, becoming both Givly's unwitting co-conspirator in a plot to get Lavon removed from office, and a party to a secret on which hung Givly's military career as well as Ben-Gurion's political future.

Specifically, Givly and Ben-Gurion starred in both parts of the Lavon Affair; Eshkol and Carmel, who became lovers, only in the second. Playing supporting but crucial roles, as both jury and judge, were Labor's veterans—including Sharett and Golda Meir, his successor—as well as Dayan and Peres. Last but not least was Isser Harel, the redoubtable second boss of Mossad, who jealously guarded Mossad's right to oversee foreign MI operations. He tenaciously fought Givly, his competitor in intelligence affairs, as well as Dayan and Peres, his rivals for Ben-Gurion's ear and succession.

The story of the Lavon affair is, finally, that of the foundation of Israel's secret service, from the wartime Haganah Intelligence Service, to the special operations of Military Intelligence, to Mossad. If the leopard can change its spots—that is, if it is possible for a people to go contrary to its history and for Jewish Israel to live in Palestine, a tiny island in an Arab Muslim ocean—partly indifferent, partly accepting, but mostly hostile—it must have excellent Intelligence and exceptional armed services, in peace and in war.

Israel's intelligence service plays a more crucial role in its society than does the CIA in the U.S., mainly because Israel depends on a system of reserves, who make up the majority of the country's armed forces. If the armed forces were constantly maintained at full strength, the country would collapse socially and economically. Thus it keeps only a small part of its military mobilized, relying on Mossad and MI to alert it to impending attack. Faulty intelligence can cost Israel its existence, as it nearly did in 1973, at time of the Yom Kippur war. This may explain the high regard in which Israelis hold Mossad and MI, knowing that were it not for them, a far larger portion of the citizenry would have to remain on active duty for the better part of their lives.

What follows is a factual account of all the narrative elements of the Lavon affair, based on solid evidence supplied by official documents—including minutes of courts, boards of inquiry, and party conferences—private letters, and interviews with most of the principal actors.

The tale about to unfold is both ordinary and extraordinary. Though primarily an account of villains plotting mischief, so common a theme in human society, it is uncommon as well. Seldom does a wrong inflicted by one individual on another, as when Givly caused the execution of Tubiansky, affect a whole society. Very rarely does a fissure open into an abyss, as it did in this particular chapter of Israel's history. In this case, not only did a government and a great leader tumble into the abyss, but so did an entire political establishment.

Whatever other lessons Israel must glean from the Lavon Affair, its moral aspect is clear. The principles of the prophets—justice, equality before the law, strict prohibition of perjury and intentional mistrial, truth, humility, mutual aid, helping the weak and not taking advantage of them—involve more than religious observance, respect for ancient teachings, or even a preferable way of life. They are mandatory for Israel's existence. Without justice and peace, it is doubtful that Israel can overcome the odds that have been against it since its birth.

In the past, the nation's citizen soldiers, unlike politicians, put their lives on the line, their willingness to serve and sacrifice being affected by the moral climate that prevailed. Not so after the Lavon Affair and the Yom Kippur War. It seems they now demand that a fissure in the moral foundation of their society be tended to promptly, before it assumes the gigantic proportions of an abyss.

Shabtai Teveth, Tel Aviv, November 1995

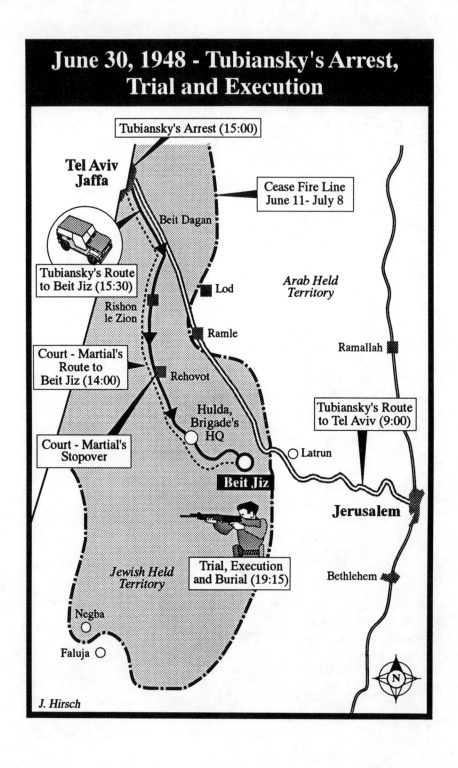

June 30, 1948 - Tubiansky's Arrest, Trial and Execution

Tubiansky's Arrest (15:00)

Tel Aviv
Jaffa

Cease Fire Line
June 11- July 8

Beit Dagan

Tubiansky's Route
to Beit Jiz (15:30)

*Arab Held
Territory*

Lod

Rishon
le Zion

Ramle

Ramallah

Court - Martial's
Route to
Beit Jiz (14:00)

Rehovot

Hulda,
Brigade's
HQ

Tubiansky's Route
to Tel Aviv (9:00)

Court - Martial's
Stopover

Latrun

Beit Jiz

Jerusalem

*Jewish Held
Territory*

Trial, Execution
and Burial (19:15)

Bethlehem

Negba

Faluja

N

J. Hirsch

Glossary

AHDUT HAAVODAH
Hebrew for United Labor, a party founded by Ben-Gurion and others in 1920, from which arose Mapai in 1930. Revived as opposition party to Ben-Gurion in 1944.

AMIAD COMMITTEE
A joint IDF-Mossad committee appointed in 1958 to investigate unit 131's falling into Egyptian hands in July 1954, and determine whether it had been betrayed by Elad, its commander, or any of its members.

CAIRO TRIAL
The trial of 13 Jews charged with spying for Israel before Egypt's Supreme Military Tribunal, which opened in Cairo on November 11, 1954. Only 10 of the accused were present: two (Dar and Elad) were sentenced to death in absentia, and a third (Binnet) committed suicide before he was called to testify. Verdict and sentences were handed down on January 27, 1955: Two sentenced to death, two to life imprisonment, two to 15 years, two to 7, and two acquitted. Yosef Cremona was found dead before the trial began, allegedly by suicide. He was an innocent man who died under interrogation.

COHEN COMMITTEE
An IDF inquiry board, appointed by COS Haim Laskov on Ben-Gurion's instruction on October 12, 1960, to look into alleged MI "forgeries," headed by Haim Cohen. It handed down its conclusions on October 15, 1960.

DMI
Director of Military Intelligence; chief of military intelligence branch or department of IDF.

ETZEL
Hebrew acronym for *Irgun Tzvai Leumi* (national army organization), a dissident Jewish underground militia, close to the rightist Zionist Revisionist party. Also known in English as "Irgun" and IZL. With the establishment of IDF it expired.

HAGANAH
Hebrew for "defense"; the underground Jewish militia in Palestine (1920–1948) that became the national army of Israel after the partition of Palestine in 1948.

HISTADRUT
Israel's General Federation of [Trade Unions and] Labor, founded in December 1920.

IDF
Israel Defense Forces, literal translation of Hebrew *Tzvai Haganah LeIsrael* (Zahal), sworn in in June 1948.

JAG
Acronym for Judge Advocate General, head of the military legal service of Haganah and later IDF.

LAVON AFFAIR
Scandal created by Lavon's demand for rehabilitation as minister of defense, and the campaign waged by him and his supporters and opponents for and against it (1960–1964).

LEHI
Hebrew acronym for *Lohamei Herut Israel* (Fighters for Israel's Freedom), dissident Jewish underground that broke away from Etzel, known in English as "the Stern Gang" and FFI. On the establishment of IDF it expired.

MA'ARAH
"Alignment," the union of Mapai and Ahdut HaAvodah, which lasted from 1964 to December 1968.

MAPAI
Acronym for *Mifleget Poale Eretz Israel* (Palestine Labor Party), founded in 1930, united with *Ahdut HaAvodah* in 1968 as Israel's Labor party (*Mifleget HaAvodah*).

MAPAM

Acronym for *Mifleget HaPoalim HaMeuhedet* (United Workers Party), founded in 1948 by the union of *Ahdut HaAvodah* and *HaShomer HaTzair* (a marxist Zionist party) as opposition to Mapai.

MI

Military Intelligence, which replaced SHAI when IDF was created in June 1948. Until the end of 1953 it was a department in the General Staff Branch (i.e., division) of the army's General Staff Headquarters. After that date MI was elevated into a branch in its own right.

MISHAP

Term used to refer to failed sabotage operations by MI's Unit 131 in Cairo and Alexandria in July 1954, which had been intended to foil the Anglo-Egyptian Suez accord. Ben-Zur's report of October 5, 1954, listed eight operations (both real and imaginary) between July 2 and 23: 1. Incendiary device placed in Alexandria's parcel post office; 2. Incendiary device placed at the American Library in Alexandria (Ben-Zur later admitted that he included these two operations in the report in order to enhance Unit 131's "credit"); 3. Incendiary device placed at the American Library in Cairo; 4. and 5. Incendiary devices activated in cinemas in Alexandria and Cairo; 6. explosive device placed at Cairo's railway terminal (said by Elad to have been a dud, this device is believed to be the product of his imagination); 7. explosive device placed at an Alexandria port warehouse (dud and probably imaginary, like 6); 8. incendiary device placed in an Alexandria cinema that went off prematurely.

MOSSAD

Abbreviation of *HaMossad Lemodiin VeTafkidim Meyuhadim* (agency for intelligence and special services).

MOSSAD LEALIYA BETH

Agency for Illegal Jewish Immigration to Palestine under the British mandatory government. It received and hid illegal immigrants and facilitated secret Jewish illegal immigration from countries that outlawed Jewish emigration. It was the foundation from which sprang Mossad.

OLSHAN-DORI COMMITTEE

Secretly appointed by Sharett on January 2, 1955, to investigate who had given the order for the "mishap." It presented its inconclusive findings on January 12.

PALMACH

Acronym for *Plugot Mahatz* (Striking Force), Haganah's elite combat force, founded in 1941.

RAFI

Acronym for *Reshimat Poalei Israel* (Israel's Workers' Ticket), the party Ben-Gurion founded and led after the split in Mapai in the summer of 1965.

SEVEN-MEMBER CABINET COMMITTEE

Ministerial Committee elected on October 30, 1960, to advise the cabinet on resolving the Lavon Affair.

SHAI

Acronym for *Sherut Yediot* (Intelligence Service) of the Haganah.

SHIN BETH

Abbreviation of SHIN BETH KAF, acronym for *Sherut Habitahon HaKlali* (General Security Service).

UNIT 131

Section of MI comprised of secret units in enemy countries, assigned to act primarily in time of war.

WAR OF INDEPENDENCE

Israel's term for the war between Jews and Arabs in Palestine, between December 1947 and May 15, 1948, and the war between Israel and five Arab states, May 15, 1948–July 1949, concluded by armistice agreements.

YERUHAM

Code name of chief SHAI officer, Jerusalem.

Chronology

I. The Tubiansky Affair

1946   APRIL:

David Shaltiel appointed head of SHAI, Isser Be'eri appointed his deputy.

1947   NOVEMBER 29:

UN resolution to partition Palestine into an Arab state and a Jewish state.

DECEMBER 2:

Arabs set fire to Jerusalem's commercial center in protest of UN resolution. On the Jewish side, this begins the War of Independence.

1948   FEBRUARY:

Isser Be'eri succeeds Shaltiel as head of SHAI; Shaltiel appointed Haganah General Officer Commanding, Jerusalem.

MARCH:

Benyamin Givly appointed head of SHAI, Jerusalem.

APRIL:

Jewish Jerusalem under Arab-Jordanian siege and bombardment.

APRIL 27:

Givly assumes SHAI command in Jerusalem.

MAY 14:

Declaration of Independence and establishment of the state of Israel.

MAY 15:

Arab armies invade Palestine. Jerusalem is officially split into a Jewish part and a Jordanian-Arab part.

MAY 21:

Haganah becomes Israel's national army (IDF).

JUNE 11:

First cease-fire becomes effective. Givly leaves Jerusalem and quits his position as Yeruham, according to one of his claims.

JUNE 16:

Tubiansky's conversation with Michael Bryant, British manager of the Jewish section of the Jerusalem Electric Corporation, seen and overheard by his colleague Aharon Eliezer Cohen and reported to SHAI.

JUNE 20:

Givly, called to Tel Aviv, is absent from Jerusalem, according to one of his depositions.

JUNE 20 OR 21:

Fritz (Dov) Sinai's first report on Tubiansky.

JUNE 22:

On this day, most likely, Givly orders Yaski to prepare a "second" report on Tubiansky.

JUNE 25:

Yaski hands in the "additional," "second," and ultimately "final" report on Tubiansky.

JUNE 25:

Most likely the date of Givly's meeting with Jerusalem commander and JAG.

JUNE 25:

In Tel Aviv, Givly hands in Be'eri Yaski's "additional" report with a covering letter signed by Givly.

JUNE 30:

Ben-Gurion present at afternoon inaugural parade of IDF's navy in Haifa.

JUNE 30:

Last SHAI meeting of senior officers, to inaugurate inception of MI; Givly is appointed head of MI1, its most important department.

JUNE 30:

Tubiansky arrested by SHAI agents in Tel Aviv and driven to Beit Jiz for court-martial.

JUNE 30:

At conclusion of SHAI's valedictory meeting, Be'eri, Givly, and two other SHAI officers set out for court-martial at Beit Jiz. At 19:15 Tubiansky is executed by a Palmach firing squad.

JULY 1:

Ben-Gurion visits Haifa aerodrome and returns by air to Tel Aviv. Be'eri reports to him in Tel Aviv on Tubiansky's execution.

JULY 8:

End of first cease-fire; the war is renewed on all fronts.

JULY 12:

Be'eri is officially appointed DMI.

JULY 20:

In response to inquiries by her lawyer, Mrs. Tubiansky is told that her husband has been found guilty of treason by a field court-martial, which has ordered his execution. The public announcement made that day omits Tubiansky's name.

DECEMBER 9:

Ben-Gurion orders Be'eri's dismissal.

DECEMBER 27:

Ben-Gurion orders JAG Hoter-Ishai to investigate Tubiansky's trial and execution, in order to bring those responsible to trial.

1949   FEBRUARY 9:

Military tribunal sentences Be'eri to be discharged from IDF in connection with the unlawful execution of Ali Kassem, an Arab SHAI informant.

FEBRUARY 11:

The general amnesty in honor of the establishment of Israel comes into force.

MARCH 3:

JAG Hoter-Ishai begins investigation of Tubiansky's trial and execution and interrogation of Be'eri, Gorali, Givly, and others.

MARCH 15:

Givly appointed MI deputy chief.

JUNE 26:

JAG Hoter-Ishai submits to Ben-Gurion his report on Tubiansky's mistrial and execution.

JULY 1:

Ben-Gurion informs Mrs. Tubiansky of her husband's exoneration and of the decision to bring those responsible to trial. On July 3

Ben-Gurion issues a public exoneration of Tubiansky and restitution of his rank and rights. On July 7 Tubiansky is laid to rest in a military ceremony in IDF's burial grounds on Mount Herzl near Jerusalem.

JULY 17:

Israeli police begin investigation of Tubiansky's trial and execution and interrogation of Be'eri, Givly, and others.

AUGUST 12:

Examining magistrate holds preliminary hearings and on August 23 refers the case to the Tel Aviv district court.

NOVEMBER 17:

Tel Aviv district court hears Attorney General Shapira's reasons for bringing to trial only Be'eri. Givly appears as a witness for the prosecution.

NOVEMBER 22:

Tel Aviv District Court finds Be'eri guilty of manslaughter committed "in the heat of battle" and sentences him "to imprisonment for one day, from sunrise to sunset." Presidential pardon given on the same day enables Be'eri to avoid this imprisonment.

1950   JANUARY:

Givly promoted to Lieutenant Colonel.

JUNE 6:

Givly appointed DMI.

1958   JANUARY 30:

Be'eri dies of heart attack.

II. The Mishap

1952   JULY 22–23:

Military coup in Egypt.

SEPTEMBER 12:

Elad accepted into Unit 131 on a trial basis.

1953   FEBRUARY 22:

Givly goes on study leave to the U.S.; Harkabi becomes acting DMI.

MARCH 30:

Elad leaves for Europe as an MI undercover agent.

APRIL:

Ben-Zur appointed commander of Unit 131.

JULY 19–OCTOBER 18:

Ben-Gurion takes a three-month leave; Lavon becomes acting minister of defense and Sharett acting prime minister.

LATE OCTOBER:

Almog meets Elad in Paris for reevaluation.

DECEMBER:

MI elevated from department status to Intelligence Branch, under Harkabi as acting DMI.

DECEMBER 6:

Dayan appointed IDF's 4th chief of staff.

DECEMBER 7:

Ben-Gurion resigns and leaves for his desert retreat at Sdeh Boker. Lavon becomes minister of defense, Sharett becomes prime minister.

DECEMBER 23:

Elad makes his first visit to Egypt as Paul Frank.

1954   FEBRUARY 24:

Colonel Abdul Nasser assumes control in Egypt.

MARCH 2:

Elad makes his second visit to Egypt under the same cover.

MARCH 28:

Givly resumes his position as DMI; Harkabi goes to Paris on a study leave.

APRIL-MAY:

In Evron's presence, Lavon and Givly discuss how to prevent an Anglo-Egyptian accord on British withdrawal from the Suez Zone.

MAY 26:

Ben-Zur leaves for Paris.

MAY 30:

Ben-Zur meets Elad in Paris, appoints him commander of Unit 131 Egypt. Elad will argue later that at this time he has been given operational orders. According to Mossad chief Harel, Elad was then already in the employ of Egypt's military intelligence.

JUNE 25:

Elad, as commander of Unit 131 Egypt, sails from Europe to Egypt for the third time.

JUNE 28:

Elad cables Ben-Zur in Israel, "Shipment Possible" (code words meaning "ready for operations").

JULY 2:

Unit 131's first operation (Alexandria parcel post).

JULY 12:

Dayan leaves for month-long visit to U.S. army and military bases.

JULY 14:

Unit 131's second operation (American Library attached to U.S. embassy in Cairo and American Library in Alexandria set on fire).

JULY 14:

Egyptian radio reports that July 2 fire was a sabotage operation.

JULY 14/15:

A "reliable source" informs MI that Anglo-Egyptian accord is to be signed on the 23rd.

JULY 15:

Weekly meeting of IDF with minister of defense Lavon. Avidar, acting chief of staff, sits in for Dayan.

JULY 16 (FRIDAY):

First Egyptian official communique on sabotage operations.

JULY 16 (FRIDAY):

Lavon's 50th birthday party at his home.

JULY 16 (FRIDAY AFTERNOON):

According to Givly, Lavon orders him, face to face, to commence Unit 131 operations in Egypt, at the conclusion of the weekly IDF meeting at Lavon's home.

JULY 16 (LATE FRIDAY AFTERNOON):

Givly orders Ben-Zur to start Unit 131 operations in Egypt.

JULY 17:

Ben-Zur sends Elad agreed-on code to "start operations" through Israel Broadcasting Authority's radio program. Broadcasts of code continue through July 25.

JULY 19:

In Alexandria, Elad negotiates sale of his car.

JULY 23:

Unit 131's operations at cinemas in Cairo and Alexandria. According to official Egyptian communique, a policeman on duty at the Rio cinema in Alexandria observed Philip Natanson's clothing set on fire by a prematurely activated firebomb.

JULY 26:

Israeli press publishes Egyptian reports of arrests of "subversive" Jews. Givly sends note informing Lavon of these arrests.

JULY 27:

Anglo-Egyptian accord is initialed. Egyptian ministry of the interior publishes description of "mishap" operations.

JULY 31:

Arrest of Shmuel Azar.

AUGUST 1:

At Givly's request Ben-Zur hands him his first "report on operations in Egypt"; Givly keeps report to himself.

AUGUST 5:

Arrest of Meir Meyuhas and Dr. Moshe Marzouk.

AUGUST 7:

Elad leaves Egypt by plane, carrying with him 131's miniature transmitter.

AUGUST 8:

Marcelle Ninio arrested in Cairo.

AUGUST 8:

Givly submits to Lavon first operational report, along with a blueprint for renewal of psychological warfare in Egypt.

AUGUST 12:

Master spy Meir (Max) Binnet arrested in Cairo.

AUGUST 14:

Elad arrives secretly in Israel and is met by Ben-Zur and later Givly.

AUGUST 19:

Dayan returns from U.S.

SEPTEMBER 2:

Elad returns to Europe, without having met Lavon or Dayan.

OCTOBER 4:

Dayan tricks Givly into flying to Europe to prepare legal defense for 131 captives in Egypt.

OCTOBER 5:

In Givly's absence Dayan orders Almog, acting DMI, to submit before sundown operational report by Ben-Zur. Ben-Zur complies; his report states that he was ordered on July 16 to broadcast "start operations" code.

OCTOBER 10:

Dayan sends copy of Ben-Zur's new report to Prime Minister Sharett.

OCTOBER 12:

Indictment of Cairo prisoners published in Egypt.

OCTOBER 20:

Givly returns from Europe.

LATER IN OCTOBER:

Dayan orders Givly to complement Ben-Zur's October 5 report by speci-
fiying on whose authority he ordered Ben-Zur to commence oprations
on July 16.

NOVEMBER 1:

Givly submits his report, in the form of a letter addressed to Dayan,
stating that Lavon ordered him on July 16 to activate Unit 131,
Egypt. At Dayan's behest, Givly reports on the "mishap" at General
Staff meeting, claiming again that order was given him by Lavon on
July 16.

NOVEMBER 4:

Lavon receives copy of Givly's November 1 letter and is informed of
Givly's account at the general staff meeting.

DECEMBER 11:

Show trial of Unit 131 prisoners opens in Cairo.

1955   JANUARY 2:

Olshan and Dori appointed by Sharett as inquiry commission and
begin work.

JANUARY 2:

Almog meets Elad in Paris to prepare his testimony before the
Olshan-Dori Inquiry Committee.

JANUARY 4:

Elad arrives in Israel and meets Givly, Dayan, and Lavon, prior to testifying before Olshan-Dori Committee.

JANUARY 12:

Olshan-Dori, unable to decide whether Lavon or Givly ordered Unit
131 to act in Egypt, submit to Sharett an inconclusive report.

III. The Lavon Affair

1954   MARCH 26:

Avriel proposes to Ben-Gurion establishment of a new party.

MAY 8:

Ben-Gurion urges Mapai to introduce "English [regional] elections"
instead of the prevalent proportional representation system.

1955   FEBRUARY:
        Elad leaves for Europe as Paul Frank, his old cover.
        FEBRUARY 16:
        LaMerhav, Ahdut HaAvodah's newspaper, reveals deliberations of
        Olshan-Dori Committee.
        FEBRUARY 17:
        For the first time, Israeli press ignores prime minister's request and
        publishes details of mishap and Olshan-Dori Committee.
        FEBRUARY 17:
        Sharett and other Mapai leaders beseech Ben-Gurion to resume posi-
        tion of minister of defense.
        FEBRUARY 17:
        Lavon confirms that his resignation from cabinet is final.
        FEBRUARY 21:
        The Knesset approves Ben-Gurion's return to the cabinet as minister
        of defense.
        MARCH:
        In Paris, Elad reveals to Harkabi his encounter with Almog in January.
        MARCH 7:
        Givly quits MI.
        MAY 2:
        In London, Dalia Carmel reveals to Harkabi that she forged the copy
        of Givly's letter to chief of staff Dayan of July 19, 1954.
        MAY 9:
        Harkabi returns to Israel from Paris; next day he tells Dayan about
        Givly's "forgeries."
        MAY 15:
        Harkabi appointed DMI. Dayan charges him with inquiry into MI
        "forgeries." Harkabi threatens to resign; Ben-Gurion and Dayan back
        down and rescind the order.
        JULY 26:
        General elections, Knesset and municipalities. Mapai loses five of its
        45 seats, out of 120. Yet Ben-Gurion is able to put together a new cab-
        inet and to resume his former positions of prime minister and minis-
        ter of defense. Sharett remains minister for foreign affairs.

1956   JANUARY:
        Elad called back from Europe because Isser Harel considers him a secu-
        rity risk, but he wins the confidence of Harkabi and Yossi Harel (his new
        commander) and sets out again for Europe, once more as Paul Frank.

JANUARY:

Ben-Gurion appoints Lavon chairman of War Emergency Economic Committee and demonstrates in other ways appreciation of Lavon's talents and political prowess.

MAY:

With Ben-Gurion's support, Lavon is elected secretary general of the Histadrut.

JUNE 6:

Sharett loses Ben-Gurion's confidence and is forced to resign as minister for foreign affairs.

JULY:

Givly appointed commander of regular infantry brigade (the Golany).

OCTOBER:

Sinai war against Egypt (known as the "collusion" between Israel, Britain, and France). Dayan becomes a national hero.

1957   JANUARY:

Ben-Gurion publicly offends Sharett. Lavon appoints Hayerushalmi as Histadrut spokesman.

NOVEMBER:

Dalia Carmel becomes Eshkol's secretary at ministry of finance.

NOVEMBER 2:

Nehemia Argov, Ben-Gurion's trusted ADC, commits suicide.

DECEMBER 12:

Investigation of Elad's contacts with Egyptian intelligence officers commences at Ramle prison, where he is in custody.

DECEMBER 26:

Aharoni and Cohen, suspecting Elad betrayed Unit 131 in Egypt, concentrate on this in their investigation.

1958   MARCH 19:

Leaks concerning Elad's interrogation by Amiad Committee constitute the initial connection between the mishap and the Lavon affair.

MARCH:

Veterans' fear of putsch, part of Lavon's laying the groundwork for his rehabilitation campaign.

MAY 25:

Dayan initiates campaign against Mapai's old guard.

JUNE 7:

Dayan's campaign dubbed "Biological Campaign."

AUGUST 26–30:

Mapai's 8th Conference.

NOVEMBER 11:

After 11 months of leave Dayan is demobilized from IDF, becoming full-fledged candidate in the coming elections for the Mapai party conference.

NOVEMBER 22:

First "reconciliation Sabbath" between Old Guard and Youth in Mapai.

NOVEMBER 27:

Ben-Gurion tells Mapai's central committee that he has been advised to set up dictatorship.

DECEMBER 12:

Second "reconciliation Sabbath."

1959   JULY 7:

Elad's trial opens in closed hearings at Jerusalem's district court. In his testimony Elad reveals that Givly, Almog, and Ben-Zur induced him to perjure himslf before Olshan-Dori Committee.

NOVEMBER 3:

General elections; Mapai's greatest victory ever (47 seats out of 120).

DECEMBER 12:

Ben-Gurion sets up his coalition government—the last he will set up—with the "youth"; Dayan is minister of agriculture, Abba Eban is minister without portfolio, and Peres is deputy minister of defense.

1960   JANUARY:

Givly leaves for London to take office as military attache to the United Kingdom and Scandinavia.

FEBRUARY 4:

Yossi Harel tells Lavon about the "forgeries."

MAY 5:

Lavon reports "Yossi's testimony" to Ben-Gurion, who orders his ADC Ben-David to examine its veracity.

AUGUST 21:

District court sentences Elad to 12 years imprisonment (commuted to 10), and in its judgment gives credence to his allegation that he was led into perjury by his commanders at MI. Excerpts of the judgment are sent by the court to chief of staff Laskov and its gist reaches Lavon.

AUGUST 18:

In light of the district court's judgment, Ben-Gurion orders Laskov to set up a military inquiry board to investigate the "forgeries" and Elad's perjury.

SEPTEMBER 12:

The Cohen Committee is set up to examine the "forgeries."

SEPTEMBER 18:

Lavon demands abolition of Cohen Committee. Ben-Gurion refuses.

SEPTEMBER 26:

Ben-Gurion meets Lavon, who demands exoneration, abolition of Cohen Committe, or at least appointment of another chairman. Ben-Gurion rejects all demands.

SEPTEMBER 29:

Mapai's central committee distances itself from the "affair."

OCTOBER 4:

Lavon's first hearing at the Knesset's Foreign Affairs and Defense Committee.

OCTOBER 10:

Ben-Gurion consults non-Mapai ministers in Sharett's former cabinet.

OCTOBER 11:

Lavon's second hearing at the Foreign Affairs and Defense Committee. Evron leaves to meet with Eshkol in the U.S.

OCTOBER 12:

Givly arrives from London to testify before Cohen Committee.

OCTOBER 15:

Cohen Committee submits its report.

OCTOBER 17:

Lavon's third hearing at the Foreign Affairs and Defense Committee.

OCTOBER 18:

Eshkol returns to Israel and starts reconciliation effort.

OCTOBER 20:

Lavon's fourth and last hearing at the Foreign Affairs and Defense Committee.

OCTOBER 22:

Givly demands a state committee of inquiry; on the 24th he hires attorney Ya'akov Salomon.

OCTOBER 25:

Sharett exonerates Lavon. Ben-Gurion demands a state committee of inquiry.

OCTOBER 30:

Eshkol wins cabinet support for setting up ministerial committee to advise the cabinet on solving the Lavon Affair (the Seven-member committee). First time cabinet votes against Ben-Gurion.

NOVEMBER 3:

Seven-member Committee begins work.

DECEMBER 6:

On behalf of Seven-member Committee, Attorney-General Hausner interrogates Harkabi and Dalia Carmel in Paris. Next day she admits having "changed" the copy of Givly's July 19, 1954, letter to Dayan.

DECEMBER 15:

Interrogated by police in Israel, Carmel retreats from testimony she gave Hausner in Paris.

DECEMBER 20:

Police expert finds copy of Givly's letter to Dayan to be genuine.

DECEMBER 25:

Cabinet endorses findings of Seven-member Committee, which clears Lavon of having given the order in July 1954 which brought about the mishap.

DECEMBER 26:

Ben-Gurion threatens to resign. Eshkol tries to dissuade him.

DECEMBER 30:

A petition calling "for cleansing of the air and restoration of confidence," signed by 50 renowned intellectuals in support of Lavon, is published in the press.

DECEMBER 31:

Givly withdraws his demand for a state committee of inquiry.

1961   JANUARY 31:

Ben-Gurion tenders his resignation to Israel's president. His cabinet is now a caretaker cabinet until he can put together a new cabinet. In accordance with Cohen Committee report, Givly is discharged from IDF.

FEBRUARY 3:

Wanting to mollify Ben-Gurion, Mapai's secretariat decides to dismiss Lavon as Histadrut secretary.

FEBRUARY 4:

Mapai's central committee votes 60 to 40 percent to ratify Lavon's dismissal.

FEBRUARY 16:

Ben-Gurion officially informs the president he is unable to put together a new cabinet; nearly all former coalition partners refuse to join. The president gives him another three weeks.

MARCH 6:

Ben-Gurion informs the president of his failure to form a cabinet. The president charges Eshkol with this task.

AUGUST 15:

General elections. Mapai is now five seats down (42 out of 120) but still the leading party.

NOVEMBER 2:

Ben-Gurion presents his new cabinet—put together by Eshkol—to the Knesset and wins its endorsement.

1963   JUNE 16:

Ben-Gurion's final resignation.

JUNE 26:

Eshkol presents his new cabinet to the Knesset, wins its endorsement, and becomes prime minister and minister of defense in his own right.

1964   OCTOBER 22:

Ben-Gurion makes public his determination to bring about establishment of a state inquiry committee regarding the mishap, which will disprove the Seven Member Committee's findings. The Ben-Gurion–Eshkol and Youth–Veteran rifts are now irreparable.

1965   MAY:

Mapai splits; Ben-Gurion and his Youth form a new party, Rafi.

NOVEMBER 1:

General elections. Ma'arah wins 45 seats; Mapai 36; Ahdut HaAvodah 9; Rafi only ten.

1966   OCTOBER 17:

Dalia Carmel admits to Ben-Gurion, at his home, that she "changed" the copy of Givly's July 19, 1954, letter to Dayan.

Ben-Gurion's Spy

The Story of the Political Scandal

That Shaped Modern Israel

1

Introducing: Givly and Friends

Among the disembarking passengers of a Russian ship that anchored at the port of Jaffa on September 7, 1906, was David Gruen of Plonsk. That same day, Gruen set out on foot for the Jewish colony of Petah Tikva, to join the workers tilling its orange groves. Eight years later, in May 1914, another newcomer reached Petah Tikva: Moshe Graniza of Briansk in the Russian-Polish province of Grodno. He too took up day-work in the orange-groves.

Both men adopted new Hebrew names in place of the ones they had borne in their native Poland: Gruen became Ben-Gurion, leader of the Jewish labor movement in Palestine and founding father of the state of Israel. Graniza became Givly, and spent his entire life in Kfar Ganim, an outlying neighborhood of Petah Tikva, where with his wife Yehudit he set up a home and farm.

Ben-Gurion and Givly might have run into one another in February and March 1919, when conventions held in Petah Tikva unified the Zionist labor movements. But they pursued very disparate paths, and it was Givly's firstborn Benyamin who came to know Ben-Gurion—but at a different time and in other circumstances.

The Givly homestead, isolated at the far end of the colony, was built entirely of wood—the family hut, the chickenrun and the cowhouse.

Kfar Ganim knew nothing of the mutual aid and cooperative marketing common in the new Jewish settlements, and the Givlys marketed their produce privately. Yehudit, a formidable woman of great initiative, ran a home dairy whose cheese and other produce Moshe delivered directly to customers' homes. The dairy required ice, whose resale provided a further source of income, with deliveries made initially by Moshe, and subsequently by Benyamin and his three younger siblings.

The Givlys reaped little reward from their labors. Their long years of hardship denied the children proper schooling—except for Benyamin, the most gifted and ambitious of the bunch. His schoolfriends recall him as a child wonder: a brilliant, diligent student, always best at sports, but equally willing and ready to help provide for his family: he was up before dawn to milk the cows, hoe the orange-grove, and deliver milk and ice on his bicycle. Except for a skin disorder that required him to keep his arms and legs covered, he was a model in every respect.

Benyamin stood out even more when he went on to a Tel Aviv trade school, which trained its students in bookkeeping and other small-business skills. Moshe's decision to send his son to such a school—with the extra cost of tuition and bus-fares—indicated his recognition of Benyamin's gifts, and his wish to see him move up in the world.

As a high-school student, Benyamin was "a good sportsman and occupied the front bench" in class. Tall and gentle, he was also thoughtful, conscientious, and self-assured. Furthermore, with the passing of his childhood skin affliction, he shed his bandages to emerge in all the splendor of broad shoulders and narrow hips. With his black hair and brown eyes, he bore a striking resemblance to Gregory Peck.

Above all, he had a unique knack—which he carried into maturity— for winning a place in the hearts of his acquaintances.

Benyamin abandoned his studies before his final year, to help support his family: initially, he did the milk-and-ice round before hiring himself out to hoe neighbors' orange-groves; here too, "he excelled." He also joined the "Haganah," the clandestine Jewish militia, and registered with Mapai, the Jewish Labor party headed by Ben-Gurion. Joining the labor sports association, Hapoel, Benyamin met the comely Esther Pinhassi; in 1940, when he was twenty-one, he married her and moved in with her family at Ein Ganim.

The marriage enhanced Benyamin's status, smoothing his path to advancement in the ruling Mapai hierarchy. Though situated near the nondescript Kfar Ganim, Ein Ganim was an entirely different world: as the first *moshav* (cooperative settlement), founded under the auspices of some of the most illustrious names in labor Zionism, it exuded great prestige. Esther's father, Ya'akov, a charter member of the moshav and a prominent member of numerous public bodies, was a founding father.

In 1941, Benyamin abandoned physical labor to enroll with the "Jewish Settlement Police"—the Haganah's legal arm—where he served till late 1944. He stood out among the other "auxiliaries" not only for his height and muscular build but for his charm and friendly generosity. In 1942, he successfully completed an infantry officers' course at the prestigious training school for Haganah command cadres, where he was noted for his articulateness, verbal and written. His fellow-cadets included future Israeli Defense Forces (IDF) generals and men who would later be his colleagues in military intelligence: Yehoshafat Harkabi, Isser Be'eri and Mordechai Ben-Zur.

Benyamin was now "one of ours," gifted and well-connected; the way was open for him to climb rapidly up the military and political ladder. He struck up an acquaintance with Petah Tikva teacher Yosef Burstein, a leading member of Mapai and the Haganah. Yosef and his wife Nehama kept open house, and Benyamin should have been a welcome guest. But Nehama treated Benyamin with a reserve verging on revulsion "from the very first moment" ("Whenever he showed up in the doorway, I'd invariably cry 'No !' "); she urged her husband to beware of him and avoid intimacy. With her sharp instincts, Nehama was the first to detect a trait which others overlooked for many years to come: behind the flawless image, Benyamin harbored a fine thread of deceitfulness. It may have stemmed from his experience as milk-and-ice retailer, which made him aware that his fine appearance and smooth tongue offered endless opportunities to take advantage of the trust and naivete of others.

In the Haganah, Benyamin opted for intelligence work, which became his specialty. In October 1946, he joined the militia's full-time staff as district officer for the Haganah Intelligence Service (SHAI), the Hebrew acronym for intelligence service, in Petah Tikva initially, and later, in the southern region. His prominence was reflected in his attendance at an April 1947 meeting between SHAI officers and Ben-Gurion, who noted Givly's name in his diary.

As SHAI South district officer, Givly's duties included safeguarding the water pipe, the lifeline for the area's Jewish settlements and a target of frequent Arab attacks. As well as supervising the paid Arab guards, he used them for intelligence purposes. In this duty, he was assisted by David Karon of the southern kibbutz Kfar Menahem.

The two men were soon friendly. They met every Friday at Givly's rented office in Rehovot, and once they had concluded their business, Karon recalls, they headed for "Friday night dinner" at a restaurant, where they read newspapers and solved crossword puzzles.

While in Rehovot, Givly lived with a new girlfriend, the wholesome, attractive Shosh Marshov. She was well-known in Rehovot, where her doctor father, a man of fine taste and profound Zionist conviction, frequently hosted leading Zionists. Marshov had begun serving with the Haganah at fifteen, performing a variety of duties. In 1939, she joined a kibbutz labor detachment at the Dead Sea potash works in Sodom—pioneering work of the highest order. After long service with the British army, she returned to the Haganah, becoming secretary at SHAI South.

Marshov fell for Givly instantaneously; their work together fostered their relationship. They had been intimate for a full year before Marshov found out that he was married and had a daughter. But even this lack of candor on his part did not diminish her love for him. Her father's warnings ("That man is neither honest nor decent, he is not the man for you, leave him!") fell on deaf ears. She believed Givly's claims that "he hadn't lived with his wife for many years, and only visited her and their daughter in Petah Tikva once in two weeks or a month" and that he was planning to get a divorce, which he deferred only because his mother "threatened to kill herself." Marshov relished Givly's company; "he had something, he could be exceptionally affable." He was "very gifted, highly intelligent and ambitious," and endeavored to fill in the gaps in his education by "reading endlessly." Occasionally they would host Givly's friend from officers' training school, Mordechai Ben-Zur, now posted to SHAI South as reconnaissance officer; Marshov found him "rather a rascal . . . not over-smart."

Of Givly's two homes, the one in Ein Ganim had smoothed his initial path; but the second, in Rehovot, boosted his ascent. Marshov was convinced that the guidance and aid she offered him was a solid investment in their joint future. She refined his conduct—"he didn't know how to use a knife and fork"—and spruced up his dress and appearance. His advancement was also facilitated by her connections with Isser Be'eri, soon to become deputy head of SHAI.

Marshov had met Be'eri in 1939 at Sodom, where he was the district Haganah commander. Noting her gifts, he made her a first aid instructor and later put her in charge of the radio communications post. Marshov admired Be'eri's "nobility and intelligence"; never, she claims, had she met anyone else of his moral stature. Friendship flowered into adulation—"To me, Isser was God !"—and lifelong loyalty.

Be'eri—tall, lean and greying—had reached Palestine in the wave of immigration immediately following World War I. He joined the northern settlement of Kfar Giladi, and was Haganah area commander from 1920 to 1929. He remained active with the Haganah when he moved to Haifa, where he found employment in construction. But a conflict with Abba Hushi, the labor council secretary, forced him to leave the city. After a three-year stint in Jerusalem (1939–42), he became aide to the head of the Haganah's northern command. In 1943–44, he was director of the Haganah's arms workshops, and later works manager at a brick factory.

In April 1946, when David Shaltiel, who had been Haganah commander in Haifa, was made head of SHAI, he made Be'eri his deputy. Be'eri invited Shosh Marshov to serve as his principal secretary at SHAI Headquarters in Tel Aviv.

Thus, Marshov became the link between her beloved Benyamin and her venerated Be'eri—a fact destined to affect the fateful developments now swiftly unfolding. In February 1948, Be'eri became head of SHAI, and in March, he made Givly "Yeruham"—code name for SHAI commander in the Jerusalem district—with Marshov as his secretary. In less than two years, Givly had advanced from subaltern in Petah Tikva, to a powerful senior post in what was probably the most important Haganah district.

That April, Jewish Jerusalem was under siege by the Arabs: food and water were rationed. A fuel shortage left the city with virtually no electric power, and it was under incessant enemy fire—sniping, machine-gun fire, and shelling. Givly and Marshov reached Jerusalem on April 20, with a convoy that made it through—at the cost of fifteen fatalities among its escort.

Aided by their friend Dubby Yaski, the pair settled into a Jerusalem apartment; on April 27, Givly assumed his position. For a month and a half or perhaps two—the period was never satisfactorily determined— Givly dominated the Jerusalem SHAI as the all-powerful "Yeruham," commanding 400 men, of whom a dozen were on full-time paid duty. The new post offered Givly a rare opportunity; determined to succeed, he embarked upon his job with great eagerness. A year later, he recalled that his "principal concern was counter-intelligence."

The besieged city, shelled and starving, was in the throes of "a spy-hunting psychosis"; malignant mistrust and a "life and death" atmosphere sparked a spate of rumors about an unknown hand allegedly directing enemy fire at vital targets. It was whispered that, even within the Jewish population, traitors were in touch with the enemy by means of a code that used rifle shots by day and light signals from the rooftops at night. The Jews' attitude toward the British was ambivalent, composed on one hand of mistrust and the suspicion that the British were spying for the Arabs, and on the other of respect for their former rulers and with an eye for future allies.

Givly's predecessor, Yitzhak Levi, told him that the SHAI office and regional command were inundated daily with reports of suspicious persons snooping around and then crossing into the British security zones beyond the Jewish-held areas. Levy offered Givly a couple of tips: "Bear in mind that Jerusalem is a tough city. The British, the Arabs, the clergymen, are all interwoven into everyday life." In other words, not every suspect—whether Muslim, Christian, or Jew—was a spy. "If you run into any problem," Levi offered, "you'd do well to consult me." But the young Givly spurned the counsel of his more seasoned predecessor, whose two years as "Yeruham" had not unearthed a single spy. Sure of his own abilities, Givly was anxious to display leadership and vigor in the hunt for Jewish spies and chalk up some real achievements.

On the morning of July 1—only two-and-a-half months after Givly's assumption of his duties in Jerusalem—Be'eri ran into Levi at GHQ, and told him: "Last night, we shot a traitor . . . Meir Tubiansky. He transmitted information to the enemy—we proved it. He confessed to the facts. He wept before his death." Having known Tubiansky from the Haganah, Levi was astonished. "Did you have proof?" he inquired.

"There was clear proof," Be'eri replied. "A document."

Levi was dumbfounded. "Along comes a new man and within the month, he uncovers the treason, . . . if such it was, that I failed to unearth over a long period."

2

Givly the Spycatcher

Soon after his appointment as "Yeruham," Givly appointed Dubby Yaski to the counterintelligence section. Yaski's only colleague there, Dov Sinai, had been on the job seven months. The two were very disparate in background and character.

Sinai—tall, slender, with black hair and moustache—had reached Palestine in 1943 from Bialystok; his speech and mannerisms still betrayed his Polish origins. He had an exceptional memory, and amazed everyone with his erudition and wit. Yaski, from an illustrious Jerusalem family, was a graduate of the city's most prestigious high school, a member of the Palmach, Haganah's crack striking force, and a natural science student at Hebrew University. Tall and balding, he looked and spoke like an intellectual, clothing any triviality in academic terms. As the elder, with longer service in SHAI, Sinai should have been the senior; but in effect they operated on an equal footing, since Yaski's intimacy with Givly gave him an edge—which, however, soon boomeranged to his detriment.

The two men were in their office on June 16, 1948, when Eitan Ron, an employee of the Jerusalem Electric Corporation, walked in with an astounding tale: "There is a traitor in our midst," he exclaimed; "we have discovered who is directing enemy shelling at vital targets!"

The Jerusalem Electric Corporation, under British ownership and management, employed Britons and Jews, but principally Arabs. To guarantee control of the company in the event that the city was divided, Michael Bryant—hitherto its secretary—was made manager of the Jewish section. On the establishment of the state of Israel, Bryant directed the corporation in the Israeli neighborhoods, running this part of it as an autonomous entity.

In late May 1948, a serious fuel shortage had obliged the corporation to cut off power over the city grid; in its place, an emergency network was installed to supply some seventy vital consumers, such as hospitals, bakeries, and food factories. Power was also fed to military locations, but their identity was concealed from Bryant by the company's Jewish employees.

On June 16, one of the latter—Aharon Eliezer Cohen, who had been with the Corporation fifteen years—was seated at his desk. A few feet away, Bryant was in conversation with Meir Tubiansky, the consumer engineer. Cohen was amazed to notice Tubiansky holding the list of the emergency network consumers and explaining the identity of each one, including some of the top secret locations. Believing that "matters were at a critical juncture," as he put it, an agitated Cohen hastened to Ron, who was adjutant of the quasi-military "electricity unit" to which the company's Jewish employees belonged, to tell him what he had seen and heard. Ron hurried to Jerusalem Judge Advocate General Gideon Hausner, in charge of military justice in Jerusalem (responsible both to IDF's legal service chief and to General Shaltiel, commander of the Jerusalem military district), who sent him to the SHAI public relations department. The department head recalled Ron turning up "one fine morning . . . in great agitation and distress," waving a sheet of paper and saying: "Study this list!" The list, comprising "objectives receiving electricity," was marked in Tubiansky's handwriting. Suspecting that "the annotations were designed to locate military targets," he directed Ron to the counterintelligence section. The following day, Ron sent Cohen there, as eyewitness to this "act of treason."

On investigating, Sinai and Yaski learned that the emergency network supplied power over special cables to vital enterprises, some of which were secret. Had that secrecy been broken? Further investigation convinced them that the secret was rigorously restricted to the Corporation's four most senior Jewish employees, who had drawn up a list—in Hebrew—of the consumers connected to the emergency network. Copies of the list were entrusted to them alone and, they claimed, had not left their possession. Other employees received only an abbreviated

Hebrew list, from which the vital locations were deleted. Bryant received nothing beyond an English translation of the abbreviated list.

Yaski later recalled that suspicions that a spy was directing enemy fire at vital targets had prompted "an attempt to plot the density of the artillery hits on a map, and to try and see if there was any pattern. . . . At a later stage, when we tried to find some rationale, someone—I don't recall who—hit on the notion that the pattern corresponded, in effect, with the emergency network." The suspicion of correspondence between the targets of the shelling and the power network was strengthened when, according to Yaski, precisely "at the height of our profound and thorough discussion—or at least we tried to make it profound and thorough . . . right in the middle . . . of all these thoughts and deliberations," along came Cohen with his story. "Plainly, it fell on ready ears, because it seemed like verification, from two sources, of a hypothesis that didn't have much going for it." The pattern of shelling seemed to "conform precisely" with the emergency network. Consequently, said Yaski, "we tried to check who was this man Tubiansky."

This statement, as the reader will observe, suggests retrospective doubt or self-justification (the discussion "we tried to make profound and thorough," the story falling "on willing ears," and the attempt "to check who was this man Tubiansky")—a note regrettably absent in 1948. More important, there are no grounds for the claim that Cohen turned up at the very moment when the possible correspondence between the shelling and the network was being discussed. The fact is that no such correspondence had occurred to the SHAI men prior to his appearance. It was Cohen who first told them about the two lists—the partial list entrusted to Bryant and the full one, known only to the four senior employees. Cohen could not have turned up "at the height" of the discussion of a correspondence which had not even been imagined. On the contrary: that discussion arose out of Cohen's tale.

Nevertheless, Yaski and Sinai went on the warpath. A few days after Tubiansky had been seen "explaining the original list to Bryant"—on either June 20 or 21—Sinai sent Givly "an initial report" entitled: "Transmission of information about military concentrations in Jerusalem to the British."

Sinai's report rested mainly on information from Cohen, who noted that Bryant was "among those roaming the Jewish [section of the] city, always feeding the other British employees information about events in the city"—a totally incorrect assertion. Furthermore, said Cohen, "he

drove to the [Arab] Old City immediately after the meeting with Tubiansky; apparently, he was apprehensive about transmitting the information
by telephone or at the Corporation office."

Who was this Tubiansky? A former major with the British Royal Corps
of Engineers and a "civilian official with [British] military engineering
bodies" in Jerusalem. "His professional colleagues' opinion of him is
poor. He is renowned for groveling to the British, taking bribes, denying
help to Jews, etc." He had been taken on at the Corporation by its British
director, Colonel Gresham, with whom he had served in the army; he
owed his job to "friendship alone, for he had no idea of the work entrusted to him." A year later, when Cohen testified under oath and was cross-
examined at Be'eri's trial, it became evident, as the court said, that he
depicted Tubiansky to Sinai and Yaski in this way out of personal ani-
mosity and jealousy.

Supplementing this character sketch, Sinai's report noted two suspicious facts about Tubiansky: first, the "locations" on the list he interpreted for Bryant were "almost totally identical with the concentration"
of enemy shell fire; second, Tubiansky had "requested an outside telephone line" from his home, to bypass the military exchange. In addition
to his work at the electricity corporation, Tubiansky was a military officer commanding Jerusalem's airstrip. This Haganah posting, Sinai
remarked in his report, had evoked "great astonishment . . . among Jewish engineers."

Sinai did qualify Tubiansky's grave suspicions, acknowledging the limited nature of his inquiries and adding prudently: "The aforementioned
drive [by Bryant to the Old City] may have been coincidental." He pointed out that the fateful June 16 conversation "was held in a public place,"
and "it can hardly be claimed that a person would deliberately pass on
secrets in so open a place." Sinai did not mention Cohen's presence at
the conversation or his part in it (Cohen had said he made warning ges-
tures at Tubiansky, trying to prevent him from giving away military
secrets). Sinai concluded his report with a recommendation for further
investigation:

> We must find out whether receipt of such information by the British
> was feasible only by way of Tubiansky. We must find out the sum of
> money in his possession. We must find out about his connections at
> the Corporation . . . how he got his airstrip appointment . . . possible
> connections with mail smuggling by planes; and, by a search of his
> home, discover any other means of communications in his possession.

Although it listed these subjects for investigation, Sinai's report made no demand for Tubiansky's arrest. None of his recommendations were acted upon by Givly, who did not even order a check of Tubiansky's bank account.

With the onset of a cease-fire on June 11, Givly went to Tel Aviv, where Be'eri briefed him on the feverish preparations for establishment of the IDF's Intelligence Department, which was imminent. Aware that the new formation would swallow up SHAI, and that the June 30 SHAI staff meeting would assign him to a new and higher post, Givly knew his days as "Yeruham" were numbered; if he was to grab the big prize—apprehension of an authentic traitor—he would have to make haste lest it fall to his successor.

It has never been established whether Givly passed Sinai's report to Be'eri; but he undoubtedly told him that the Jerusalem SHAI, under his command, had unmasked Tubiansky as traitor and spy. Be'eri, it should be noted, had known Tubiansky when the latter was an engineer with the Dead Sea potash works, while Be'eri was the area's Haganah commander.

Although Be'eri normally pursued investigations of traitors and spies himself, he entrusted the Tubiansky investigation—as a reward, perhaps—to Givly. As was revealed in October 1949 when Be'eri was brought to trial for Tubiansky's execution, Be'eri ordered Givly to submit "a further report." It seems, however, that Givly resolved to do so without additional investigation, which would entail a lengthy and tiresome process during which the prize was liable to slip through his fingers.

It is evident in retrospect that, had Givly troubled ahead of time to scrutinize the suspicions which ultimately cost Tubiansky his life, he would have found little difficulty in unearthing facts which became quite plain when it was too late. Above all, he would have encountered chronological inconsistencies totally demolishing the alleged correspondence. The emergency network was installed on May 30, the day the list of its consumers was drawn up: any correspondence with the shellings could thus have existed for no more than twelve days—from May 30 to June 11, when the cease-fire went into effect. But the Tubiansky-Bryant conversation did not occur until June 16. How then had Tubiansky contrived to direct Jordanian artillery shells fired *prior* to the cease-fire?

When that question was put to Be'eri at his trial, he replied: "I try to ask myself, of course it's only a hypothesis, that had the late Tubiansky pointed out . . . 'You accuse me of transmitting to the enemy information that brought on the bombardment, [but] the conversation with Bryant was on June 16, during the cease-fire,' we would undoubtedly have thought about that point." In saying this, Be'eri knowingly disregarded the fact that Tubiansky was given no opportunity to put forward any defense.

David Shaltiel, who became Jerusalem commander at the same time that Be'eri was appointed to head the SHAI, told the court that the shelling of Jerusalem prior to the cease-fire had been "indiscriminate," excluding only the borderline neighborhoods. "There may have been espionage," he said. "But I never sensed it. . . . " Refuting the claims in Sinai's report, Shaltiel asserted that the Eden hotel, where he had his headquarters, was not a target of the shelling, suffering only sniper fire which persisted till May 14; after that date, "I don't think the Eden hotel constituted a particular target." The Jewish Agency buildings likewise were not bombarded "in particular." Yet these two structures played a key role in the alleged "correspondence."

Had Givly tried, he would also have learned that the external appearance of the emergency network marked it off from the regular grid, which consisted of underground lines and overhead, uninsulated cables. The emergency network, consisting of cables with red-and-black insulation, was consequently easy to pick out, and could not be regarded as secret; it was moreover connected to the existing meters, making it necessary only to locate the active meters to discover who was receiving power.

Furthermore, the network could not have been operated without the knowledge of the corporation's manager. Had Givly interrogated the senior Jewish official, Alexander Singer, he would have learned—as Singer conceded at the trial—that it was out of the question to conceal the complete list from Bryant; in fact, that July Singer himself, after consultation with the Haganah, sent Bryant the complete list.

Givly might also have deduced that the seeming veil of secrecy shrouding the emergency grid—in the form of the two separate lists of consumers—was designed, among other things, to inflate the status and importance of Singer, the organizer of the "electricity unit," to whose command he nominated himself (the aforementioned Ron was his adjutant). Tubiansky did not join the "electricity unit," for he was a military officer ranking far higher than Singer and, as Givly would have known if he had examined Tubiansky's relations with his colleagues as thoroughly as he should have, the IDF disapproved of the quasi-military "Singer force": its activity was suspended for two weeks in May, and it was disbanded finally on August 1.

Had Givly, moreover, done some snooping in Singer's outfit, he would have encountered an ambience of rivalry and envy surrounding power struggles for the positions that would open up when the fledgling state reorganized the corporation. He might even have surmised that Singer, abetted by Cohen and other cronies, was trying to prevent Tubiansky from getting Bryant's job, which they feared was intended for him—a point made glaringly obvious at the trial.

Nor did Givly trouble to verify whether Bryant did drive to the Old City after his June 16 conversation with Tubiansky. Neither did he probe any of the other subjects Sinai had recommended, nor investigate Tubiansky's actions as commander of Jerusalem's only airstrip, nor try to find out whether he smuggled secret documents or black market goods on airplanes. Yet his airstrip position should have enabled him to provide the enemy with data far more vital and crucial than the list of power consumers: the planes carried the confidential correspondence of the Israeli provisional authorities, the Haganah command, and, on occasion, the SHAI itself.

Relying on Sinai's psychological diagnosis, Givly ascribed Tubiansky's supposed perfidy to "his loyalty to the British, his stupidity, and largely to . . . his naivete and apprehensions about his fate and that of his family in the grave circumstances then [prevailing] in Jerusalem." The only action Givly took was "a talk with the district commander" wherein he told Shaltiel of his suspicions of Tubiansky, and warned of the use he was liable to make of the phone line he had requested. Shaltiel, however, responded that Tubiansky was worthy of "command of all our airforce installations" and claimed that his job "justified" his request for a direct line.

In his trial testimony, Shaltiel said that the "evidence" Givly had presented was insufficient "to remove Tubiansky from his post." He simply instructed Givly to keep Tubiansky under "constant surveillance" and to "consult with and confide in the Jerusalem JAG," Gideon Hausner.

In his trial testimony, Hausner vividly remembered this conversation with Givly at Shaltiel's office. "Givly said further investigation and inquiry would be carried out in Tel Aviv. I objected" in view of the "regional confines of jurisdiction" laid down in IDF military justice regulations. An accused person must be tried within the area where he committed his offense, "and I still didn't know whether he committed an offense, because the results of the investigation had not been conveyed to me. But if he committed an offense, and there was sufficient evidence to file an indictment, that should be done in Jerusalem. We had a judicial apparatus, and we had set up courts here. Whereupon Givly objected, saying the SHAI command insisted it be done in Tel Aviv."

Givly was disgruntled by the results of this conversation. Shaltiel had not been convinced that Tubiansky was a spy, and Hausner insisted he be tried in Jerusalem by the existing military justice regulations. All he could extract from them were instructions to keep Tubiansky under surveillance.

Hausner's testimony confirms that Givly had an interest in moving Tubiansky out of Jerusalem, so as to detach him from Shaltiel's command and Hausner's jurisdiction.

This conversation took place no later than June 24; promptly thereafter, Givly ordered Yaski to draw up "an additional report." Only one day later Yaski handed in this second—and final—report, entitled "Transmission of information on military power supplies in Jerusalem to the British." To give the report a professional look, it was embellished with three appendices:

a. An authorized Hebrew list of power consumers that "constituted confidential material of the first order," since it was "capable of giving a full picture of the extent of the establishments engaged in war production, and of the locations where soldiers concentrate, and where other activities vital to the war effort are conducted." Attaching it to the report supposedly established Tubiansky's guilt.

b. A report on Tubiansky.

c. A report on Bryant.

The entire report was largely a paraphrase, in the academic jargon Yaski favored, of Sinai's earlier account. Givly cannot possibly have failed to notice that it furnished no new information, and thus by no means constituted an "additional report." It is consequently difficult to understand why he elected to act upon it—unless he had himself taken a hand in its drafting.

"After comparison of the sketch of the bombardment of Jerusalem, with the diagram denoting the locations receiving electricity . . . there appears to be a great similitude between the two," Yaski wrote. He stressed that the emergency network was secret; "according to Jewish technicians with the Corporation, there is no possibility of pinpointing the locations consuming electric current by a check of the main meters" (a patently inaccurate statement that exposes the superficiality of this "additional report"). According to Yaski, Bryant drove to the Old City "a few days after his meeting with Tubiansky"—not immediately, as Sinai had claimed. Yaski reviewed in detail Bryant's extensive connections with Jews, then noted that, as company manager, he possessed documents granting him "entry and exit at will"; accordingly, he "generally contrives to cross into the Arab area and return, no one knows how."

Yaski went on to smear Tubiansky with gossip garnered from his envious Corporation rivals: "During his period in the country, Tubiansky has worked at the Dead Sea, the Electric Corporation, the army, and back at the Electric Corporation." While working at the Electric Corporation "as foreman . . . he worked alongside the Briton Gresham. Gresham cultivated him, also cultivating an Arab." Irrefutable proof of espionage.

When World War II broke out, Gresham and Tubiansky both joined the Royal Engineer Corps; Tubiansky became a major. His treatment of his subordinates was "bad," as was "the general opinion of him." After the war, Gresham, now Jerusalem Electric Corporation director-general, gave Tubiansky a job "at a salary higher than those of all other Jewish employees, although his experience and qualifications fell short of theirs."

Finally, Yaski described Tubiansky's posts with the Haganah and IDF, noting "the 'foulups'" that attended his previous command, whereupon "he was transferred to command of Jerusalem's airstrip."

Yaski's elaborations upon Sinai's report were less important than his omissions. He did not mention that the fateful conversation was held in public; that Bryant's drive to the Old City might have been coincidental; that Tubiansky was also suspected of espionage in relation to his command of the airstrip. Above all, he omitted Sinai's recommendation for further investigation. But Givly attached no importance to the disparities between the two reports. It seems that Yaski's report met his requirements; with no further investigation, he set about implementation.

On the same day Givly received Yaski's report—June 25, 1948—he presented it to Be'eri, with a covering letter affirming that the detailed explanations and data Bryant had received from Tubiansky were enough to enable the recipients to "plan the shelling of the city."

Pretending that Hausner had shared in his decision, he wrote: "In a conversation with the judge Advocate [Hausner] *we resolved* (italics added) to convey the attached material to your attention, further handling and investigation thereof to be conducted in Tel Aviv." Givly went

further: "*In our opinion*, Tubiansky should be detained and the investigation begun outside Jerusalem. If you agree with our proposal, it will be
up to you to notify [Shaltiel], by means of the [GHQ] Judge Advocate
General office, that Tubiansky is required to show up in Tel Aviv at the
earliest possible time, where he is to be detained and the investigation
launched. Either way, I await your notification; for certain reasons prevailing in the city, it is vital to deal with this forthwith." The letter concluded with the comment that "the [Jerusalem] district commander and
attorney-general have been notified of this matter."

Givly's implied claim that Hausner shared in the decision to interrogate Tubiansky outside Jerusalem was false. Hausner shared in no "decision" or "opinion"; he never gave his consent to such a course, nor did
he authorize anyone to propose it on his behalf. Givly appears to have
made the claim on the assumption that neither Shaltiel nor Hausner
would ever see the letter; indeed, their first glimpse of it was at the Be'eri
trial.

The "certain reasons" prevailing in Jerusalem, which made it "vital" to
conduct Tubiansky's interrogation far from the city and "forthwith,"
appear to have been the objections from Shaltiel and Hausner to
Tubiansky's detention. If there were other reasons, Givly never gave
them. After all, the sole location appropriate for an investigation worthy
of the name was Jerusalem: it was there they could find Tubiansky, and
Bryant, and their colleagues; it was the seat of the Jerusalem Electricity
Corporation, and the scene of the shelling. All the witnesses and evidence were right there, in Jerusalem.

3
Without Mercy

The fledgling army—now dignified as the Israel Defense Force (IDF)—took advantage of the ceasefire to formally induct its soldiers. One swearing-in ceremony, held on Monday June 28, 1948, was conducted by Captain Meir Tubiansky, CO of the Jerusalem airstrip. In the crowd were his wife Lena and eleven-year-old son Ya'akov. The boy took several snapshots of his father, who was elated over being given the great honor of presiding over the ceremony. That evening, he told his wife and son that he was going to Tel Aviv the following morning for two days and would bring back provisions. He had no idea that this was a fateful move, for by now Shaltiel was his only protection, and Jerusalem the only safe place for him.

That same day, in Tel Aviv, Be'eri showed the Sinai report, and Yaski's report with the covering letter, to Dr. Avraham Gorali, the IDF's Judge Advocate General (JAG), seeking his counsel concerning the Tubiansky case. It is unknown precisely when Givly submitted "the file" to Be'eri, whose trial a year later established only that this must have been between Friday June 25 and Monday June 28. The difficulty in pinpointing Givly's timetable and movements is typical; he invariably contrived to cover his tracks.

According to Be'eri, Gorali told him that the Haganah's military justice regulations did not provide adequately for due process in the case of "grave offences" carrying the death penalty, since a court of appeal had not yet been established. Accordingly, only a field court-martial, in which guarantees of due process did not apply because the procedure was intended to be conducted in the heat of battle, could try Tubiansky. The Be'eri trial judges determined that Gorali's counsel was misleading, for it was construed by Be'eri as license for a field court-martial.

In justification of the advice he gave, Gorali argued that he was refer-ring "mainly to investigation" [1] of the suspect after he was brought from Jerusalem, and to his ensuing indictment, in case the investigation called for one." He claimed he had advised Be'eri first "to conduct the investigation" and that was the purpose of the warrant Gorali issued for Tubiansky's arrest. Gorali stressed: "I considered it self-evident that the prisoner would be brought to me" for investigation, and "there was no talk of what was to be done subsequently." To Be'eri's question: "What about a trial after the investigation ?" Gorali said he had replied that, should the investigation substantiate the espionage charges, Be'eri "would have to see to a field court-martial." According to Gorali, then, he envisaged two distinct stages: first, an investigation; then, a field court-martial, should the investigation prove it necessary. Be'eri, for his part, claimed that they had discussed only one stage: the immediate con-vening of a field court-martial.

We cannot know which man spoke the truth, but we can assume that, just as Givly was scheming to remove Tubiansky from Shaltiel's com-mand by transferring him "out of Jerusalem," Be'eri was trying here, on similar grounds, to remove him from the JAG's jurisdiction. His person-al ambition matched his Socialist Zionist zeal; he wanted to prove his own worth and that of the SHAI in the building of the new Jewish state. From the outset, Be'eri too was intent upon a field court-martial in which he would be able to determine the sentence and order its imme-diate execution. Indeed Givly cleverly manipulated his boss's craving for action. He knew Be'eri had complete trust in him, and he abused it. It was Givly's duty to caution Be'eri that the investigation was still at an early stage.

Further evidence of Be'eri's intention is provided by recent testimo-ny from Lieutenant Colonel Daniel Magen, the first commander of the IDF military police (MP), whose duties included execution of military

---

1. Author's note: the Hebrew word hakira is a broad term denoting either "investigation" or "interrogation"; the precise meaning must be deduced from the context.

sentences. Gorali advised the MP commander that "a death sentence on a traitor is awaited, and it is the MP's duty to carry it out; will you be willing?" Unwilling for the military police to be identified as responsible for carrying out death sentences, Magen flatly refused.

That course blocked, Be'eri sought another way of procuring Tubiansky's execution. He confided to deputy chief of staff Major General Zvi Ayalon [2] that he possessed "a mass of evidence and prima facie proof which incriminate Tubiansky, or at least place him under grave suspicion, of passing military information to the enemy"; he asked Ayalon to order Shaltiel to hand Tubiansky over to the SHAI. Ayalon was puzzled as to why Be'eri needed such an order: as SHAI chief, "he is authorized to act, and moreover, bound to act" on his own in such circumstances. Be'eri told him that a GHQ order was required "to prevent unforeseen delays." Contrary to the insinuations of Givly's covering letter, it is clear that Shaltiel and Hausner opposed Tubiansky's removal from Jerusalem, and could be induced to consent to it only by an express order from GHQ. For reasons best known to himself, Ayalon gave Be'eri a note in his own handwriting, addressed to Shaltiel:

> Personal—confidential
> June 28 1948
> To David S.
> In accordance with Yeruham's conversation with you, it has been decided that you are to hand over Tubiansky to the bearers of this letter, who are SHAI officers.
> *Boaz* [Ayalon's codename]

Armed with this letter, Captain Shmuel Ganizi—head of the SHAI "suspects department"—drove that same day to Jerusalem. He arrived that evening, but discovered that Tubiansky had already departed for Tel Aviv.

On the morning of Tuesday June 29, Be'eri approached Palmach commander Major General Yigal Alon, who was "in charge of the Jerusalem corridor sector" and to whom he was politically close, to solicit his assistance in prosecuting a traitor by field court-martial. This was a period of coolness between the Palmach command—linked socially and politically to the kibbutz movement and the left-leaning Mapam party—and the IDF's other officers, of whom most had served with the British

---

2. Chief of staff Dori was on sick leave.

army during World War II. However, considering Be'eri "one of us" and therefore trustworthy, Alon directed him to the Palmach's Yiftah brigade, entrusting him with a note in his own handwriting:

> To Mula or Itti
> The bearer, Isser Be'eri, is to be assisted in all his requests. He may ask for an escort of a number of men. He may want you to form a field court-martial to clear up a grave matter etc. I am advised of the matter, and his decisions in regard thereof are to be respected.
> 08:45 June 29 1948 Yigal P. [3]

On Wednesday June 30, Be'eri instructed Ganizi to lay charges against Tubiansky with the JAG General Headquarters and draw up a warrant for his arrest, then "to locate Meir Tubiansky who is accused of high treason and detain him."

On arrival at the JAG office in Tel Aviv at 9 that morning, Ganizi was awaited by Gorali's deputy, who advised him in spelling out the charges: "Tubiansky who is posted with the airforce in Jerusalem is suspected of transmitting information to the enemy. I received a file in this regard from Yeruham. Witnesses to the above are Ganizi and Be'eri. I request you remand him for ten days, for interrogation." Ganizi signed the charges, and was issued an arrest warrant addressed to "Military police commander / OC Tel Aviv military prison":

> June 30 1948
> Please detain:
> Name: Tubiansky
> Rank: Air force unit (sic !)
> Place: Tel Aviv—Jerusalem.
> For a period of 10 days, incommunicado barring special permission.
> The above is suspected of transmitting information to the enemy.

Ganizi and his escort drove off in their jeep to detain Tubiansky. They found no one home at the apartment of his brother, engineer corps Captain Aryeh Magen, nor was Magen at his office. Eventually they determined that Tubiansky and his brother had lunched at a beachside hotel with Magen's daughter Elisheva; she and Tubiansky then went shopping in the Carmel market. Heading there, Ganizi had no difficul-

---

3. Mula and Itti were Yiftah officers. The "P." in the signature refers to Alon's former name, Paicovitch.

ty in identifying Tubiansky, a well-pressed "English type" with knee-length khaki socks, crepe-soled shoes, officer's cane and pipe. Informing Tubiansky that he was "summoned to an urgent meeting with Shaltiel," Ganizi consented to drive Elisheva and her purchases to her parents' home, waiting while Tubiansky helped her carry the bags indoors. Tubiansky arranged to take her to the movies that evening, and she gave him the apartment key knotted in a handkerchief. While he waited, Ganizi called Be'eri: "We have the man. We're on our way." Tubiansky got back into the jeep, and drove off, never to return.

On reaching the outskirts of the city, Ganizi informed Tubiansky that he was being detained for investigation. Stunned, Tubiansky inquired as to the grounds. Ganizi responded that "he would be informed in due course" and asked him to hand over his weapon, a small ivory-inset P.B. pistol, and his cane. Hitherto a proud officer, Tubiansky was now a humiliated prisoner.

It was a two-hour drive to Yiftah headquarters at Hulda in the Jerusalem highway combat zone. On arrival, Ganizi presented Alon's letter, receiving in return a note addressed to Matitiyahu Goldman, commanding officer of a company stationed at the abandoned Arab village of Beit Jiz, half an hour's drive by jeep. Ganizi handed the note to Goldman, who directed him to an isolated house at the edge of the village, where Tubiansky would be held until the "interrogators" arrived.

The routine midday SHAI staff meeting on Wednesday June 30 was festive in mood. Be'eri announced the formation of the newborn state's secret services and their division into three branches: he would head military intelligence (MI), reporting to the IDF chief of staff and the defense minister. Givly would lead MI's most important division: operations and combat intelligence, making him third—after Be'eri and his deputy, Chaim Herzog—in MI's chain of command. It was a remarkable leap forward; if the occasion struck Be'eri as worthy of celebration, he seemed to know just how: by executing the Haganah's and Israel's first Jewish traitor, he would prove the secret service's effectiveness.

When the meeting adjourned, Be'eri requested Givly to stay on for "a minor consultation," along with Avraham Kidron, just appointed to head field security and counterintelligence, and Levi Avrahami, MI's new chief for the north. Givly's buddy from Rehovot, David Karon, who was waiting in an adjacent room, was also invited.

The three men testified later that Be'eri asked them to join him for an expedition to the south, though without disclosing where, or for what purpose. Be'eri contended that he took Kidron and Karon along as "observers" or "apprentices" for "beneficial instruction"; in other words, they were to receive an object lesson in conducting an interrogation. Avrahami, whose work prevented him from coming, revealed that at this consultation Be'eri and Givly made references to the traitor Tubiansky: Avrahami claimed that had he realized what was afoot, he would have opposed the execution, and moreover, prevented it.

Givly claimed that Be'eri told him only that this was "a special assignment"; not until they neared Rehovot did Givly learn that "I would have to interrogate" Tubiansky. He told how the foursome, not having had a bite to eat since morning, "lingered" in Rehovot for a snack "at one of the coffee houses"—probably the one he and Karon cherished in memory of the Friday evenings they used to spend there.

On arrival at Yiftah headquarters, Be'eri, discovering that the brigade and battalion commanders were away, inquired whether "any other officers" were on hand. They went on to Beit Jiz, where Captain Goldman, the senior commander available, told Be'eri he had an order from the battalion's deputy commander "to make myself available to the people who are to come." At his trial, Be'eri recalled Goldman's words as proof that he had relied on Alon and the brigade commander to "allot" Yiftah officers for the field tribunal, asserting that it was only when he realized that the Yiftah commander had not followed Alon's instructions that it occurred to him to "appoint the three officers who had accompanied me from Tel Aviv . . . to constitute a tribunal."

At this juncture, Karon testified, "Be'eri told us the man was accused of treason and transmitting information to the enemy, and said he was appointing us to be a field court-martial, and we would try the man." Asked who would preside over the tribunal, Be'eri replied: "It was understood that Givly was senior . . . in other words, the court president." The newly appointed judges headed for the house at the end of the village.

Tubiansky, who was seated in the doorway, saw the approaching four officers; to quote one of the soldiers there, " 'Bigwigs' with three-quarter length khaki pants and military pistols dangling down to their knees." At his trial, Be'eri testified: "I charged Tubiansky with transmitting information to the enemy . . . he realized he was being indicted before a court." This was how Tubiansky first learned that he was facing a field court-martial.

That June 30, 1948, Tubiansky's judges were self-confident, none foreseeing the day when he himself would face a court, as accused or witness. But a study of their testimony at the Be'eri trial raises suspicions of a concerted fabrication concocted to create the impression that Be'eri was following Gorali's counsel by initially interrogating Tubiansky, and only then bringing him before the field court-martial.

Such a study, in fact, demolishes their story, since it reveals that no investigation at all preceded the "trial." It is evident, moreover, that Be'eri and Givly intended this all along; for Be'eri had probably foreseen that the Yiftah commanders would not be willing to participate in a field tribunal for an outsider. Thus the three subordinates Be'eri brought along—who were neither "observers" nor "apprentices" as he claimed—were meant to constitute his kangaroo court. Otherwise, what was stopping him from delaying the trial for a day or two, until Yiftah fulfilled Alon's instructions? Be'eri's haste reflects a fear that, unless it was carried out that same day, the death sentence would never be executed; this explains why he appointed the tribunal ahead of time, and conducted the trial in a manner that denied Tubiansky any chance of defending himself. At his own trial, Be'eri claimed that Tubiansky could have denied his guilt; but Be'eri was caught off guard by a devastating question flung at him by one of the judges: "What witnesses did you prepare in the event of the accused's denial?"

Be'eri: "There were no witnesses."

Neither was there an attorney for the defense.

Be'eri handed Givly the documents he had previously received from him, and requested him to commence the prosecution. Tubiansky rose to his feet, but observing his judges seated on the steps, he likewise sat down again. Then Givly—who was seeing Tubiansky for the first time—stood up, and the trial commenced.

Following some routine questions—name, rank, place of employment, duties in the Haganah and IDF—Givly informed Tubiansky that he was "charged with transmitting information to the enemy." Tubiansky denied the allegation. Givly then produced the full list of consumers linked to the emergency power network, in an English version bearing various annotations, and affirmed that Tubiansky had delivered it to Bryant, and that it had served the Jordanians in aiming their artillery. Horrified, Tubiansky seized his head, mumbling: "What have I done?" This reaction was construed as a full admission of guilt. The trial was at an end.

As the tribunal members later agreed, the trial was a one-man show by Givly: Kidron and Karon remained silent, and Be'eri contented himself with one or two questions. Givly's colleagues agreed likewise that he played his role with considerable flair: catching Tubiansky unprepared with the list of power consumers, he proved—so they said—that its delivery to Bryant constituted complicity in espionage, cracking Tubiansky's resistance and extracting his confession.

According to Givly's testimony, Tubiansky conceded that the list's annotations in Roman letters were in his handwriting, and admitted that, in passing it to Bryant, he had engaged in espionage. "One of the larger weapons workshops which had been heavily shelled, was shelled again one day after being relocated."

Attorney General Ya'akov S. Shapira, prosecuting, asked him: "Tubiansky denied [the accusation] and only confessed after being shown his handwriting on the list?"

Givly evaded the question: "He confessed in the course of the interrogation, but he denied it initially."

Shapira: "In fact, he denied [the existence of] any list?"

Givly: "He denied transmitting information."

The members of the field tribunal all agreed in their testimony that the trial lasted about an hour. But when it emerged that the evidence comprised nothing more than Yaski's report, district court president Dr. Nathan Bar-Zakai asked Karon: "Why did the interrogation last an hour? Regarding what did you interrogate him?"

Karon: "At the beginning of the interrogation and for quite a time . . . before the document was shown to Tubiansky, he denied giving Bryant . . . any list with markings . . . and that took time; later, when he saw the list, he broke down, that's what took time."

Judge Bar-Zakai: "Up to this breaking point, what questions did you ask him?"

Karon: "It was always the same questions, repeated in one form or another. . . . the denials went on until the list was produced."

Be'eri likewise recalled "with utter certainty" Givly showing Tubiansky the list of consumers, with vital military locations marked. "What I remember is that it was in English, and he was asked whether the insertions were in his handwriting. . . . that was the breaking point. . . . he admitted it was his handwriting. . . . he was shocked. . . . he admitted it was the list he showed Bryant, and that he had noted for Bryant, in his own handwriting, the nature of those locations . . . and he admitted . . . that he now saw the great harm inflicted upon Jerusalem, or certain locations in Jerusalem, due to transmission of the information."

The reader will probably have noted the discrepancies glaring from these statements. Both Yaski's and Sinai's reports specified that "in mid-June, a Jewish engineer in the company's employ, by the name of Tubiansky, was seen *explaining* to Bryant . . . *the complete Hebrew list.*" (italics added). That list was appended to Yaski's report, which stressed furthermore that the Hebrew list alone was complete, rendering it so confidential that only four copies were made, for the Electric Corporation's four most senior Jewish officials, who claimed that the lists "did not leave their possession." Bryant received nothing more than an English translation of the abbreviated Hebrew list; a complete list did not exist in English. Yaski based his suspicions of Tubiansky entirely upon the charge that he had told Bryant the identity of the consumers omitted from Bryant's abbreviated list. If so, how did the complete Hebrew list get transformed into a complete English list at the Beit Jiz trial? And how did it acquire annotations in Tubiansky's handwriting? On what grounds did Givly accuse Tubiansky of having *given* the list to Bryant? And if Tubiansky had indeed given the list to Bryant—how did it turn up in Givly's possession?

When Be'eri was asked by defense attorney Ya'akov Salomon whether he had believed that Tubiansky "*gave* the list," Be'eri replied: "He admitted it."

Prosecuting attorney Shapira noted the incongruity. "You say Tubiansky admitted he gave the list to Bryant?" he asked Be'eri who, apparently aware of the snare, replied: "I wouldn't say 'gave,' rather, that he explained . . . from it, by means of it . . . in the course of a conversation, or conversations, that took place between them about this list, he added the explanation in his handwriting."

Shapira: "In the course of the conversation?"

Be'eri beat a hasty retreat: "I couldn't say whether it was at the same time or not."

Similarly, Bar-Zakai lashed out at Karon: "Didn't you ask yourself how the list came into Givly's possession? If it was conveyed to the enemy, how did it reach him?"

Karon: "The question didn't occur to me."

Bar-Zakai: "How did it not occur to you? Did the enemy glance at the list, say thank you, and return the list? I do not rest content, Major Karon, with expressing amazement, I want an explanation."

Karon: "I am unable to explain."

Since the decisive proof of Tubiansky's guilt lay in the list allegedly conveyed to Bryant, Givly should have attached it to his report on the field court-martial and the execution. Hence it is quite bizarre—as the Be'eri trial judges also found—that the list should vanish. At the trial, it was referred to as "the vanished list."

Attorney Shapira: "Well, Mr. Be'eri, I put it to you that the list you said was before the Beit Jiz tribunal in fact didn't exist at all." For his part, Judge Bar-Zakai indicated his opinion of the list by referring to it as a "bordereau." [4]

What list did Givly have at Beit Jiz? The Be'eri trial exhibits included a number of lists of consumers—in Hebrew and English—collected from Electric Corporation employees who had received them to use in their work. Singer testified that he had himself drawn up a complete Hebrew list of power consumers—which was attached to Yaski's report; and that, in July, he had, with Haganah approval, handed over its English translation to Bryant. That copy featured X's marking locations which had yet to receive power. Such a list was indeed delivered to the SHAI, and a copy was submitted as an exhibit at the Be'eri trial. If Karon's and Be'eri's testimony was correct, this may have been the list in Givly's possession; but this would mean that Singer had given the list to Bryant—or Givly—prior to June 30 and thus was lying to the court.

Be'eri stated in his trial testimony that the three Beit Jiz judges saw the list Givly exhibited to Tubiansky. However Givly, when asked during preliminary interrogation by an examining magistrate whether he showed Tubiansky the full English list, complete with annotations, replied: "*I do not remember whether I showed it to him—I do not remember whether I showed it to him.*" (italics added) This striking inconsistency raises the suspicion that the list shown to Tubiansky was not an incriminating document, and did not prove his guilt; it is therefore not unthinkable that it was spirited away so as to remove evidence of Tubiansky's innocence, and his judges' culpability. The only conclusions are that the list brandished in the face of the hapless Tubiansky was the one Givly had received from Singer, whose X marks it bore; or alternately, that it was just a plain sheet of paper—a trick familiar to any devotee of courtroom movies.

All the possible solutions to the riddle of the list reinforce the deduction that Tubiansky's conviction on treason and espionage rested upon false charges.

---

4. Bordereau—French term for a docket or schedule. Ever since the Dreyfus trial—where the conviction rested upon a forged "bordereau"—European languages use this term to denote a forged document which does not stand up to judicial scrutiny.

Be'eri was less than accurate in stating, at his own trial, that the Beit Jiz court heard no witnesses. There was one: Givly. Having personally experienced the shelling in Jerusalem, he testified to noting a correspondence between the power lines and the locations shelled—as though the alleged correspondence was adequately established by his mere affirmation. Karon testified that "Givly . . . who closely observed the course of the enemy bombardments . . . on vital command and industrial locations in Jerusalem . . . *knew* that those locations were especially affected. *He testified thereto*" (italics added).

On top of giving Givly the stage to act as prosecutor, the Beit Jiz drama also cast him in the supporting role of prosecution witness.

With Tubiansky's guilt supposedly established by the first and only interrogation he underwent, Be'eri and the three tribunal judges now convened to deliberate on a verdict. They gathered beside the house, Karon testified, and "Be'eri asked whether we found the man guilty. The reply of each one was . . . guilty . . . each one of us said yes. Be'eri too said yes." Be'eri's memory was less distinct: "I think I also expressed my opinion afterwards [after his three subordinates] that in my view too, he's guilty." Be'eri then "raised the question of the sentence . . . I demanded the death sentence." The other tribunal members concurred.

Givly now proceeded to discharge the duties of presiding judge. He informed Tubiansky that the tribunal had found him guilty, and that its verdict was immediate execution. "He said it in a loud voice," Karon related. With tears in his eyes, Tubiansky begged for his life, imploring consideration for his twenty-two years with the Haganah, and his eleven-year-old son who would be orphaned. But Givly ignored his pleas.

Striding to the office of company commander Goldman, Be'eri—"in the doorway," as Goldman related—told him Tubiansky "has to be done away with" and he must "prepare the men to shoot him." Goldman asked whether they should "turn out" in uniform. Be'eri said this was unnecessary, and Goldman instructed the company's first sergeant to prepare "a detail of soldiers to carry out the death sentence." Accompanied by "six or seven soldiers," casually dressed, Goldman marched to the house where the trial had been conducted. He notified his men "that a death sentence has to be carried out," and told them that "anyone who thinks he won't be able to execute it, is dismissed." Exercising this privilege, two soldiers refused the assignment. The sergeant led Tubiansky—two soldiers before him, and two behind—to a fruit grove at the village border, stationing him with his back to a stone fence. The detail lined up facing him.

It was 7:15 in the evening. Givly strode toward Tubiansky, tore off his epaulets, removed his belt and hat, and stepped back. As Karon testified at the Be'eri trial, his words confirmed by Givly himself: "Benyamin Givly proclaimed . . . the sentence . . . from memory . . . Meir Tubiansky, 22 years a member of the Haganah, had been found guilty of transmitting information to the enemy, and was therefore sentenced to death."

Kidron recalled Tubiansky's last moments. "He begged for mercy, with tears in his eyes. He behaved like an old woman, anyway, not the way I imagined the conduct of a man, a Haganah officer. After we announced the verdict, he was pale as chalk, his lips quivered, but he tried to pull himself together, he overcame the trembling of his teeth and lips, and behaved very well, drew himself erect, and I must say I was impressed by his conduct."

Karon testified: "He walked with trembling knees, all the time complaining and begging, 'Have mercy on my wife and my child.' Mainly he mentioned the child: how would the child be brought up, how would he grow up, and what would they tell him about his father . . . at the last moment, when the officer asked whether he wanted his eyes bound, he did not request it, and stood erect awaiting the 'Fire' order, snapping to attention."

Goldman ordered his men to load their rifles, which they aimed at Tubiansky's chest. Givly nodded to Goldman, who cried: "At the traitor, one round, fire!" "Tubiansky collapsed and fell," Givly related. It did not occur to the judges to ascertain whether he was dead or alive. "The officer gave the order ['Fire'] and we went to the car," Karon related. Goldman recalled Be'eri shaking his hand and saying "Well done" or something of the sort: "I don't remember his precise words."

The company sergeant determined that Tubiansky was dead and conducted his burial. One of the soldiers removed his wristwatch and emptied his pockets of their contents: the key tied up in a handkerchief, a pipe and tobacco pouch, identity card, a Jerusalem Electric Corporation pass, a checkbook, money, fountain pen, and a bundle of snapshots. Without removing Tubiansky's clothing and shoes, the soldiers dropped the body into a pit scooped in the rocky soil; after filling it in, they left it unmarked. The forty-five-year-old Tubiansky's own version of his investigation and trial went with him to the grave.

That grave of dishonor housed Tubiansky's remains for a year and a week, until July 7, 1949.

Givly's final role was as clerk of the court, taking it upon himself not to record the facts, but to establish them. Again, it is a mystery how, where, and when Givly drafted—in his own handwriting, on a single sheet of paper—the following spurious document:

Report on the interrogation of Meir Tubiansky of Jerusalem, June 30 1948
Meir Tubiansky, an officer and commander of the airfields in the Jerusalem district and a senior official at the Jerusalem Electric Corporation, was charged with transmitting information to the enemy, which furnished target points for the bombardment of Jerusalem by cannon- and mortar-fire.

The accused was interrogated on June 30 by Isser B. and confessed his guilt:

a. Disclosing the location of the Etzel [arms] factory at Ochshorn House.

b. Disclosing the location of the Lehi factory.

c. Disclosing the location of the Defense Force factory.

d. Disclosing the address of the Eden hotel as base of operational headquarters.

All the aforementioned objectives were targets of enemy shelling. Most of the aforementioned military factories were damaged thereby.

A field court-martial at the scene of the investigation, composed of Kramer A., Givly B., Karon D., issued a sentence:

Sentence: Execution in situ!

Sentence was executed on June 30 1948 at 1915 hours, in a military ceremony, at one of the bases, by a military unit.

[Signed]

Prosecutor: 1. (—) Isser Birenzweig. [5]

Tribunal: 1. Kramer A. (—)

2. Givly B. (—)

3. Karon D. (—)

June 30, 1948

Israelis felt a powerful impetus to give their utmost to the war for independence and statehood. Staff and intelligence officers, recognizing that they were not as exposed to danger as combat troops, made an enor-

---

5. Avraham Kramer changed his name to the Hebrew "Kidron." For some reason, Isser Be'eri signed under his former name.

mous effort to excel in their jobs, as if to compensate for their easier service. Some, like Be'eri, no doubt did so from a sense of moral obligation; others, because such was the accepted behavior, the proper pose. In either case, this state of mind may explain, at least in part, Be'eri's and Givly's zeal. Capturing spies and putting them on trial would be the ultimate justification of their feathered beds and pressed uniforms.

Given the atmosphere then prevailing in Jerusalem, Givly and Be'eri must have been convinced that they had laid their hands on a traitor. Had they conducted a proper investigation, their haste would have been forgiven and forgotten. Instead, they started down a slippery path that led them, finally, to eliminate any possibility of allowing Tubiansky a proper trial, with defense counsel and witnesses. There seems hardly a doubt that they were blinded by ambition.

4

Taking Responsibility

The night after the execution, Be'eri said at his trial, his conscience gave him no rest. The following morning, July 1, 1948, he requested an urgent audience with prime minister David Ben-Gurion, who was also defense minister, to "tell him about the matter" and show "the evidence," Yaski's report with its appendices and the "Report on the interrogation of Meir Tubiansky of Jerusalem on 30.6.48" in Givly's handwriting. Be'eri said that they met "before noon," but did not claim that his actions received Ben-Gurion's blessing.

Ben-Gurion's diary makes no mention of the meeting—which does not necessarily prove it did not take place, for Ben-Gurion had an unusually heavy schedule that day.

Gorali testified to having heard from Be'eri that same day that he had "called [Ben-Gurion] out of a [cabinet] meeting" to tell him of Tubiansky's trial and execution, and that "the prime minister listened and made no reply." Their encounter was evidently quite brief. Responding to a question from defense attorney Ya'akov Salomon, Be'eri related that Ben-Gurion had asked who the judges were, and he had named them. Gorali's testimony confirmed this.

Nehemia Argov, Ben-Gurion's military secretary, testified that Givly's report on the Tubiansky trial, which Be'eri had given Ben-Gurion, was passed on to him, together with Ben-Gurion's instruction to "conduct an examination regarding the interrogation and sentence."

Despite the enormous burden imposed on him by the resumption of hostilities—the ceasefire came to an end on July 9—Ben-Gurion gave consideration to the trial's shortcomings and the necessity of preventing a recurrence. On July 5, he summoned Gorali for a broad discussion of the 1948 military justice regulations, which should, he thought, be replaced by "a new law"; his diary notes that "Gorali undertook to prepare a draft within a week." This haste indicates that Ben-Gurion may also have instructed Gorali "to examine the matter of the interrogation and sentence" of Tubiansky. If so, it was a timely move: rumors about the execution of a traitor from Jerusalem were making the rounds, and signs of puzzlement and protest were appearing among the public.

Yitzhak Levi, learning of the execution from Be'eri on the morning of July 1, reported it to Shaltiel. The latter "leapt up in fury, saying: 'I was told that Tubiansky is required for some duty in Tel Aviv.'" Having heard nothing from the SHAI, Shaltiel "did not keep the secret . . . somehow or other, the matter became known in the city, reaching Tubiansky's friends who alerted . . . the widow."

Tubiansky's wife and brother, and his other relatives, demanded to know what had become of him. Mrs. Tubiansky retained the services of Attorney Asher Levitzky; on being approached by him, Shaltiel sent Ben-Gurion the following cable, dated July 8; it refutes the claims of Givly's covering letter:

> To this day, I have received no notification regarding the fate of Meir Tubiansky, who was arrested by the SHAI. Rumors are circulating throughout the city which I can neither confirm nor deny. The lack of any authoritative formal announcement on the matter is causing great harm. I request reply and instructions forthwith.

Gorali testified to having urged Ben-Gurion to publish a press communique about the execution of a spy—without naming him—"because the public knows about the case, and the absence of an official statement denies the benefits to be attained thereby for the civilian population"; he also advised that Attorney Levitzky be notified. Be'eri claimed that, in his conversation with Ben-Gurion, he expressed the view that it was "desirable and vital to publicize" the trial. Although he denied any part in wording the communique, Gorali claimed that he and Be'eri wrote it jointly. The communique, signed by Ben-Gurion, was published in all the papers on July 20:

It is hereby announced that, on June 30, 1948, a summary field tribunal composed of three officers sat somewhere in the country to issue a sentence of death upon a spy for the enemy. The spy transmitted to the enemy details about the IDF's industry in Jerusalem, and also revealed . . . an IDF operational headquarters base. As a result of the aforementioned transmission of information, these objectives were attacked by the enemy. The death sentence was executed at an IDF base by a military unit.

On July 13, Gorali submitted his findings to Ben-Gurion. His conclusions largely coincided with his own legal counsel to Be'eri before the Tubiansky trial: the 1948 military justice regulations made no provision for trials of the type called for in this instance. However, in view of "the evidence" which "was apparently most trustworthy," and of Tubiansky's "confession," "there can be no doubt that the [Beit Jiz] court was bound to issue the verdict it did issue." In conclusion: "As long as there is no regular military law to establish the essential principles for the conduct of major trials like the aforementioned, there was and will be no possibility of conducting trials of the aforementioned type other than the way this one was held."

Two days later, Gorali submitted "proposals for laws on detention and treason," but they failed to satisfy Ben-Gurion, who again noted in his diary: "A military law is required." At this time, Ben-Gurion appeared to be contemplating replacing Gorali, and the name of Attorney Aharon Hotter-Ishai begins to appear in the diary. On July 17, Ben-Gurion consulted with Hotter-Ishai about "military jurisprudence," noting that Hotter-Ishai "is willing to undertake the task."

And in fact, on November 29, 1948, Hotter-Ishai was appointed in Gorali's place. While not due directly to his misleading advice to Be'eri, or his retroactive endorsement of the Beit Jiz trial, the decision to dismiss Gorali was undoubtedly hastened by these actions. Evidently Ben-Gurion was aware of the miscarriage of justice in the Tubiansky trial, and certainly he disapproved of it. But his interest was not restricted to that specific case: anxious to prevent a recurrence, he took steps to speed up the enactment of new military justice regulations.

On July 20, at Ben-Gurion's behest, Gorali sent Mrs. Tubiansky confirmation that her husband had been put to death on June 30, 1948, in an action "arising out of the verdict of a court," and warned her against "publishing [the confirmation] or any part thereof." The family, stunned, made no response. It seemed then that the Tubiansky affair was over. But Tubiansky did not rest peacefully. His blood cried out from his unknown grave, granting his widow no repose; on November 18, she plucked up the courage to break her silence in a letter to Ben-Gurion:

> Mister prime minister,
> I, Haya (Lena) Tubiansky, widow of the officer and engineer Meir Tubiansky, take the liberty of addressing this request to your honor, in the hope that you will give it sympathetic study . . . On Monday July 7, I learned of strange rumors circulating in the city that my husband had been arrested in Tel Aviv . . . Days passed and I received no news. . . . Then came the heavy blow—the press report about Tubiansky "the traitor" . . . and I, his wife, am the wife of a "traitor," and his only son Ya'akov, is a "traitor's" son. . . . Initially I did not know how I was to go out and show myself to our numerous acquaintances; principally, I did not know how I was to explain the fact to my only son, who adulated his father, and whose father loved him as himself. Afterwards, I set my life's course. I told my son the facts, promising to do everything to uncover the truth and [seek] justice. As for myself: despite my age, I enlisted with the army (under the name of Bentov) so as to resume, with my feeble strength, his service. I declare to your honor, by my solemn word, my utter certainty that there has been a bitter, tragic and painful error, and that my husband was innocent. It is unthinkable that he was a traitor, and I do not believe he was guilty of the terrible allegations made against him.
> . . . I have yet to receive any formal official notification about the circumstances of his death . . . I have received no death certificate, and have not been informed of his place of burial . . . I have not received my husband's personal effects, nor been informed whether he left a will, letter or note for me or for his son. No official authority has notified me whether, where or how a trial was held, whether a verdict was issued, what that verdict was, and in what manner he was put to death.
> . . . I fail to understand why I was told nothing regarding the trial, or at the very least, about the verdict issued against him, so that I could see him before his death. After all, the worst of criminals is granted a final request. . . . I am convinced your honor will agree there was something untoward here, and my husband's blood cries out from the earth over the injustice visited upon him. Accordingly, I venture to approach your honor with the request that you examine the matter yourself. . . .
> In addition to the above, I request your honor to issue instructions that formal notice of his death be conveyed to me, with a death cer-

tificate, so as to enable me to settle his civil affairs. In addition, I request notification as to his place of burial so that I can at least lay flowers of commemoration and shed my tears over his grave. In addition, I request you issue instructions for the restoration to me of his personal effects which were with him at the time of his death; also, to notify me whether he left a will or letter for me.

. . . And finally, with regard to my son: who will provide for him now? I will continue my service with the army until the war's end, and then I will find employment—but what will become of my son ?

I look forward to your honor's reply, and hope you will not let me down . . .

With my deepest respects,
Lena (Haya) Tubiansky (Bentov)

This letter reached the defense minister's office on November 23, but remained unanswered. On December 23, she sent a reminder, and on December 27, Ben-Gurion wrote his reply. Argov, Ben-Gurion's military aide, watched Ben-Gurion drafting it, "suffering with the woman. . . . That woman somehow shook his faith in the rectitude of the court and the sentence it had handed down," Argov noted in his diary. "He appears to wish to rectify a great injustice."

Ben-Gurion replied:

I deeply regret that my reply has been delayed till now. I wished to clar- ify the matter to myself as far as possible, and it was not easy to find the time; forgive me.

I have no doubt as to the sincerity of your words. Words of truth can be recognized. It does not lie within my power to pass verdict upon your husband; but I examined the procedure of his trial, and discov- ered it was not in order—possibly because the habits of clandestinity persisted in army circles that emerged from the Haganah, and the state has not yet managed to enact laws and impose its authority upon all concerned. But the matter undoubtedly calls for review, and I have instructed the IDF chief of staff to order an examination of the trial and the appointment of a new court-martial. I have also given instruc- tions for formal notification of your husband's death to be sent to *you*, and for issuance to you of the necessary documents—and if any pos- sessions remain, they will be returned to you.

The government will continue to be responsible for the education of your son, and whatever the outcome of the trial, clearly no hint of blame falls upon you or your son—at the moment, it does not lie within my power or prerogative to pronounce . . . whether or not your husband was guilty of anything; that must be left to a new trial which will not be long delayed.

With respect and esteem,

David Ben-Gurion.

That same day, Ben-Gurion also wrote to chief of staff Dori:

To the chief of staff,

I attach herewith the letter from Tubiansky's widow, and my reply to her.

Consult with legal experts and appoint a court to review the accusations against the deceased. Plainly, the trial that took place was not in order—and likewise did not comply with the regulations prevailing in the Haganah before the foundation of the state.

Also, an official document is to be issued to the widow about the death of her husband, and if any of his possessions remain, they are to be returned to his widow.

The army is required to continue to take charge of the son's education, and should it transpire that there was a mistake and the man was executed without adequate cause—the army will have to pay ample compensation.

During this period, Be'eri contrived to embroil himself in three further scandals: the detention of Abu Laban, the murder of Ali Kassem, and the Abba Hushi—Jules Amster affair.

In September 1948, it was learned that a clandestine Arab group active in Jaffa was secretly stocking arms and maintaining contacts with outside parties. Before any official decision could be reached about how to respond, Be'eri, acting on his own authority, arrested Abu Laban, a leader of the clandestine group. A furious Ben-Gurion noted in his diary: "I shall tell Isser that such conduct is unthinkable."

Ali Kassem, an Arab landowner and orange-farmer, was an informant for the SHAI and the IDF military intelligence department. One day, he fell under suspicion of planning to slip across the Jordanian border. Kassem was well-briefed on Israeli affairs, and his superiors were aghast at the information he could bring to the enemy, and the damage he was liable to inflict upon Israel. Be'eri ordered his arrest. Shortly afterward, Kassem's bullet-riddled body, which had been tossed into a ravine on Mount Carmel, was discovered accidentally; it turned out that he had been executed without trial on November 16, 1948, on Be'eri's orders.

On December 6, Ben-Gurion directed chief of staff Dori "to appoint a fact-finding commission"; and upon reading its report, he ordered Be'eri put on trial.

The trial was held in camera in January 1949, before a special military court made up of three judges with the rank of lieutenant colonel. In detailing the circumstances of his actions, Be'eri did not duck responsibility for the order he had issued nor did he call defense witnesses.

In his defense, Be'eri argued that during wartime, the head of the intelligence service was equal in authority to an officer of his rank on the battlefield, being likewise required, on his own responsibility, to reach—and immediately implement—fateful decisions affecting the lives of his subordinates. Intelligence work was no less of a battlefield, he claimed, and it was not always possible to resort to a court conducted according to ponderous rules unsuited to combat conditions.

Be'eri also contended that by nature an intelligence service operated against the law and that if it did otherwise it would cease to serve its purpose. He tried to make his point with examples of operational circumstances in which law and morality conflicted with the need to swiftly execute a vital operation, balancing the life of an individual against the security of the state.

In its verdict, the court took Be'eri's principles and his conscientious motives into account, but affirmed that no individual or group stood above the law of the land. Notwithstanding the extraordinary circumstances in which the intelligence service operated, and that Israel was at war, it said, no offender should suffer punishment—certainly not the death penalty—other than by verdict of a duly-constituted court.

The court passed sentence on February 9, 1949. In view of Be'eri's "record, devotion, service and duties," and the time and circumstances of his offense—"a period of national revolution, and transition from underground to legal national existence"—the court unanimously sentenced him to "dismissal from any command, without reduction in rank."

Subsequently, the court's president commented: "Be'eri was dismissed for killing an Arab . . . I believed it was only to the credit of the state of Israel that, with battles in progress, a man of the rank of lieutenant colonel was legally demoted, by a military trial . . . precisely for killing an Arab, not because of Tubiansky or . . . Amster."

The appointment of a court "to review the charges" against Tubiansky was, on Ben-Gurion's instructions, delegated by the chief of staff to IDF Judge Advocate General Hotter-Ishai, who had been the prosecutor in Be'eri's court-martial. When that trial ended, Hotter-Ishai may have hoped at last to devote himself to an examination of the Tubiansky affair; but the chief of staff then saddled him with an urgent examination of yet another episode involving Be'eri.

In May 1948, not long after he was appointed to head the SHAI, Be'eri had unlawfully arrested Yehuda (Jules) Amster, who had served as liaison with the British on behalf of Abba Hushi, mayor of Haifa and Mapai party boss in the north. Interrogated at a secret installation, Amster was subjected to brutal torture and humiliation: his teeth were extracted, he was singed with a soldering-iron, water was dripped on his head, and he was plunged into salty sea water during hot summer days. This was done in an unsuccessful attempt to extract a confession which would have incriminated Hushi in connection with accusations by adversaries of Mapai that Hushi had given the British advance warning of a 1946 Palmach operation against British police vessels hunting illegal Jewish immigrants. After failing with Amster, Be'eri, who had carried on a smoldering vendetta against Hushi since the thirties, ordered Captain Haim Ya'ari, head of the SHAI technical department, to forge three telegrams—"exact facsimiles" of those used by British counter-intelligence—whose text named an informant with Hushi's initials.

In July, Be'eri submitted the telegrams to chief of staff Dori and reported to Ben-Gurion that he had just acquired decisive proof of Hushi's perfidy. But Ya'ari revealed the forgery to his superior, who demanded an internal inquiry. In January 1949, Ya'ari admitted to having forged the cables on Be'eri's instructions, and the matter was submitted to the JAG for formal investigation. On March 6, 1949, Be'eri confessed to having commissioned the fabrications.

On March 18, the JAG submitted a final report to the chief of staff, depicting Be'eri's conduct as "criminal" and "a breach of the trust placed in him." However, "the offense having been committed before February 10, 1949, it falls under the amnesty [1] and there is accordingly no possibility of bringing him to trial." At the same time, in view of "the unique nature of the offense," the JAG recommended that Be'eri be discharged from the army and voluntarily cede "his IDF entitlements and

---

1. On February 11, 1949, a general amnesty went into effect. It covered all offenses committed before February 10 except for murder or other offenses for which the maximum penalty was death or life imprisonment.

rank." Nevertheless, on the orders of the chief of staff, Be'eri was discharged from the army on May 15, 1949, without forfeiting either rank or entitlements.

Now that he had cleared his desk, Hotter-Ishai could turn his attention to the Tubiansky affair. He began to collect testimony, commencing on March 6 with Givly, who was followed by Kidron, Shaltiel, Karon, and Gorali. Investigation of Yaski's Electric Corporation informants was delegated to the police. By the 16th, Hotter-Ishai had already reached firm conclusions, which Ben-Gurion noted in his diary: "It turns out that there were no grounds for accusing [Tubiansky] of espionage; at most, he spoke imprudently." But submission of the inquiry report was delayed "for a painful reason." Despite Ben-Gurion's insistence, "no adequate efforts had been made" to locate Tubiansky's grave. "I found it impossible," Hotter-Ishai wrote, "to submit my opinion, with its recommendations, before we were able to show the widow the site of the grave, and permit her to transfer the body to another location."

Thus it was not until July 1 that Ben-Gurion wrote to Mrs. Tubiansky that her husband "was innocent, and the verdict, and its execution, were a tragic mistake"; he assured her that "those responsible will stand trial." To redress as far as possible "the regrettable and painful injustice," Tubiansky would be posthumously awarded the rank of captain in the regular army and interred with full military honors at a military cemetery. His innocence would likewise be proclaimed at "a special parade" to be held at Ya'akov Tubiansky's school, "so that your son's friends know that his father fell by error, and his child will be able to take pride in the service of his parents—his late father, and his mother (long may she live)—over many years in defense of our homeland." The widow and her son would likewise receive appropriate financial support.

On July 7, 1949, Tubiansky was interred at the Mount Herzl cemetery with full military honors, a year and a week after Givly had ripped the epaulets off his uniform.

The following day, July 8, a warrant was issued for Be'eri's arrest for his role in Tubiansky's execution; on the 17th, he was indicted before the justice of the peace in Ramleh (whose jurisdiction included Beit Jiz), who acted as examining magistrate in a preliminary investigation, as then required by law. On August 23, the justice of the peace referred the case to the Tel Aviv district court. On November 22, 1949, the three district court judges unanimously convicted Be'eri of manslaughter. In their reasoned judgment, they wrote:

> It is clear to us beyond any doubt that this conclave of SHAI officers, which issued sentence of death against Meir Tubiansky that evening at Beit Jiz, cannot possibly be termed a court. It is unthinkable that the image of that malicious field tribunal should remain etched in our minds as the likeness of a court entitled to convict a 'soul in Israel.'

But in passing sentence, the judges took account of "the defendant's record, and his service to his people." In their view, the General Amnesty Ordinance failed to draw a distinction between criminals and "persons . . . of the Jewish security forces and the IDF"; anyone who committed an offense in the heat of battle deserved "a law of absolution,"[2] even if that offense carried the death penalty or life imprisonment. Finding "the defendant worthy of benefiting from the law of absolution, had it been enacted," they sentenced him "to imprisonment for one day, from sunrise to sunset . . . unless the president of the state sees fit to pardon him."

In view of that recommendation, the new chief of staff, Yigael Yadin, wrote to President Chaim Weizmann, requesting a pardon for Be'eri "who has served many years in the Haganah and IDF, during arduous periods and in responsible posts, and has been sufficiently punished by the mere fact of his trial and conviction." Following procedure, Yadin sent his letter to the defense minister; Ben-Gurion conveyed it to the president, appending the comment that he "supports his request." With his approval, the defense ministry also bore Be'eri's legal costs.

Although pardoned by the president, Be'eri remained broken in spirit and defeated. His wife Gita died a few months later, and Be'eri lived on for nine years—in "sorrow and desolation," to cite his defense attorney—before succumbing to a coronary seizure on January 30, 1958.

---

2. Analogous to the British "Act of Indemnity."

5

Alone in the Dock

Even though Ben-Gurion's letter to Mrs. Tubiansky, as well as the press communique proclaiming Tubiansky's innocence and terming his execution "a tragic mistake," had pledged that "those responsible will be placed on trial," Be'eri was the only defendant named in the Tubiansky indictment.

It seems to have been largely his own fault. Each of the scandals in which he was implicated featured him as a man who considered himself above the law, permitting himself to hand down flagrantly unlawful orders. The revulsion aroused by this image detracted from the guilt of his subordinates, who appeared to be innocently following their superior. In his opening address to the Tel Aviv district court, Shapira elaborated on the judicial consideration involved:

> The situation of the three judges was different, in one important aspect, from Be'eri's situation. They acted . . . albeit unlawfully . . . on the orders of a superior officer, whose subordinates they were. And it was at a time of bitter fighting. They faced a conflict . . . between disobedience and breaking the law. Under the law of this land, the order of a superior officer is no justification in a criminal trial. . . . On the other hand, had they refused . . . Be'eri's order . . . they would have risked court-martial [for refusal of orders]. . . . [Under] the accepted procedure regarding soldiers who break the law in the honest convic-

tion that they must obey orders . . . [the authority] to direct that they not be placed on trial is vested in me. I [accordingly] found fit not to place the three judges on trial.

Shapira reverted to this line of argument in 1955, when defense minister Lavon questioned him about Givly's conduct in the Tubiansky affair: "The entire Beit Jiz trial was not in order, and it cannot be said that Mr. Benyamin Givly was guilty to a greater or lesser degree than the other two judges. The alleviating circumstance of having acted on the instructions of their superior, Mr. Be'eri, applied to all three judges equally. That fact was also my sole consideration in deciding at the time to place Mr. Be'eri alone in the dock."

Shapira was wrong. He overlooked the fact that Be'eri never demanded blind obedience of his subordinates. Givly, who was more familiar with the charges against Tubiansky, and enjoyed special status as Be'eri's "younger brother"—to use his own term—could have opposed each step taken against Tubiansky. But instead, as has been shown, Givly exhibited great zeal in preparing the "trial," at which he played every imaginable role. A thorough investigation would have established beyond all doubt that Tubiansky's life had lain in Givly's hands no less than in Be'eri's.

Another reason why public opinion appears to have focussed on Be'eri was that the Hushi affair smacked of party politics. While Be'eri did not belong to any party, he was known for his close social and ideological links with the Ahdut HaAvoda movement, then a component of the far-left Mapam party.[1]

Equally well-known was the conflict between Ahdut HaAvoda and the followers of Abba Hushi—dating back to the days when the two groups had vied for hegemony within Mapai. In this context, the Hushi affair was perceived as a further chapter in the titanic, long-raging struggle between the two rival labor parties, which was further exacerbated by the 1949 election campaign. Mapai leaders regarded the Hushi affair as a Mapam bid to turn the electorate against them, while Mapam leaders suspected that Be'eri's indictment was an odious ruse to discredit them. Even within Mapai's own ranks, some believed the trial to be politically inspired.

---

1. Initially an opposition faction within Mapai, Ahdut HaAvoda broke away in the mid-forties, later joining other socialist movements to found Mapam.

Undoubtedly aware of the political undertones, the three Tel Aviv judges conducted Be'eri's trial as a criminal case, confining it strictly to the terms of the indictment. Thus, Be'eri's accomplices found a haven on the witness stand, as public attention homed in on him alone.

At the same time, this exclusive focus was largely Be'eri's own doing. Just as in previous instances, he shouldered the full burden of responsibility. Furthermore, he waived the appearance of all fourteen defense witnesses that his lawyer had lined up—including senior IDF officers eager to stress his unsullied intentions, and his good character. Alone in the dock, Be'eri was also the sole defense witness.

The cornerstone of the defense strategy was the portrayal of Be'eri as selfless, clean-handed, dedicated to his vision of Israel as a Socialist republic with a strong central government, conscientious in his way, and utterly loyal to his subordinates and the IDF. To emphasize this aspect of his character, defense attorney Salomon led Be'eri to testify: "My qualms were awakened about . . . the procedure . . . after execution of the verdict. The question was: had I been fair, above all to my subordinates? Was it fair to impose such heavy responsibility upon three of my subordinates?"

Be'eri declared that he was still troubled by this remorse, which had been "aroused, I think, that night, or the following morning." Did he say this merely because his attorney had coached him to? At one point Judge Gavison asked, "You said it was plain to you that Tubiansky's conversation with Bryant brought about the shelling; but that conversation was on June 16, at the beginning of the ceasefire! How could it have brought about shelling *before* the ceasefire?"

Be'eri could have replied that this discrepancy ought to have been brought to his attention by Givly. But, electing to stand behind his subordinates, he replied: "Had the late Tubiansky pointed to this, [saying]: You accuse me of transmitting information to the enemy that brought on the bombardment, [but] the conversation with Bryant was on June 16, during the cease-fire—we would undoubtedly have considered that point." All in all, he came across as a man torn between loyalty and honesty, unhesitatingly conceding that he was consumed by doubts as to whether he had been fair toward someone who bore responsibility for the execution.

Givly testified in the Be'eri trial as a prosecution witness. He made a dismal impression on the court, as the prosecutor hinted during his summing-up. "You have seen him," he told the judges, "you have seen his conduct, and you probably have your own assessment. I hope it coincides with my own. . . ." Salomon drew upon Givly's testimony to further stress Be'eri's fairness toward his subordinates: in spite of having acted upon information submitted by Givly, Be'eri cast no part of the blame upon him, nor did he hold him to account for setting in train the process that had led to Tubiansky's death. Again he was displaying "fairness and conscience, and that is to his credit." No doubt the court and prosecutor were aware of Givly's role, but if they had laid too much stress on it they might seem to be calling for a new trial. Salomon made the most of this, telling the judges: "It is the defendant's judgment of Givly that counts"—and Be'eri had judged the three Beit Jiz judges to be "honest, brave and loyal."

Be'eri's indictment as sole defendant, and his acceptance of full responsibility for Tubiansky's trial and execution, left Benyamin Givly in the shade. His multiple roles in the field tribunal—presiding judge, prosecutor, witness, executioner, and record-keeper—were overlooked by court and public alike. Furthermore, even though the trial revealed Givly's faults in deed and conduct, Be'eri's guilt was so evident that public opinion was inclined to believe he had led Givly astray.

But it may be proper to speculate what the verdict on Givly would have been, had he been a co-defendant. The question was hinted at during the trial, when presiding judge Bar-Zakai expressed his astonishment to Be'eri: "Someone comes along and says that Tubiansky takes money, that he takes bribes, that he fawns on the British, and so on—and you did not consider it your duty at least to call the man who wrote that report and elicit from him the grounds on which he makes these statements?"

Be'eri: "There were those in the SHAI who were required to deal with this matter, and did so—not I." He referred, no doubt, to Givly, whose task it indeed was. Had Givly been a co-defendant, the question would have been directed at him, and Sinai and Yaski would have been called to the witness stand. Their interrogation would have proved that Givly had made no effort at all to substantiate their reports, and had likewise failed to note that, neither one having seen Tubiansky, they had both relied exclusively upon rumor. Both men would have testified that they had recommended to Givly—not to Be'eri—further investigation, and that they were unaware of his covering letter. Furthermore, they would have testified to being thunderstruck at the news of Tubiansky's execution.

Had Givly been a co-defendant, his culpability in Tubiansky's trial and execution would have become blatant. But instead, Be'eri was the target for questions which ought to have been directed at Givly.

Among the trial's revelations was the fact that Be'eri had played no part in the Tubiansky investigation—that he had neither directed Givly nor checked whether the investigation had been properly conducted. Be'eri gave Givly his full trust: the broad scope of the authority delegated to Givly emerged from the disclosure that Be'eri had learned of his subordinate's suspicions of Tubiansky only on receiving Yaski's report from him, some time between June 25 and 28. As to Sinai's report, Be'eri heard its content from Givly. He probably saw it for the first time at his trial.

Had Givly been indicted, he would have had to concede his failure to pursue any of the matters whose examination Sinai had recommended. For example:

SHAPIRA: Did you follow up the recommendation in Sinai's report, to
    investigate Tubiansky's connections at the Electric Corporation?
BE'ERI: Personally, I didn't.
SHAPIRA: Did anyone?
BE'ERI: I can't say.

Givly would have had to admit that he did not pursue such an investigation, nor instruct his subordinates to do so.

SHAPIRA: Was a search conducted at Tubiansky's home, as Sinai recom-
    mended?
BE'ERI: I can't say.

Givly would have had to admit that no such search was conducted.
Bar-Zakai asked Be'eri whether he did not find it "strange" that, upon learning from Givly of his suspicions of Tubiansky, Major General Shaltiel did not remove him from command of Jerusalem's airstrips: Be'eri replied: "It is undoubtedly strange."

Had Givly been asked that question—and given a truthful answer—he would have had to admit that Shaltiel did not consent to Tubiansky's being interrogated outside Jerusalem. He would also have had to admit his own failure to probe Tubiansky's actions as airstrip commander, questioning nothing beyond his request for a direct telephone line. In his cross-examination of Givly, defense attorney Salomon asked: "In your questioning of him about the telephone, didn't he give a satisfactory answer?"

Givly stated: "I can't remember that."

Shapira pointed out to the court that Be'eri had overlooked Givly's failure to pursue, or to order others to pursue, any of the suspicions raised in Sinai's report. The discovery that "he had no money" was made after his death. "And it's in Tubiansky's favor," said Shapira.

The Sinai and Yaski reports both cited "Jewish technicians" to affirm that, without Tubiansky's disclosures, the locations consuming power from the secret network were undetectable.

Shapira cast doubt on that assertion by asking Be'eri whether he had tried to identify the experts who had made it. Be'eri replied he had not.

Had Givly been a defendant, Sinai and Yaski would have testified that the "Jewish technicians" were Tubiansky's Electric Corporation colleagues (notably Cohen, the man who set the wheels in motion against him), who were resentful of his rapid promotion. That point probably occurred to presiding judge Bar-Zakai, who asked Be'eri whether he had questioned "this wretched man Cohen."

Be'eri: "I have only seen him here."

Had Givly been questioned on that point, he too would have had to admit that he failed to interrogate Cohen.

In response to Shapira's asking whether he had tried to verify the alleged correspondence between the targets of the bombardments and the vital plants consuming electric power, Be'eri replied: "Personally, I didn't."

In questioning Givly, Salomon read out a portion of his earlier testimony—"The bombing and shelling were directed at vital plants in the city, and that induced us to launch an investigation"—and asked him to verify that assertion.

Givly's response: "I can't recall, but to me, the very possibility of [finding] the two sketch-maps identical was a decisive point in directing the investigation. If we take a sketch of the Electric Corporation supply line drawn on transparent paper, and lay it over a sketch of the bombardments, we will see that the two correspond."

Shapira, seeming to cross examine his own witness (he considered requesting that Givly be declared a hostile witness): "You personally do not know whether or not the facts recorded in [Yaski's] report are correct?"

GIVLY: I don't know. I have considerable faith in Yaski's work, and when a finding emerges from his investigation, I give it a high degree of credibility.

SHAPIRA: You consider it correct only to that degree, no more?

GIVLY: I could not get involved in all the details relating to each case.

SHAPIRA: And you would not be surprised if some of the facts [in the report] were incorrect?

GIVLY: I wouldn't be surprised.

This highlighted the profound difference between Givly and Be'eri. Givly accepted no responsibility: neither his own, nor that of his subordinates or superiors.

It was undoubtedly Givly's covering letter that convinced Be'eri the charges against Tubiansky were valid. Be'eri would not have acted as he did had he not believed that Shaltiel and Hausner shared the conviction that Tubiansky was a spy, and thought action should be taken against him—outside Jerusalem, and without delay. Be that as it may, had Givly been a co-defendant, he could have been confronted on that point with Shaltiel and Hausner, whereupon it would have become obvious that he had lied, and that it was he who had an interest in the investigation being conducted outside Jerusalem.

The riddle of the list in English allegedly handed to Bryant by Tubiansky would also have been open to elucidation if the indictment had included Givly—the only man who knew the contents of the sheet of paper that induced Tubiansky to break down.

Givly testified four times about the Tubiansky affair. Since he spoke as a witness, rather than as the accused, his statements did not reflect his degree of guilt; but they do shed light on his conduct toward superiors and subordinates, and largely foreshadow his future behavior.

Later on, Shapira classified his statements into four stages, in which his initial great fear of being indicted himself progressively decreased, until he discovered that he would not be prosecuted. He appears to have lied more at the beginning and less later, when he felt safer. His first testimony, on March 6, 1949, was given to the JAG just twelve days before the latter recommended Be'eri's discharge from the IDF minus rank and entitlements. Givly was in a state of anxiety at the time, uncertain who would go on trial for Tubiansky's killing—Be'eri, he himself, or both. His defense required that his story coincide with Be'eri's; and indeed, both men claimed—in contrast to Sinai and Yaski, who had charged only that Tubiansky *explained* the list to Bryant—that he had *given* it "to the British officials" of the Electric Corporation. They also claimed that Givly was a judge at the court-martial, while Be'eri acted as interrogator or prosecutor. Givly added: "I wrote the record which noted the words of the prosecutor, and the defendant's replies. . . . I'm not sure, I think I wrote down his replies."

HOTTER-ISHAI: What became of the record and the verdict?
GIVLY: We handed them over to Isser Be'eri.
HOTTER-ISHAI: Was there a presiding [judge], which of you was he?
GIVLY: There wasn't one. It was like what they call a field tribunal. . . .
   After deliberating among ourselves, it was decided that the man had
   committed treason . . . and deserved death. The decision was unan-
   imous, all three judges.

Shunning any responsibility beyond that arising from his role as one of the judges, Givly related, "At that time, I left Jerusalem because I had been called to Tel Aviv. On one of the days I was in Tel Aviv, between June 20 and 30, 1948, I was summoned by Isser Be'eri; he told me I would have to appear as a member of a military court, against Meir Tubiansky. That was midday June 30." If he had not been in Jerusalem on June 20, he could have had no part in the developments leading to Tubiansky's arrest. But this was a plain lie, as shown by his talk with Shaltiel and Haus-ner and his instruction to Yaski to prepare an "additional report."

HOTTER-ISHAI: Why was sentence executed immediately?
GIVLY: I'll tell you. In the ambience of that time, when I [had just]
   returned from Jerusalem where I was hungry for bread, with the city
   under siege and daily bombardment and all that entailed, and unexpectedly this admission of guilt came out, to me that was certainly
   one inducement to decide on an immediate execution.

But there had been no admission of guilt; and Givly completely forgot that June 30, the day of the execution, was the twentieth day of the truce. For nearly a fortnight there had been plenty to eat and no shelling.

HOTTER-ISHAI: Did you know which law you were judging him by?
GIVLY: As far as I recall, Isser informed us prior to the trial that, should
   we find him guilty, a court of this composition was empowered to
   sentence him to death. I did not inquire which law contained that
   provision.

Givly testified for the second time to the police on July 12, 1949, after Ben-Gurion had granted Tubiansky complete public rehabilitation, and Shapira had ordered a criminal investigation of Be'eri. But because Ben-

Gurion had used the plural ("those responsible will be placed on trial"), Givly could not be certain that he would not figure in the indictment. Therefore, he tried to pass the buck to Be'eri. Givly stated that the "Report on the interrogation of Meir Tubiansky of Jerusalem on June 30, 1948" in his handwriting "was dictated to me by Isser Be'eri . . . on the same occasion, we all signed the document." He added: "No record was kept of the proceedings." Had he forgotten about telling Hotter-Ishai in March that he had kept a record "which noted the words of the prosecutor and the defendant's replies"?

Givly claimed he was not to blame for the actions leading up to Tubiansky's execution, for the whole affair "was closed to me from the time I left Jerusalem, up to that day, June 30, 1948." Only after that day's SHAI staff meeting in Tel Aviv had "Isser Be'eri informed me that I was to be ready to travel with him on a certain matter"; in the course of the drive, Be'eri had notified him, along with Kidron and Karon, that he was appointing them as judges in a field court-martial and "that it would be up to me to interrogate him." Givly did not seek the role of interrogator "*because the evidence, and my acquaintance with the matter, were slight* (italics added) but "Isser told me [the information I possessed] was adequate."

His testimony to the police also offered a different description of the sentencing and execution:

> Isser asked us to step aside, and while we were standing there, he informed us that by virtue of his authority to appoint us as judges, we were endowed with the authority to sentence Tubiansky to death should we find him guilty. Immediately after, Isser, who considered himself responsible for conducting the whole matter, turned to us and said: Is it agreed that Tubiansky is guilty? As far as I recall, the response of each of us three was that Tubiansky was indeed guilty. . . . Isser informed us that, as we had found him guilty, "his punishment shall be death." We accepted that on the clear assumption that it was his prerogative to decide on a verdict of one kind or another.

Givly added: "*As far as I recall, the immediate implementation of the sentence was not part of the verdict we decided upon* (italics added) . . . for myself, I thought it wasn't up to the judges to decide when the sentence was to be executed. . . . When I saw that the sentence would be executed immediately, I was convinced that this must lie within Be'eri's power."

Givly had found a way of justifying his own acceptance of the sentence's immediate execution:

I went through the siege of Jerusalem and saw the sufferings of its inhabitants; each day, I personally experienced the suffering and distress of every soldier and civilian in Jerusalem. Therefore I did not have the spiritual stamina at that moment to try and examine Isser Be'eri's authority to decide on immediate execution of the sentence.

But Givly and his fellow judges—who had not suffered the siege—had all been fresh and alert enough at the SHAI midday conference to discuss in detail the reformation of the secret services. Givly had the mental and physical strength to understand exactly what was taking place at Beit Jiz—if he had wanted to. He claimed, however, that before he had time to reflect, "Isser requested me to announce the court's decision again to the defendant, and then Isser gave the company commander the order to execute the sentence."

As will be recalled, it was Givly who gave the order with his nod to company CO Goldman.

Givly made his third deposition to the Ramleh examining magistrate on August 12 of that same year—by which time Be'eri alone had been named in the indictment. Nevertheless, Givly prudently adopted a common enough defensive tactic: camouflage. He came across as a professional officer without initiative, obediently fulfilling the orders of his superiors. The following version is based entirely on his testimony as recorded in the magistrate's handwriting:

On the afternoon of June 30, Be'eri instructed Givly, Karon and Kidron to join him on a drive, without specifying any assignment or destination. "It was only between Rishon-Lezion and Ness-Ziona that Be'eri told me I would have to conduct an interrogation." Even then, Givly did not know whom he would have to interrogate; but he felt no surprise, because he had expertise in interrogation. "Among my other duties," he told the magistrate, "I used to engage in interrogation." Did Be'eri not indicate that the interrogation was linked to Tubiansky? Givly searched his memory: "We may have discussed the Tubiansky case along the way. But I don't remember any talk thereof." What remained imprinted in his mind was that "while we were still on our way, [Be'eri] delegated me to prosecute . . . *a man accused* (italics added) of transmitting information to the enemy."

To explain his fuzzy memory Givly added, "At that time, I was in a state of weariness after months under siege in Jerusalem." He lopped nine additional days off his stay in Jerusalem, stating: "Until the first ceasefire,

June 11, 1948, I think . . . I was head of the Jerusalem SHAI. Then I was transferred to military GHQ in Tel Aviv." This meant he would not have been in Jerusalem on June 16, the day of the fateful conversation between Tubiansky and Bryant; nor would he be responsible for Sinai's report, Yaski's report, or the covering letter; nor would he be present for the conversation with Shaltiel and Hausner. Givly was not the man to fall into the trap of specifying exact dates, so he was quick to add: "On about June 26, 1948, I finally left Jerusalem" to take up his new position with military intelligence, after handing over his command to his successor as Yeruham.

It was only at Beit Jiz that "Be'eri handed me documents, and I studied them, and embarked upon Tubiansky's interrogation."

MAGISTRATE: "Was there talk of a court prior to the interrogation?"
GIVLY: I believe a "court" was first mentioned after the interrogation.
MAGISTRATE: Was a record kept?
GIVLY: "To the best of my recollection, no record at all was kept."

The JAG and the police had heard Givly testify that there were three judges, but he now claimed that there were four: "The four of us, I, Karon, Kidron, and Be'eri, moved away from Tubiansky and . . . summarized the interrogation. . . . I remember Isser in this exchange using the term 'military court' or 'field court' in relation to the four of us."

MAGISTRATE: Who said, and when, that it lay in the power of this court to sentence Tubiansky to death?
GIVLY: I can't remember at what stage Be'eri said that it lay in the power of this panel of judges to sentence Tubiansky, if found guilty, to death. The court concluded—in other words, the four of us talked with one another quite freely—that Tubiansky deserved [the] death [penalty]. . . . we spoke about death in a general fashion, not how or where. Similarly, "there was no talk. . . . of execution of the sentence on the spot." Only "when the firing squad approached did I grasp that the sentence would be executed on the spot. . . . Be'eri summoned the firing squad when I was not present." But being obedient, he heeded Be'eri's order and proclaimed "the sentence before the firing squad from memory." In other words, both the verdict and the execution came as a surprise to him.

Givly testified for the fourth and final time on October 17, 1949, at Be'eri's Tel Aviv district court trial. As a prosecution witness, he was questioned solely on Be'eri's responsibility for Tubiansky's killing, not on his own share in it. Givly's characteristic fuzziness manifested as a frequent resort to I-don't-remember answers, though his memory improved miraculously whenever the question related to Be'eri. Shapira wished to know where the "Report on the interrogation of Meir Tubiansky" was written—in Tel Aviv or Jerusalem?

GIVLY: I can't remember exactly, either Beit Jiz or Tel Aviv.

SHAPIRA: Before Tubiansky was shot or later?

GIVLY: Later.

JUSTICE BAR-ZAKAI: May one inquire how much later?

GIVLY: I can't remember sir.

BAR-ZAKAI: A matter of days, weeks or hours?

GIVLY: I can't remember exactly.

SHAPIRA: If it was written at Beit Jiz, it was shortly after the incident, because you did not linger there long after the shooting. Don't you know whether it was written in Tel Aviv?

GIVLY: No.

SHAPIRA: Was it that same day or not?

GIVLY: I don't remember.

SHAPIRA: Who drafted the report? Did you write it, or was it dictated to you?

GIVLY: It was dictated.

SHAPIRA: By whom?

GIVLY: By Isser.

SHAPIRA: Did he dictate it word for word, or was it all said to you, and you wrote it yourself?

GIVLY: The wording is mine, but the content was dictated to me.

SHAPIRA: When you left Tel Aviv, were you told by Isser Be'eri for what purpose you were going?

GIVLY: It was said, not in so many words, but in essence, that we were going on a special duty. I do not remember the wording.

SHAPIRA: What happened then?

GIVLY: I can't remember exactly, but at some juncture, we were told that . . . the four of us constituted a field court-martial. That was said by Be'eri. . . . On top of that, we were told that by virtue of this office it lay within our power, should we find the man guilty, to sentence him to death.

SHAPIRA: Who instructed the company commander to give the 'Fire' order?

GIVLY: I don't remember.
SHAPIRA: Was it you who instructed him?
GIVLY: Possibly, I don't remember.

In spite of having testified earlier that "Tubiansky admitted at Beit Jiz to having given Bryant the list on June 16," Givly said at the trial, "I don't think Tubiansky said he handed over the list on a specific date. I only learned of a specific date yesterday, from the prosecutor." Was Givly foolish enough to expect people to believe that—despite the reports from Sinai and Yaski, and his own covering letter—it was October 1949 before the date of the Tubiansky-Bryant conversation came to his notice? More likely, he laid his trust in the foolishness of his listeners.

In his district court testimony, Givly again insisted that there were four judges at the field court-martial. His intention is transparent: he wished to shift the responsibility for the verdict onto Be'eri, thus diminishing his own role. Be'eri had testified that Givly was "the senior . . . in other words, the court president"; Karon and Kidron also maintained that "Givly presided." But if there were four judges, Be'eri, clearly senior to Givly, bore responsibility.

JUSTICE REICHART: Before me lies a copy of the report on the interrogation of Tubiansky, in your handwriting. . . . Isser Be'eri is recorded as prosecutor. According to your testimony [to the examining magistrate], you were the prosecutor. How do you explain that?
GIVLY: I repeat, I was the interrogator. Not being responsible for procedure, I received the order of my superior and wrote the report as dictated to me. I considered Isser Be'eri responsible for the matter.
PRESIDING JUDGE BAR-ZAKAI: Why did you not send the death sentence to be confirmed by IDF's high command?
GIVLY: I regarded all action in the sphere of deliberation and implementation [as lying] within the unique authority of Isser Be'eri.

[Justice Bar-Zakai repeated his question.]
GIVLY: I regarded Isser Be'eri as my superior, as the man who instructed me to interrogate Tubiansky, as a man who had long been a commanding authority for me, as [bearing] unique power and responsibility to determine each detail, from the beginning of the . . . interrogation until its termination. I did not regard myself at liberty to voice my opinion beyond what I was requested to do, and I regard-

ed all action in the sphere of deliberation and implementation [as lying] within the unique authority of Isser Be'eri.

BAR-ZAKAI: What were the grounds for hastening execution of the sentence?

GIVLY: The reason for my failure to prevent execution of the sentence was the psychological influence at work upon me after nearly three months I spent in Jerusalem, the harsh siege conditions I experienced, hunger and thirst, the incessant bombardments, the tension that defense of Jerusalem imposed upon me by virtue of my position, and also Tubiansky's confession to having transmitted the list.

Here too, Givly stood apart. Be'eri had told the court of sleepless nights and torments of conscience. David Karon likewise later repented: "This question ate away at me, because it went very much against the grain—what happened, and how it came about, including the ways the interrogation [was conducted] and things were done." Givly alone experienced no scruples; his conscience was clear.

6

The Lesson Not Learned

Foreseeing the significance of the Be'eri trial as the cornerstone of a law-abiding Israel, prosecutor Ya'akov Shimshon Shapira commented: "We have this to be grateful for, that the [proceedings] were not conducted in camera."

In January 1955, on the basis of his "personal handling" of the Be'eri trial, then defense minister Pinhas Lavon solicited Shapira's legal opinion "on the role of Mr. Benyamin Givly in that affair." Unaware of Lavon's purpose, Shapira submitted his opinion on February 6. Givly, he wrote, was "the Jerusalem intelligence officer who, on June 25, 1948, submitted to Isser Be'eri a report on the basis of which Mr. Be'eri drew the conclusion that Tubiansky had engaged in . . . espionage and treason . . . whereupon a 'field court-martial' was held on June 30, 1948, at Beit Jiz, and . . . Tubiansky was executed in situ. . . . The source of the accusation was the report Mr. Benyamin Givly submitted to Mr. Be'eri."

Shapira did not use such unequivocal terms at the time of the Be'eri trial, probably because he did not then hold such a view. Only in retrospect, it appears, did Shapira realize that his own misjudgment had precluded a thorough investigation of Tubiansky's execution, and of Givly's role in it.

Givly's conduct in the Tubiansky affair raises a crucial question: Why did Ben-Gurion sanction his subsequent promotion to a rank just short of DMI? The answer—that military intelligence was at the time only a department of the General Staff Branch, and the promotion of a major was not the concern of a cabinet minister—is unsatisfactory, for it in turn raises another question: why did Ben-Gurion not have Givly investigated? Such questions are endless; and whatever the answers, they all depend on the differing principles governing different spheres of operation. The military rationale is unlike the judicial one, and those wise after the event claim a rationale all their own.

The vacuum left at military intelligence by Be'eri's removal was filled by his deputy, Haim Herzog. But the SHAI veterans who predominated in MI felt little liking for Herzog, who had served as an intelligence officer with the British army. Herzog recalled that it took Ben-Gurion "to ram me in by force" because "Yadin and his little coterie . . . didn't want a man from the British army." On his elevation to chief of staff in November 1949, Yadin proposed that Herzog go to Washington as IDF military attache; another officer would assume his place as head of intelligence. But Ben-Gurion insisted on Herzog, who recalled the parties concluding "a package deal, namely, they came and told me: Benyamin Givly is Number 2, and you're Number 1."

Yadin made Givly deputy DMI; the appointment, approved by then chief of staff Ya'akov Dori, took effect on March 15, 1949, predating the decision to try "those responsible" for Tubiansky's killing. In addition to his post as deputy, Givly retained his previous job as head of Intelligence Service 1, comprising the corps' most important section: combat intelligence and research. It was agreed further that he would also serve as "MI representative with the General Staff"—which in Herzog's interpretation meant assigning Givly as "Yadin's intelligence officer." His closeness to the chief of staff was further manifested when he was installed at GHQ in Ramat Gan, while Herzog was kept at a distance, in Jaffa. According to Herzog, "Givly dominated the entire administrative side, right from the outset." In short: although he was "Number 2," Givly wielded enormous powers, and was widely regarded as an early candidate for "Number 1."

During his tenure as DMI, Herzog prepared for civilian life by taking time to study law. Every morning from 5 to 8, a tutor helped him prepare for his bar examination, and he returned to his books each evening.

Givly devoted all his time and energies to the service, winning the esteem even of Herzog, who regarded him as a tough and thorough officer noteworthy for his initiative and honesty and his flair for human relations. "He maintained the entire administrative side of the service, at a time when it was one great mess and nothing was organized."

Herzog passed his examinations in 1950. When Yadin again offered him the job of military attache in Washington, he leaped at the opportunity. He became attache on April 16, 1950; that same day, on his warm recommendation, Givly was made acting head of the MI.

Givly's rise in the intelligence hierarchy was evidently unimpaired by the Tubiansky affair and the Be'eri trial; on the contrary, these events appear to have expedited his advancement. Enjoying wide esteem, Givly was regarded as a superb officer with a clean record.

A prime example is provided by Herzog himself, who had been directly touched by the Tubiansky affair when Lena Tubiansky, in her distress, approached his father, Chief Rabbi Yitzhak Halevi Herzog. "Father called me and said: 'Mrs. Tubiansky has been to see me, to demand justice for her husband. What do you know?' I told him: 'I know nothing, but I'll go and find out.'" Herzog claims to have turned up nothing. One day he accidentally discovered "in a drawer in one of the rooms [at headquarters in Jaffa] the beret, pipe and other effects of Tubiansky"—but Be'eri declined "to talk about it."

On July 8, 1949, Herzog advised Ben-Gurion against trying Be'eri for Tubiansky's execution, lest "Be'eri try to wash the [dirty] linen." When Givly took the witness stand at the Be'eri trial, his testimony held no interest for Herzog, who commented later: "To tell the truth, I knew very little beyond what was published in the papers . . . I got the impression that [Givly] was not given prominence. Isser was." Givly's role in the affair evoked a similar measure of indifference and disinterest in Yadin and his deputy Mordechai Makleff: neither found any fault with Givly.

On the contrary: as Director of Operations, Yadin had been struck by Givly's diligence and strength of character. His sole defect, Yadin and Herzog agreed, was his lack of schooling, both military and general. Herzog recommended he be sent abroad for advanced studies to broaden his horizons. Yadin became chief of staff in November 1949 and in January 1950 granted Givly the rank of lieutenant colonel, retroactive to December 1, 1949—just one week after the Be'eri trial verdict was handed down. In the spring of 1950, Herzog asked Yadin who would replace him as head of MI when he left for Washington; the chief of staff replied unhesitatingly: "Givly." Yadin did indeed give Givly that position, which he assumed on June 1, 1950; a few days later, he was promoted to full colonel.

Givly was due to receive brigadier general's rank after one year, then the minimum term for promotion. Within that year, as recommended by Yadin and Herzog, he was to complete his studies in Israel and abroad. Prior to his departure in February 1953, he was signed on for five further years of regular service—clear evidence of the esteem in which his superiors held him.

As chief of MI, Givly succeeded where Herzog had failed: he convinced Makleff (who became chief of staff on December 7, 1952) and acting defense minister Lavon (standing in for Ben-Gurion, who was on leave before retiring to Sdeh Boker) to elevate intelligence from a department to a GHQ branch. It was his greatest coup. On December 28, 1953, chief of staff Moshe Dayan and defense minister Pinhas Lavon—both newly installed—endorsed the creation of the Military Intelligence Branch, with Givly as its first director—a post customarily filled by a brigadier general. It was a dizzying leap.

No lesson had been learned from the investigations pursued by the JAG, the police, the examining magistrate, or the court. There was no demand—whether from General Staff, the intelligence corps, or the civilian authorities—for expert scrutiny of the Tubiansky affair. The heads of the army and the intelligence service knew very little of what has been recounted thus far in these pages. Those who sensed the presence of dry rot believed it had been excised by Be'eri's removal.

History teaches that a failure to learn lessons entails a heavy toll of recurrent error. But that leads us to a new and still more complex affair.

7

Faces Old and New

Givly's lover Shosh Marshov had a life full of ups and downs. The ups came first. When the fledgling IDF first introduced ranks in August 1948, she was made head secretary at MI, with the rank of lieutenant; thanks to Givly, she was soon promoted to captain, and subsequently, to major. Her influence in the intelligence corps was such that even as a mere lieutenant, "I discharged the duties of a lieutenant colonel." "I was like a queen," she boasted: "I did whatever I wished."

Givly and Marshov indeed conducted themselves like a royal couple. They set off together each morning to their jobs at MI headquarters, returning together in the evening to their apartment. Givly had two homes: with Marshov in Tel Aviv, and with his wife and daughter in Petah Tikva. Marshov had come to terms with this situation.

But their relationship was haunted by the anguished figure of Isser Be'eri. Marshov, who idolized Be'eri, was tormented by a growing suspicion, which turned into conviction, that Givly had betrayed him. Be'eri had "raised him, made a 'mensch' of him, fought to make him head of Intelligence Service 1"; but instead of coming to his aid, Givly was the only one "to bear witness against Isser." On top of that, "he also lied . . . in order to protect himself, because his guilt exceeded Isser's. If there had to be a trial, he should have been in the dock."

Marshov watched Be'eri languish in despondency—he was "depressed, his wife fell gravely ill, and he too had a heart attack"—while Givly went from strength to strength, the embodiment of health, success, and well-being. Marshov found it increasingly difficult to reconcile her heart, which followed Givly, with her conscience, which cried out for Be'eri. Over time, her eyes were opened to Givly's true character: "not fair, not honest, not candid . . . not the man for me anyway." She began "to mistrust him"; one evening in 1951, she told him, "the story's over." She resigned from the army, and Givly returned to his wife.

Givly was fond of familiar faces, and Marshov was not the only SHAI veteran in his immediate circle. Shmuel Ganizi, for example, received the rank of major and command of the General Staff intelligence base.

Another SHAI graduate was Mordechai Ben-Zur, an acquaintance of Givly's from the old days in officers' school and Rehovot. Unwittingly, and to his own detriment, Ben-Zur was to find himself at the epicenter of a crucial juncture of Israeli politics; it is thus necessary to introduce him in some detail.

Ben-Zur was fifteen when he came to Palestine from his native Poland. In November 1941, after a period of kibbutz life, he began five years of Palmach service. In November 1946, he went to Iraq on a Haganah mission which he completed without distinction after eighteen months. From May 1948 through June 1949, he served as intelligence officer with the Palmach's Harel brigade in the Jerusalem sector and at Southern Command headquarters. He was made captain in January 1949; that June, he was attached to the intelligence corps and stationed in Jaffa as investigations officer charged with collating intelligence from overt sources, and with interrogations of war prisoners and immigrants from Arab countries.

His promotion made good sense. He was experienced—he had spent a year and a half in Iraq, had visited Syria, and made a brief expedition to Iran. He also had a knowledge of languages—perfect Hebrew and Yiddish; written and spoken Arabic; and written Polish, German, and English. Later he was appointed, on Givly's recommendation, to base commander, with the rank of major. In February 1950 however, Givly, citing "personal acquaintance," made him head of Section 13, planning and operations; and, in April 1953, he took command of Unit 131, which was entrusted with all undercover operations in enemy territory.

Enshrouded in a romantic mantle of secrecy, 131 was the spearhead of the intelligence corps, its finest and most sought-after unit. Did Ben-Zur possess the qualities required of its commander? An elite unit operating in enemy territory demands a leader of exceptional talent and instinct, supplemented by a high level of intelligence, finely tuned learning skills, a sophisticated mind, and rapid adaptability to changing circumstances. Given these needs, Ben-Zur certainly was not the man for the job.

Indeed, with the wisdom of hindsight, it can be affirmed that he was totally unfitted for so important and sensitive a command. Givly had, in fact, no reason to believe that Ben-Zur had the necessary education, gifts or experience in "planning and operations." In giving him the job, Givly set Ben-Zur and his unit—and, ultimately, the government of Israel—on a course to disaster.

A bearlike 210-pound six-footer, Ben Zur was clumsy and convivial. His grey-green eyes, nestling under chestnut hair, shone with goodwill and camaraderie. One MI colleague rated him as a modest officer, loyal and honest, and devoted to his superiors, though "cool" toward them; another recalled him "exuding charm." His acquaintances from this period agree that he was inexhaustibly energetic, a trait some construed as eagerness for initiative and action. But he did not possess "a brilliant mind," nor did his gifts extend to concocting sophisticated scenarios, or to exercising remote control of espionage networks in enemy territory. He was regarded as "mediocre"—according to some, "less than mediocre"—a judgment reflected in his grades in various courses, which were never high: in the first phase advanced officers' course he attended just before taking command of 131, he was graded below average.

Admittedly, the military has a rationale of its own. Not everyone who distinguishes himself in courses goes on to make a good soldier. In promoting its personnel, the army takes account of their traits overall, attaching great weight to courage on the battlefield, to perseverance and dedication. Ben-Zur's dedication—universally recognized and acclaimed— may have played an important role in his advancement, inducing his superiors to overlook his lax discipline as a cadet (at the advanced course for intelligence officers, his grades for conduct and discipline were a modest B-C).

Givly appointed Ben-Zur to command 131 before he left for his year of study. The nomination ran into opposition at the General Staff Personnel department, which had to approve ranks above Major. Lieutenant Colonel Yehoshafat Harkabi, who was standing in for Givly, saw it as his duty to ram the nomination through and did so, knowing this was what Givly expected.

Doubts as to Ben-Zur's fitness for the command were subsequently expressed by a board of inquiry headed by Justice Haim Cohen, which was established in 1960 to look into the Lavon affair (see chapter 18). Its members were inclined to attribute Ben-Zur's perjured testimony before them to "his stupidity." Nor did Givly disagree: among his intimates, his nickname for Ben-Zur was "the fat dummy."

Why, then, did Givly give Ben-Zur command of 131? The answer, if there is one at all, may lie in the fact that in the military hierarchy, dedication and loyalty sometimes make up for a mediocre mind and a lack of originality or imagination. Perhaps the answer was merely that Givly wanted to keep 131 under his own control—impossible if it had been led by an intelligent and strongly independent officer. Indeed, Givly did set limits on Ben-Zur's authority by appointing Avraham Dar to recruit personnel for Unit 131 in Egypt.

Dar was a veteran of the Palmach's naval unit, with experience in running illegal immigrants through the British blockade. Re-enlisting with the IDF in 1950, he joined the intelligence corps to serve with its "Arabist" unit; at his own insistence, he was dispatched to Egypt to recruit volunteers for psychological warfare operations, from April 1950 through August 1951, and in January–February 1952. The recruits he picked out in Cairo and Alexandria were sent to Israel for formal enrollment with the IDF and training at the 131 base. Thus, just before he went on leave in mid-February 1953, as Dar testified at the hearing, it dawned on Givly that although there were volunteers, their unit existed in name only, lacking an operational organization and clear chain of command. As Dar saw it, Ben-Zur had been unable to develop an operational concept or translate it into an effective formation. Thus Givly offered Dar command of the Egyptian volunteers, under the overall command of Ben-Zur. After some hesitation, Dar accepted.

Ben-Zur's version is different. He claimed that Givly advised him that the volunteers training in Israel would come under Dar's "charge," making him "autonomous within my unit." Ben-Zur objected to "a kind of joint or subsidiary command" in his unit. Aside from being concerned to preserve a unified command, Ben-Zur said, Dar "didn't go for my methods, and I didn't go for his"; accordingly, "I didn't want Avraham Dar, or the way Benyamin wished to saddle me with him." But Givly dismissed Ben-Zur's protests and redefined Dar's duties: he would supervise the Egyptian volunteers during their training in Israel, and issue orders to them that came directly from Givly. Givly was thus positioning himself as an arbiter between Ben-Zur and Dar, retaining complete control over both. In February 1953, when Givly went abroad, Dar quit 131, claiming that his differences with Ben-Zur made it impossible to work under his command.

As Ben-Zur claimed later, Givly "played a double game." He and Dar agree on one point: by means of the ongoing confrontation he fomented between them, Givly sought to keep 131 under his own control.

There is no better testimony to Givly's prestige and status in the intelligence corps, or the army's great expectations of him, than the study program drawn up for him, which was unequaled in the annals of the IDF. Initially, at the recommendation of Yadin and Herzog, he was selected for phase 2 of the IDF's advanced officers' course; designed especially for senior officers, it covered six months, in late 1950 and February–May 1951. Subsequently, he was awarded fifteen months of study abroad: nine months at Princeton, three or four months with the U.S. army, and another three or four months to be spent either at an advanced course in administration at Harvard, or at the British army's advanced officers' course at Henley. The associated requirement that, instead of the usual three years, he had to sign on for five years of service, likewise reflected his superiors' confidence in him.

On February 22, 1953, accompanied by his wife Esther and daughter Tamar, Givly departed for the United States. In two semesters at Princeton's Woodrow Wilson school of international relations, he followed a non-degree program, taking "horizon-broadening" courses designed for U.S. Administration officials and military officers; this enabled him to attend lectures and submit papers on a wide range of subjects. From January 4 through March 6, 1954, he attended an administrative course at Henley in Britain. The rest of his program was curtailed by cutbacks in Israel's defense budget; on March 19, after an absence of thirteen months and two weeks, Givly and his family returned to Israel.

Givly's foreign studies evidently broadened his view of the world. But he had nothing to learn from anyone in the cultivation of personal connections, as indicated by his extensive correspondence with his superiors and subordinates in Israel. He shared his experiences with them, and expressed his affection in his readiness to meet requests for goods and appliances unavailable in austerity-ridden Israel. But he was equally swift to solicit assistance, for example in getting the intelligence corps to fund his purchase of a car for use in the U.S., or obtaining customs concessions on his return to Israel. He seems to have had few equals in establishing mutual commitments along the lines of "I'll scratch your back, you scratch mine."

On March 28, 1954, Givly was appointed Director of Military Intelligence (DMI). Harkabi, now departing to study in France, left him with a staff full of new faces. Noteworthy in the present context are his aide-de-camp Aluf Hareven, and his secretary Dalia Carmel; both were enamored of their charming new boss.

Hareven—thin and bespectacled, studiously earnest and conscientious, his gifts and ambitions inclining to scholarship and literature—had served initially with the research department; after completing an infantry officers' course, he moved to the armistice department. In April 1954, he leaped at Givly's invitation to serve as his aide-de-camp. Hareven recalled later: "I found him a superb superior, energetic, authoritative, gifted; an excellent man of action. . . . I trusted him."

Dalia Carmel was striking in appearance: tall, athletic in build, with chestnut hair and grey-green eyes. Born September 1, 1935, she was the only daughter of Dr. Yosef Wieser, a Jerusalem TB specialist; when she was a child, her family moved to Tel Aviv. On graduating from high school, she worked as a volunteer at the foreign ministry's consular archives. As she relates, she took a special interest in music, literature and diplomacy; she had a mastery of English and German, and spoke a little French and Yiddish. Enlisting for her compulsory military service in 1953, she landed a posting with military intelligence. Her high grades in the course for intelligence personnel, along with recommendations saying she was fit "for secretarial duties at the highest level," got her a clerical job at the office of the DMI during Harkabi's directorship.

Carmel was soon noted for her aptitude, keen understanding, and initiative; she was an exemplary worker. Her total identification with her job evolved into a sense of partnership and collegiality with her superiors.

When Givly replaced Harkabi, a new luminary irradiated Carmel's cosmos: "Benyamin . . . he was a giant with beautiful hands." She idolized him from the outset, and more intensely as time passed. When she first began working with him, "I walked around like I was doped, so I was told. For example, my father used to tell how if Givly came to our house, I behaved as though God had arrived." Besides visiting her parents' home, Givly also invited her to his own. "It was open house for artists and everyone who was anyone. People would come for musical evenings. He would invite me to his house, and then drive me back to my parents.' "

But as a rule, she said goodbye at the door, "because my father detested him with a murderous hatred. Father sensed that he was taking advantage of me." Was Dr. Wieser afraid that his daughter would get herself mixed up with a married man sixteen years her senior? Knowing her well, Dr. Wieser appears to have detected her partiality for older men. Indeed, her first lover was a married man fourteen years her senior; she went on to a romance with a widower forty years older than herself; and her present husband is twenty-one years older. But with regard to Givly, Dr. Wieser was mistaken: despite gossip, their relationship never went beyond friendship and veneration.

Still, Carmel's adoration was blind: as she concedes, she looked upon him "as one contemplates God." She knitted a sweater for his birthday, hung his photograph in her room and carried another in her purse. What was the secret of his charm? In Carmel's words: "He made you feel like you were the only person in the whole wide world. He would remember things, always asking after my mother and sending flowers." At the same time, if Dr. Wieser was apprehensive that his daughter would be exploited in other ways, he was quite right: Givly was to involve Carmel in Israel's greatest political earthquake.

Unlike his subordinates, who were mostly old acquaintances, Givly's superiors on the General Staff and in the defense ministry were entirely new to him.

During Givly's year-long leave of absence, Ben-Gurion had begun preparing for his retirement. He did not make his intentions public initially, but merely sought cabinet permission for a special leave of absence to study basic defense needs and the structure of the army. On July 19, 1953, the cabinet approved Ben-Gurion's nomination of Pinhas Lavon, until then minister without portfolio, as acting defense minister; foreign minister Moshe Sharett became acting prime minister. These nominations took effect on August 15, when Ben-Gurion left for his two-month leave, which was mostly devoted to a study of defense problems, and a tour of the IDF's various units, so as to draw up guidelines for his successors.

On October 18, Ben-Gurion returned to his office. The next day, he submitted his defense proposals to the cabinet—which endorsed them unanimously—along with an announcement of his own immediate resignation. On October 25, Mapai's political committee, disregarding Ben-Gurion's recommendation of finance minister Levi Eshkol, nominated Sharett as prime minister.

Ben-Gurion remained in his two positions until Sharett had staffed his coalition cabinet, which included Lavon as defense minister. On December 6, Mordechai Makleff resigned as chief of staff; that same morning, Ben-Gurion appointed Moshe Dayan to succeed him. On December 7, Ben-Gurion submitted his own resignation to the state president, taking leave of the nation in a radio broadcast. A week later, he and his wife Paula moved to Kibbutz Sdeh Boker, in the southern Negev wilderness.

Mapai's senior ministers were irked by Lavon's appointment as defense minister, which in their eyes showed favoritism toward someone who was their junior in both age and party hierarchy and also elevated him over their heads to the status of heir to Ben-Gurion. Keeping these private resentments to themselves, they did however tell Ben-Gurion of serious misgivings which focussed exclusively on Lavon's character. Their disapproval was summarized in a somewhat cryptic quote attributed to Mapai's departed mentor, Berl Katznelson, who allegedly had characterized Lavon as "a brilliant mind in a murky soul." But it was not until February 1965, at Mapai's tenth convention, that Golda Meir publicly voiced the vigorous objections she and her colleagues had conveyed to Ben-Gurion back in 1953: "A not inconsiderable number of colleagues" had considered Lavon unfit for the job and objected to his appointment; but "Ben-Gurion did not heed our suggestion."

Lavon's appointment was also the main reason for the resignation of Makleff, who complained of the new minister's disdain for the army, and his treatment of its officers as clerks in uniform (Lavon reportedly described the officer corps as the strongest trade union he had ever encountered). Makleff also objected to Lavon's intemperate activism; he responded to the most trivial of border incidents by pressing for far-reaching reprisals. At the time, Ben-Gurion ignored Makleff's warnings; not until eight years later, in January 1961, did Ben-Gurion confide to Mapai's central committee that Lavon had issued to Makleff and Dayan "certain 'adventurous' military directives whose implementation was forestalled only because, to our good fortune, these chiefs of staff realized that such hazardous adventures must be prevented."

Ben-Gurion conceded later that Lavon was "a mistake"; but in 1953, he insisted on his appointment, which created a novel state of affairs: no longer did the prime minister simultaneously officiate as defense minister; now, Lavon had to toe the political line laid down by Sharett, who doubled as foreign minister and was renowned for his moderation. With respect to the cabinet and prime minister, as well as his subordinates—chief of staff Dayan and director-general Shimon Peres—Lavon maintained a stance of mistrust, if not outright hostility. Not only did he fail to observe proper procedure; in a quest for political independence, he also withheld controversial matters from Sharett's knowledge and from consideration by the cabinet.

Pinhas Lavon will probably remain a riddle. Lean and willowy, his hair a premature silver, he had too great a taste for brandy, a weakness offset by an erudition and swift wit which set him intellectually head and shoulders above most Mapai leaders. He had reached political maturity in the Histadrut trade unions, and his elevation to the defense ministry brought out previously undetected traits. From being an outspoken pacifist, "among the most consistent of anti-activists . . . opposed to a mailed-fist policy which might jeopardize existing [achievements]," once in his new post Lavon turned into a hardline advocate of force; from scholar and authority on Socialist theory, he was transformed into a man of action avid for military exploits; from champion of internationalism, he became a nationalist who despised Arabs; from prophet of social justice and the general welfare, he metamorphosed into a powerseeker who reacted to any encroachment upon his status or dignity with a readiness to wreak havoc, even if it harmed the state.

From the outset, Lavon pursued a policy of excessive force, expressed in vigorous reprisal raids that exacerbated Israel's relations with its Arab neighbors; it was matched by his "line of violent activism toward the Western states." Sharett noted in his diary that Lavon "incessantly advocated acts of lunacy, inculcating the army command with the diabolical notion of igniting the Middle East, fomenting dissension, bloody assassinations, attacks on objectives and assets of the Powers, acts of desperation and suicide."

Ben-Gurion and Sharett did not always see eye to eye politically, but their invariably strict observance of proper procedure underpinned their relations with mutual trust. Lavon introduced new patterns of conduct. A defense minister who defies the prime minister overtly and covertly—feeding him reports verging upon falsehood and inspiring the army with disdain for him and his policies—probably suspects that he is himself the object of similar treatment by his own subordinates.

The IDF had changed beyond recognition during Givly's thirteen-month absence. Yadin had gone, and so had Makleff; above all, Ben-Gurion was no longer there. In their places were Dayan and Lavon; the latter had promoted Shimon Peres, the defense ministry's acting director general under Ben-Gurion, to full director-general; military secretary Nehemia Argov, who had been ardently cultivated by Givly, was replaced by Ephraim Evron, formerly private secretary to Sharett and Ben-Gurion. It was an army unfamiliar with Givly, and to Givly.

The stage was set for the second act. When the bell sounded and the curtain rose, Givly could again look forward to a leading role.

8

Unit 131 Strikes

In his new capacity as Director of Military Intelligence (DMI), Benyamin Givly was now a full member of the IDF General Staff. The faces he encountered around the table at his first meeting on April 5, 1954, were youthful. Back in 1949, Ben-Gurion had bypassed the Haganah veterans to give supreme command to Yigael Yadin, then thirty-two, with Mordechai Makleff, three years younger, as his deputy; Makleff's replacement by Moshe Dayan took the rejuvenation of the military command a step further. Director of Operations Major General Yosef Avidar was now the sole GHQ member over forty; the others were all colonels around thirty years of age. At thirty-five, Givly was the oldest of them.

The defense ministry received a similar infusion of young blood with Ben-Gurion's nomination of Lavon, forty-nine, a step widely regarded as foreshadowing Lavon's eventual accession to the prime ministership. Plainly, the days of the state's aging leaders were numbered; the stage would soon be dominated by a younger generation born in the twentieth century, and by Sabras (native-born Israelis). If extended to the ruling Mapai leadership, Ben-Gurion's drive for revitalization would soon fill the top political slots with younger men and women, the first in the line of succession being the heads of the army and the defense establishment. The future prospects of chief of staff Moshe Dayan and his thirty-one-year-old ally, defense ministry director-general Shimon Peres, also appeared bright.

Quick to observe the new order in the making, Givly poised himself to snap up a choice position. His keen instincts swiftly identified the Lavon-Dayan-Peres trio—Ben-Gurion's handpicked proteges—as the future national leadership upon whom his own advancement would depend. Givly "was convinced he would join the troika," claimed Rehavia Vardi, a senior MI officer and Givly's friend. Vardi's perception is supported by Mordechai Ben-Zur, who noted "three individuals discontented with what they had: Givly, Dayan and Lavon": the first—as Givly himself admitted—wanted to become chief of staff; the second, defense minister; and the third, prime minister. "This pursuit of office distorted their judgement."

Luckily for Givly, the Lavon-Dayan-Peres idyll was short-lived. The initial fissures appeared when the unrelenting covert rivalry between Dayan and Peres made the ever-mistrustful Lavon suspect each of them of "using" him to enlarge his own foothold within the defense establishment. In the words of Lavon aide Ephraim Evron: "Lavon suddenly began to think: 'they aren't telling me the whole truth, and I don't know exactly what's going on.' " As his suspicion grew, Lavon became ravenous for information above and beyond the reports Dayan gave him; departing from Ben-Gurion's practice, he went behind the chief of staff's back, meeting privately with GHQ branch chiefs, heads of regional commands and army corps, and staff officers.

Lavon also made himself freely available to Givly, probably for two reasons. First, he anticipated an advantage in enlisting as ally and confidant a gifted, promising intelligence officer renowned for his daring and imagination, and credited with numerous triumphs such as Unit 131's success in penetrating hostile territory—Egypt in particular—and the operational options this penetration opened up, which had been hailed as "extraordinary achievements in the international arena."

Second, Givly offered solutions for Lavon's most pressing problem. Ever since the July 1952 military coup in Egypt—particularly after February 24, 1954, when Colonel Abdul Nasser took control of that country—its stance toward Israel had hardened, as strikingly evidenced in its tightened blockade on Israeli shipping in the Tiran Straits and Suez Canal. Worse, the Egyptian junta's improved relations with the British government made it increasingly probable that the latter would withdraw its garrison stationed at the Suez Canal under a 1936 Treaty. As a result the British military buffer between Israel and Egypt would be removed; British installations would be handed over to the Egyptian army; the British units would be relocated to Jordan, whose border with Israel was extremely troublesome; Egypt would become eligible for U.S. military aid; and Arab states would be invited to join a regional defense pact under the aegis of Britain and the U.S.

Seeing such developments as a menace to Israel's very existence, Lavon sought ways of preventing the British withdrawal. In Lavon's penchant for bold decisions and striking action—whereby he hoped to rise to equal, if not surpass, Ben-Gurion—Givly discerned the opportunity for an operation of historic proportions. In the words of Rehavia Vardi: "I think he wished to distinguish himself greatly, to stand out." Dayan too believed that this operation, which became the focus of the Lavon affair, was initiated by Givly, though not exclusively by him.

Before describing it we can already point to similarities between the episode about to be described and the one discussed in previous chapters. As he had done in the Tubiansky case, Givly responded to a superior's craving for action by submitting a proposal his boss would find appealing; as before, the plan was conceived in haste and inadequately scrutinized; as before, its implementation was calamitous; as before, it took its toll of human life; and as before, the entire episode was incompletely investigated. But there was one major difference: this time, the undertaking hurled Israel into a giddying maelstrom unequaled before or since. The parallel also extends to the issue of responsibility: when the chips were down, would Givly manage to divert attention to a superior behind whom he would take cover? Would he again contrive to get off scot free?

The answer to that question hinged upon a critical change in the supervision of Unit 131. Designated for action in hostile countries, 131 was initially placed under political control, exercised by a two-man committee comprising the head of the "Mossad," who answered directly to the prime minister, and the IDF's deputy chief of staff, who was then in charge of military intelligence. As long as Ben-Gurion was both prime minister and minister of defense, Unit 131 came under his purview. But when he resigned and his powers were divided between Prime Minister Sharett and Defense Minister Lavon, the latter, envious of the undivided control wielded by his predecessor, proceeded—without consulting Sharett—to do away with the supervisory committee.

But Isser Harel, now head of the Mossad and chairman of the secret services' coordinating committee, was reluctant to yield his supervisory role, and called for renewal of the two-man committee. On February 18,

1954, the defense minister and the chief of staff rejected this request. Dayan later explained that his opposition to Sharett's policies—which he shared with Lavon—lay behind his objections to the revival of the two-man committee: "Bringing in Harel" (who was answerable to Sharett) "entailed bringing in the prime minister." Lavon was to claim that he objected in principle to placing an operational unit under such joint supervision because it "opens up the way for an absence of responsibility by any minister." He conveniently forgot that Sharett was not just "any" minister.

The bottom line: 131 now lay under Lavon's exclusive control.

Concluding their training in Israel at the end of 1953, Unit 131's recruits returned to Egypt to await instructions. In the meantime, they were ordered to keep in regular touch with Israel by means of transmitters entrusted to them; to concoct explosives from materials on sale at pharmacies; and to pick out objectives for sabotage in the event of war.

On February 18, 1954, Harkabi's request for an increase in 131's complement and budget came up for consideration. Dayan objected on principle, arguing that the unit was reserved exclusively for operations in times of war. He also questioned 131's operational capacity, and the fitness of its CO, Ben-Zur. Adopting Dayan's view, Lavon ordered "a significant reduction" in the resources Harkabi demanded.

Lavon's ruling was issued on February 25. The next day, Mossad chief Harel—warning the defense minister of the foolhardiness of drawing upon a single source of information, particularly in relation to cross-border operations—again offered to help supervise the unit. According to Harel, Lavon responded arrogantly that "He didn't need help, and would supervise the unit personally and directly." Harel said that was "a one-sided arrangement," to which Lavon retorted: "In that case, one-sided it shall be."

During Harkabi's term as acting DMI, these arguments and differences were purely theoretical: "There was no talk of activating the men of 131." But when Givly resumed his position, debates over the unit and its tasks soon became distinctly practical. The removal of any formal hierarchical barriers between Givly and Lavon, compounded by lack of supervision by the prime minister, had paved the path to disaster.

Lavon's eagerness to activate Unit 131 dovetailed with his newfound hawkish stance, reflected in his public statements, and even more in his authorization of a series of cross-border reprisal raids. Givly was familiar with Lavon's opposition to Sharett's policies and his habit of bypassing the prime minister by withholding information or submitting incomplete reports. Undoubtedly, Givly also knew that Lavon had given his blessing to a number of reckless schemes: "crazy," he called them later (most remain classified to this day). Eager to court favor with the defense minister, Givly embraced Lavon's bellicose line, along with his disdain for the prime minister, and the head of Mossad.

The lack of cooperation between Sharett and Lavon was all the more notable in the light of ongoing diplomatic moves: under U.S. pressure, Anglo-Egyptian talks on Britain's evacuation of the Canal Zone, broken off in October 1953, were to resume in June 1954. The threat this posed to Israel riveted the attention of Lavon and Givly, who were now directly exchanging information and ideas.

Could Israel do anything to prevent or at least delay the British withdrawal? Working papers from MI's research department, sent to Lavon by Givly, argued that the only chance was to fan the opposition to the pullout then prevalent in the British Parliament. It was doubtful whether "it lies within our unaided power to foil an agreement on the Canal withdrawal," Givly wrote in a memorandum dated June 16; such a goal "will not be achieved by routine diplomatic means." However, "our actions, in concert with other parties, are capable of deferring or swaying attainment of the agreement."

To this end, Givly proposed five "feasible and desirable" operations, two by the IDF and three by the foreign ministry:

First scheme: sending a ship under the Israeli flag through the Tiran Straits or the Suez Canal. On June 21, Givly, together with Dayan, presented Lavon with a proposal surmising that "if Egypt halts the vessel in defiance of the Security Council resolution, and Israel responds with military action, an immediate response will come from opponents of the agreement in the British Parliament. In consequence thereof, the agreement may be delayed. If Israel were to occupy the Canal straits in response to the vessel's seizure, security will be undermined throughout the region, making the situation unpropitious for conclusion of an Anglo-Egyptian agreement. Even if an agreement is achieved, it will be influenced by this state of affairs." Lavon promptly endorsed the plan, urging MI "to purchase this vessel" and prepare it for its voyage.

Second scheme: "Psychological warfare operations in Egypt," intended to make the Egyptians believe that the British were not offering withdrawal, "but rather, replacement of military uniforms by civilian [clothing], with the American element superimposed upon the British element already installed in Egypt." Lavon claimed to have scrawled on this proposal the comment, "It can be done, but its usefulness is questionable."

Givly also proposed three lines of diplomatic action, which Lavon—or so he later claimed—did not endorse. Regarding a proposal to engage in propaganda in Britain, in conjunction with groups opposed to the Canal withdrawal, he commented: "These things are being done, they are of scant value." About a similar campaign in France, he wrote: "A broken reed." He made no response to Givly's third proposal, for "propaganda in the United States, stressing the instability of the military regime and the army's Communist leanings."

Because the memorandum made no reference to sabotage by MI's operational units, there was no call for comment or response from the chief of staff. The subject was however discussed privately by Lavon and Givly, in a conversation destined to plunge Israel into enormous upheavals and changes.

Givly claimed subsequently that this exchange occurred "at the end of April or early in May." Evron, who sat in on it, said it took place in May or early June; but eventually, he too dated it to April or May. The two men differ on the substance of the conversation. In Givly's version, "Lavon said: 'Benyamin, we have to be *ready to act* (italics added) against British objectives.' I asked: 'In Cyprus too?' He replied: 'No, only in the Arab countries.' " According to Evron, Givly submitted a broad outline of action, and Lavon replied that they would reconsider it when Givly had boiled it down into a clear-cut operational plan. Wherever the truth lies, that conversation became the subject of fierce differences between Lavon and Givly, and the facts surrounding it remain obscure to this day.

On July 12, 1954, ignorant of what Lavon and Givly were concocting in private, Dayan flew to the United States for the first-ever tour of American military installations by an Israeli chief of staff. His replacement during his thirty-eight-day absence was Director of Operations Major General Avidar.

From this point on, a distinction must be drawn between incontrovertible facts, and those which are in dispute. The former will be presented as objective narrative, the latter as the conflicting versions of the participants.

On July 14 or 15, a "reliable source" reported that the signing of the Anglo-Egyptian agreement was expected to occur on the 23rd. Although there had been numerous intimations of an imminent turnaround in relations between the two countries, the report struck MI like a bolt from the blue. (The report turned out to be only partly correct. The agreement was initialed on July 27; but not until October 19 1954—matching MI's original projection—was the treaty signed. The last British soldier left Egypt in June 1955.)

It was discussed at the defense minister's weekly meeting on Thursday July 15, attended by the regular participants: Lavon, acting chief of staff Avidar, defense ministry director-general Peres, and Lavon's chief aide, Evron. Although Givly was not on Evron's list of participants, there is no doubt that the DMI attended at least part of the meeting. According to Dayan, when he returned from the U.S., Avidar reported that "Thursday July 15, there was a weekly meeting and afterwards Lavon asked Givly to remain. . . . It irked him. . . . It stuck in his memory." Avidar agreed. The only person who did not insist that Givly had attended the meeting was Givly himself.

With an eye to those Westminster parliamentarians opposed to the Suez withdrawal, the deliberations weighed the feasibility of some Israeli action that might prompt Tory M.P.'s to rebel against the cabinet, in an attempt to put off the agreement. The scheme of sending an Israeli vessel to Eilat by way of Tiran was set aside for the moment. That left only one way to foment an eleventh-hour crisis of confidence between Britain and Egypt: direct action by MI's operational units.

In the event, Unit 131 did carry out a series of actions between July 2 and 23. These efforts bore no political fruit, achieving nothing beyond: two hangings; two suicides; the extended incarceration of three young men and a young woman; and ignominy heaped upon Israel and its intelligence service. Who advocated this course? When and where was it debated? Who authorized it? Who ordered its implementation? These questions were to rock Israel with tempestuous discord that sapped the young state's foundations, exposed Ben-Gurion and Lavon to private and public travail, sundered Mapai and reduced the political arena to utter chaos. Israel would plunge into agonized strife over the relentless question: "Who gave the order?"

According to Givly, on Friday July 16, the day after the weekly defense meeting, a more restricted conclave at Lavon's home weighed "the significance of the British withdrawal from Suez." Afterward, Givly claimed, he conferred in private with the defense minister, who ordered him directly, and without informing the acting chief of staff about this astounding scheme, "to activate the 131 teams against British . . . objectives" in Egypt. For his part, Lavon totally denied Givly's story.

Meanwhile, 131's commander, Ben-Zur, had been in Europe between May 26 and June 29, 1954. Ben-Zur later testified that it was a routine trip, long scheduled and merely deferred until Givly's return to his job. Givly claimed—discrepancies were rife in his account, just as in Lavon's—that on resuming his duties, he found "the [131] teams in a dysfunctional state. I began to doubt their operational fitness and organization, and I instructed Ben-Zur to go abroad and study the situation." In Lavon's version, Ben-Zur went—without his authorization—to issue operational orders to activate 131's teams in Egypt.

In fact, Ben-Zur's principal assignment was to meet Avraham Seidenberg (Avry Elad), an undercover agent posing as a German businessman in Egypt. But the mission he assigned Avry proves that Ben-Zur's journey was far from routine, and could have been scheduled only after Givly and Lavon held their private talk in April or May.

Who was this Avry Elad? Some information is verifiable:

Avraham (Adolf) Seidenberg was blond, blue-eyed, and ruggedly handsome. Known to all as "Avry," he was born in Vienna in 1925. Reaching Palestine as a boy in 1938 or 1939, he finished school and then trained as a motor mechanic at a trade school. Settling in Haifa, he married in 1948 and had a son.

The rest of his claims, however, are replete with falsehoods. For example, he never was a member of the Haganah's full-time staff. Nor did he serve with the Palmach from 1942 onward; in fact, after a mere two-and-a-half months with the Palmach's "German company," he was dismissed for "unfitness," and stealing from his comrades. He was not a volunteer with a British commando unit, as he claimed; in fact, he was a driver with a British military transport outfit, where he earned notoriety as a "shirker and malingerer," was tried for making a false statement to a superior officer, and got caught stealing a camera from a fellow soldier. He was not a cadet in a 1947 Haganah officers' course, but merely a driver there.

In 1948, he wormed his way into the Harel brigade, but he was not in command of its headquarters company—merely its administrative officer with lieutenant's rank—until it came out that he was selling food and kerosene from brigade stores on the Jerusalem black market and getting paid for running civilians out of the besieged city in military vehicles; he was also caught stealing money from a fellow soldier. He was never a combat officer, either with Harel or the IDF paratroop unit formed late in 1948; in fact, he was dismissed from the latter outfit when it transpired that he had become a parachute instructor without having ever jumped himself.

Nevertheless Avry contrived to enroll in an IDF battalion commanders' course, winning a posting as second-in-command—not officer commanding, as he claimed—of 128 Battalion, a unit composed largely of jailbirds released under the February 1949 general amnesty. He equipped his Haifa home with a brand-new refrigerator filched from his unit; in the bleak days of 1951, amid austerity and shortages, the appliance was a rare luxury. This time, he was court-martialed, reduced in rank, and dismissed from the army. Following this downfall, he and his wife divorced.

With a forged letter of recommendation, Avry now got a job at the Kaiser-Fraser vehicle works in Haifa, where he found a savior in the form of Ben-Zur, a former comrade-in-arms in the Harel brigade. Aware of the setback Avry had suffered with dismissal from the army and loss of his rank, and considering him an ideal candidate for a solo mission as secret agent with Unit 131, Ben-Zur brought his name to Givly's attention. Givly, for his part, subscribed to the notion that people with a criminal record could be profitably employed in intelligence work if they were willing to seek rehabilitation by volunteering for tough and perilous tasks. As both officers later claimed, they were convinced that Avry would willingly undertake a mission into enemy territory as a way of regaining his honor and rank; they perceived his eagerness as justification for selecting him for a dangerous assignment.

Liar, thief, braggart; unscrupulous and irresponsible; without respect for his comrades or unit, Avry's only distinction was as a poseur who invariably managed to save his own skin and come out on top. Thus he passed off the looted refrigerator as the sole blemish on an otherwise untarnished record; neither Givly nor Ben-Zur troubled to run any additional check. What was more, Ben-Zur ignored the warnings of a senior officer who remembered Avry from his service with the British army, and also bypassed the personnel department chief who cautioned against reenlisting him and giving him the 131 posting, recalling his dishonesty about the battalion commanders' course as well as a penchant he had for car-theft.

Already in training with 131 since September 1952 on a trial basis, Avry finally got his formal posting to the unit. On March 23, 1953, while the personnel department chief was on furlough, his deputy was induced to sign Avry's service contract, which restored his former rank.

Avry took the code-name "Elad," which he later adopted as his surname. On March 30, he left for Switzerland; and in April 1953, he took up residence in Germany. MI had assigned him to Egypt, where he was to pursue his covert mission as former Wehrmacht officer "Paul Frank," commercial agent for the Faust & Stolberg company, one of numerous Germans currently seeking their fortune in the Arab countries. Avry's reinstatement had restored the affections of his former wife, and the couple remarried. He was, supposedly, a reformed character. Elad had reenlisted at Ben-Zur's initiative; his assignment and cover were supervised by Givly; and his trial period in Germany was sponsored by Givly's stand-in, Harkabi.

In only a few weeks it became evident that Avry had not reformed at all. He showed no haste about leaving for Egypt, and did nothing to set up "Faust & Stolberg," which was supposed to appear as a thriving company. Instead, compounding irresponsibility with extravagance, he breached every rule of prudence and secrecy: without authorization, he bought a brand-new Plymouth convertible in an eyecatching shade of green—and made a habit of parking it across from the Cologne offices of the Israeli purchasing mission, which was under surveillance by the German security police. He gossiped expansively with the mission's women employees, rewarding those responsive to his advances with a drive in his car. Without permission or advance notice, he also drove to France; it is unclear whether he went alone, or with a female companion.

There was nothing secretive about Elad, who told his women passengers, like other Israelis he encountered, that he had to ferry the car to Israel to be fitted with a transmitter, "for operational requirements" for his mission to Egypt. He regaled a secretary at the Cologne office with an account of "the entire content of his mission and task," and also "spilled everything" to three Israeli military men. His hearers reported these indiscretions, and the story got back to Ben-Zur, who snapped: "Is he a whore, does he have to sleep with anyone he runs into?" and "I don't believe that a 'brave' man has to be so careless and so stupid."

Ben-Zur cautioned Elad, but the man was unequaled at dredging up excuses. Assuring Ben-Zur that "he understood" his failings, he thanked him for "the opportunity to make amends," vowing henceforth to conduct himself appropriately.

But as Ben-Zur wrote to Lieutenant Colonel Mordechai Almog, MI's second in command and the head of its senior department, Elad "breaks his promises shamefully." Neglecting his instruction to harden his cover as representative of "Faust & Stolberg," he chose instead to establish it by means of a partnership with "a smart, nifty Jew" who "exploits Avry brazenly"; through him, Elad "has moved into the business of acquiring German military surplus for sale in Arab countries." Avry's partner knew about "all his movements," and his ties to the Mossad representative, whom "he visited regularly"; he also had the phone number of the representative, from whom he was to pick up "diplomatic mail or money due to arrive" for Avry.

That was not all. A visiting MI officer was among those who heard that Avry was "expecting a large sum of money from Israel." At the same time, Elad made scant use of diplomatic mail and was very tardy in mailing his financial and operational reports.

In view of Elad's mounting excesses, Almog was dispatched to Europe, to scrutinize his fitness for the secret mission to Egypt. In a letter to Ben-Zur dated October 11, Almog advised that Elad be summoned to meet him in Paris. Ben-Zur ordered Elad to leave immediately for Paris to meet Almog and cabled Almog "to withhold approval for [Elad's] plans and money. . . . I'm sending him no money, and don't you give him any either until his account is settled . . . up to October 1, 1953." In a letter to Almog dated October 25, he listed all the facts recounted above "so you can examine matters in the light of the man's replies and . . . assess his stories," and requested Almog to find out "precisely what is this business of . . . income tax in the sum of 800 Deutschemarks, that he writes he is required to pay; isn't that in fact payment for the car?" Ben-Zur added:

" . . . I write with a heavy heart, in sorrow at the disgrace this man has caused us . . . neglecting all security measures and the entire course of action he began with, without which I don't believe he'll have any success in his task."

Ben-Zur's next words were a flash of foresight:

" . . . In my eyes, the man is a lost cause. Maybe nothing has happened as far as security goes, and no-one knows about him. But if it hasn't happened yet, it will. As far as I'm concerned, you are authorized (should all this be true) to send him back to Israel immediately. . . . I'm glad I haven't tied Elad in with anyone else, so that if he is cut off, nothing will collapse."

Ben-Zur then clutched briefly at false hopes: "Great mortal danger in a hostile land may teach Elad a lesson and induce him to mend his ways. . . . I see only one possibility: he must sell the car immediately and contact the Faust firm, or otherwise, leave immediately, within a month at most, for Egypt. Otherwise, we should not waste time on this mug who'll only pile more disgraces and failures on top of these."

Yet Ben-Zur still seemed convinced that individuals anxious to erase a criminal record could be of service to MI: "I want you to speak sharply with him . . . tell him . . . if he's to make good for what he's done to me, only an exceptional deed will do."

Little is known about Almog's meeting with Elad in Paris. Almog probably reprimanded him, yet Elad managed to convince his superiors that he was fit for the mission. Accompanied by Almog, he returned to Germany, where, on October 30, he and his "cover" partner signed a contract with the company they were to represent in Egypt. That same day, Almog mailed a letter announcing he had decided to give Elad another chance. Defying all logic, Ben-Zur, with Almog's backing, sent Elad on his mission, blazing a one-way trail to calamity and perdition.

Predictably, Elad reverted to form: instead of selling his car, he brought it ashore in Alexandria, Egypt, on December 23, 1953. By January 2, 1954, he was preoccupied with gliding. On January 7, for no obvious reason, he sailed for Europe, leaving his car at the disposal of a newfound friend: Baron Theodor von Bechtoldsheim, head of the German naval mission.

Back in Germany, Elad pursued his business and the initial "commercial offers" he had received. But it is questionable whether he informed his superiors that his wife and son were living in Vienna, where he visited them from time to time. On March 2, Elad returned to Egypt; this time, he remained for two months and a day. In Alexandria he rented an apartment on Adly Pasha Street which he shared with Bob Jansen, a young German he had encountered, whom he promptly recruited as his loyal retainer.

Having regained possession of his ostentatious car, he now proceeded—without so much as a by-your-leave to anyone—to build himself a new cover, in the manner of "sewing a suit to match a button": no longer a drab technician, he now became a dynamic, well-connected entrepreneur representing German industrial agents, as well as dabbling in surplus military equipment—even though that brought him into contact with official representatives of the Israeli government and the Jewish Agency. Since this new identity still fell short of his aspirations, he dignified himself with the additional title "qualified mechanical engineer"—an easy-to-detect fabrication. This new "Paul Frank" bore absolutely no resemblance to the cover constructed by Givly and Ben-Zur.

Early in May 1954, Elad was summoned to Paris to meet Ben-Zur. On May 3, he embarked on the *Achilles* for Europe. Having taken his car along this time, Elad was out of touch for two weeks during which he toured Italy, Austria, France, Germany and Belgium. It was not until May 19 that he showed up in Paris.

He arrived, however, bearing negatives depicting components of a missile that German experts were developing in Egypt. These made a profound impression on Ben-Zur, allaying his misgivings and greatly reinforcing his trust in Elad. Years passed before it was learned that the negatives were worthless, being images of drafts of mechanical parts that represented nothing new—as Elad was well aware. He had gotten them from a German photographer "short of money" who hoped he "would find a buyer in Europe" for them.

Elad and Ben-Zur met from May 31 through June 3. To review their conversations is to tread a tricky path. Their own accounts, which they coordinated before testifying to the Olshan-Dori inquiry commission (set up in January 1955 to investigate the disaster in Egypt), are untrustworthy, having been tailored to obscure that they had met in order for Ben-Zur to give Elad his instructions.

The two depositions accordingly differ very little. Both men said that Elad was ordered to contact the Alexandria team (Elad noted that Ben-Zur had put him in command) and instruct its members to: initiate communications with Israel, prepare explosives, and reconnoiter suitable targets. Ben-Zur added that Elad was also charged with "preparing them for the purpose of the assignment."

What was the assignment? To undermine Western confidence in the existing regime by generating public insecurity and actions to bring about arrests, demonstrations, and acts of revenge, while totally concealing the Israeli factor. The team was accordingly urged to avoid detection, so that suspicion would fall upon the Muslim Brotherhood, the Communists, "unspecified malcontents," or "local nationalists."

Ben-Zur and Elad agreed on a "code for radio communication," "a standby link by way of Israel radio," "a fallback address" in Europe and "a tentative date for making contact." On Elad's return to Egypt, he was to send a cable whose coded wording—"Shipment possible"—would prompt coded transmissions over Israel radio, and dispatch of mail using the agreed-upon code and address. The choice of targets was left to Elad—who was supposed to bear in mind "the possible outcome in the light of current circumstances."

Elad was in no hurry to return to Egypt. It was June 25 before he set sail from Naples, with his car, on the Turkish ship *Iskandron*; he disembarked at Alexandria on the 28th. That same day, he met with von Bechtoldsheim, and sent the "Shipment possible" cable to Israel by way of Europe. The "shipment"—operational instructions—was sent on July 17 and 18; as we shall see, it prefaced a tragic drama with an attendant enigma.

The list of people with whom Elad struck up an acquaintance in Egypt, some of whom became close friends, is astonishing. In addition to Baron von Bechtoldsheim, they included well-known German experts employed by the Egyptian military. Egyptians on the list include politicians and senior officers such as navy commander Admiral Suleiman Azazath; Colonel Osman Nuri; and Elad's most spectacular espionage coup, Zacharia Muhi a-Din, interior minister and head of Egypt's security services. The last two were introduced to Elad by Mahmud Hassan, an Egyptian counterintelligence officer posing as liaison with the German experts.

On his first visit to Egypt, Elad had noticed that his hotel room had been searched and his valise tampered with. He thought it would be useful to make the acquaintance of the man who was keeping him under surveillance—the aforementioned Mahmud—and before long they became fast friends; in the company of their German acquaintances, they went on pleasure trips to Libya and the Red Sea, lavishly bankrolled by Elad.

Elad's indiscretions in Europe were matched by his rashness in Egypt: instead of blending into the local German colony, he made himself conspicuous with his flashy car, his attendance at every scintillating social function, and the extravagance of a man whose business is flourishing, even though he had yet to make a single deal. But—not to belittle his gifts as an impostor—the source of this remarkable success was the fact that both the Germans and Egyptians soon blew his cover and identified him as an Israeli spy.

In 1980, former Mossad chief Isser Harel—whose suspicions, aroused as early as 1955, had brought about Elad's indictment in Israel on security offenses—proved publicly that Elad had been uncovered by Egyptian intelligence shortly after his first arrival in Egypt. Faced with a grim alternative, Elad presumably opted to play along with the Egyptians as a double agent. At the end of May 1954, when he met Ben-Zur in Paris and received command of the team that was to carry out the sabotage attacks, he was already in Egypt's employ, and "his actions were instigated and directed by the Egyptians themselves."

Indeed, on June 28, when he returned to Egypt with his new commission, he disclosed everything he knew about the 131 teams to Egyptian intelligence; then, after sending his "Shipment possible" cable to Ben-Zur, he activated the Alexandria team. Operating under the watchful eyes of Egypt's secret police and at its direction, the team carried out the following actions, not one of which was directed at a British installation:

July 2: the torching of a parcel office mailbox at Alexandria's central post office.

July 14: "bombs"—eyeglass cases stuffed with explosive—laid in the reading room of the American library, a wooden structure flanking the U.S. embassy in Cairo, and in the reading room of the American library in Alexandria.

July 23, Egypt's "Revolution Day": "bombs"—eyeglass cases again—laid in two Cairo movie theaters and two Alexandria movie theaters. In addition, an operation belonging entirely to the realm of fantasy: a valise filled with explosives "in an amount sufficient to cause a thunderous explosion, but without injury to persons" was supposedly deposited at the Cairo railway station's checked-luggage counter.

These "explosions" caused no harm, and failed to disrupt Egypt's relations with Britain or the United States. But they were to wreak enormous havoc in Israel.

9

July 16

From both an operational and a political standpoint, the Egyptian operation was a dreadful blunder. But years elapsed before it sank in at MI that the undertaking had labored under an enormous handicap right from the start: Elad, Givly's choice to lead 131, had been "turned" to work for the Egyptians and had conducted the network's operations under the directions of his Egyptian spymasters.

With 131 in its clutches, Egyptian intelligence set about confounding its Israeli adversaries with disinformation. The July 2, 1954, arson attack on the Alexandria post office was not made public; but on July 15, an Egyptian press report, making no mention of arrests, stated simply that "the library attached to the U.S. embassy in Cairo, and the American information office in Alexandria, were yesterday set on fire." The item reached the Israeli press—what coincidence!—on July 16.

On the 24th, Israel's intelligence chiefs were stunned to learn that the previous day, six members of "a Zionist gang" who had laid bombs at Cairo theaters and "set fire to the American propaganda offices" in order to "disrupt the course of the Anglo-Egyptian talks on Suez" had been arrested. On July 26, it was reported further that three Jews "in possession of incendiary materials resembling those used to torch the two American institutions" had been arrested in Alexandria; "a fourth Jew," arrested July 23, was charged with "setting a bomb" which "was discovered five minutes before detonation" in a movie theater.

If Givly and Ben-Zur were bewildered by these exploits by "Zionists" who had apparently jumped the gun on Lavon's operational orders of July 16, their perplexity ended on July 27, when Cairo radio broadcast an official communique stating that on July 14, fire had been set at the U.S. consulate library in Alexandria and the U.S. embassy building in Cairo, by means of eyeglass cases stuffed with incendiary material. On July 23, according to the communique, a policeman on duty at the Rio cinema in Alexandria observed a young Jew, Philip Natanson, whose clothing was on fire; in his pocket was an eyeglass case containing similar materials. A search of his home turned up large amounts of combustible chemicals. The police discovered eyeglass cases with similar materials at Cairo's Rivoli cinema, and at the Alexandria Rio. Two other Alexandria Jews, Victor Levi and Robert Nissim Dassa, were also arrested. The trio, all active Zionists well-known to the police, confessed to perpetrating these acts of arson. This communique, like the earlier reports, made no mention of the July 2 operation.

Givly and Ben-Zur lacked any reliable information about events in Egypt. No radio contact had ever been established with 131; the sole, tenuous link was by way of Europe, with coded letters and cables. The coded messages transmitted over Israel radio remained unanswered, and it was unknown whether they were being received.

Nevertheless—at least in Givly's version of events—on July 16, Lavon—disregarding the absence of communications as well as the reports that the team had already taken action and been apprehended—had ordered the activation of 131; and Givly instructed Ben-Zur to transmit the order. Using the code he had agreed on with Elad in Paris, Ben-Zur sent out the first transmission on July 17, repeating it fourteen times until July 25:

> One. Commence immediately action to prevent or delay the Anglo-Egyptian agreement. The targets are: 1. Cultural and propaganda institutions; 2. Economic institutions; 3. Official representatives, their cars, British representatives or other Britons; 4. Anything further that can bring about a rupture of diplomatic relations.
>
> Two. Notify us about the feasibility of action in the Canal Zone.
>
> Three. Listen for us every day at 7 hours Greenwich time, on frequency G.

On July 18, Ben-Zur also sent this message via "a letter carried by special courier." It also went out over Israel radio's "housewives' choice" program. That day, Israeli housewives heard "a recipe for a dish, at the request of Mrs. Shula Zarhi" (Elad, whose wife's name was Shula), which featured the words "dish" (operational instructions); "first course" (public place); "green pepper" (casualties); "soup" (reconnoitre); "salt herrings" (military personnel); "boiled fish" (leaders); "hamburgers" (Cairo), "frankfurters" (Alexandria); and "meat" (port). If Elad and his radio operator in Alexandria picked up this recipe, he was to decode it to read: "Act against the British to forestall the Cairo agreement. Also possible: Alexandria and the Suez region."

The first sign of life from Elad came on July 25, at 11 P.M., in a cable received via Germany: "Cease all further contact with the 'Henri Pierre' company. They are bankrupt. Will do my best to salvage the company, but no prospect of cash. Merchandise in hands of believers."

"Henri" and "Pierre" were Philip Natanson and Victor Levi; the "believers," the Egyptians. In other words, two Alexandria team members were in Egyptian hands, and Elad, while pledging his "best," saw no prospect of freeing them.

On July 26, Givly sent Lavon a handwritten note:

To: the defense minister
From: DMI
    1. The details on the Suez transit will only reach me in the late afternoon. The officer familiar with them is in Haifa, and could not be reached last night.
    2. This morning I received a first cable reporting our people among those arrested in Alexandria. Details and circumstances of the arrests are not included in the cable. We have meanwhile taken precautions to forestall further mishaps.
    B. Givly

This astonishing communication, its receipt confirmed by Lavon's initials, shows him and Givly continuing to promote the project of sending a vessel through the Suez Canal. The reported arrests of "our people" are relegated to second place as a mere "mishap" against whose recurrence precautions had been taken. Everything proceeded as though it were still possible to deploy the unit in Egypt, the capture of three operatives being a fair price to pay in the espionage game.

On July 30, a letter from Elad, mailed in Alexandria on the 25th, reached Paris. Its text—"giving notice that Pierre and Henri are very tired"—was instantly cabled to Givly. The following day, Ben-Zur radioed a request to the Alexandria team to report whether or not they were picking up the transmissions from Israel. There was no reply.

Prime minister Moshe Sharett, having received no information or explanation from Lavon, was puzzled by the media reports. He wondered whether the defense minister had taken action in Egypt behind his back, in defiance of his own explicit demand for advance notice of any such initiative.

On July 29, Sharett summoned labor minister Golda Meir to his Tel Aviv office. She told him she had heard from Shimon Peres that Lavon had given instructions "to liven things up" in the Mideast by fomenting explosions in Arab capitals. Peres had repeated this to Ben-Gurion, who "seized his head in his hands" as he realized the "shocking blunder" he had made in nominating Lavon. Meir added that she intended to tell Ben-Gurion he must instruct Lavon to resign.

Mossad chief Isser Harel also told Sharett that he knew of the operations in Egypt exclusively from the press, "but my impression is it's our doing." When he inquired on Sharett's behalf, Givly replied: "Our people did it. There were no operational instructions, there were instructions to be on standby, to plan."

Givly told the defense minister about Harel's questions, whereupon Lavon growled: "If the prime minister wants an inquiry, he should approach me, not do it by way of Isser." If Givly also confided to Lavon the excuse he had given Harel, it offered them both a formula for explaining away the "mishap." Lavon would adhere even more firmly than Givly himself to the assertion that no operational instructions had been issued to Elad and the 131 team, who had merely been placed on standby and ordered to make plans.

Sensing that he would be required to submit an account, Givly got ahead of the game by demanding one from Ben-Zur. On August 1, he received Ben-Zur's "report on operations in Goshen (Egypt)," comprising: 131's manpower complement in Egypt; provisions for communications; details of the assignment Ben-Zur had given Elad in Paris; Givly's operational instructions to Ben-Zur on July 16; the date and mode of their transmission to Egypt; the exchange of letters and cables with Elad; and the Egyptian media reports which, it will be recalled, omitted the July 2 operation.

On August 8, Givly sent Lavon a report on "Operations in Egypt, July 1954." It was in two sections, the first comprising descriptions of the operations drawn from Egyptian media reports, and the solitary cable from Elad on the 25th. Givly's only input was to comment that the three detainees named in the press reports were "Egyptian Jews we brought to Israel two-and-a-half years back for a year's training, and sent back on an assigned mission."

The report's second portion, headed "Instructions," lists orders issued "immediately"—no date specified—after the arrests:

1. The immediate departure from Egypt of . . . Marcelle Ninio, who served as liaison, and whose arrest was liable to entail further arrests.
2. Cessation of radio links, and of resort to the old addresses.
3. Concealment of all the sabotage materials and equipment prepared on our instructions.
4. The departure to Europe of . . . Elad.

With respect to the instruction that Ninio leave Egypt, a remark was written in: "We have yet to get confirmation whether she received the warning before being arrested." That comment is doubly puzzling: first, because it emerged later that Ninio had been arrested by Egyptian counterintelligence on August 8, the day the report was written. Second, Givly and Ben-Zur foresaw that interrogation of the three detainees would extract all they knew—including the identity of the liaison Ninio, a Cairo resident who was also the only person in Egypt aware of the true identity of MI's most important and successful agent at the time, Max Binnet. Yet Binnet was not warned, nor was Dr. Moshe Marzouk, former head of the Cairo team, nor Shmuel (Sammy) Azar of the Alexandria team. The omission would cost the three men their lives.

Givly's report to Lavon concluded: "The feasibility of extending legal aid to the detainees is being studied." Remarkably enough, although the detail that was to elevate this incident in Egypt into Israel's "Lavon affair," was specified in Ben-Zur's report, Givly omitted it: he did not mention receiving his operational instructions from Lavon on July 16.

The report elicited no comment from Lavon—no request to Givly for additional information, and, most notably, no question about the purpose of the operations or the authority that had approved their execution. Neither Givly nor Lavon seemed excessively perturbed over the seizure of 131's agents by the Egyptians. On Sunday August 8, the day the report was drawn up, Givly pursued "business as usual" with a new plan for "renewal of psychological warfare" aimed at "destabilization of the regime" and "encouragement of elements hostile to foreigners" in

Egypt—proposals Lavon took seriously. He also enlisted Givly to pro-mote the Suez Canal scheme.[1]

Despite the grim news from Egypt, the Lavon-Givly relationship attained new levels of intimacy. This was distinctly evident at the July 27 General Staff meeting, where Lavon summed up his first year at the defense ministry—as acting, then as full minister. Having routinely bypassed prime minister and military chain of command alike, while sub-verting the status of the chief of staff and eroding standing procedures,[2] Lavon now prided himself on having elevated the IDF into an army with a firm allegiance to the state. Portraying his predecessor's tenure in a somber light, he claimed much of the credit—which had previously gone to chiefs of staff Makleff and Dayan—for boosting the IDF's standards of planning and discipline, and its combat skills. Air force commander Dan Tolkovsky listened to Lavon in "amazement blended with derision, and I assume I wasn't alone in thinking so." Even greater astonishment greet-ed Lavon's announcement that—contrary to the custom of entrusting such matters to the chief of staff, or his deputy, or the Operations Branch—the task of studying past operations and drawing from them lessons for the future would instead fall to "intelligence and operations": in effect, to DMI Givly, who knew little about actual warfare. Yitzhak Rabin later recalled that "a honeymoon prevailed between Givly and Lavon. . . . they bypassed Dayan . . . the General Staff was largely aware of it."

Not until late August did Israel learn of the arrest of Shmuel Azar (July 31); Meir Meyuhas and Moshe Marzouk (August 5); and Marcelle Ninio (August 8). In the second week of September, it became known that master spy Max Binnet had been apprehended on August 12.

But even as information streamed into MI, Givly tried to conceal it from Lavon. It was September 23—the day Israeli papers published a report about an IDF "colonel" [Binnet] posing as "an expert with an Egyptian company" who was about to stand trial on espionage charges, along with "a doctor [Marzouk], a lawyer [Azar], and a young woman [Marcelle Ninio]"—before Givly responded to a demand from Lavon by advising him of Binnet's arrest. Even then, he did not reveal that Binnet

---

1. The vessel Bat Galim reached the Suez Canal on September 28 1954; Israel made no response when its entire crew were arrested. They were released on January 1, 1955 through diplomatic intervention by the Western powers and the UN.
2. Sharett's diary frequently refers to Lavon's "malignant role . . . in running riot with state morality in the army, and introducing a regime of untruthful relations in it."

might have been saved, had he been warned in time—and that this omission was causing great agitation at military intelligence.

In fact, the network's collapse became known only on October 12, 1954, with publication of indictments against thirteen defendants—two, Elad and Avraham Dar, in absentia—which showed beyond doubt that Cairo was preparing a show trial. The full extent of the calamity emerged on December 11, when the trial began. It put an end to the myth glorifying Givly as an intelligence chief of imagination and daring; what had been ascribed to bold sophistication would now be revealed as the reckless escapades of a charlatan.

To fill in the gaps in MI's knowledge about the events in Egypt, and in preparation for an eventual inquiry, Givly ordered Elad back to Israel. According to Elad, on August 5 he received instructions from Givly to come to Paris on the 11th. He left Egypt on the 8th. From Rome, his first stop in Europe, he sent the tiny radio transmitter to Israel, then went on to Austria, Germany, and France, to take care of his business affairs. He reached Paris on the 11th, and three days later flew to Israel, landing at Lod in the late evening of Saturday August 14. On September 2, he returned to Europe. These are the sole credible facts which can be established from the written and oral testimony of Elad, Ben-Zur, and Givly.

Elad's debriefing was conducted by Ben-Zur, without witnesses or stenographer; to this day it remains their exclusive secret. Elad later said that he spent the next two days cooped up in Ben-Zur's home, composing his report; even his wife did not know he was in Israel. Strangely, Givly, who had summoned Elad to Israel, and whose own home was close by, claimed not to have seen Elad until one, or possibly two, weeks after his arrival. Only when the report was finished did Ben-Zur take Elad to see his wife and son in Haifa.

Unlike Elad's, Ben-Zur's reconstruction of their encounter was hazy. "I don't remember where I met him to take his testimony," he told the inquiry commission. "I didn't write his testimony down." Elad recounted "how our people were captured," specifying "the possibilities of rescuing them, the girl particularly." Only then, in Ben-Zur's version, did Elad write his report "On the episode of the teams," which Ben-Zur "gave the DMI to read."

But in the report itself, Elad specifies that "it was mostly written from memory, immediately upon my return to Europe [that is, before he returned to Israel], drawing upon brief notes in my work journal." Upon arrival he presented the original report, in his own handwriting, to Ben-

Zur, who conveyed it to Givly, who had it typed up by his loyal secretary Dalia Carmel. According to Elad, however, a number of later drafts were typed, with various details modified, before Ben-Zur submitted the report, in its sole extant version, to the Olshan-Dori inquiry board in January 1955. Even in its original form, there can be no doubt that Elad's report was false, for he designed it from the outset as a cloak for his perfidy.

The version submitted to the inquiry commission did not mention the operations of July 2 and 14, though they did feature in its first draft, where Elad explained them away by blaming his subordinates' lack of discipline and enthusiasm for action—which, as we shall see, is the explanation Ben-Zur used in an October 5 report to Dayan. In November, Givly likewise would tell Lavon and the General Staff that "our people acted on their own authority." At Elad's subsequent trial, and in the book he later published, he made this claim without reservation. The first two operations may have been omitted from Elad's report at the behest of Ben-Zur and Givly, as Elad claimed in his own defense; or they may have deleted them on their own initiative.

The omission certainly suited Elad, for it matched the false claim in his own report that, after his Paris rendezvous with Ben-Zur, he returned to Egypt on July 4 (as opposed to the true date, June 28). It also dovetailed perfectly with Givly's needs; his claim to have received the order from Lavon on July 16 gave him a stake in establishing that the July 2 and 14 operations were not 131's doing. Elad's report also claimed that the operations had all been authorized by the orders he picked up from the Israel radio broadcasts of July 18 and 22. Perhaps to compensate for concealing the first two operations, Elad dreamed up an additional—an utterly imaginary—exploit at the port of Alexandria on July 23.

Elad's report depicted his subordinates in Egypt as rash and reckless, and implied that they had betrayed one another. For example, he claimed that Philip Natanson went to his assigned theater without troubling to buy a ticket for the first performance ahead of time and was unable to get in. While he waited for the second screening, the delayed action fuse went off in his pocket, and the charge caught fire. "The network went [to the devil] because of a cinema ticket," Elad remarked. In fact, Natanson had gone in for the first showing, only to be detained by a policeman lying in wait for him; but he was in prison, unable to refute his superior's slanders.

At the time, the operations before July 16 were dismissed as an enigma that Givly and Ben-Zur, finding it convenient, did nothing to elucidate.

Givly told the Olshan-Dori commission that "Elad too was unaware of their being carried out." Of the July 16 reports of arson attacks at the U.S. information offices, he commented, "Such reports appear all the time."

When the inquiry commission asked Givly why he had failed to pass Elad's report on to Lavon, he replied: "Because its substance had already been conveyed to him in previous reports." He also claimed to have suggested that Lavon "see Elad and draw a direct impression" but "the defense minister did not wish to see him." But Lavon told the commission: "I did not know he was in Israel."

In August 1954, then, Elad's superiors regarded him as a hero who had ventured into the lion's den, contriving to emerge unscathed by virtue of his resourcefulness, courage, and coolness. He had, it was believed, run the risk of sneaking into the Alexandria team's safe house, which was under surveillance, to remove incriminating evidence, including the tiny transmitter, which he supposedly smuggled out, heedless of the danger of detection by Egyptian customs, which searched all luggage. Only much later did the truth emerge that the "cleansing" of the safe house had in fact been carried out by Shmuel Azar—which may explain why Elad's report failed to mention his arrest but instead smeared him with slanderous insinuations. Azar was executed; unlike his colleagues, he did not live to expose Elad's treachery.

Elad claimed, further, that he was "ready to risk his life" by returning to Egypt to rescue Marcelle Ninio who if arrested was liable to break down under interrogation and put her captors on the trail of Max Binnet. Ben-Zur—who like Givly did not know that Elad had already turned her in—bought the idea, and began preparing passports; but Givly dismissed the plan as perilously rash. All the same, he too was gratified by such dauntlessness.

Could there be any better vindication of the belief that a miscreant, if given a chance to clear his name by an act of daring, will turn into a hero? Why then did Givly not show off MI's bright star before chief of staff Dayan on his return from the United States on August 19, 1954?

The day after Dayan's return, his temporary replacement, Avidar, gave him a rundown of events during his absence, including the detention of 131 personnel in Egypt; Avidar noted that the chief of staff's office had never been apprised of their actions. Dayan promptly embarked upon an investigation. From this point on, the Lavon-Givly honeymoon was in jeopardy.

On August 22, Dayan asked Givly into his office for a private talk, of whose content nothing is known. But Dayan's testimony to the inquiry commission indicates that, at the time, he believed Givly's version of events: that the instructions to activate 131 had come from the defense minister, and that Givly "had no knowledge" of the July 14 operation. However, apparently sensing the evasiveness of Givly's replies, Dayan directed him to submit a report.

On August 25, Dayan, following routine procedure, submitted a request to Evron to have "the operation in Egypt" put on the agenda for the defense minister's weekly meeting; but Lavon refused. By late September, rendered increasingly suspicious by Lavon's puzzling failure to respond to any of the reports that reached him, as well as by Givly's failure to submit the requested report, Dayan resolved to crack the tripartite conspiracy of silence by isolating its weakest link: Ben-Zur. Dayan proposed that Givly go to Europe to supervise the legal defense of the Cairo accused. Aware that Avraham Dar had been in Europe since September 1 for that very purpose, Givly swallowed the bait, taking Dayan's proposal as a declaration of confidence. Lavon too was unaware of the snare.

Givly flew to Europe on October 4. The following morning, Dayan summoned acting DMI Mordechai Almog and dropped a bombshell: Ben-Zur was to submit, by that evening, a full account of 131's operations in Egypt. Ben-Zur, who had heard from Givly that Dayan intended to dismiss him, received the order at 11:30 and presented the report to Dayan within two hours. Departing from the line agreed on between Lavon and Givly, according to which the 131 teams had been ordered merely to plan and prepare, Ben-Zur claimed in this report that he had received operational instructions from Givly on July 16. Dayan had not erred: in Givly's absence, Ben-Zur fell into the trap.

The most striking innovation in the October 5 report—which makes it appear, of all Ben-Zur's accounts, the closest to the truth—was its acknowledgment that the Alexandria team had carried out a total of eight operations,[3] including those of July 2 and 14, as well as an entirely fictional incendiary device which Elad's report had said was "planted" in

---

3. 1. Alexandria parcel post; 2. the American library in Alexandria; 3. 1. the American library in Cairo; 4. Alexandria cinema; 5. Cairo cinema; 6. Cairo railway station (the device failed); 7. Alexandria port warehouse (the device failed); 8. incendiary device at an Alexandria cinema (the man was arrested).

an Alexandria port warehouse. Ben-Zur depicted with gratification and pride the zeal and eagerness for action displayed by his unit. Dayan promptly sent a copy of the report to Lavon; on October 10, he presented a summary to the prime minister.

Instead of returning within the week, as scheduled, Givly stayed in Europe until October 20. He reported the following day to Dayan's office for a private talk. Of the four items they discussed, legal aid for the Cairo defendants appears to have been the first. Then they took up Givly's promotion, Ben-Zur's report, and the latter's immediate dismissal.

Dayan rejected out of hand Givly's request for major general's rank. Givly agreed with Dayan's resolve to remove Ben-Zur from command of 131, and on December 12, Dayan notified Ben-Zur in writing that his commission would expire on January 1, 1955. Dayan replaced him with Lieutenant Colonel Yossi Harel, who was recalled from Boston.

The Ben-Zur report was undoubtedly the principal item at the Dayan-Givly meeting. Remarking on Ben-Zur's failure to specify who instructed the DMI, Dayan ordered Givly to fill in the gap with a further report—thereby shrewdly forcing Givly to break his and Lavon's conspiracy of silence by submitting a report of his own about the order's origin.

However, drawing up a report which would reconcile the discrepancies of all its predecessors was an impossible task. Apparently, therefore, Dayan consented to accept a letter instead. But, finding the letter he received some days later obscure, Dayan suggested—or perhaps, demanded—that Givly rewrite it to be succinct and clear. The new version focussed on the essential facts: the giving of the order, its date and its content.

General Staff
Intelligence Branch
678/a131
November 1, 1954
Chief of staff

a. In response to your request, I hereby append the following details in relation to the operations in Egypt, and the mishap that occurred there.

b. July 16, 1954, after a discussion at the office of the defense minister on . . . "the significance of the British withdrawal from Suez," the defense minister instructed me to activate the 131 teams against British elements and objectives in Egypt.

The objectives I specified, which were endorsed by the minister, included attacks on installations of the British delegations, British institutions and vehicles. Attacks on British soldiers seemed impractical, mainly because their movements were restricted exclusively to the Canal Zone.

c. Immediately after the meeting, I summoned to my home the commander of Unit 131 and the commander of X [Rehavia Vardi—S.T.] (the latter was called in to consider the feasibility of X operations in the Canal Zone itself).

I told the aforementioned of the overall purpose, whereupon the commander of Unit 131 advised me that his people were in a position to take action, since his most recent meeting with the people from Egypt had stressed the need for heightened preparedness. Subsequently, I instructed him to issue appropriate operational instructions, by suitable means of communication. The commander of X was unable to offer any concrete proposal, and I delegated him to study the options.

B. Givly, Colonel
Director of Intelligence Branch

Exploiting this initial breakthrough of the Givly-Lavon conspiracy of silence, Dayan proceeded to a second one. At a General Staff meeting that same Monday, November 1, he requested Givly "to recount details on a number of subjects." The abruptness of this invitation enabled Dayan to avoid expressing a point of view that Givly might adopt, thus becoming an unwanted ally. In response, Givly described the entire course of the operations in Egypt. His account was confused and incoherent, as though he had been taken by surprise. He said that the teams had been activated on instructions received from the defense minister on July 16 after a discussion of the significance of the British withdrawal. The instructions stated explicitly that action was to focus on British objectives, but garbled transmission led to operations against Egyptian and American targets. Furthermore, Givly went on, there was a malfunction when an incendiary device caught fire on one of the men in an Alexandria movie theater. The man was arrested, prompting extensive investigations and arrests. The first two operations were carried out before the 16th. Only when concrete reports arrived did it become known that "they were carried out by our people, who did not wait for an order," acting on the strength of instructions merely to prepare, given 3–5 weeks earlier.

In response to questions, Givly added "that the fellows confessed to everything," and that "most of the network has collapsed."

In this manner, Givly apportioned the blame between the defense minister and an operational mishap.

A GHQ meeting is no forum for discussion of secret operations beyond Israel's borders; certainly not of the defense minister's responsibility in relation thereto. Dayan evidently made his unprecedented move with the calculated purpose of clearing himself, and the General Staff, of responsibility for the Egyptian operations, and casting it entirely upon the defense minister. Dayan later stated:

> When the Suez withdrawal seemed imminent, . . . there was the initiative of the DMI who presented us with a memorandum for actions he suggested we undertake so as to disrupt the Suez withdrawal. . . . I had my reservations regarding the memorandum. . . . On my return from the United States, I discovered that the unit had been activated, and Major General Avidar who filled in for me was likewise not asked about the activation of the unit. It was an order from the defense minister to the DMI. The object was to disrupt the Suez withdrawal by means of actions made to look as though they had been instigated by the Egyptians, which would create tension between the Egyptians and the British.

Dayan had no need to brief Lavon on the General Staff meeting, where the minister was represented by his principal aide, Evron. But seemingly anxious to establish beyond all doubt where responsibility lay, Dayan wrote Lavon the following letter, appending the Ben-Zur report and Givly's letter:

> Chief of staff's office
> November 3, 1954
> Defense minister
> re: Activation of 131
> As the DMI was out of the country when the report concerning the activation of 131 was written, I requested him to complete the gap in the section dealing with the giving of the order to activate the unit.
> Attached is a copy of his letter in respect thereof, which should be appended to the aforementioned report.
> *Moshe Dayan*, Lieutenant General
> Chief of the General Staff

From that moment on, Israel would never be the same.

10

Line of Defense

On November 4, Evron brought Lavon Dayan's letter and appendixes, as well as the minutes of the November 1 meeting, which included Givly's account of the Egyptian operations, while remarking that Givly's account contained "some inaccuracies." Lavon read the papers, commenting: "They're more than inaccuracies." Later he claimed that this response proved "that he was shocked to read the letter," and rejected its version of events. But the Olshan-Dori commission did not find Lavon's response "clear proof" that he did not give the order.

Throughout November, Givly's claim that the order had emanated from Lavon drew no comment from the latter, whose relations with the DMI remained cordial. It was, no doubt, the expansive show trial launched in Cairo on December 11, 1954, that made Lavon aware that an inquiry was inevitable and that he urgently needed to prepare for it. He took his first step the following day, summoning Dayan and Givly to his office to tell them that "such circumstances demand that colleagues come forward"; he suggested that "we agree among ourselves on a line."

According to Givly, Lavon proposed that "we adopt the prime minister's line" (as will be recalled, this line had been formulated by Givly, not Sharett) "whereby authorization was given for planning but there was a mishap in the execution"; Givly claimed that he and Dayan received this suggestion "in silence" that was construable as "affirmative or negative."

Subsequently, however, during a conversation in the car, Dayan said that "if he were to adopt that position, he would have to appear [before an inquiry] and defend it, and that went against his conscience." Lavon told the inquiry commission that he had suggested the line to Dayan and Givly only upon learning that the foreign affairs and defense committee of the Knesset was determined to discuss "the sorry business."[1] But on learning of Dayan's negative response, Lavon told the inquiry commission, "I dropped it."

Once Dayan's stubbornness put an end to Lavon's "line," Lavon realized that clearing his own name would require casting the blame on Givly. Preparing to do battle for his honor and political survival, Lavon solicited Evron's aid. Evron found himself caught among five distinct loyalties: he had been secretary to Sharett and to Ben-Gurion, and he was Lavon's principal aide, a position he had landed through his friendship with Dayan and Peres. However, his loyalty to Lavon appears to have prevailed. He testified that Lavon invited him to his home to ask whether he remembered "a meeting held at his home," thereby "letting me in on the secret."

For a time, Evron was indeed alone in sharing this secret: that Lavon had designed a ruse to crack Givly's story. Lavon claimed to possess "absolute proof" that the conversation with Givly had taken place on July 31, four days after the conclusion of the Anglo-Egyptian agreement. Scrutinizing his wife's diary, he found that on July 16, 1954, his fiftieth birthday, he had spent the entire afternoon at home, helping her prepare a festive family banquet for thirty guests. He acknowledged that he had spoken in private with Givly directly after a meeting held July 31, but no one could argue that he would give instructions to activate the unit at a time when reports had reached Israel that it had already taken action and several of its people were detained. The inescapable conclusion was that Givly, not Lavon, had issued the order.

To establish this version, Lavon needed written confirmation from all the participants that a meeting had been held at his home on July 31, at the end of which he and Givly met in private. (Those attending the meeting were: Lavon, acting chief of staff Avidar, director-general Peres, the new deputy DMI Lieutenant Colonel Yuval Ne'eman, Lavon's adviser Colonel Shalom Eshet, and Evron himself. Givly told the Olshan-Dori

---

1. Author's note: Details of the Egyptian operation and its ramifications were initially suppressed by Israel's military censor, so that the episode and its heroes were referred to by code words. Overall the debacle was known as "the sorry business."

commission that he remembered giving Ne'eman a ride. Ne'eman confirmed that Givly had driven him to the meeting at which the significance of the British withdrawal was discussed, but insisted that the meeting had been held on July 31.)

Evron, who took it upon himself to obtain the affidavits, claimed later that Lavon had asked him to do this on December 16, 1954. But Evron was already assembling the affidavits on that date. Furthermore, his testimony failed to mention his presence on December 12 at the meeting with Dayan and Givly where Lavon proposed his "line" for their reports to the foreign affairs and defense committee. Hence Evron was "in on the secret" with a vengeance.

On December 14, Lavon invited Givly to his home. It was the first of four meetings designed, as Lavon told Givly, "to give you one more chance to tell me the whole truth." As a rule, Lavon elaborated, he was not vindictive, but there was one thing he could not condone: a resort "to lies and fabrications to embroil me." Givly's report and his account to the November 1 General Staff meeting were "replete with incorrect facts which distort things from A to Z."

For his part, Givly testified to Olshan and Dori that he recalled telling Evron that Lavon "isn't behaving fairly, he's trying to pass the buck," and that Lavon invited Evron to his home only after Evron complained about this. Givly charged Lavon with "seeking to evade responsibility for the instructions," to which Lavon replied: "I hold myself responsible, and will bear full parliamentary and political responsibility for what happened in Egypt."

On December 23, Lavon staged a second confrontation with Givly, at his own office. Givly told the commission that Lavon "called me into his office with a smile: Tonight I'm going to tie up the matter [of the inquiry commission] with the prime minister, but I'm short on a number of points. Could you give me a few points in writing?" Lavon confessed that he "was rather sadistic." He asked Givly who had attended the July 16 meeting, incidentally mentioning Colonel Shalom Eshet, who had written to Lavon that he had been at his father's deathbed in Vienna from July 6 through the 28th. Givly, who knew nothing of Eshet's letter, rashly confirmed that Eshet was present. That same day, Givly sent Lavon a letter stating: "In the light of our conversation this morning, I recall that Lieutenant Colonel Eshet" attended the July 16 meeting.

At Lavon's request, Givly provided written replies to several further questions, claiming that he first learned of the operations carried out before July 16 from the Egyptian press and Cairo radio, and "later also from Elad," who was however equally in the dark; "we have no information . . . as to whether our people decided to act on their own authority."

Lavon demanded further elucidation. On December 27, Givly sent him an additional letter, in substance reiterating his earlier statements. Lavon promptly summoned Givly to his office for a third confrontation. He demanded to know why it was "August 8 [before you told me] . . . two weeks after you knew . . . that the operations had been carried out, and that the people had fallen [into captivity]? Why didn't you notify me earlier?" On December 23, he said, he had given Givly "another chance to tell me the whole truth" and had received only "an infantile answer."

On December 28, saying he still required "a few points," Lavon summoned Givly for the last time. To Givly's consternation, a stenographer entered the room. It was a stinging insult; as Givly told the inquiry commission, "In my entire career, I have never experienced anything like it." Lavon, evidently considering himself "on firm ground," was obviously preparing evidence for an inquiry.

Lavon told Givly that he was seeing the prime minister that night for "a conclusive talk" on the inquiry commission, and considered himself bound to tell Givly why he had "kept silent all this time." There were two reasons: "a. in a disaster situation, one must not indulge in intramural arguments and investigations" which could cause turmoil. "b. I was silent, but not inactive; without any [investigative] apparatus, I examined the matter" and concluded that your "entire story" was "a fabrication." For according to Givly himself, half the operations were carried out before "the decisive date" of July 16. "I asked you several times: How come? And you kept saying you know nothing about it, you can't explain it." It was inconceivable that "people would carry out such operations on their own authority. . . . I don't believe those people decided, out of a mere sense of adventure, to blow up the American information office or set fire to the Alexandria post office. That's out of the question."

Lavon now came "to the crux": "Benyamin, I advise you formally that there was no meeting on July 16, 1954, and no conversation between us. I have the testimony of all the participants at the meeting. . . . On the other hand, I have evidence, completely independent and absolute, that [the meeting concerning the British withdrawal] took place many days after the 16th."

GIVLY: May I ask what is "many days"?

LAVON: After the people were arrested in Egypt, is that enough days? I have the date fixed and established. Believe me, I'm telling you this with a broken heart.

GIVLY: I am unable to believe you, minister, I'm very sorry.

LAVON: I have to draw one of two conclusions: Either you did the entire thing as of July 2 on your own exclusive authority; or it wasn't on your own authority—in which case, whose?

GIVLY: I think I've lost any residue of trust [in you]. . . . On one point I am clear: After the meeting held at your home, I got the order to activate the teams from your own lips.

LAVON: Benyamin, permit me. I'll let you say it if you wish, but I advise you not to get in any deeper, I beg you not to get in any deeper.

GIVLY: I may already be in deep enough.

LAVON: It could get deeper.

GIVLY: There's no hanging in Israel. I have the date that Ben-Zur transmitted the report, it was on the 17th. . . . On the 16th, Friday, I was at your home.

LAVON: I entreat you again: the conversation you refer to didn't take place on July 16.

GIVLY: It's not the meeting that interests me, it's your attitude. If the minister wishes to ignore that, go ahead. I'll know how to take it.

LAVON: One moment—the meeting didn't take place on July 16. It was held at the end of July, after you had learned that the whole business was finished. I didn't know—[but] you did. When you issued the order on the 16th—you had no authority to give it.

GIVLY: Good, I accept the verdict, all right.

LAVON: This meeting is over.

Once Dayan demolished the agreed-upon line, neither of the two adversaries knew what his friend-turned-foe had up his sleeve. Givly may have gathered that Lavon wanted to strike a deal to create a new version. Lavon may have wondered what line Givly would adopt, and what evidence he would use to "prove" it. That may be why he held the first three confrontations without a stenographer, for a record of those conversations might have restricted his freedom to argue his case before the commission. Only after squeezing all he could out of Givly, and polishing his own new version to a fine sheen, did Lavon summon the stenographer. Lavon thereby gained a considerable edge over Givly, who was taken totally by surprise. Givly told the commission that it was only after December 12, when Lavon's proposal to coordinate their stories fell by the wayside, that his "forebodings were aroused regarding the defense minister's position." But when Givly mentioned those misgivings during their first encounter on December 14, Lavon reassured him that his "fears were groundless." Only at their fourth confrontation did Givly learn that Lavon "denies giving the orders."

Like market peddlers proclaiming their wares, Givly and Lavon each endeavored to project the image he hoped to impress upon the commission when testifying about the confrontations between them. Lavon came across virtuous and pious. Givly took on the role of the man of truth, reviled and betrayed: a soldier honest and loyal, ever since the Tubiansky trial, willing to put himself on the line to save his professional honor.

Realizing that Lavon had made the stenographic transcript for their benefit, Olshan and Dori did not fall for the image it projected. They wondered why the four questions Lavon asked Givly in December had not been asked in August. Lavon's reply—that Givly had not yet disclosed the information he possessed—fell far short of satisfying them. He should have demanded a report and ordered an investigation. Furthermore, why did Lavon focus his questions exclusively on the operations of July 2 and 14? After all, he claimed equal ignorance of the later operations. Finally, Lavon focused on proving that his private talk with Givly took place on July 31; he did not reveal its subject.

The commission did consider the hypothesis, which Dori expounded to Dayan, that Ben-Zur went to Paris "in an ambience of readiness to begin action in Egypt," giving "the local commanders" freedom of action, but "no clear orders limiting the onset of the operations or their extent." It was not out of the question "that Givly, relying on the defense minister's backing, would embark upon such an operation without waiting for the chief of staff's opinion, particularly if he knew that the chief of staff is not wholeheartedly in favor of the scheme." Taking account of Lavon's style of operating, "Givly's personality," and the fact that "the line between preparation and action was blurred," was it not "possible that the order executed on July 16 had matured earlier?"

The commission's findings implied that if the understanding reached by Lavon and Givly in their talk of April or May subsequently unfolded into a tragic venture, this was because as the planning orders descended the chain of command, each echelon stepped them up to an operational level. That seemed to be the underlying meaning of Givly's comment to Harel in July, of which there were two versions, both acceptable to Lavon: "There were no instructions for action, the instructions were for preparedness and planning" and "Instructions were given for planning, but there was a snag in the execution."

The theory presented here is that the Lavon-Givly alliance broke down only when Dayan made the DMI afraid that the minister would deny his responsibility, and thus demolished their tacit understanding. Ever after, each had sought to save his own skin by incriminating the other. This hypothesis draws upon two sources: Evron's testimony and the chief of staff's journal.

On December 28, 1954, Lavon told Dayan his version of the story: that his talk with Givly took place on July 31, when 131 "was already in Egyptian hands"; that "it was the only conversation between him and Benyamin concerning 131, and in it he authorized planning of the operations in Egypt, but not their execution"; that "Benyamin apparently wanted retroactive authorization"; and that "there was no earlier meeting with Benyamin to discuss the issuing of operational orders."

These quotes, noted in all their fragile inconsistency in the chief of staff's journal,[2] seem to indicate that rationality is not the only yardstick for measuring the conduct of Lavon and Givly. That same December 28, Dayan solicited Givly's comments, which were also recorded in the journal:

"Benyamin claimed initially that he received instructions to act. On learning [of Lavon's claim] that the meeting took place on July 31 after their execution, he came up with the notion that he had an earlier meeting with Lavon on July 16, when he received the order."

Even the information that everyone else who attended the meeting at Lavon's home remembered it taking place on Saturday July 31 failed to budge Givly from his version, which in turn rested upon the fact that his operational order to the unit in Egypt had been transmitted on July 17.

---

2. The chief of staff's journal was typed up daily in two copies by his secretary. When he left office, one copy was entrusted to the defense minister; the other remained in Dayan's possession. The journal entries for the period under study were written by Dayan himself, his aide-de-camp, and his secretary.

Thus Givly dug in his heels, insisting that he got the order from Lavon on the 16th.

In an attempt to fathom the truth of what went on and when it occurred, Dayan's journal entry for December 28 includes a "Sequence of principal events," which commences: "May 1954, Benyamin instructed [131] to prepare for execution of operations to disrupt [Egypt's] relations with the *United States*; Benyamin claims the instruction was issued at Lavon's directive"; and ends on August 8, the day Givly submitted his report to Lavon on events in Egypt.

In conclusion, Dayan noted, "Whatever develops, outwardly no drastic measures must be taken before the Cairo trial ends." Consequently Dayan, who had sought to get Givly transferred as far back as April, now, in late December, resisted Lavon's demand to do so.

But it was a long time before Dayan reached his own opinion as to "who gave the order." On February 20, 1955, at his son's bar-mitzvah, Olshan told him that Sharett had testified to hearing from Lavon that "Benyamin tried to elicit retroactive authorization" on July 31. Dayan appears to have been persuaded that this was so, but he kept this view to himself until 1964, when he revealed it in a letter to Ben-Gurion.

Evron's account was not free of discrepancies and inaccuracies. He testified that Lavon "did not respond, and gave me no instructions, after getting Givly's note of July 26" (with the news that "our people are among those detained") and the report of August 8. Apart from Lavon's comment on November 4 that Givly's report, and his statement to the General Staff, contained "more than inaccuracies," Evron recalled no other reaction or reservation from him. Moreover, Lavon had ducked any discussion of 131's operations, rejecting Dayan's demand that he do so. Until December 16, Lavon had "expressed no surprise, to me or to others."

On December 16, when Lavon brought Evron "in on the secret," and they discussed "Givly's claims" of having received the order from Lavon, Evron, by his own account, had remarked: "The only conversation to which I can attribute anything approaching instructions was the one in May or June." Dayan too told the inquiry commission that Evron had said to him: "I was present at a conversation where instructions were given for planning, but not for action." Lavon, said Evron, did not recall that conversation, but asked Evron to give him written certification of it. Before Lavon's first testimony to the commission, Evron gave him this "affidavit":

At the end of one of the meetings you held with Colonel Givly, one day in May or June of this year [Evron's dating of this meeting "fluctuated" from April–May to May–June and back again—S.T.] the DMI brought up the option of activating the teams in Egypt. He told you the teams had reached a level of complete preparedness and for that level to be maintained, it would be desirable to give them some assignments.

In response to your question: "What assignments?" Colonel Givly replied that they were capable of fomenting tension and riots inside Egypt, etc., and, by attacks on foreign elements, could even cause postponement of the signature of the Anglo-Egyptian agreement.

You told him that, of all the options, you would only consider attacks on British installations in the Canal Zone, and asked him to check whether it was at all feasible to plan such a thing. He promised to do so.

My clear impression was (taking part in the conversation were: you, Givly and myself) that the reference was to a remote possibility; should it prove practicable, it would be submitted to you for consideration.

With the resurgence of the "Lavon affair" in 1960, Evron would observe an error in his initial dating of this fateful exchange; it could not have taken place in June, for it was, Evron argued, the source of Givly's authority for instructing Ben-Zur to activate 131 in Egypt—and Ben-Zur had left for Europe on May 28. Hence, Evron reverted to April or May as the date of the conversation.

It appears that Evron's account of the conversation did not arise fortuitously, and that the memorandum he wrote was designed less to jog Lavon's memory than to support his version of events. It seems to have been Evron's idea, brought up as they were considering how Lavon's testimony would reconcile the discrepancy between the planning order and the ensuing action. As far back as October 28, Evron had told Sharett "about the conversation held late May or June, and I said it was strange that Givly could have interpreted instructions for preparations as an operational order." In that case, could Evron have waited until December before sharing his hypothesis with Lavon? More probably, Evron acted on Lavon's behalf in propagating that version.

Furthermore, maintaining a state of preparedness could hardly justify the deployment of a military unit—particularly a secret one in an enemy country—in operations of far reaching diplomatic significance. Ben-Zur had testified that 131's level of preparedness was not high, and that the unit was fit only for "minor" operations—a claim repeated in

Givly's testimony. Be that as it may, Evron's version—to which Lavon adhered until December 12—dovetailed with Dori's theory that each echelon upgraded the original order, until mere planning was transformed, seemingly by its own momentum, into concrete action.

Unhappy with Evron's testimony, Olshan and Dori assailed it.

DORI: How do you explain that no one summoned . . . the person responsible to demand an explanation?

EVRON: Maybe . . . on this matter, which was disagreeable to Benyamin, I waited for him to broach the subject.

This show of consideration for the feelings of a colleague failed to convince Olshan and Dori, but Evron insisted, "I had qualms about discussing the matter with Benyamin."

DORI: Reports of the debacle had already arrived on July 26. Why did no one call Givly to ask what had gone wrong? I fail to comprehend this Olympian serenity.

EVRON: The only explanation, from my viewpoint, is that I was not required to ask. I don't remember whether I advised the defense minister to go into the matter.

DORI: If there is no explanation, one can only assume that the responsibility lies with everyone, and there is therefore no need to question Givly in particular.

This conclusion—that Lavon and Givly bore joint responsibility, and had therefore entered into a conspiracy of silence—was precisely what Evron had gone to such lengths to conceal, and it was extracted from his testimony over his resistance. It can thus be reasonably assumed that he was in fact "in on the secret" from the outset, and that his conversations and his testimony to the commission were designed to support Lavon. This became the commission's ultimate view.

While Givly had the opportunity to refute Lavon, he missed his chance. If he claimed that he had received Lavon's order on July 15, rather than the 16th, located their exchange at Lavon's office rather than his home, and dated it as a sequel to the routine weekly meeting, rather than the discussion on the British withdrawal from Suez, his version would have been incontrovertible. It would have simultaneously jibed with his own instructions to Ben-Zur on the 16th and disarmed Lavon's claim that he had not issued the original order. The fear that Givly might redate their talk to the end of the weekly meeting on the

15th explains why Lavon pursued the subject of the dates. When it became evident that Givly was insisting on the 16th, Lavon could rely upon his own version, in view of the solid evidence he possessed that they held no conversation on the 16th, and the evident implausibility of the notion that he should give orders to activate the network on July 31, after it had been captured. If it was on the 16th that Givly ordered Ben-Zur to activate the teams, he had to have done so on his own authority.

The possibility that the conversation took place after the meeting on the 15th also came up before the commission. Although Givly's name was not on Evron's typewritten list of participants, Peres and Avidar claimed that he did attend. Lavon himself prudently testified that Givly might have attended part of the meeting, but did not remain till the end, and thus could not have met with Lavon afterward. Evron affirmed unequivocally: "Givly did not attend."

Unaware of the opportunities offered by this complex weave of dates, Givly claimed only that "I attended most weekly meetings [during July and August] . . . I don't suppose there was a meeting involving the *Bat Galim* [the ship that was to be sent through the Suez Canal] without me." He also claimed to have held numerous private talks with Lavon, and "I was not in the habit of telling Evron of my conversations with the defense minister." Evron rejoined: "I attend all of the defense minister's conversations, including those with the chief of staff. . . . rarely did the minister meet with anyone without my being present. . . . I know of no other instance [apart from the July 31 meeting at Lavon's home] that he saw Givly in my absence." But the commission rejected this claim. Olshan and Dori wrote in their findings:

> We do not cast doubt upon the account of Maj.-Gen. Avidar, who was very cautious in his testimony, and who evidenced his impartiality. With that, in view of Lavon's claim that Givly attended part of the meeting:
>
> We are unable to determine whether the defense minister's private talk with the DMI, according to Maj.-Gen. Avidar's account, relates to the July 15 meeting or some other meeting.

This inconclusiveness left its fateful imprint upon the commission's findings.

11

Before the Commission

On the evening of December 28, 1954—the day that saw Lavon's decisive confrontation with Givly, and Sharett's "conclusive conversation" with Lavon—the prime minister drafted the terms of reference defining the scope of the investigation to be carried out by a "confidential commission of inquiry." It was charged with answering three questions: 1. Were the operations in Egypt carried out on instructions from Israel? 2. Were any other such actions carried out, also on instructions from Israel? 3. By whom were these instructions issued, on whose authority, and to what end?

Aware that the inquiry commission would be set up within days, and that his testimony before it would be fateful, Givly sensed that he had to act swiftly. His mainstay was the support of his subordinates at MI, his own loyal office staff in particular; Lavon's allegation that the DMI alone had issued the order descended upon them calamitously. As Givly's aide-de-camp Hareven would put it, MI's officers were unanimous in the conviction that "Benyamin is the saint, Lavon the villain."

Dalia Carmel expressed great concern. Beyond being a devoted admirer of Givly, she was his confidential secretary; she typed all his letters and all the documents relating to "the sorry business" in Egypt. The debacle, the arrests, an attempt by Marcelle Ninio to kill herself, the sui-

cide of Max Binnet, the Cairo trial and the harsh sentences expected—
all these plunged Givly's staff, along with the rest of the MI command,
into gloomy frustration. Like everyone, Carmel was eager to lend a
hand; accordingly, when Ben-Zur—who supervised the care of the Cairo
defendants and their families—asked her to do some typing, she leaped
at the opportunity.

Of the tasks he gave her, two remained in her memory. One was the
alteration of the carbon copy of a two-page letter from Givly to Dayan,
dated July 19, which she had typed herself. According to what she told
Gideon Hausner, now Israel's Attorney General, on December 6, 1960,
the letter was filed in Givly's office safe; if so, he alone could have sanc-
tioned its retrieval. Ben-Zur directed her to retype the entire second
page of this letter, making a change in the second paragraph, which
referred to the operations in Egypt. The original began with the words:
"In accordance with conversations which were held," or "In accordance
with instructions issued"—she did not remember precisely. In retyping,
she was asked to replace those words with a phrase handwritten—she
could not recall whose writing it was—on a sheet of paper: "On Lavon's
instructions." She did the job in the evening, when the office staff had
all gone home.

Assisted by Ben-Zur, Carmel took great pains to make the second page
resemble the first. The freshly unwrapped copy paper struck her as look-
ing too new; the sheets in her drawer "looked a little more worn. So I
used the older paper, to give it the same color." She used "several sheets
of copy paper, to get the grey, faded effect so it would more or less"
resemble the copy of page 1. "I put in several papers, with the carbons in
between, and finally I found the most suitable one."

Carmel also scrutinized the copy thoroughly. She was aware that, in
those days of manual typewriters, typists had their own "signatures"—
divisions, spacing, recurrent errors, letters interchanged, stronger and
weaker keystrokes, and the like; even the same typist's "signature" varied
from day to day. Carmel related: "I pinpointed the recurrent errors I had
made on July 19 on page 1; if I'm not mistaken, there was some characteristic error with a particular letter. As I retyped page 2, I tried to repro-
duce the 'signature' from page 1."

Carmel had reason to be proud of her handiwork: when Givly submitted this retyped copy to the inquiry commission as proof of the veracity of his testimony, experts affirmed unanimously that the copy was no
forgery.

The other alteration Carmel remembered involved the "notebook"—
an ordinary elementary school composition book—where she entered,
in her own hand, every document submitted to Lavon's attention: subject matter; reference number; the date and hour of its release from
Givly's office and its return there. In this case, the alteration was
designed to convince the commission that the DMI kept Lavon fully
briefed, with documentation, on all the developments in Egypt. "I
changed the list of documents issued to Lavon's office," she testified.
Lifting out the notebook's binding staples, Carmel extracted the two
middle pages, intending to substitute two new sheets that she had filled
out. But when she tried to insert the new pages, they "wouldn't go in
because they were from the middle, they were too big, the holes too; and
when I tried to realign the middle of the notebook, it didn't fit and I did-
n't know how to fix it." Convinced that Hareven knew what was going
on, she asked him how to insert the pages. Staring at her in astonishment, he "asked me what I was doing; I told him the look on his face was
killing me."

Hareven had a different story. According to him, Carmel told him she
had been requested to rewrite the notebook's two inner pages, which
were then reinserted by the documentation department. Hareven
claimed to have told her, "it's stupid to do such things," and ordered her
"not to talk about it."

Carmel had just turned nineteen; in her youthful adulation of Givly,
she thought her forgeries would help "to save us all"—that is, all of MI.
Convinced that Givly was being framed by Lavon, she saw nothing wrong
in fighting back "lie for lie." Learning of her belated confession, Rehavia
Vardi commented, "I guess it's true," adding that Carmel was not alone
in being "spellbound by Givly, and ready to do anything for him . . .
everyone was. . . . Ben-Zur would have gone through fire and water for
him. If someone had come to Rehavia Vardi and told him alterations
were needed, he wouldn't have blinked an eyelid."

Ben-Zur did not deny the forgeries either. When Carmel first published her story in 1989, he commented: "Dalia Carmel was not my secretary. She was Givly's secretary. Therefore, if she forged that letter or
any other evidence, as she says, she probably did so at her boss's request,
not mine."

On January 2, 1954, Sharett, with Lavon's consent, nominated the members of his "confidential commission": Supreme Court president Yitzhak

Olshan and Ya'akov Dori, the IDF's first chief of staff. The commission heard its first witness, Lavon, that same day.

The inquiry hinged upon the question Olshan posed to Isser Harel: "Is it conceivable that Givly . . . would not seek authorization, and act on his own authority?" Harel replied that Givly should have "learned prudence" from the Tubiansky affair with regard to unlawful acts; but "when he knows that the defense minister conspires against the prime minister, and operations are launched without [prior] notification," it was not surprising that he too should act on his own. Harel added that, had the operations succeeded, Givly "would have shouted them to the rooftops. Lavon would have glorified them further." In other words, Givly had been counting on Lavon's backing.

Givly was the commission's second witness, testifying on January 3, 1955, and again on January 9. His testimony makes it doubtful whether he did learn anything from the Tubiansky case. Just as at the Be'eri trial, his preferred tactic was camouflage. He tried to come across as the obedient, professional soldier, short on initiative, invariably deferring to his superiors and carrying out their instructions. Once again, he cast slurs on everyone around him.

He depicted himself as a "subordinate to the chief of staff" but also to the defense minister, "who would summon me occasionally." This dual allegiance "had landed him in endless conflict between [Lavon] and the chief of staff."

Olshan and Dori wanted to know under whose command 131 fell, and who was authorized to give the green light for its activation.

Givly: "131 falls under my command . . . I would need authorization for its activation either from the chief of staff or the defense minister."

From whom did Givly take his orders in Dayan's absence?

Givly: "I did not inform the acting chief of staff of the defense minister's instructions. In effect, the defense minister himself stood in for the chief of staff."

Was 131 not designated to operate exclusively during times of war?

Givly: "We have recognized that in view of the [im]balance of forces between us and the Arab states, we would have to commence action before the zero hour of hostilities."

Olshan asked, "Did the notion of . . . sabotaging the [British] withdrawal by means of operations in Egypt originate with you?" Givly replied that such operations rested "upon the defense minister's political judgment. I didn't go into that judgement, and I won't do so now."

Quoting from Evron's "affidavit" regarding the Lavon-Givly conversation and its references to fomenting tension and disorders in Egypt and to attacks on British installations, Dori requested Givly's comments. Givly replied that he had never proposed "any options for activating 131." On his return to Israel, he had discovered that the 131 teams were "in dysfunctional condition," which made him "doubt their operational fitness and organization"; he accordingly instructed Ben-Zur "to go abroad and study the situation."

Stressing Lavon's bent for unorthodox and intemperate action, Givly recalled that "the defense minister was disappointed in the West's stance and its desertion of Israeli interests"; accordingly, in early April, Givly had directed MI's research department "to gather material on British objectives in the Middle East."

Givly thus glossed over his own initiative, which he had outlined in (among other places) his June 6 memorandum to the chief of staff and defense minister, and to which Dayan had alluded at the General Staff meeting of the previous November 1. He did not trouble to inform the commission that he had sent Lavon a memorandum by the MI research branch which asserted: "Our activity, in concert with other parties, is capable of delaying or swaying attainment of the agreement" but "it is unimaginable that this task . . . will be accomplished by routine diplomatic means."

In short, in Givly's account, any ideas of or plans for clandestine operations in Egypt and other Arab countries (he listed several) arose in Lavon's mind; and he, as DMI, was required to act in accordance with "the defense minister's mindset and inclination." Did Givly report about this to the chief of staff? He replied cautiously: "I believe I told the chief of staff about the defense minister's most recent ideas and the steps he took against the British." But he added that, on Dayan's return from the United States, he "spoke with me, saying he had always dreaded the defense minister's eagerness to lay hands on 131. . . . one should be cautious."

Givly asserted further that Lavon's order to activate 131 was given orally. Why had he not demanded it in writing? Givly replied: "It isn't my habit to work like that. . . . I don't record the substance of meetings with the defense minister, unless there are operational instructions. Even in those instances, I destroy the notes."

Dori asked Givly whether he felt equally responsible with Lavon; Givly replied: "All echelons bear responsibility, each at its own [level]."

OLSHAN: When a certain operation involves a military aspect, and a political aspect, who decides?

GIVLY: One of the greatest dangers is when intelligence bodies impinge upon political considerations—that's what ministers are for.

OLSHAN: If there is a risk of political repercussions, aren't you bound to receive instructions from someone so authorized?

GIVLY: I don't have to exercise judgment. I have to analyze possible repercussions and results, but I take no part in decisionmaking.

DORI: You activated 131, which is a combat unit; you should have objected to jeopardizing it—if not on political grounds . . . on jeopardizing a unit MI cherishes.

GIVLY: Had I been asked, I would have voiced my opinion.

Yet, although his opinion was not solicited, the obedient Givly "had no shadow of doubt" about obeying the defense minister's instructions regarding operations against the British.

Givly claimed that Lavon, ever eager to dabble in intelligence affairs, phoned him frequently, and saw him sometimes "three times a week." This intimacy was not to Givly's taste; but, being unswervingly responsive to his superiors' requests, he fulfilled this wish too. When rumors reached him that Lavon intended to make him the fall guy, he did not heed them. Prior to the decision to set up the inquiry commission, "I had no inkling that the defense minister was liable to pass the buck." Consequently, he was taken aback when Lavon said, "in the presence of the stenographer, that I was lying."

The commissioners questioned Givly repeatedly about his reports to Lavon. At the first news of the arrests, demanded Olshan, "Did the defense minister ask you about it right away?"

GIVLY: I don't remember, but I talked about it with him a few days later. There is a routine procedure for conveying information from my office to the defense minister's.

OLSHAN: The reports appeared initially in the press. You should have taken notice and run a check to find out if these were your people.

GIVLY: The reports appeared as far back as July 16—about persons unknown lobbing bombs at the American information offices. We only began taking the matter seriously after the broadcasts [about the arrests—S.T.] from Cairo on July 24 and 25. When the defense minister inquired on July 27, we said we didn't know, and were making inquiries.

OLSHAN: On August 8, you sent the defense minister a report. . . . after that report, was there an approach to you, or any steps regarding you?

GIVLY: There was no approach, no question, no demand for an inquiry.

If Givly had learned of Max Binnet's arrest in late August, asked Dori, "why was the defense minister only informed of it on September 23?" Givly replied that the report was a summation that "must have been preceded by other reports to the defense minister. Binnet was important to us." He did not specify the "other reports."

The commission asked why he had not passed Elad's report on to Lavon: "Because its substance had already been conveyed to him in previous reports. I suggested the defense minister see Elad and draw his own direct impression. The defense minister did not wish to see him." Lavon contradicted that claim: "I didn't know Elad was in Israel." He learned this only on receiving Ben-Zur's October 5 report to Dayan. Givly also resorted repeatedly to "don't remember" replies.

DORI: Around the time of Ben-Zur's departure for Paris, did you not speak with the defense minister about his mission or its purpose?

GIVLY: I think not. I am not in the habit of reporting to him on such missions. I can't remember.

Givly did have clear recollections from the Friday he transmitted the order for the operation in Egypt, July 16. "I remember the conversation with the defense minister. . . . When I came to his home on July 16, we spoke about the evacuation, then went on to the activation of 131." On receiving the order from Lavon, he summoned Ben-Zur and Vardi to his home. But at this crucial juncture, Givly's memory again went haywire—or had it been thrown off balance when Lavon unexpectedly produced a conflicting version? In his first testimony, Givly clearly remembered

> the defense minister asking what can you do, and I replied: only minor things that will raise some dust, like attacks on institutions or vehicles. We also talked about troops, but that fell by the wayside. After that, he gave instructions to activate 131. Over the past two weeks, the defense minister has managed to extract from me a number of documents which are liable to obfuscate matters. In the process, a talk between us held on July 31 *intruded upon my memory* (italics added).
>
> I remember Friday evening July 16. . . . When I re-examined my memory, I realized I had *confused* two unrelated conversations. I admit

I didn't clearly remember the date of the conversation. The July 16 conversation was just between the two of us, I don't remember whether it was at his home or the office. I think it was at home. . . . From the scene of that conversation of the 16th, I sent an urgent summons to the commander of 131 . . . to come to my home at 5.

In Givly's second testimony, he claimed to remember the July 16 conversation:

I rang [Ben-Zur] from somewhere or other, on my way home. . . . I am liable to *confuse* the circumstances. I am in no doubt that the meeting with the defense minister was on a Friday afternoon. At his home, I *think*. Logically, it should have been at his home, at 3 or 4 in the afternoon.

On one occasion only did I say that the conversation [with Lavon] ensued from an earlier discussion of a certain subject [the British withdrawal]. . . . I can't recall, but *I think* we didn't just switch to that topic haphazardly; rather, it was in consequence of some previous discussion. I don't think there was an earlier discussion in a broad forum. The defense minister tried to draw me into giving details which would fit in with the July 31 discussion.

DORI: "How is one to explain that the defense minister's order was given on July 16—neither earlier nor later?"

GIVLY: . . . Obviously, the matter did not happen fortuitously. Our memorandum was [submitted] on June 16. Frequent reports were coming in that signature of the agreement was imminent, there was talk of August 1. Plainly, there was a discussion of the matter.

When asked if he had notified Lavon that his operational order of July 16 had been conveyed to Egypt, Givly replied that "The minister asked me whether the orders had been issued, and I told him they had. That was between July 16 and 26."

When asked if the discussion on the Suez withdrawal had taken place at the minister's home or in the office, Givly replied: "There was a discussion about Suez, with the participation of the defense minister, Avidar, Peres, Yuval Ne'eman perhaps, and myself. I don't remember the date. I think it was at the office. If it was at the office, Evron was there too. It's hard to remember."

But the commission members knew that Yuval Ne'eman, head of the Director of Operation's planning department, had attended only the

July 31 meeting at Lavon's home. Did Givly remember attending the weekly meeting at Lavon's office on July 15? Could this have been the meeting that preceded his conversation with Lavon?

Givly did not recall such a meeting "in particular," but:

> I remember a number of instances when I remained alone with the defense minister. I'm almost certain there was an instance when the defense minister asked me to remain behind. I remember the July 31 meeting well. And the meeting's agenda. I remember Shimon Peres wasn't there. It's highly probable I remained alone with the defense minister after that meeting.

But Peres was at the July 31 meeting, and at the one of July 15 too. Could Givly's recollection have been so faulty? Carmel stated later that his memory was excellent. His extensive resort to I-don't-remember replies appears to have been calculated to obscure dates and circumstances, to make his July 19 letter to Dayan seem a valid, credible document proving that Lavon gave the order on July 16.

That letter—of which Lavon said that "in whole or part, it must be a forgery"—was indeed accorded considerable weight by Olshan and Dori. Of 22 pages of handwritten findings, the commission devoted two to the paragraph fabricated by Ben-Zur and Dalia Carmel:

> On Lavon's instructions, we have sent the Hundred thirty-one group into action. Even if it were plain that—notwithstanding the growing opposition of the young Conservatives—an agreement cannot be prevented, Lavon believes it may be feasible to postpone or delay it, and thus gain some diplomatic profit. In spite of all our apprehensions, it will be a test, even if only in minor operations. I hope that on your early return, we will be at the final phase of all the operations.

The commission noted that Givly had sent Dayan typewritten letters, whose receipt was confirmed by Dayan and by Herzog, the military attache in Washington. But "they did not remember the substance of the letters, and could neither confirm nor deny" their contents. Dayan testified that he had destroyed them on security grounds.

Besides the possibility that the letter was genuine, Olshan and Dori entertained two alternative hypotheses: Either the DMI "wrote the letter from the outset with the intention of being able to fall back on it in the future"or "that the copy shown to us was typed later, with the addition of the aforementioned passage which did not appear in the original."

This uncertainty induced the commission "not to perceive the letter as decisive proof" that Lavon gave the order on July 16; however, it "contributed towards inspiring us with doubt as to the charge" that Givly lied. Yet, had the commission summoned Givly's aide-de-camp Hareven, and Carmel, it might have learned that its second hypothesis—forgery—was the unvarnished truth.

Givly's testimony denigrated 131's Alexandria team: "Had those fellows been well-disciplined," he said, "they would not have commenced operations before July 18." But he laid the blame for the bungled operation mainly on 131 commander Ben-Zur.

It is clear that Givly induced Ben-Zur to provide a version that reinforced his own testimony, thereby setting Ben-Zur up as the fall guy for "the sorry business." Ben-Zur played his role with inexplicable eagerness. The Lavon-Givly faceoff did not affect him at all; and the operation's failure preoccupied the commission less than its authorization, whether by Lavon or by Givly. Moreover, Ben-Zur had already paid the price of failure, having lost command of 131 and retaining no prospects of promotion.[1]

Why was Ben-Zur so compliant in backing up Givly's story? This question has no definitive answer. Whatever Ben-Zur might come to realize later, his prospects at the time seemed bound up with Givly's fate. In short: instead of diminishing Ben-Zur's dependency upon Givly, his removal from the command of 131 increased it.

But while Ben-Zur's future seemed to hang upon Givly's vindication, Givly's future depended to no small degree upon the inculpation of Ben-Zur. That may be why Givly went to great lengths to inculcate in Ben-Zur a sense of profound guilt, as though he were to blame for everything: the botched operation, the capture of the network, the suicides, the prison sentences, and above all, the eventual ruin of Givly himself. But Givly forgot that a bungling accomplice can wreak greater harm than a gifted foe.

---

1. Ben-Zur never won another command. After a number of temporary assignments, and having achieved only mediocre grades at the IDF staff command college, he left the army in April 1958 and was later relieved of any active post in the reserves. Unlike other officers terminating their service, he was not helped to find employment, and ultimately landed a job through a "Help Wanted" ad in a newspaper.

Given the facts that came to light later, Givly and Ben-Zur probably would have blamed Elad for the operations of July 2 and July 14, of which they had no prior knowledge, for he had initiated these on Egyptian orders. But instead of admitting their ignorance of those operations to the Olshan-Dori commission, they both blamed the 131 teams in Egypt.

On December 28, the chief of staff asked Ben-Zur, "How come operations were carried out on July 2 and 14, and how did we come to lump them all together?" Ben-Zur retorted that "when listing 131's operations, he had included those carried out before July 16, because, in his haste, he copied the reports from the press without verifying whether the dates tallied." Dayan recalled that Ben-Zur had said: "I wrote in that manner because that was the mood at the time, and no instructions were given to carry out the actions of July 2 and 14." In his testimony Ben-Zur conceded that he had prepared the report "in haste," only to discover later that "it did not correspond with the facts." When the commission asked why he had relied on Elad's report to state "with absolute certainty" that there had been eight operations, Ben-Zur replied: "I was under the impression of the charges, and the publications from sources." He did not elaborate on that cryptic statement.

Givly belittled Ben-Zur in his testimony, saying, "He lacks elan," and implying that Ben-Zur was entirely to blame for the Egyptian debacle. One example:

DORI: If the defense minister referred to the British, why didn't Ben-Zur specify [in the transmission to Egypt] that the operations were to be directed exclusively against them?

GIVLY: I told Ben-Zur to act against the British.

DORI: If so, why were American institutions torched?

GIVLY: There are mysteries here which baffle us too. We received no reports or information from the people in Egypt about the July 2 and 14 operations. Elad likewise did not know of their execution. I asked Ben-Zur why he listed eight operations.

DORI: I get the impression that they acted according to the briefing [they received].

GIVLY: I'm not sure. Ask Ben-Zur.

OLSHAN: When did you initiate radio contact with the men in Egypt?

GIVLY: I suggest Ben-Zur answer on that.

But the commission wanted Givly himself to say when the teams were activated.

GIVLY: Prior to the briefing by Ben-Zur [in Paris] and Elad's arrival [in Egypt], the teams were not activated, maybe just for the sake of keeping them on their toes. Ben-Zur should be asked about that.

That is, what might seem to the commission like operational orders amounted only to a dry run, to heighten their morale and alertness. Givly also told the commission: "Only on learning from Ben-Zur that [the Alexandria team] was capable of such action, did I give the order."

Ben-Zur testified on January 5 and 9. Dori, believing that Ben-Zur's instructions to the unit in Egypt "bear a closer resemblance to operational orders than to advance standby instructions," asked: "Before your departure for Europe, did the mood prevalent among you extend to . . . the necessity of action in Egypt, that it would be profitable . . . ?"

BEN-ZUR: No, definitely not.
OLSHAN: Did the DMI ask you specifically about the feasibility of activating the unit?
BEN-ZUr: Not specifically.
DORI: Did you give Elad instructions to be ready for operations in advance of the withdrawal?
BEN-ZUR (*lying*): Not in advance of the withdrawal.

Living up to expectations, Ben-Zur's description of Friday July 16 supported Givly's testimony. He had been summoned to Givly's home between 5:00 and 6:30. How did Ben-Zur know Givly had received the order from the defense minister?

"As a rule, Benyamin doesn't refer to those above him, but this time, he spoke for the defense minister." Thus he had been shocked on learning from Givly that the defense minister denied giving the order.

But as his testimony proceeded, Ben-Zur's rehearsed story did not stand up. Under pressure from the Commissioners, he mixed his rehearsed version with off-the-cuff answers, making a very poor impression. The commissioners were dubious when he claimed that Givly's order had taken him by surprise. "Is it conceivable," Olshan asked, "that Givly would think up a scheme like that without consulting you?"

"I think he wouldn't have tried to plan it without consulting me," Ben-Zur responded. Before giving the order, Givly had "asked me whether it was feasible to activate the unit," and Ben-Zur had said it was, though he would have preferred "them to have more time . . . . it would have been better to entrust them with such an assignment three months later." In that case, why did he not say so to Givly?

Here Ben-Zur fell back on a reply which also featured in Givly's testimony, and in the copy of his letter to Dayan: "That Friday July 16, I said the unit was up to carrying out only minor actions. There had been no previous talk on the subject."

On this point, Ben-Zur's testimony plainly did not jibe with Givly's. Givly had said that, before giving the order, "Lavon asked: what can you do, and I replied: only minor actions which will raise dust, like attacking institutions or vehicles." But Ben-Zur testified that Givly had not consulted him before meeting with Lavon that Friday. How then did Givly know, during his conversation with Lavon, what Ben-Zur would tell him subsequently?"

Asked to explain why the Alexandria team acted against American and Egyptian institutions, in spite of clear orders to attack British objectives, Ben-Zur took the blame upon himself, telling the commission that it stemmed from a faulty English translation of the cable, which "was not sufficiently precise or specific. It does not clearly refer exclusively to the British."

All the commission's witnesses were cautioned to keep their testimony confidential; but it is only Givly whose response—that he "knows that the hearing is secret and must not be disclosed"—is recorded. If the commission suspected him of attempting to influence witnesses, their misgivings were borne out by Ben-Zur's deposition, in which Supreme Court president Olshan—a seasoned judge skilled in distinguishing genuinely spontaneous testimony from the pre-orchestrated variety—was quick to discern Givly's influence. His suspicions were reinforced when Ben-Zur, asked whether he had discussed his testimony with Givly, replied: "This morning [January 5, 1955—S.T.] I talked with Givly, who told me I was to be called to testify." With the over-eagerness of a man harboring a guilty secret, he hastened to add: "I understand the whole matter stems from my [October] report, and it's my fault."

With an opening like that, there was little difficulty in cracking so hapless a witness. When asked why he thought it was his fault, Ben-Zur replied: "Some time ago, Givly asked me what were the sources for my report, and I said: 'That's how it looked to me.' " That is, he claimed he told Givly that his sources were press and radio reports, and the report reflected what he gleaned from them—whereas in fact, he had used Elad's August report.

OLSHAN: When did you learn that we two would conduct the inquiry?
BEN-ZUR: On Sunday [January 2] from Givly. We spoke only of the report. He told me I'd find it difficult to explain my style of operating.

What was the commission investigating?
Ben-Zur replied, "I know from Benyamin that the question you're investigating is whether the minister gave an order to Benyamin on July 16." In their findings, Olshan and Dori wrote:

> We were unfavorably impressed by this officer's testimony before us, and were unwilling to draw any conclusions on the strength of his statements. His replies to several questions were so confused and vague as to make it hard to distinguish facts from wishful thinking.

It would not be the last time Ben-Zur came in for harsh words in an inquiry's findings.

12

Almog's Mission

Lavon's testimony did nothing to resolve the commission's perplexity over his five-month-long silence, which therefore largely colored its findings: his denial of having given the order could not be reconciled with his failure to demand any explanation, either before or after the collapse of the Egyptian network; his claim of having received no account from Givly merely highlighted his failure to demand any. The commission's findings express astonishment that Lavon remained passive even after receiving Ben-Zur's October report, which "explicitly states as fact that instructions were issued to the commander of 131 by the DMI"—refuting the latter's claim that "there was just a matter of planning and the boys lost control."

Lavon claimed that since the controversy "had not surfaced," it never occurred to him before November 1, 1954 that the instructions to activate 131 were being attributed to him. The commission responded: "How is one to explain the defense minister's failure, in the period preceding November 1, to express his indignation to the chief of staff and the DMI, over the latter activating 131 on his own authority?"

Lavon argued that the Cairo defendants might have been jeopardized by the commotion liable to arise from investigations at that stage. Here too, the commission responded with a question: "Why did he nevertheless commence—during the second half of December, at the height of the trial in Egypt—collecting signatures on affidavits concerning the date of the discussion on the significance of the Suez withdrawal?"

Lavon replied: "a. After November 1, on first learning" that the order had been attributed to him, he "began to seek out evidence" regarding the date of the discussion; "by the time he managed to assemble concrete proof that the discussion was held on July 31, considerable time had elapsed. b. The trial in Egypt was approaching its final phase, and he thought the time had come to start figuring out what had happened."

The commission noted that "this explanation is acceptable"; however, "a distinction should be drawn between the period preceding November 1 and the period thereafter." After that date, Lavon, suspecting that "a libel" was being concocted against him, preferred to remain silent until he could "assemble evidence to refute it." But "that motive does not apply to the period" before November 1, particularly after receipt of Ben-Zur's October 5 report which, before any controversy occurred, "explicitly states" that he "received instructions from the DMI on July 16."

"Hence," the commission's findings noted, "the defense minister's conduct likewise renders it impossible to draw a firm conclusion one way or the other."

Furthermore, in view of the close ties between Lavon and Givly, it was unimaginable that a matter of such vital importance evoked no exchanges between them. There was no explanation for Lavon's failure to react to Givly's August 8 report, whose receipt he had confirmed by initialing it; or to Givly's proposal that day to "renew psychological warfare" with the aim of "destabilising the regime in Egypt." Similarly, the various explanations Lavon proposed, particularly his reference to "a snag in the execution," could not be reconciled with his professed ignorance of any operation in Egypt. It was also probable that Lavon knew that Givly had told Isser Harel: "Our people did it, there were no instructions to act, merely orders for preparedness and planning." Lavon was unable to explain why press reports about the arrests in Egypt prompted prime minister Sharett to seek an explanation, while he himself failed to react.

Why then did the commission decline to accept Givly's contentions, or pronounce in his favor? The commission drew up a kind of balance sheet, weighing the arguments for and against each of the adversaries. In Givly's debit column they recorded that the date he said he had received the instructions—Friday July 16—"had no basis in fact because there was no discussion whatsoever that day, or with the participants he specified"; that operations had already begun on July 2 "and are listed in Ben-Zur's reports as having been carried out by our people after receiving 'assignment instructions'"; that the Cairo defendants had "confessed to committing the sabotage acts of July 2 and 14, on Elad's orders, and it cannot be assumed that they would admit to acts they had not committed." Hence it was probable that "Givly is lying to save his skin," and that the copy of the July 19 letter to Dayan was "a forgery or a prearranged alibi." Finally, even Givly maintained that "he received orders from the defense minister to act against the British, whereas the instructions sent from MI refer to general—not merely British—objectives." It was thus possible that "Ben-Zur too is lying" and "may be subject to pressure and extortion by Givly."

The commission also listed arguments that seemed to show "why it is reasonable to believe that Givly issued the instructions on his own authority." Among them: the chief of staff was out of the country "and Givly felt free to act at will"; "he assumed that such operations were to the defense minister's liking, and should he succeed, he would earn praise"; he was under pressure because "the teams in Egypt demanded action"; he gauged that "time was short till the withdrawal agreement was signed"; and by nature, he was "a reckless gambler who inclines to running risks, and enjoys the sense of his power to carry out actions which bring major results." Finally, Givly initially issued "instructions to carry out easy minor operations, as training exercises, first mailboxes, then the [U.S.] libraries, and in light of their success, ordered more decisive operations . . . [on July 23]. There was a snowball effect."

On the credit side, the commission considered the possibility that he "confused two meetings . . . a private conversation, which appears to have been held on July 15, after a weekly meeting; and another conversation, on July 16." The commission also noted that "there is no proof or report from our own sources that the July 2 and 14 operations were carried out by our people": the Cairo trial confessions might have been extracted "by coercion." Elad too doubted that our people "acted without instructions because . . . they are well-disciplined"; however, if they did carry out the operations, they did so of their own accord, not "on orders or directions from MI." Finally, as Ben-Zur had admitted, "the wording of the orders may not have been apt."

Ironically, an important argument in Givly's favor was his flawed memory: had he issued instructions on his own authority and attributed them to the defense minister, "he would have to be alert to any slip liable to expose the lie"—whereas in fact, "he was imprudent, getting himself enmeshed needlessly" with regard to the date.

The commission also noted arguments for casting the blame on Lavon: "In the past likewise, he had given instructions for acts of sabotage" which "conform with his views on the use of force in reprisals and harassment against the British." In July, Lavon was "particularly full of bitterness towards the West" because of "reports of the signing of the withdrawal agreement on August 1"; at the same time, he heard from Givly "that the teams are fit for minor operations." However, putting all these considerations together, the commission was still unconvinced that Lavon had given the order. His silence until November 1, for example, could be explained by his not knowing "that the . . . order was being attributed to him"; not till then did he begin "seeking evidence to refute the libel, meanwhile refraining from investigation so as not to cause commotion and publicity as long as the trial lasted." Having thus refuted its own contentions, the commission was powerless to reach a conclusion one way or the other.

On January 12, 1955, the commissioners submitted their findings—handwritten for the sake of confidentiality—to Sharett. Drafted by Olshan on behalf of them both, the findings were inconclusive:

> In conclusion, we regret that we are unable to answer the questions presented to us by the prime minister. We find no possibility of stating anything beyond [the fact] that we have not been convinced beyond all reasonable doubt that the DMI did not receive instructions from the defense minister; with that, we are not certain that the defense minister did indeed issue the orders attributed to him.

Yet, while condemning neither of the two, the commission did not exonerate either one. As Dori remarked, if it remained undetermined who was responsible, "one can only assume that the responsibility belongs to all"—that is, both. Though only indirectly, the commission thus hit upon the truth while falling short of its task by not specifying positively that Lavon and Givly bore joint responsibility for the debacle in Egypt, and shared the blame for its tragic outcome.

The commissioners finished their work in ten days, having heard only fourteen witnesses. These included five civilians (the prime minister, minister of defense, the latter's principal secretary, the director-general, and the head of the Mossad) and nine army officers (the chief of staff, his deputy, the military attache in Washington, Haim Herzog, the DMI, two

MI department heads, 131's commander, and the heads of its teams in Egypt, Avraham Dar and Avry Elad). The commission's work was hasty and sketchy. While admitting it could not accomplish its assigned task, it failed to call witnesses who could have helped solve the riddle: Mordechai Almog, Rehavia Vardi, Aluf Hareven, Dalia Carmel, and other MI and IDF personnel.

The commission's greatest oversight, however, was its failure to detect that it had been duped by Givly, who coordinated Elad's testimony with his own.

On January 1, 1955, Ben-Zur instructed Elad, who was in Zurich, to go to Paris and contact "the usual number," while telling no one of his movements. The next day, Elad reached Paris and registered at the cheap Avenue Wagram hotel assigned to him.

That morning, Givly sent his deputy and righthand man Mordechai Almog on a one-day trip to Paris. Almog received his passport and tickets at the airport, where Ben-Zur entrusted him with a letter to Elad: a single handwritten sheet in a sealed envelope. Meeting near the Arc de Triomphe, Elad and Almog headed for Almog's hotel room. According to Elad, Almog cautioned him to tell no one he was in Paris. (Breaking with custom, Almog himself did not visit the Israeli embassy; he also ignored his former commander, Harkabi, when he spotted him on the street.) Having drawn the shades, Almog gave Elad Ben-Zur's letter; he watched as Elad read it and, at his bidding, tore it to shreds and flushed it down the toilet. Almog told Elad only "that he was to come to Israel immediately."

Ben-Zur's letter, Elad wrote in 1976, commanded Elad to "forget" the instructions he had given him at their Paris meeting in early June 1954, as well as the operations before July 23. "The instructions were confined to communications and planning. Nothing else!" Before departing, Almog took Elad's hand in both of his, saying: "Leave for home at the first opportunity . . . and forget you heard or saw me, or even my ghost. Shalom and good luck."

Almog, who had helped Ben-Zur advance in the army, was also the man who, in October 1953, had found Elad fit for his assignment. Givly had chosen Almog as his messenger not merely because he was his confidant and MI's highest-ranking officer after himself, but also because Elad was afraid of him and would probably comply with his instructions.

On January 4, Elad landed at Lod airport; there, outside the passenger terminal, "among the night shadows" as he later wrote, he found-

Ben-Zur waiting to drive him to Givly's home. As with Elad's previous trip to Israel, this stealth was vital if he was to cover effectively for Givly.

The three men spent the night rehearsing the spurious tale Elad was to relate to Dayan, Lavon, and the Olshan-Dori commission: that he had received the radioed instructions to act on July 18 and 19; and that the July 2 and 14 operations were not carried out by our people. Givly said goodbye to Elad at 4 in the morning, saying: "You didn't see us tonight—either of us." Ben-Zur now drove Elad to his hotel for two or three hours' sleep.

Givly reported Elad's arrival in a phone call to Dayan's aide-de-camp, Eli Zeira, who made an appointment for him to see Dayan at 7:30 in the morning of January 5, "to discover what [Elad] knows of the operations of July 2 and 14," as Zeira noted in the chief of staff's journal after driving Elad to the meeting. Indeed, Dayan had just one question to put to Elad: who was responsible for the July 2 and 14 operations? Elad's reply, recorded in the journal: "Those operations were not carried out on our instructions, or by our people."

Sometime later, Dayan discovered that Givly had sent Almog to Elad—in defiance of the chief of staff's explicit order that before testifying to the commission Elad "is to see only me." Dayan fumed, "My trust in Givly has collapsed."

Going on to a lengthy interrogation at Lavon's office, in Evron's presence, Elad piously recited his memorized lesson. It was afternoon before he finally came before Olshan and Dori—the appearance for which he had been called to Israel. Olshan later expressed his indignation over Lavon's failure to "notify us beforehand" that he was meeting Elad. "It was a serious defect. But we did not take it seriously at the time because Lavon was not on trial before us."

The commission's first question to Elad was: when had he arrived, and whom had he seen? Almost a full day after landing at Lod, Elad launched into his testimony with his first lie: "I arrived this morning . . . I have seen Major Zeira, the chief of staff, Benyamin [Givly], Ben-Zur, Lavon." From here on, his rehearsed falsehoods flowed unchecked.

The commission discovered that the testimony had been cooked on January 10, 1955, two days before Olshan began writing its findings (except for Almog's role, which was not found out until May 1955). Teddy Kollek, director-general at the prime minister's office, told Sharett that Givly and Ben-Zur had "grabbed [Elad], coached him in detail about what to reply—incidentally instructing him to lie—and overall saw that the testimony matched so as to tighten the incriminatory noose around Lavon." Alerting Olshan and Dori, Sharett learned, as he noted in his diary, that "the cooking of the testimony" was "clear to them, anyway Lavon himself takes care it is clear to them." Inexplicably, Olshan and Dori disregarded this point in their findings, even asserting that Elad was "a man who did not impress us as a liar."

A more generous tribute to his probity had never come Elad's way.

By accepting Elad's account, Olshan wrote in his memoirs, the commission gave its imprimatur to the denial that 131 carried out the July 2 and 14 operations.

Let us move ahead of our story to record that in 1957, suspicions were aroused regarding Elad's contacts with Egyptian intelligence officers in Europe. He was lured back to Israel and interrogated, beginning on December 16. His interrogators—Zvi Aharoni of the general security service, and his assistant, Victor Cohen—suspected him of having had a hand in the downfall of the Egyptian network.

It was March 19, 1958 before Elad consented to tell his interrogators "the whole story of his links with the network." He admitted that, at the Paris meeting of May 30, 1954, Ben-Zur had instructed him "to take action the moment he returned to Egypt." On his arrival there, he had sent his "Shipment possible" cable which—according to this new version—signaled that the unit was ready to act. It was he who instructed the 131 personnel to carry out the July 2 and 14 operations. He confessed further that Givly, abetted by Ben-Zur and Almog, had solicited him to perjure himself before the Olshan-Dori commission.

On April 20, 1954, during his stay in Egypt, Elad reported to Ben-Zur that he had discovered "unmistakable signs of a thorough search of my letters and effects." His valise was searched five times. He notified the Egyptian police, and "an officer arrived to take depositions." To Aharoni and Cohen, this suggested that the Egyptians had suspected Elad from the moment he stepped on their soil.

The interrogators now discovered that Elad had set off for his May 30 rendezvous in Paris with Ben-Zur on May 3, without notifying anyone. He spent four whole weeks touring Italy, Austria, France, Germany and Belgium. On May 23, Elad noted in his diary,[1] in large, underscored let-

---

1. Elad's diary was obtained from his mother in Vienna, while he was under arrest in Israel. The method used to secure the diary is still a Mossad secret.

ters: "It's impossible to meet Mohab." Elad had become friendly with Colonel Mohab, head of Egyptian military intelligence and subsequently military attaché to Brussels and Bonn, after meeting him at the home of his German friend Baron von Bechtoldsheim. But Elad could not recall why he wanted to see Mohab in Brussels, whether it was to deliver a letter or just pass on regards "at the request of the Baron, or Engel, or on my own account." This, then, was the purpose of his Brussels trip, of which there was no mention in the reports he submitted to MI. After meeting with Ben-Zur, Elad did not return to Egypt till June 28.

According to his diary entries, Elad met Mohab again on September 13, 1954, when he made Mohab "an offer." Only a month had elapsed since his "escape" from Egypt, and his interrogators wondered why he showed no apprehension about meeting with Mohab, who must have known of his links with the recently captured network. Elad had no adequate explanation for this, and he fended off questions about his diary entries from late July 1954 onward.

Suspicion also focused on Elad's association and correspondence with Mahmud Hassan, whom he had met through the German consul in Alexandria on December 25, 1953, only two days after first arriving in Egypt. He reported to Ben-Zur that the Germans in Egypt regarded Mahmud as a helpful friend, but suspected him of being the security police officer charged with supervising them. Elad too suspected Mahmud of belonging to the security police, but befriended him because he regarded him as a key to contacts with the Germans. During his stay in Europe, Elad kept up the connection by correspondence, both before and after the network's collapse.

Aharoni and Cohen's investigation led them to two conclusions: Elad had connections with Egyptian intelligence personnel; the Egyptians had an informant within the network. Put together, these conclusions pointed a finger at Elad. Suspicion was heightened by Elad's lack of fear, both before and after the network's capture. In his contacts with the authorities and the German experts, and with the personnel of 131, his conduct "was marked by striking imprudence, testifying that he acted with almost total absence of fear." Following are only a few examples.

In his assumed identity as "Paul Frank," Elad told his German friends that he had previously worked for German intelligence, and was still in contact with his former superiors. He displayed an extravagance quite inappropriate to his cover as a businessman: he spent lavishly, kept a luxurious car, and took his friends on costly pleasure trips—without making a single deal that could justify such munificence. Neglecting the business on which his cover was based, he made no effort, not even for appearance's sake, to solicit commercial orders and was late replying to communications from the German firm he supposedly represented, eliciting a letter of severe rebuke.

As will be recalled, when Elad left Egypt on August 7, 1954, he took the tiny radio transmitter to Rome, where he delivered it to his contact. He explained away the risk this involved by saying, on one occasion, that the transmitter was expensive "and it was a pity to waste it"; on another, that he was afraid it would fall into Egyptian hands; and on yet another, that he did it "so as to be believed." But, confronted with Shmuel Azar's testimony before the Egyptian court that sentenced him to death, Elad admitted it had been Azar who, on July 24—the day after the mishap at the cinema, when it was learned that Victor Levi and Philip Natanson had been arrested—removed the transmitter from the apartment that served as the team's safe house. Azar dumped two of its components; Elad insisted on taking the third and vital piece from him.

Elad was unable to explain why he was not afraid of keeping, for two weeks, an object so incriminating, and which could be of no use to him. Nor could he remember whether he had concealed it on his person, in his luggage, or elsewhere. His interrogators deduced that he had nothing to fear—possibly because he had smuggled it out with the assistance of Egyptian intelligence.

What was more, after the July 23 operation failed and the arrests began, Elad showed no haste to make a getaway. His diary entries between July 25 and August 6 reflect his preoccupations while his subordinates and friends were undergoing interrogation and torture: morning and afternoon trips to swim in the sea; dancing and concerts in the evenings; a dinner with Willy, the missile photographer; a birthday party; a lunch at Malki's; a movie matinee; buying a belt and earrings for his wife.

Between July 25 and August 3, the names of Egyptian military intelligence chief Osman Nuri, naval intelligence officer Ragib Fahmi, and Captain Fawzi, who was connected with Fahmi, appear in the diary. Elad could offer no satisfactory explanation of these entries.

Overshadowing all the rest was the fact that he had made no effort to rescue his people. The only defense he offered—that he had to follow his regular habits in order to ward off suspicion—was not very credible.

On reaching Rome on August 7, he told his liaison that he was ready to return to Egypt to try to save Marcelle Ninio, which contradicted his contention during his interrogation that he had left Egypt that day for fear of being arrested at any moment.

Most dubious of all was his assertion that he decided to sell his car only after the arrests began; several diary entries, and some of his actions, indicated that he was preoccupied with selling it as far back as July 16, when he inquired about the customs duty he would have to pay when he did so. Clearly, his behavior was governed by the knowledge that he was about to leave Egypt.

Was this the conduct of a man in mortal danger, whose subordinates were under arrest on serious charges? Aharoni and Cohen concluded that Elad was the informant within the network, and that, at the time he met Ben-Zur in Paris, he was already in the employ of Egyptian intelligence. Aharoni's report to his superiors concludes:

> The cumulative effect of the suspicions we have raised against Elad in this matter: his conduct during interrogation; the hints he dropped . . . the results of his polygraph test; his persistent efforts to conceal his original diary of that period from us;[2] his fantastic attempts to blame the network's betrayal on others, such as Shmuel Azar, who was executed in Egypt . . . and a thorough scrutiny of his past and character . . . have led us to the final conclusion that, beyond all doubt, Elad directly and knowingly engineered the destruction of the network in Egypt.

In addition, material from covert sources in Egypt and Germany convinced Aharoni and Cohen of Elad's treachery. In their opinion, he had acted out of fear. "He was scared of commanding a sabotage detachment," Aharoni said. "If you're caught [at that] in an Arab country, it's the death sentence—unless you finger [the others]."

Aharoni and Cohen contended that, if Givly had debriefed Elad thoroughly as he should have, and if he had summoned him to Israel in August 1954 for that purpose, rather than to coach him in giving per-

---

2. During this interrogation, Elad claimed to have rewritten his diary to reflect his perjured testimony to the Olshan-Dori commission; but Victor Cohen is convinced that the diary he showed the interrogators was authentic.

jured testimony, suspicion about Elad's role in the network's destruction might have been aroused earlier. The questions put by Elad's interrogators in 1958 should have been asked then.

But Givly never asked what Elad did, or where he went, between May 3 and his return to Egypt on June 28. The DMI did not probe the circumstances surrounding the smuggling out of the transmitter; he did not ask Elad why he defied instructions by keeping his car; he did not inquire why Elad neglected his business responsibilities, or why he jeopardized his cover with his extravagance and imprudence. When Elad requested compensation for the loss he incurred from selling the car, Givly should have closely scrutinized the entire matter. Indeed Elad's own reports could have alerted Givly to all the questionable behavior described above. In striking contrast to the Tubiansky affair, it is one of fate's grim jests that, in Elad, Givly came up against a genuine traitor—but let him slip through his fingers.

Had Elad been a trustworthy individual of proven dedication, perhaps no such investigation would have been necessary. But the circumstances of Elad's recruitment hardly justified this blind faith in him. Almog's assertion that he deserved another chance did not relieve Givly of the obligation of inquiring whether Elad had passed the test.

Why did Givly not take any such steps? There can be only one answer: he was anxious to conceal the truth, not clarify it. That was the only reason why Ben-Zur kept no record of the account Elad gave when he was secretly summoned to Israel; why Elad's report was repeatedly retyped; why Givly and Ben-Zur endorsed that fraudulent account and its false claim that Elad returned to Egypt on July 4—when they had in their possession his "Shipment possible" cable dated June 28.

Givly hastened to keep Elad out of Israel, glorifying him as a hero to justify sending him back to Europe, as though his "Paul Frank" cover had not been blown. Givly had only one purpose in mind: protecting the line he and Lavon had worked out together to explain away the debacle in Egypt.

13

Sharett in Torment

Prime minister Moshe Sharett was graced with virtues rare in a politician: a passion for truth, honesty, and fairness as well as a nobility of soul. His physique, however, was frail. Small wonder that he was prone to sinking into distress, or that a perennial stomach ulcer plagued him.

Sharett now found himself caught in a labyrinth, entrapped by three separate constraints. First, for fear of further compromising the Cairo defendants, he felt bound to shroud the Olshan-Dori commission in a thick cloak of secrecy, precluding an appeal to public opinion. Second, diplomatic necessity forced him to deny flatly that Israel had instigated acts of sabotage at U.S. installations. Third, the national interest made it imperative to find a fitting response to the debacle in Egypt.

But these considerations were all overshadowed by political calculations, for 1955 was an election year in Israel, with polling set for July 26. "The country has plunged into the electoral vortex," Sharett observed in his diary when Lavon urged him to set up an inquiry commission. The issue of that inquiry's terms of reference—which hinged entirely upon party interest—tormented Sharett, putting him at odds with himself. It was an ominous harbinger of his vacillation in days to come.

The projected inquiry evoked opposition that united Mapai factions otherwise locked in mutual rivalry or outright hostility: on one side, finance minister Levi Eshkol and his director-general Pinhas Sapir; on the other, the party's younger leaders and the group known as "Ben-Gurion's whizkids." Eshkol and Sapir cautioned that an inquiry could entail "the most malignant" consequences for Mapai; on the threshold of the elections, the public would be made aware of "the terrible rivalry prevailing within the top defense echelons" when "the recriminations they hurl at one another" were published. The younger leaders, while arguing that the public was already familiar with "relations within the defense leadership," claimed that an inquiry would fan feuds that would leave the participants "incapable of working together." Although they all opposed an inquiry, Eshkol and Sapir demanded that Lavon be retained, while their younger rivals urged that he be fired immediately, given what Sharett termed "the malignant role he played in undermining the army's morale and instilling standards of untruthfulness." Although Sharett was even more eager than they to see Lavon go, he realized that diplomatic considerations made dismissing him no "simple matter," for doing so would constitute an effective admission that "we had a hand" in the Egyptian operation, thus delivering "the [Cairo] defendants into the hangman's hands."

As spokesman for the national interest, and for the principle and practice of sound administration, Sharett had insisted initially on a full-fledged formal inquiry, duly constituted; but, because Lavon had objected, he chose to appoint Olshan and Dori as a "personal" commission to help him uncover the facts and draw the necessary conclusions.

Sharett's genuine concern for the national interest competed with party interest; indignation vied with disillusionment; and underneath lay his natural urge for survival. "All these days," he noted in his diary, "I have paced about like a sleepwalker, plagued by horror and astray in the labyrinth, totally at a loss."

Nevertheless, Sharett did not doubt that Lavon was guilty. "Let us suppose," he wrote in his diary, "that Givly acted on his own authority. . . . even then, does moral responsibility not devolve upon Lavon, who incessantly advocated acts of madness, and inculcated the military leadership with the diabolical notion of igniting the Middle East, fomenting disputes, bloody assassinations, attacks on objectives and assets of the Powers, desperate and suicidal acts?" As the inquiry neared its conclusion, the commission's secretary, who was Sharett's loyal principal secretary, informed him that "the picture overall goes against Lavon." Sharett appears to have received this news gratefully.

As Sharett dithered, the factor in his calculations which, it can be argued, overrode all others, was Ben-Gurion, and the close "Big Brother"-like scrutiny he maintained from his remote Sdeh Boker retreat. According to a trickle of reports and rumors, he had tired of Mapai and was hatching schemes to reform the country's electoral system and political constitution. Incessantly wondering whether "Ben-Gurion is indeed intent on returning to the government," Sharett was at the same time convinced that he intended to do precisely that.

Should Ben-Gurion return, Sharett affirmed, "I'm out. I will not be up to embarking upon a new chapter of struggles with Ben-Gurion, only to capitulate to him. Finished!" Worrying that Ben-Gurion was liable to prevent him from discarding Lavon—and with his fear of Ben-Gurion reflected in his every move—the prime minister held extensive consultations, beginning with his senior cabinet and party colleagues: Levi Eshkol, Golda Meir, Zalman Aran, and other veterans. Born in the previous century, they all, to a greater or lesser degree, believed Ben-Gurion was intent on dumping them so as to revamp the party and government leadership by enthroning their younger rivals. They construed the awarding of the defense portfolio to Lavon—who, born in 1904, stood halfway between them and Dayan—as a first step toward implementation of this plan as well as the anointing of Lavon as Ben-Gurion's heir.

Sharett also conferred with the younger party leaders and "Ben-Gurion's whizkids": Teddy Kollek, director-general of the prime minister's office; and Ehud Avriel, former director-general to the prime minister and finance minister, and at the time a senior official at the foreign ministry. From them Sharett sought information regarding Ben-Gurion's intentions and what was going on at Sdeh Boker. They further sharpened his suspicion that Moshe Dayan and Shimon Peres had been tapped for senior posts in the projected "youth cabinet," which, Kollek predicted, would include "no more than three or four" incumbent ministers.

Sharett also consulted former aides like Evron and Yona Kesseh, one of Mapai's two party secretaries and an intimate of both Sharett and Lavon. Evron and Kesseh appear to have worked in concert to throw Sharett into a panic. Invited to dine at Sharett's home on January 5, 1955, Kesseh told of Lavon's "threat to kill himself," and of his conviction that Dayan and Peres were conspiring to "publicly annihilate him." Lavon had likened Dayan to Colonel Adiv Shishakly, head of Syria's military junta, as "being capable of bulldozing anyone standing in his path."

A week later, Evron told Sharett "of the malignant conspiracy between the army brass and top ministry officials [i.e., Dayan and Peres—S.T.] against Lavon, who, surrounded by enemies, is now totally isolated." To underline his point, Evron sent Sharett "a signed note clearly hinting that if Lavon is pronounced guilty, he will not rest content with mere resignation, and might be driven to an act of despair." The note worked its desired effect: Sharett recalled Lavon telling him that "if he comes out [of the inquiry] guilty, he will put an end to his life." This "suicide threat" would from now on impinge on Sharett's judgment.

With Sharett thus on the alert for bad news, his numerous advisers fed his fears by passing along ominous reports from Sdeh Boker. This multitude of advisers indicates that Sharett did not possess a single true friend whose counsel he could trust. He was in need of such a friend as never before when he began to entertain the notion of dismissing Lavon, and supplementing his tasks as prime minister and foreign minister by assuming the defense portfolio until the elections. But he hesitated before taking such a step, as his January 9 diary entry reveals: "God of Gods, how can I master three such enormous tasks? And what will happen if I am incapable of thoroughly grasping military matters?"

Then it occurred to him that Shaul Avigur, his wife's brother and a long-standing ally, could assist him at the defense ministry. On January 11, Sharett cabled Avigur in Zurich, instructing him to return immediately to Israel. In his diary, Sharett noted: "I face decisive consultations—with the colleagues in the cabinet on the one hand, and on the other, Ben-Gurion—and it is my wish to have Shaul by my side, all the more so in view of the role awaiting him in any future reshuffle at the defense ministry." Avigur could indeed offer Sharett an extensive familiarity with the defense establishment, as well as political and diplomatic acumen; but neither he, nor anyone else, could endow Sharett with decisiveness.

Ever since January 1954, when they took up their positions of prime minister and defense minister, Sharett had been aware that he was not getting truthful accounts from Lavon; instead, the defense minister undermined Sharett's authority, defying him by implementing intemperate policies that placed the state in jeopardy. Consequently, Sharett believed he had "the moral right—obligation, perhaps—to demand his removal." But "the colleagues" were reluctant to countenance such painful surgery: Lavon's dismissal would generate a serious crisis within the party, which as yet knew nothing of Lavon's "reprehensible deeds" or "the sorry business" in Egypt. They were supported by Ben-Gurion who, in Tel Aviv on January 8, received successive visits from Lavon, Sharett, and Dayan. Sharett told of his "convoluted relations with Lavon," and reported on the Olshan-Dori commission. Ben-Gurion conceded that "the Cairo affair is the setback of his lifetime," but told Sharett he "must freeze [the status quo] and work."

Sharett was also troubled by the fact that "dismissing Lavon now would totally annihilate him." Yet he also lacked the fortitude to maintain this compassionate attitude; a suppressed vindictiveness, reinforced by the rationale of national interest and plain common sense, pushed him the other way: "Not to dismiss him is to cover up his evil, courting the destruction of the defense ministry and the total corruption of the high command." Figuratively raising his arms in supplication, Sharett wrote in his diary: "What shall I do, what shall I do? I am maddened by my thoughts, the depth of my depression and a dearth of counsel and resourcefulness. I am stifled within, and lack the fortitude to shake off the distress of my spirit."

To understand the complex circumstances surrounding Sharett's wavering, we must revert to December 8, 1954. That day, the Syrian army captured a five-man team of IDF soldiers as they attached listening devices to a telephone line in the Syrian heights. Four days later, Israel's air force intercepted a Syrian civilian airliner over the sea beyond Israeli airspace, forcing it to land at Lod airport, with the aim of exchanging its passengers for the five captives. The incursion into Syrian territory and the aerial hijacking, both undertaken without the cabinet's knowledge—along with false claims by the IDF spokesman that the soldiers had been seized inside Israeli territory, and that the plane was intercepted within Israel's air space—infuriated Sharett. In a fierce letter to Lavon, he condemned the interception as "an act unprecedented in international conduct" and "in total defiance of explicit standing instructions." He was astounded, Sharett wrote, by "the narrow-mindedness and myopia" of "our army chiefs," who seemed convinced "that the state of Israel is entitled—or even required—to conduct its international relations by the laws prevailing in the jungle." He concluded by warning: "It has to be clear to all concerned that the government does not intend to tolerate such manifestations of 'independent policy' by its security forces."

Seeking to free the five captives, Sharett resorted to diplomatic channels befitting a law-abiding state: the foreign ministry, the Israeli-Syrian mixed armistice commission, and the chief of staff of the UN observers.

He forbade the IDF to procure their release by hostage-taking; at his vigorous insistence—backed by the protests of an international community outraged over Israel's aerial piracy—the Syrian plane and its passengers were released on December 14, 1954. Aware that his policy was not widely acclaimed, Sharett sensed a storm brewing around him. He consoled himself with the hope that his policy would lead the IDF and the Israeli public toward prudence and responsibility; furthermore, he could claim to have decreased the level of violence. As he noted in his diary, "for weeks and weeks, not a single person has been murdered." But on January 13, 1955, it was learned that one of the five IDF captives, nineteen-year-old Uri Ilan, had committed suicide in a Damascus jail. When his body was brought back to Israel, notes in his handwriting, discovered between his toes and in the folds of his clothing, proclaimed that he had defied his interrogators and revealed no secrets.

The tidings came as "a dreadful shock" to Sharett. His heart went out to the "young boy sacrificed for nothing," and this innocent victim lingered in his thoughts for many days to come. But being a politician, he could not avoid a further, "inadvertent" reflection: "Now they'll say of course that the boy's blood is on my head—had I not given orders to release the Syrian plane, the Syrians would have been obliged to free the lads, and the boy . . . would be alive still." Sharett also feared a setback to his policy. "If the Syrians release the four, it shall not be said that they were freed by resort to the channels of international diplomacy; rather, it will be evident that the release came about as a result of the suicide." As it turned out, this fear was misdirected; for Uri Ilan's four comrades were returned to Israel on March 29, 1955, in exchange for forty Syrians whom the IDF—in defiance of Sharett's policy—had captured in reprisal raids and abductions.

January 14, 1955, was a painful day for Sharett. Uri Ilan was interred at his kibbutz home; and outraged public opinion pointed an accusing finger at the prime minister, just as he had foreseen. Anguished and plagued by doubt, trusting no one, Sharett closeted himself in his office with Mossad chief Isser Harel for a long talk. Visually, the exchange must have resembled a scene from the Charlie Chaplin movie *The Kid*. The pale Sharett, with his dark hair, moustache, and benevolent, alert eyes, evoked the renowned vagabond; while Harel, a five-footer with clear, innocent blue eyes, represented Chaplin's youthful companion. Like Ben-Gurion before him, Sharett found nothing statesmanlike in Harel who, he wrote, was remarkable for "his earnestness and rectitude, but his thinking, almost inhumanly one-dimensional, sometimes renders his counsel deficient in concrete realism." Nevertheless, a seemingly bewitched Sharett surrendered to Harel's influence, unaware of the impropriety of this political consultation with the head of the secret service. He confided to Harel his plan of action regarding the Olshan-Dori commission's report: "First of all, I shall, with the assistance of . . . [my personal aide] master all the material from the inquiry; I shall then hold consultations with Golda, Eshkol, and Aran, in conjunction with Harel. After that, I shall go to Ben-Gurion—or Golda and Aran will go to him."

Harel greeted this confidence with a torrent of persuasion verging upon intimidation; and in his distress Sharett, departing from the ground rules of governmental protocol, in effect bestowed quasi-ministerial status upon a state employee he believed loyal to himself. He was led on by Harel who, envious of Dayan, Peres, and Ehud Avriel, considered their prospective enthronement in Ben-Gurion's "youth cabinet" an intolerable slight. Harel's own craving for a cabinet post led him to abuse his official position and its wide-ranging influence to promote his ambitions; but he was encouraged by Sharett's show of weakness. In fact, Sharett had no one to blame but himself for Harel's permitting himself to adopt such a tone.

As Sharett revealed his innermost feelings and solicited Harel's counsel, Harel seized his chance and threw Sharett into a panic with fearsome predictions. He began by warning of what lay in store for the prime minister as a result of Ilan's suicide: "A vicious onslaught is developing, against which a bulwark must be erected. Particular concern must be addressed to the army; riotous excesses must be forcefully prevented."

It is obvious now that the "vicious attack" existed solely in Harel's fantasy. But, trusting to Harel's renowned rectitude, Sharett accepted his words without question or second thought. He also told Harel that he was disappointed with Olshan and Dori, who "declined to condemn the harmful political trends which have overtaken the army leadership, not least under the influence of the defense minister . . . and its total disregard for the duty of obedience to the prime minister's political authority." He also confided his intention of "taking the most extreme measures with respect to Lavon—in other words, demanding his immediate resignation."

Thus did the prime minister and a state employee subordinate to him inexplicably share decisions regarding cabinet and party, with Harel assuming the mentor's role and making pronouncements on matters of principle. Sharett's diary entries abruptly switch to first person plural [italics added]:

> After thorough deliberation, *we both agreed* that we cannot forgo recti-fying this intolerable situation merely for fear of a further tragedy. The first precept, supplanting all others, is to save the army. *Harel laid down three principles:* effective and vigorous enforcement of government authority; subordination of the army to civilian control and suppression of any adventurous urges there; *enlisting the party's moral backing* to achieve these objectives.

The two men went on to consider the most pressing issue: who would replace Lavon? Sharett shared a further secret with Harel: failing all other options, he would himself—without relinquishing his duties as prime minister and foreign minister—take over the defense portfolio, with the assistance of Shaul Avigur and Ehud Avriel.

Harel favored neither of these prospective aides. He had long resented Avigur; and Avriel, besides being his rival for Ben-Gurion's confidence, was also Dayan's candidate to replace Givly as DMI. Apparently upset at the mention of these two names, Harel "rebuffed the notion with all the decisive cogency of which he is capable," Sharett noted in his diary, and suggested that the defense portfolio be offered to Golda Meir—with whom he was to forge an alliance against Peres; should she refuse, it should go to Eshkol.

The discussion now turned upon the makeup of the cabinet and the nomination of ministers, and the two men, on terms of apparent equality, considered the greatest obstacle in their path. "*We both* agreed," Sharett noted in his diary (italics added), "that *we can* expect grave difficulties on the part of Ben-Gurion, who has already voiced his view in favor of freezing matters at the top levels of the defense establishment, without any shakeup until an opportune moment. Likewise *we both* agreed that Ben-Gurion has no moral right to sway the decision, because he sees matters from the outside and from a distance."

Finally, they turned to Givly and Dayan. Sharett argued that Givly too must go, and "*we both* agreed that the chief of staff is not to be touched . . . granted, he is capable of serving God and Satan equally, but *we* have no choice other than to presume that, in the near future, he will do that which is righteous in the eyes of the Lord, controlling his urge towards running risks and casting obloquy upon supreme authority, to raise himself to the level of his responsibility to the nation, which he is surely capable of properly comprehending."

Sharett was obviously right to characterize this intimate parley as "a lengthy and gravely significant conversation, highly incisive and far-reaching in its conclusions." In any case it reassured him: the following morning, which was the Sabbath, he slept till 10:30.

The Olshan-Dori commission's report reached Sharett on January 16, 1955, offering no definitive ruling with respect to Lavon's dismissal. The fact that "evidently there is a bitter disappointment for Lavon" was small consolation for Sharett. Within days, his response crystallized into a wish and a quasi-policy; yet by his own acts, he thwarted the policy's implementation.

On January 17, Sharett forwarded the commission's findings to Lavon. He did so not without misgivings, as he put it, "because the findings are a setback for him"; but there was also the gratifying belief that they would reinforce Lavon's "inner readiness to step down from his office."

Without a clearcut verdict, Sharett had to draw his own conclusions. First, he affirmed that Lavon, Dayan, and Givly must not retain their present offices. Next, he asserted that "the army must undergo, not reorganization, but rather—total regeneration, with the single aim being, first and foremost: *truth*." Finally, he concluded that the nominee for defense minister "should be a man who is masterful and also highly moral," while the nominee for chief of staff must be "a soldier-of-the-line, neither partisan nor political dilettante. Prototype: Haim Laskov."

Shaul Avigur returned to Israel on January 17 and came the following day to Sharett's home "just in time for the consultation" Sharett had scheduled with Eshkol, Meir, Aran, and Harel. That morning, Sharett had been hit by "a thunderbolt," as he put it: two kibbutz members plowing their fields had been murdered by Arab infiltrators. After a long period of quiet, "all of a sudden, it seems that a tidal wave of blood has again erupted." Sharett was certain he would have to approve a reprisal action; there is little doubt that Harel's warning of "a vicious attack" in preparation against him was among the influences that induced him to consent:

> I have braked and blocked much in recent months, preventing several volatile actions and exposing the public to great tension. I must not overstrain their patience. Tension must be defused, otherwise there

will be an outbreak of fury which many of my colleagues will share; by overreaching myself, I shall fail in the attempt to educate the people, achieving the opposite.

Nevertheless he was tormented at having authorized the reprisal raid (which, as it turned out, was called off when Sharett learned that the four murderers had been arrested in Jordan and would go on trial), telling his wife Zippora that "the structure I have stubbornly built these many months, and all the brakes and fences I have erected . . . are liable to be swept away at a single stroke."

Sharett thus called the Mapai leaders—Eshkol, Meir, Aran, and Avigur—to the aforementioned consultation, which he opened with a brief presentation regarding the inquiry commission "and everything that has been woven and entangled around it." Harel, who had also been invited to this high-level meeting, was the first to speak, and "let fly," as Sharett put it, with a scathing condemnation of Lavon, audaciously demanding his prompt dismissal, going so far as to "remind" his hearers that "he had demanded it of us before the Egyptian abomination came about." The participants, all wise and intelligent individuals, nevertheless disregarded the fact that they were being addressed by a man who would forgo no opportunity to settle scores with rivals and adversaries. As Sharett recorded, [italics added] Harel

> also vented his fury at Dayan, over how he is debauching the IDF by condemning the cabinet in the presence of its officers; on the surface, he proclaims the duty of total obedience to its political authority, but he is careful to explain further that he and his colleagues requested authorization to take such-and-such action, and had they been permitted, would have saved us; but the cabinet decided otherwise, and since, though they are certain that the cabinet's course will lead to failure, they are disciplined military men, they accept the verdict. *Such a form of instruction in the duty of obedience is effectively instruction in mutiny . . . a continual process of leading the army to disaffection.*

How did this tirade against the chief of staff, from a state employee involved in cloak-and-dagger operations, strike the Mapai ministers? Sharett notes that "everyone welcomed Avigur's presence among them with gratification"—but says not a word about their reception of Harel. Did he find that his colleagues thought that, as an employee of the state, Harel had no business at an inner party conclave? In any case Sharett's diary records that "when Isser concluded his portion, I requested him to take his leave, whereupon the debate amongst us commenced."

Avigur, whose support Sharett had so eagerly awaited, also pronounced "the most severe verdict against Lavon"—not merely with regard to the Egyptian debacle, but also, as Sharett notes, "because of his character and his approach and his lack of earnestness and responsibility and his total unfitness for his office and the relationships he generated and the moral depravity he instilled." Aran recalled Berl Katznelson's characterization of Lavon as "a brilliant mind in a murky soul" and rather wildly pronounced what was in effect "a death sentence in every moral and public sense." Next, "Golda beat her breast," as Sharett said, in remorse over her failure to insist on Lavon's dismissal "when she first realized the course he was taking, and what calamities he was liable to inflict upon the state."

The path now seemed clear for Sharett to proclaim Lavon's removal and announce his own assumption of the defense portfolio; but still he stalled. After analyzing "all the pros and cons regarding Lavon's dismissal," he proposed that "Eshkol, in addition to the finance ministry, take upon himself the defense portfolio with the assistance of Avigur." Eshkol rejected this idea outright, as well as "the notion of replacing Lavon . . . at this time," so near the elections. Even now, Sharett balked at telling his colleagues he intended to take over the defense portfolio— apparently out of fear of Ben-Gurion, who, it will be recalled, advocated a freeze of the status quo. Keeping Sdeh Boker in the corner of his eye, Sharett left himself a line of retreat from the dismissal of Lavon: he concluded the conclave by saying, "we must consult Ben-Gurion" and that in the meantime, Avigur would "go over all the written material from the inquiry and offer his opinion."

Sharett's colleagues appear to have feared that Lavon would steal a march on them by announcing his resignation. Sharett should perhaps have welcomed such an outcome, which had been his goal; but with elections in the offing, the Mapai leaders seemed terrified at the mere thought of the scandal involved in the resignation of a senior minister. This prospect also perturbed Sharett, as indicated by his statement at the end of the meeting that he would notify Lavon in no uncertain terms that "he is to cast aside any thought of resignation of his own accord, and await the considered conclusion of his colleagues."

These "colleagues" were Ben-Gurion and Avigur; the latter was not only studying "the evidence" but also conducting additional inquiries of his own. Lavon, vehemently opposed to this procedure, sent Sharett two notes. The first declared that "as a minister, I'm not prepared to be the object of examination by all kinds of honest citizens. I made one mistake [in requesting an inquiry] and that is quite enough for me." His second note warned that once the verdict in the Cairo trials was announced he would "feel free to take what measures I choose." But Sharett was powerless to halt the course of events, principally the growing stream of pilgrims beating a path to Sdeh Boker. All he could do was keep his eyes and ears open to the signals emanating from Ben-Gurion's retreat.

Avigur was the first to come up with the idea of recalling Ben-Gurion to the ministry of defense. Concluding his inquiries on January 26, he affirmed to Sharett that Lavon must go; moreover, since the responsibility "for selecting Lavon as his successor" rested with Ben-Gurion, it was his "sacred duty" to return to the government "and take . . . the defense portfolio." Avigur thus put an end to the notion of Sharett taking over the defense ministry.

But this meant setting Ben-Gurion on course for a return to office—the eventuality Sharett so greatly dreaded. This may explain why the prime minister was now inclined, like Ben-Gurion himself, to leave Lavon in place. Having rehearsed for Avigur all the reasons to dismiss him, Sharett went on to list seven reasons against doing so "at this time": it would constitute implicit admission of Israel's responsibility for events in Egypt, "which we have vigorously denied"; it would advertise abroad "the downfall of the activist line" which—although Sharett rejected it—he had "no interest in subjecting to a conspicuous defeat"; it would be "a bombshell fomenting dissent and upheaval in the party whose situation is anyhow precarious"; the scandal could be exploited "in the most malignant manner against the party" in the elections; Lavon would not accept the verdict, and would create a public explosion "to maximize the destructive effects, internally and externally"; he was liable to carry out his suicide threat; and finally, "there is no one to replace him."

The following day, Avigur drove to Sdeh Boker to persuade Ben-Gurion to remove Lavon and return to the cabinet as defense minister. This proposal, Ben-Gurion told him, was "not open to consideration." Having heard Avigur's diagnosis and conclusions, Ben-Gurion was "dumbly miserable and depressed," but "adopted no clear position with regard to the inevitable conclusion." Avigur "pressed him to the wall" for a definite answer on "removing Lavon or retaining him," but Ben-Gurion declined "most vigorously" to express his opinion, arguing that replacing Lavon "presents no problem" because supervision of the defense ministry could be entrusted to a committee. On hearing this report, Sharett wrote in his diary: "The man who created the defense ministry contemplates the administration of this vast ministry, and command of the IDF . . . by committee . . . "

Sharett could not have known that on January 26 Ben-Gurion had sent Lavon a handwritten letter of congratulation: "Well done on your speech in the Knesset yesterday."

In a debate on the killing of the two kibbutz farmers, Lavon had warned of the prospect of growing border violations, adding: "Israel, like any state, lives by two laws . . . international law, and the state of Israel regards itself . . . bound to live by that law; but it also lives by . . . the natural law of self-defense."

Lavon's words were directed mainly at Sharett's address during the January 16 Knesset debate on the interception of the Syrian airliner. Condemning the IDF's "factual misrepresentations" about it, and rejecting the claim that hostage-taking was the only way IDF captives had been freed in the past, Sharett had offered Israel the choice "of being a state either law-abiding or rapacious; either prudent and foresighted, or recklessly riotous of instinct."

Ben-Gurion's note of commendation to Lavon made the rounds and was construed as a signal matching earlier messages: Ben-Gurion wished Lavon well. On January 25, Ben-Gurion's diary records Dayan telling him "that if Pinhas Lavon remains defense minister another half year, they could achieve a correct relationship . . . even though past damage cannot be undone. Dayan opposes the candidacy of Avigur . . . because he is regarded as a has-been. Dayan proposes Levi Eshkol. I do not approve."

Dayan had most likely calculated that, while Ben-Gurion had conceded his error in nominating Lavon, he was not demanding that Lavon be replaced; hence, Lavon would probably remain in office, and from Dayan's viewpoint, he was better than any of the alternatives advanced by Sharett and his advisers.

The congratulatory letter to Lavon left "Ben-Gurion's boys" disgruntled. "Pinhas Lavon needed no better medal of distinction," Nehemia Argov noted in his diary, "and it's hard to contain the bitterness within one's heart." He summarized some of his colleagues' comments: Ben-Gurion supported Lavon; he had nominated him, "he had made him heir" and would not allow him to be destroyed. "If Lavon doesn't go—that means others will; if the others go, that means havoc to . . . Israel's security." It was plain to all that, of those "others," Peres would be the first to go.

On January 27, 1955, the Cairo court published its verdicts, which were stunningly harsh: two defendants were sentenced to death, two acquitted, and the rest received prison terms ranging from seven years to life. In addition, Max Binnet had committed suicide in his cell on December 21, 1954, while Armond Karmona, though unconnected with the network, was arrested and tortured to death and his demise disguised as suicide. At the end of that day's session of Mapai's political committee, Lavon told Sharett that "there can be no further postponement of a decision"—which, to him, meant the dismissal of Givly and Peres; it seems his self-confidence had been boosted by Ben-Gurion's message. Sharett, who as yet knew nothing of Ben-Gurion's note and still awaited "an echo from Sdeh Boker," replied evasively that "there has to be a consultation . . . I will try to arrange it without delay."

When Sharett did learn, on January 30, that Ben-Gurion, while "sharply critical" of his own Knesset speech, had sent felicitations to Lavon, he realized that Ben-Gurion favored the defense minister's policy and saw no grounds for removing him. Determining that he had been wise to give up the notion, Sharett felt that, however unappealing the prospect, it was now vital that he meet with Ben-Gurion in person. Accordingly he scheduled an expedition to Sdeh Boker with Meir, Aran, and Eshkol, "for a consultation." That day, when he returned to his home, "its light and warmth" restored his spirits; but it is not surprising that, although he followed a strict diet, he was subject to increasingly frequent ulcer attacks.

Before the expedition to Sdeh Boker, Harel earnestly urged Sharett "to demand Lavon's removal come what may." He went on to assert that Sharett's colleagues now supported him with more confidence than ever (Sharett did not inquire how he could be so certain) and that many considered him a success as prime minister. He now faced a cardinal test, "in the army's eyes particularly"; if he did not dismiss Lavon, "it will be seen as a mark of weakness . . . flinching from consequences, giving priority to apprehensions about the fate of an individual over concern for . . . the future of the IDF"; Sharett's honor would be trampled in the mire, his moral authority destroyed.

But if Harel intended to embolden Sharett for his meeting with Ben-Gurion, his exhortations had the opposite effect: they "made me shudder," Sharett recorded in his diary.

On January 31, Dr. Moshe Marzouk and Shmuel Azar were executed in Cairo. Tormented over the fate of "the Jewish boys in Cairo jail, delivered for nothing, nothing at all, into the hangman's hands," Sharett scourged himself with thoughts of what they were undergoing "in these hours as they prepare, in their loneliness, for their face-to-face encounter with a bitter death."

14

Lavon Resigns

On February 1, 1955, Sharett, Eshkol, Meir, and Aran, accompanied by Avigur, went to see Ben-Gurion at Sdeh Boker. Like other convocations held there, this one ended inconclusively. As Ben-Gurion told Nehemia Argov: "The colleagues did not reach a decision, each voiced his opinion." He added that Aran and Eshkol opposed "Lavon going now"—which suggests that Sharett, Meir, and Avigur held the opposite opinion. Had Ben-Gurion leaned toward their view, Lavon almost certainly would have been removed. It probably follows that Ben-Gurion expressed no opinion, leaving the decision to his colleagues. This is indicated by his diary entry: "Only our colleagues in the cabinet can decide [on Lavon's removal—S.T.], for they will have to bear responsibility for the outcome, whether the decision is affirmative or negative."

This was the "echo from Sdeh Boker" Sharett had awaited so anxiously. On his return to Jerusalem, he met with Aran, who again argued for retaining Lavon, on the grounds that his dismissal would "destroy the man" and the party. Aran told Sharett that "Golda regrets" demanding Lavon's removal. If the balance was tilting, it was in Lavon's favor. The score now was four in favor of Lavon's retention, one (Avigur) for his dismissal, and Sharett wavering.

On his way back to Jerusalem, Sharett had resolved to summon Lavon to "a private talk" the following day. But that same Wednesday, February

2, Lavon took Sharett by surprise with a letter of resignation, with copies sent to his cabinet colleagues and Ben-Gurion. The substance of the letter, and the list of addressees, indicate clearly that Lavon was reacting to the Sdeh Boker meeting, and not to the scheduled "private talk"—which may not have taken place.

Lavon, of course, learned of the Sdeh Boker conclave from the press. *Haboker*, for example, cited a "reliable source" to report the five-hour "sudden" consultation, dealing "mainly with security problems," but also raising "the possibility of a reshuffle of Mapai cabinet ministers." Even in those early days of Israel's statehood, the axiom applied: there are no secrets in politics. But then as now, gossip and leaks were frequently both inaccurate and misleading.

It was information of this nature that induced Lavon to send his resignation letter, and word it so strongly. Two points roused his ire. First: he had not been invited to the Sdeh Boker consultation, of which he had only learned "from the press." His cabinet colleagues were treating him as a leper, an "untouchable" someone who is "an object of pity, or a settler of scores." Second, he fumed, the conclave had sealed his fate even though he had been vindicated by "a mass of solid facts"—Lavon listed them one by one—none of which Olshan and Dori had refuted. "Any unprejudiced person not interested in profiting from my discomfiture" would agree that "in effect, *the investigation of this affair has ended.*" Why did his colleagues then resort to additional deliberations behind his back?

It was here that misinformation wrought its mischief. Had Lavon known that no decision had been reached at Sdeh Boker, and that four of the six participants had not demanded his removal, he might not have elected to resign that day.

Lavon's letter lists the sins of Sharett and his colleagues: disregard for the ground rules of comradeship, and of ministerial and party solidarity; discussions and consultations behind his back; opening up the Olshan-Dori inquiry to "an investigation embracing everything in . . . the defense establishment" and thereby also "to lies, half-truths, and defamations aimed at obfuscating *the particular matter* under consideration"; and finally, "breach of trust."

The letter concludes on a note of defiance and menace and a pledge of revenge:

> a. I am no longer prepared to be a comrade to persons who have demolished their comradeship with me. I hereby notify you of my

resignation from my office as defense minister and member of the cabinet . . .

b. I reserve the right to bring the grounds for my resignation to the attention of the party and the Knesset foreign affairs and defense committee. I am not prepared to bear public responsibility for the Egyptian affair, and no party discipline will bind me to bear that responsibility.

The letter left Sharett in dismay. Having once hoped Lavon would concede guilt and step down, he now rejected outright a resignation based on reproaches which, being difficult to refute, would resonate widely both within the party and among the general public. Sharett's trepidation may perhaps explain why he made no entry in his diary for the first five days of February. When he did, he noted that his "tension and nervousness" had caused his ulcer to trouble him both night and morning, as well as during the February 6 cabinet meeting.

Most likely, Lavon's resignation letter was merely a ruse to bolster his position, submitted in the hope that it would not be accepted, so that he could—as he indeed did—dictate his terms for staying in office: the removal of Givly and Peres, and curtailment of Dayan's powers.

Lavon's hostility toward Peres had arisen mainly from two episodes. In May 1954, Lavon had clashed with Dayan over the latter's desire to acquire French weapons systems whose quality Lavon questioned. Without notifying Dayan, Lavon thwarted this transaction by directing Peres—whom he evidently trusted sufficiently to draw him into "conniving" against the chief of staff—not to sign the contracts, which had been negotiated with considerable effort and were already initialed.

Lavon was astounded to learn that Peres had told Dayan about this move. When Lavon refused Dayan's request to discuss the arms deal, and then froze the purchase of the tanks, Dayan twice submitted his resignation, which Lavon twice rejected. Although they effected a quasi-reconciliation on June 18, Dayan noted in his diary: "The crisis is resolved. The issue isn't."

Having regarded Peres as loyal and devoted, and having made him his director-general to act as he directed, Lavon did not forget this treachery. Their relationship was totally disrupted; henceforth, each knew that his own advancement was predicated upon the other's downfall.

The final rupture occurred when Peres testified before the inquiry commission. It was unheard of for a director-general to offer character testimony against the minister who had appointed him, or address military matters lying outside his purview. On January 5, Dayan recorded in his journal Peres's account of having testified about "all the episodes known to him concerning Lavon, which show up his lies, and his disavowals of operations he himself had previously authorized."

On February 12, 1955, Lavon notified Sharett "that no party discipline can bind him to work with persons who are his sworn foes"—that is, Givly and Peres.

Lavon's colleagues were initially sympathetic to the demands in his resignation letter; Sharett agreed that "Shimon Peres should be removed," and Eshkol "did not mince words in condemning the chief of staff." However, they put off implementing the demands. Had Lavon settled for more modest gains, he might have won the day.

His letter did achieve one of his objectives, when a confidential committee of Mapai's top five ministers (Sharett, Eshkol, Meir, Aran, and Lavon—Sharett called them "the fivesome") was revived and charged with "resolving the Lavon issue." All agreed that Givly must leave MI; but they differed on Lavon's two other demands. Sharett declared categorically that "under no circumstances will I take responsibility for Peres's dismissal, and for revolutionary reforms in organization of the General Staff" which would have the effect of curtailing Dayan's powers. But Lavon, equally categorical, announced that "under no circumstances will he stay if he is not permitted to carry out these reforms." Meir and Aran supported Sharett, as did Eshkol, though less strongly. But with respect to "Lavon's objectionable methods" of conducting defense policy—regarding the defense establishment and his cabinet colleagues in particular—they prudently avoided "speaking the whole truth," as Sharett noted, "for by so doing, we would have forced him, by our own utterances, to resign."

Aware of his colleagues' reserve, Lavon did not contest their assertion that, since "the horror of Egypt" was his responsibility "from a moral point of view," it was out of the question that he be authorized—"as though he had passed the test of responsibility and emerged victorious"—to indulge in dismissals and reorganization. He merely reiterated that "he could not be expected to work with persons who plot and grumble against him, incessantly fomenting intrigues and enveloping him in trickery and deception." When Sharett presented him with an ultimatum—either accept the status quo or resign—he retorted that "he would not go on with Shimon Peres" as director-general, or "in utter dependence" upon the chief of staff.

Sharett stuck by his ultimatum until, at the last moment, he deferred to Eshkol, "who supports Lavon's position regarding Peres and totally refuses to compromise with regard to his removal." In his diary he cited a Russian proverb: "The morning is wiser than the evening."

During the three days that elapsed before "the fivesome" met again, Sharett tormented himself for not having insisted from the outset on "Lavon's resignation, and be done with it." If he had, he would have achieved "a foundation in principle and moral validity"; whereas now "that I have given way on the main issue and consented to his retention, while rejecting his terms, I find myself seemingly fighting for Shimon Peres's status, and against a minister's prerogative to replace his director-general as he wishes—a position claiming no great majesty."

Meanwhile, Evron came up with a possible compromise: "Postponing Shimon Peres's dismissal for two or three months." If this were done, the cabinet would remain unaware of the undercurrents swirling through Mapai, since after the time had elapsed, a plausible reason for Peres's transfer to another office could be found. Sharett liked this notion, for his advisers had filled him with dread of the scandal likely to erupt, given that Mapai's coalition partners were demanding a share in considering the entire affair. "It is liable to bring about Lavon's dismissal under pressure from without, and that would be an incomparably greater disgrace than if he were to resign on his own initiative."

"If the Cairo affair is discussed in cabinet," he told Eshkol and Aran, the whole issue would enter "the inter-party arena with all the threat of publicity." Furthermore, how was he to explain the Egyptian affair to the cabinet? "Should I indeed immerse myself in falsehood by covering up for the abomination committed there?" If he did not, Lavon would have to resign under pressure, when he had refused to do so voluntarily; and this would supply Mapai's adversaries with ammunition for the election campaign.

During the discussion, a proposal "gradually gained acceptance" for Shimon Peres to switch jobs with the defense ministry's Paris representative for the six months until the elections, taking over "supervision of arms procurements" in Europe. He would not be fired, nor stripped of his title; but Lavon would be rid of a subordinate whom he did not trust. Sharett did not take easily to this compromise, but his colleagues managed to talk him into accepting it. Approaching Lavon during a recess

in the following day's Knesset proceedings, Eshkol got him to agree to
the switch.

Using the English phrase "administrative necessity" as a justification,
Sharett braced himself to advise Givly that he was being transferred out
of MI, and Peres that he would be displaced from his position as head of
the defense ministry.

In "a private conversation" on Friday February 11, 1955, Sharett
recorded in his diary that he was, "desperately overcoming inner obstacles." He told Givly that, even if instructions to activate 131 had emanated from Lavon, the fact that he, as DMI, had sought authorization for
such an operation "makes it impossible to leave him at the head of MI,
and he would be transferred to another post in the army." Givly's reaction stunned Sharett: "his entire being erupted in fury and offense over
this injustice," and he bombarded Sharett with disconcerting questions:
Was he to be the scapegoat? Was he to be condemned as the sole culprit?
Was this the reward he deserved for all his work and devotion? He would
not willingly take the blame for launching the operations which cost four
lives, he declared; demoting him was equivalent to moral annihilation;
and, finally, was this a finding of the Olshan-Dori commission?

Sharett was dumbfounded, for Lavon had assured him (lying once
more) that the chief of staff supported Givly's reassignment and had
already informed him of it; it was only as a token of decency that Sharett
had decided to see him in person before his formal reassignment. But to
Sharett's stupefaction, Givly, taken by surprise, was furiously indignant.
Sharett foresaw disastrous consequences he had not expected, for the
Olshan-Dori commission had not found Givly solely responsible, nor recommended he be disciplined. Sharett summoned the chief of staff, finding it hard to look Givly in the eye when the latter snapped to attention,
saluted, and strode out.

Dayan arrived right away, claiming that "nothing had been settled"
between him and Lavon regarding Givly's reassignment. Dayan too
inquired whether the commission had recommended Givly's removal; if
not, why was he being singled out for punishment? The entire officer
corps would be up in arms if it turned out that his dismissal—which
would be construed as affirming his guilt—did not ensue from the commission's findings.

The same was true for Peres, Dayan went on: his banishment to
Paris—clearly "in retribution for his testimony" against Lavon—would

be seen as a recommendation of the commission. Peres would not take it lying down, either; he too would stand up for himself, with all the attendant consequences. How could the findings of the Olshan-Dori inquiry allow for conclusions the commission itself had not drawn? So concluded Dayan's argument.

Then in an instant, "as though the blanket of thick fog had been lifted from the entire landscape," Sharett glimpsed a solution:

> Either one way or the other: either overall imposition of consequences—or everything frozen until an opportune moment. Givly has to leave MI, though not now, but rather, in time. Shimon Peres must remain in place for now. Lavon, if he wishes to remain, must accept this verdict and renew a working relationship with the two men, even if it makes him gnash his teeth. It is unavoidable.

This decision, which in effect was identical to the position Ben-Gurion had taken from the outset, was "a total reversal of the plan seemingly signed and sealed," as Sharett acknowledged. Before falling asleep, he offered up a prayer "that this will be the last change, and that I will find the fortitude to insist on the conclusions I have reached today."

On the afternoon of February 12, the "fivesome" met at Sharett's home to hear him state, again "resolutely," that the solution agreed upon two days earlier "is liable to bring calamity upon the government and the party." After listing his reasons, he declared that "until an opportune time . . . both Peres and Givly must be left in place."

Lavon promptly announced his resignation. He would not be defense minister after the elections; and soldiering on until then would require him to come to terms with a state of affairs he could not tolerate a single day longer. Completely disregarding having misled Sharett about Dayan's position, Lavon complained that the prime minister, in telling Givly he would be transferred and then backing down, had capitulated to pressure from the chief of staff, establishing a precedent "which must inevitably lead the state to ruin."

"Ruin," Sharett retorted, "would have ensued from creating a situation that demonstrated to the officer corps that the prime minister had offered one of them up as a scapegoat to cover for the defense minister, because of either party or personal friendship."

Meir, and this time Eshkol too, took Sharett's side. Lavon—again amazing Sharett "with his nimble mind and perception"—discerned their true motivation: "To tell the truth—let's speak candidly—you aren't totally certain of my innocence."

Cajoling Lavon to accept the decision, Eshkol tried to meet him halfway by suggesting that Givly be replaced in four to six weeks, instead of two to three months. But Lavon remained adamant: Olshan and Dori had perverted judgment, flouting any legal rationale. He launched into a defamatory tirade against Givly, incidentally revealing that Ya'akov Shimshon Shapira, the prosecutor at the 1949 Be'eri trial, had, at his request, provided him with an opinion regarding Givly's testimony in the Tubiansky case, which "sets his personality in a nightmarish light." Lavon thus was exploiting the Tubiansky affair as a kind of liquid asset: he had been aware of Givly's role in the case, but used it only now when they had fallen out.

This time (possibly, after hearing Lavon mutter, "So what, I won't kill myself") Sharett plucked up the courage to tell him: "This terrible thing happened in your ministry, during your term of office. Does that not leave you with the responsibility? How can you permit yourself to cast it off?" Meir added: "And cast it upon us?"

Lavon stuck to his guns, in the process providing his colleagues a glimpse of a habit that exposed his weakness—and simultaneously, his strength: during the meeting, he repeatedly went over to the liquor cabinet to help himself to generous shots of brandy. To his colleagues, accustomed to sipping lemon tea, "it was shocking," as Sharett put it, "to observe a man in his shameful sin."

The meeting continued until Lavon, in Sharett's words, "gulped down the last drop in his goblet" and abruptly declared: "I believe that, for me, the matter is closed." Rising to his feet, he departed. Interpreting this as confirmation of his resignation, his colleagues resolved to refer the issue to a joint meeting of the party's ministers and executive officers. Sharett, Eshkol, and Meir then went on to consider preparations for the elections.

Party interest thus emerged in all its sordidness. A crime committed in Egypt had cost the lives of four Jews and resulted in lengthy prison terms for six others; Israel and its army had been humiliated before world opinion. But because of the approaching elections, the Mapai ministers, for reasons of political expediency, did not insist on penalizing those responsible.

Standing by his ultimatum to Lavon, and anxious to see it go into effect with the least damage to party or state, Sharett sought swift ratification of it by Mapai, so as to forestall an uncontrolled cabinet discussion that was liable to make his political adversaries aware of the disgraceful relationship between himself and Lavon, the party's two senior ministers. If there had not been leaks to the press, his intricate maneuver might have succeeded. On February 15, the subject was discussed by "Our Colleagues" (a Mapai forum comprising senior state officials and party leaders) with fourteen people in attendance, including all the Mapai ministers except Lavon, who reported in sick. It was, Sharett recorded, "the first time the issue of the secret group in Egypt, and the Cairo trial, was raised for consideration in so wide a party circle." The conclave granted virtually unanimous approval to Sharett's proposal that if Lavon "is willing to stay on unconditionally, well and good; if not—he has leave to go." Two days later, Lavon acted upon that "leave" and resigned from the cabinet.

On the afternoon of February 16, 1955, Dayan went to see Lavon at his home, "finding him physically and spiritually drained. At his bedside lay his gear: a bottle of brandy and the Tubiansky review" by Ya'akov Shimshon Shapira.

For six months, Sharett had refrained, for reasons of confidentiality, from putting "the sorry business" on the cabinet's agenda. Incredible as it may sound nowadays, not merely the findings of the Olshan-Dori commission, but its very existence, remained secret. But as the days passed, in response to the press leaks and parliamentary rumors, Mapai's coalition partners demanded that the matter be brought up for debate, and Sharett consented to do so in the February 16 meeting of the cabinet committee for foreign affairs and defense.

Sharett began the proceedings by impressing the necessity of Lavon's resignation upon the non-Mapai ministers. One of these latter spoke in a statesmanlike way of ministerial responsibility. Another "poured fire and brimstone upon Givly, whom he recalled from the Tubiansky trial," but hastened to agree that there was nothing to gain from simply "dismissing some officer"; the minister was answerable and should pay the price, "and Lavon must therefore resign." Pinhas Rosen of the Progressives expressed disappointment in Sharett's conclusions, "but did not challenge them."

The following day, the entire Israeli press launched a campaign for Lavon's dismissal, thereby sealing his fate. Lavon was condemned as bearing sole responsibility for "the sorry business."

Sharett realized that he and his government faced a crisis of confidence, requiring a decision that transcended personal or party accountability. It was a moment of truth: Ben-Gurion must be persuaded to reassume the defense portfolio. Here Isser Harel helped stiffen Sharett's resolve, reassuring him that the party leadership now shared his "awareness that the surgery is urgent." Even the Knesset Speaker—a veteran adversary of Ben-Gurion—stepped forward to convince Mapai's lingering skeptics of the need to "discard Lavon and recall Ben-Gurion."

Sharett now acted swiftly and decisively; early on Thursday February 17, he dispatched Nehemia Argov to Sdeh Boker with a message begging Ben-Gurion to come to Tel Aviv that same morning. Failing that, "several colleagues will come to him at Sdeh Boker."

Ben-Gurion's diary records that Thursday as "a sleepless day":

At 8 in the morning, Nehemia arrived. Sharett asked him to come to me with all dispatch, to advise me that Pinhas Lavon insists on resigning and submitting his complaints to the cabinet and the [Knesset] foreign affairs [and defense] committee. Avigur refuses to assume [the defense portfolio] and there is no other candidate. . . . In the early evening, Golda and Namir came unexpectedly. Crisis in [the] defense [establishment]. Lavon is definitely going, and there is no one [to replace him], it is proposed that I return. I was moved. I decided I must accede to the demand and return to the defense ministry. Defense and the army override all else.

Even before receiving Ben-Gurion's reply, Sharett informed Lavon of the steps he had taken and accepted his resignation. Lavon released the news for publication by the Government Press Office and Israel radio:

On February 2, 1955, I notified the prime minister in writing of my resignation of my cabinet membership. After discussions pursued with me ever since, I notified the prime minister today that my resignation is final.

I will convey the grounds for my decision to the cabinet and the Knesset foreign affairs and defense committee.

At 8 that evening, Meir brought the tidings to Sharett: "Ben-Gurion accepts!" In Sharett's words, "a wave of joy engulfed me" and he promptly worded a communique for Israel radio. Thus, only two and a half hours elapsed from the airing of Lavon's resignation at 8:30 to the newscast at 11 reporting his replacement by Ben-Gurion. Sharett gave himself credit for not "leaving a state of vacuum." Meir praised his decisiveness, which had shielded the public from anxiety and insecurity. We all live in this country, she opined in her unique style, and we can all appreciate what went on when it became known that Lavon had resigned, and what it meant, for the country and its people, when the second report was broadcast at 11:00. The next day, Sharett cabled Ben-Gurion: "Admire your step as model of noble citizenship and testimony to profound comradeship amongst us. I know what you sacrifice. May joy of the nation and army be your consolation. Be strong! Moshe."

Lavon's resignation, and his replacement by Ben-Gurion, were made public on February 17, before the cabinet's weekly meeting. It is thus understandable that the February 20 meeting was awaited eagerly. Indeed, as Sharett noted, the cabinet convened on a note of "high tension." All 16 ministers[1] were present; Pinhas Rosen had risen from a sickbed and another minister cut short his vacation. But if the ministers expected fireworks, they were in for a disappointment.

Sharett launched the proceedings by announcing Lavon's resignation, then giving him the floor to defend it. Amid somber silence, Lavon read out a brief statement, which began by listing the achievements of the army and defense establishment during his tenure of office, before going on to declare that: "As defense minister, I bear parliamentary responsibility for the setbacks, even if I am not morally responsible for them, just as I bear responsibility for the achievements, even if many hands, in the army and defense ministry, toiled to attain them."

Lavon claimed that the Egyptian operation had been launched without his authorization or knowledge; as Sharett's diary described it, "he purged himself of all blame, shunting it onto the DMI." At the same time, "he displayed a monstrous picture of discipline running riot, and utter license for criminal adventuring." Lavon, he said, "naturally denied his own responsibility—even though previously he had acknowledged it—for eliminating the . . . arrangement"—a reference to the two-man supervisory committee which, if it had still existed, would have made the prime minister and Lavon himself aware of what was going on at a much earlier stage and thus averted the calamity.

1. The cabinet included nine ministers from Mapai, four from the General Zionists, two from Hapoel Hamizrahi, and Pinhas Rosen of the Progressives. Another coalition faction, Poalei Agudath Israel, had no cabinet representative.

Lavon concluded by declaring that "such setbacks cannot be averted, nor can control of the armed forces be guaranteed . . . without quite radical reforms in the structure of the entire defense establishment, and in the powers of its various branches"; however, since his proposals for such reforms had been rejected by the prime minister, he considered it impossible to bear continued responsibility for defense affairs, and therefore was resigning. Lavon had shifted his ground: his February 2 resignation letter had protested his shabby treatment by his party colleagues, not the rejection of his proposed reforms.

When Lavon finished, Sharett announced that Ben-Gurion had consented to return to the defense ministry. Lavon sent Sharett a note: "I suppose I'm free to get out." Sharett voiced "words of esteem, and expressed regret at his departure," as well as "the hope that he would yet serve the state with his gifts and experience." Both rose, and Sharett went over for a vigorous handshake. "Exiting erect of stature," as Sharett put it, Lavon terminated three and a half years of cabinet office: a year at agriculture, a year-and-a-half as minister without portfolio, and a final year at defense. However, Sharett's announcement did not prompt the promised discussion, so that Lavon's resignation and the reappointment of Ben-Gurion were both reduced to mere formalities.

With Ben-Gurion's nomination unanimously approved, Sharett drove to Sdeh Boker "at record speed." That Sunday, he noted in his diary, was his first day in many weeks without distress from his ulcer: there was no knowing whether it was a new medicine he was taking, or relief at Ben-Gurion's return. Still, an inner voice warned him that Lavon's resignation had not put an end to the affair. Lavon himself had predicted that sooner or later it would become clear that, like Tubiansky, he had been falsely condemned by "a vile libel" and that "*not all* those guilty" had been brought to account.

The responsibility for the great vexation still in store may be assigned to Sharett's failure to submit the affair to the scrutiny of his cabinet. The price of that error—like that of his abandonment of his initial plan to set up a state commission of inquiry—would be paid by his successor as prime minister: David Ben-Gurion. An intimation of what lay in store was expressed by Aran when he warned his cabinet colleagues: "I think that we shall all meet again with minister Lavon . . . this affair is not yet over."

15

Ben-Gurion Returns

Ben-Gurion and his wife Paula had settled at Kibbutz Sdeh Boker in Israel's southern Negev wilderness on December 14, 1953; six months later, the kibbutz admitted them as full-fledged members. In a "broadcast to the nation," Ben-Gurion quoted from the Hebrew poet Bialik to declare that he now felt himself "at one with" the eternally humble, dumb souls meek in thought and exploit, nameless dreamers spare in words but great in deed. The Sdeh Boker work roster obliged by sending him to tend the sheep.

No doubt Ben-Gurion hoped that shepherd's duty in the clear desert air would soothe his soul; snapshots of him clutching a day-old lamb were no mere publicity stunt. But it is equally certain that his self-proclaimed oneness with the meek and humble smacked of hyperbole. He did not seek peace for his spirit; rather, he sought to fortify it to confront new challenges. During his sojourn there he espoused a variety of causes, the most important being the scrapping of Israel's proportional representation system and replacing it with regional elections on the U.S. or British model. From this and other indications, it seems that Ben-Gurion had set aside no more than two to three years for his voluntary retirement; and certainly he kept in touch with events in Jerusalem.

Ben-Gurion was in no haste to support the ouster of Lavon. His comments to Sharett and others, backed by his vigorous refusal to step into

Lavon's shoes and his opposition to the nomination of Eshkol, and capped by his willfully absurd proposal to replace the defense minister with "a committee," indicate that, up to February 17, 1955, Ben-Gurion inclined toward retaining Lavon.

His motives were many and varied, but it will suffice to note two: the difficulty of publicly admitting his mistake in nominating Lavon in the first place and his reluctance to end his retirement prematurely. Ben-Gurion had been sixty-eight when he stepped down, and would be seventy-one at the time he intended to return to the public arena; he needed reinvigoration before tackling the last great project he had assigned himself: reform of "the regime." Sharett was thus totally accurate in surmising that Ben-Gurion wished to launch "a revolution in electoral law, and reform of the system of government-by-coalition"; when he achieved that transformation, he would end his retirement and return to "the government of the new regime."

Addressing party, cabinet, and Knesset, Sharett defended his appeal to Ben-Gurion to reassume the defense portfolio by pointing to the havoc wrought in the army during Lavon's tenure—"a state of disenchantment . . . of bitterness . . . of mistrust . . . of lack of inner confidence." He referred to "the supreme need" to fill the vacuum left by Lavon in a way that would reinforce "internal stability within the army." He claimed that only "the man who was Israel's first defense minister . . . who created the army, molding its form, and inspiring it with the spirit we all wish to see prevail within it" could achieve that purpose.

All the opposition parties, as well as the influential newspapers, insisting that Ben-Gurion was taking advantage of the defense establishment crisis to regain office, dismissed these claims. Some papers did not flinch at making the senseless assertion that the operation in Egypt, and Lavon's resulting resignation, were nothing but a ruse, or "covert initiative," designed to deliver Ben-Gurion from his feigned withdrawal to Sdeh Boker and also rescue Mapai in the upcoming elections. However, the press had not invented the notion that returning to the cabinet would "save" Ben-Gurion; it was inspired by his own intimates, who wanted him back. Argov, for example, claimed that Ben-Gurion's aches and pains were caused by his anguish over developments in the defense establishment, and would pass when he returned to active life.

Sharett reacted to sarcastic comments in the press with words from the heart—and mind—when he addressed the cabinet on February 20:

"Had it been [Ben-Gurion's] wish to return to the post of prime minister . . . he could have done so overtly, without resorting to any ruses to smooth his path."

On Monday February 21, 1955, Ben-Gurion left Sdeh Boker for Jerusalem. He paid a courtesy call to Sharett's office at 3:00; at 4:00, he attended the Knesset, which was asked to approve his appointment. The Knesset held no debate, but each party delivered a statement. The opposition parties—Mapam, Ahdut HaAvodah, the Communists, and Herut—proclaimed their opposition to Ben-Gurion's appointment. The Orthodox "Agudath Israel" party declared that, in view of "the perilous deterioration of security," it would vote for the motion. Ben-Gurion's appointment was approved by 74 votes to 22, with one abstention—his own; he signed the oath of office, and joined the cabinet.

With Lavon gone, Dayan quipped about the likely fate of his right-hand man "Eppy" Evron in English: "This is a happy end, and the end of Eppy." On the morning of Tuesday February 22, 1955, Ben-Gurion returned to the defense ministry in Tel Aviv, accompanied by his veteran aide-de-camp Nehemia Argov. After a festive welcome from the ministry staff he spoke with Lavon, then with Dayan. In the afternoon, he met with Peres, "and again with Dayan, and again with Lavon," as he recorded in his diary. According to Lavon, Ben-Gurion asked to hear the proposals for "radical reforms" of the defense establishment whose rejection had triggered his resignation. In that exchange—as Lavon would write to Ben-Gurion five-and-a-half years later when the "Lavon affair" was revived—"I told you . . . that two persons should be removed from the defense establishment: Givly and Peres." Ben-Gurion's diary entry for that day notes only that Lavon put forward "a series of reasonable proposals."

Ben-Gurion ignored opposition demands for an inquiry into "the sorry business." He had already resolved to hold off any such probe, claiming that "I did not even find cause to read all the inquiry material which was before me" because:

> I knew, and greatly esteemed, [Olshan and Dori] . . . and as they had not uncovered the whole truth—I reached an inner resolve not to deal with this "affair." I found it fitting to grant Lavon the benefit of the doubt, and continued to treat him as a colleague. Regarding Givly, I found it fitting to be strict—out of that [same] doubt. He was an officer in a service that demands great trust, and I decided to transfer him to another post.

Ben-Gurion would spend the rest of his life reiterating that view, and paying a heavy price for his error.

Givly's more than six-year reign at MI thus neared its end. On March 28, 1955, he attended his final General Staff meeting as DMI. On April 7, he went on leave, with Yuval Ne'eman acting as his stand-in; on May 15, Harkabi took over the command. Givly was to assume a new post as Northern Command's chief of staff on June 1; but before quitting MI, he took a brief and mysterious trip to Germany, whose purpose emerged later. In addition—operating, as always, through others—he engineered two separate stratagems to remove from Israel two people who might reveal his secrets: Avry Elad and Dalia Carmel.

In February 1955, Elad had again left for Europe. With his rare flair for bamboozling others, he had managed to convince 131's new commander Yossi Harel, and incoming DMI Harkabi, that he could continue to be of service to Israeli intelligence under his old cover of "Paul Frank." This return to clandestinity under a cover publicly blown in the Cairo trials undoubtedly flouted every principle of intelligence work. Elad's departure could be of benefit to only two persons: himself and Givly.

In 1955, Yossi Harel, Harkabi and Dayan all still believed that Elad had followed instructions in Egypt and was entitled to esteem and reward for his coolheadedness, resourcefulness, and pluck. Only Givly and Ben-Zur knew that he had lied—at their behest—in his reports and in his testimony to the Olshan-Dori commission, to hide the fact that the July 2 and 14 operations had been carried out by 131, on his orders. For Givly, keeping Elad content and at a distance was preferable to having him nearby and disgruntled. Givly did not foresee that Elad's mission to Germany would ultimately expose them both: Elad as a turncoat who had betrayed his own subordinates, and Givly as a liar and solicitor to perjury. The only person with the extraordinary professionalism to mistrust Elad and oppose his dispatch to Germany was Isser Harel.

Dalia Carmel was to complete her obligatory army service on May 3, 1955; in February, however, she was offered a job with Israel's military attache in London. This posting was proposed in a recommendation submitted to the GHQ Manpower Branch by Hareven and endorsed by Givly's signature. "There's a proposal I go to London," Dalia told her parents. "I don't really go for it." However, she knew that "Benyamin was leaving" and "everyone said it was worth my while. So I agreed." On March 30, she signed on for an extra year of army service; and on May 11, "with rather mixed feelings," she flew to London. Soon afterward, however, she realized that she had been "expelled" to "get me out of the way"; completing her two year's service in London—one as a military and one as a civilian employee—she resigned from her post and returned to Israel.

In August 1954, when Dayan had first learned of the operation in Egypt, he decided to act on a longstanding resolve to replace Givly and inject fresh blood into MI. His journal mentions assigning Lieutenant Colonel Yuval Ne'eman to MI as early as August 27, but a long delay ensued, the fruit of Givly's efforts to limit Ne'eman's authority exclusively to research. Dayan rejected the notion, again resorting to English wordplay: MI, he said "is called 'intelligence' in English, and therefore they need someone 'with intelligence.' " Ne'eman too insisted that he would accept the job "only with comprehensive responsibility" embracing intelligence-gathering. He became deputy DMI in mid-December. On January 18, 1955, Givly, fighting to secure his preserve, demanded that his henchman Mordechai Almog, who had been head of MI's Intelligence-gathering Department, should stay at this post, possibly as a reward for his mission a mere two weeks earlier to instruct Elad before his deposition to the Olshan-Dori commission. Dayan consented, and so did Ne'eman.

Ne'eman retained clear recollections that on his arrival at MI, "various persons" confided to him "some fairly limited tidbits" concerning the Egyptian debacle, its examination by the Olshan-Dori commission, and "suspicions about . . . falsification of documents, signatures and testimonies." What he heard induced him to look into why Max Binnet had not been tipped off when he might still have had time to flee. Inviting in Binnet's widow Jane, who had been brought to Israel some two weeks before her husband's suicide, for a talk, Ne'eman found her embittered over the way Givly and Ben-Zur had treated her. Her story, Ne'eman said, "took me deeper into the matter." He reported it to Dayan, asking "whether or not we're doing anything about it." The May 3, 1955, entry in the chief of staff's journal notes that "Dayan instructed Ne'eman to prepare a conclusive report on the 131 affair"; in other words, to conduct an internal inquiry. As soon as Ne'eman took the first step in setting up this inquiry, Givly got wind of it.

At this point Dayan learned of Almog's trip to Paris to coach Elad, whereupon he lost any lingering trust he still retained in Givly. Aware that Elad was back in Germany, and apprehensive that Givly would again try to coordinate testimony with him, the chief of staff personally ordered Lieutenant Colonel Ya'akov Hefetz—MI's staff chief, whose duties included supervision of foreign travel—"not to handle" any trip abroad by Givly or any of his cronies without Dayan's approval. Then it became known that Givly had secretly departed for Germany. The chief of staff's journal for May 11 notes: "Ne'eman says it has been hinted in MI that Givly's current journey to Germany was to finish 'organizing' testimony" with Elad.

It turned out that his fare had been paid with a check drawn on the MI bank account, and signed by Hefetz. Summoned in haste to the chief of staff, Hefetz found him out for blood; he was saved from summary dismissal only by convincing Dayan that he had known nothing of the trip. A brief investigation revealed that MI's bursar, a great fan of Givly's, had "a wad of emergency blank checks signed by [Hefetz] . . . which he used to give Givly a check to cover his travel expenses."

Harkabi, who was studying in Paris, received a letter from Dayan in February 1955, notifying him that Ben-Gurion had decided to make him DMI. While tying up loose ends, Harkabi agonized over whether it would be better for the intelligence corps, and for himself as its new chief, if he were to investigate "the sorry business." His suspicions of something amiss at MI had been reinforced in early January, when Almog pretended not to see him as they passed one another in a Paris street. In response to a question, 131's Paris liaison revealed to him in utter confidence that Almog had come "to deliver something to Elad."

Meeting Elad in Paris in March, Harkabi learned from him that Almog had come to "give me instructions with regard to my journey to testify to the commission." Harkabi responded, "I find it strange that a man is sent to tell you something prior to your testimony," but "Elad reiterated his story." On May 2, during a visit to London, Harkabi encountered Dalia Carmel, who told him of the "alteration" she had made to Givly's July 19, 1954 letter to Dayan; he was convinced she was telling the truth.

In this manner, Harkabi discovered that improper "things had gone on"; but even before returning to Israel, he resolved against further ravaging "a demoralized [intelligence] corps" with investigations. He was convinced that MI remained unsullied: "It isn't the corps that lies and forges, it's Benyamin. . . ." Consequently, any investigation would focus upon Givly, which meant it could be interpreted as a new commander's vindictiveness against his beloved and admired predecessor.

On May 9, 1955, Harkabi returned to Israel; within hours, he was stunned to learn of the goings-on at MI. He told Hareven of Carmel's story about falsifying Givly's letter to the chief of staff; citing the same source, Hareven told him of the notebook that had been tampered with. Meeting with Dayan and Ne'eman on the 11th, Harkabi recounted all he had learned about Elad's perjured testimony to the Olshan-Dori commission, and the documents altered or concealed from it.

Dayan ordered Harkabi to "replace everyone linked to this matter. . . . Elad too will have to return" to Israel; furthermore, the new DMI was "to investigate [the matter of the testimonies] down to the minutest details, by the system of direct command as commander of MI, not as inquiry commission."

Harkabi objected, but Dayan insisted: "Harkabi has to get to the bottom of it" as well as question MI's bursar about his use of checks signed by Hefetz for Givly's trip to Germany. Ne'eman too was instructed by Dayan "not to ignore matters, but to go into them thoroughly."

Dayan conferred with GHQ's Director of Operations and the head of its Manpower Branch about whether "to conduct a vigorous special investigation" or "delegate Harkabi and Ne'eman to investigate on their own." Further, should Dayan hold back on appointing Givly to his new post, or "put him into his job even if it turns out the charges have merit"? Both officers agreed with Dayan "that it would be better at the present stage to conduct an investigation by means of Harkabi and Ne'eman, and not delay Givly's assumption of his job for the time being"; when "they report on their findings, we'll reconsider."

Because of Harkabi's reservations, Dayan needed the backing of the defense minister. At their weekly meeting on May 12, Dayan reported to Ben-Gurion on what he had learned from Harkabi, adding: "I won't agree—you certainly won't—that someone at MI should think he can run a double set of accounts, writing here and deleting there, whether it's for the defense minister, the chief of staff or the commission."

"It's a grave matter," Ben-Gurion responded. "I regret to hear it."

The two agreed "beyond any doubt" that there had to be "a purge" at MI, to render it "totally clean." Dayan pondered aloud how to "clear up these suspicions": an internal inquiry by Harkabi, or "doing it with drums"—that is, by means of a full-fledged military board of inquiry. Tipping the scale in favor of the instructions he had already given Harkabi, he added that an inquiry board "means delaying Givly's appointment . . . bringing people from abroad, that's a major production."

This way of presenting the issue undoubtedly took the heat off Ben-Gurion, who was determined to maintain his hands-off stance. He conceded that "the matter has to be completely cleared up"; but it was preferable "for the present not to create an inquiry commission, nor delay Givly's reassignment." As a first step, "Harkabi will set to work and investigate" and "submit a summary of the matter. From the summary, we'll see" whether there was need for a second step.

However, nothing came of it, for Harkabi refused to investigate, even threatening to resign. On Saturday May 14, he and Dayan discussed "the 131 affair" and came up with an effective compromise: Harkabi would talk to Ben-Gurion about "the overall question"; while conducting no probe at present, he "will write a report about all he knows currently. Should he uncover further data, he will report to Dayan."

For his part, Harkabi found himself "in an awful fix" as he took up Givly's legacy: "a devastated corps, which had suffered an awful ordeal" and whose rehabilitation was his first duty. He knew that "something improper" had happened at MI, but had no idea which of its personnel or sections were implicated. He also feared being seen as one who, "having inherited Benyamin, now sought to bury him." In his distress, Harkabi reflected: "Perhaps I shouldn't have gone and told them about the matter." Considering his own strained relations with Givly, and his status as newly installed DMI, charging him with the task of investigating his predecessor struck Harkabi as verging on "irresponsibility."

Harkabi began his new job some six weeks after a February 28 retaliation raid by the IDF in Gaza, an action that sent shock waves throughout the region and the world at large, ushering in the "period of reprisal actions" which prefaced the Sinai campaign. The raid exacerbated tensions between Israel and the Arab frontline states, and Harkabi had his hands full. He knew, he said, that conducting an investigation now would put him "out of commission" for regular MI tasks for months. "I see no way of ceasing to be DMI and launching an investigation," he told Dayan. "I can't take it on." Dayan passed the buck: "Go to Ben-Gurion," he told Harkabi, "and tell him you're unable to run an investigation." After listening to Harkabi's misgivings, and hearing his determination to resign should he be required to make such a probe his first task as DMI, the defense minister told him: "Drop it."

Harkabi had expected a different decision: he thought Dayan and Ben-Gurion should have appointed an examining officer, or even a properly constituted inquiry board. Ben-Gurion's acquiescence in disregarding suspicions and charges of improper conduct would tarnish his reputation as a defense minister whose concern extended to the army's moral standards; moreover, he would pay for this lapse with his public standing and prestige. Just as in the Tubiansky affair, the only man to profit from the failure to investigate the Egyptian debacle would be Benyamin Givly.

16

Fears of a Putsch

The balance in the 1948 War of Independence had been tipped in Israel's favor by the youthful officers and soldiers who braved the perils of combat. With that victory, the elevation of young officers to senior IDF commands, highlighted in the November 1949 appointment of thirty-two-year-old Yigael Yadin as chief of staff, reflected Ben-Gurion's faith in the competence of the younger generation, and his intention of entrusting it—under his own supervision—with national security. However, as we have seen, one effect was to awaken fears among the older Mapai leadership that Ben-Gurion intended to catapult younger men over their heads to the top slots in the party and Histadrut, perhaps even the government.

Their fears were intensified in November 1950, when the difficulties created by an influx of 700,000 new immigrants prompted the decision to "send the IDF into the immigrant camps," to help with maintenance, food delivery, and medical treatment. Where civilian groups had failed, the army soon claimed major success. Brushing aside the officials and party hacks who often neglected real needs in favor of incessant intrigues against rival agencies or parties, the soldiers came to seem like guardian angels. It was widely agreed that in "saving the immigrants," the IDF—young, professional and adroitly businesslike—had earned the accolade "people's army" in the noblest sense of the term.

Accordingly, the Mapai leadership feared an equally broad consensus that saw the IDF as the sole body capable of pulling off any national task. This prospect heightened the elder leaders' fears of a "putsch"—their term for a takeover of top government posts by "the young men" acting with Ben-Gurion's blessing, and in total disregard for their own seniority and rights. In fact, on two separate occasions, "two persons of public standing" did approach Yadin and urge him to "try a putsch"; Yadin turned them down. He declined to name the persons concerned, whose identities remained an enigma.

The Mapai leadership therefore could not remain indifferent to the emergence of two groups of "young men": one made up of holders of state office, the other deriving from the party's "youth section." Ben-Gurion's aides belonged to both groups.

Created in response to the herculean tasks confronting the fledgling state, as well as widespread criticism of governmental impotence in dealing with them, the officeholders' group reflected a desire for rapid creation of a strong central authority that would be up to the job. Ben-Gurion attended the group's October 28, 1952, meeting, whose participants he listed in his diary: along with the police inspector-general and senior reserve officers, they included: finance ministry director-general Ehud Avriel; the prime minister's director-general, Teddy Kollek; defense ministry acting director-general Shimon Peres; the OC of the IDF Southern Command, Major General Moshe Dayan; and the director of the Jewish Agency's Absorption Department, Dr. Giora Josephtal. The meeting's host, Ephraim Evron—Ben-Gurion's political secretary at the time—listed two further names: Reuven Shiloah, special political adviser to both prime minister and foreign minister, and Mossad's first chief; and Colonel Katriel Shalmon, military attache in London.

According to Kollek, "We spoke about . . . matters not being well-managed, and the need to handle them differently. . . . it was a kind of consultation." Ben-Gurion recorded in his diary: "Most of the time, they spoke about why the group [is needed]; part of the time, they criticized the state of affairs in the country. The aim was to ask whether I was in favor of the group, and what was its purpose." He admonished his listeners, who held executive posts of such importance: "In place of criticism and complaints, show your ability in practice, for things depend upon you." However, Ben-Gurion *"refrained from expressing any opinion* as to whether [the group] is needed or not, and if it is *permissible* at all." (italics added)

Although this was in fact the final meeting of the officeholders' group, echoes of it reached the ears of cabinet ministers. According to Ehud Avriel, Isser Harel denounced the group to Lavon as "anti-party, somewhat putschist and menacing." Harel denied saying this; but his warnings against Avriel and Moshe Dayan appear repeatedly in Sharett's diary.

The other group, scions of Mapai's "youth section," survived longer; it emerged in a direct challenge to the party old guard or "Bloc," which had long dominated the party apparatus and controlled its selection committees so that internal democracy did not exist. Denied the hope of attaining senior positions, the "youth section" group called for replacement of Israel's proportional representation system by regional elections and urged selection of party candidates by internal primaries.

In 1951, Moshe Dayan had addressed "the youth section," condemning Mapai's veteran functionaries and arguing that the party should be an instrument serving the state in deed, rather than in word. He proposed that the young people of the older settlements must move to the new immigrant villages, with newcomers taking their old places. The native Israelis would help the new immigrants surmount the arduous circumstances they faced, instructing them in farming techniques and the Israeli way of life, stiffening their morale and helping them strike roots in their new home. During his tenure as chief of staff, Dayan sponsored a new "Sons of veteran settlements" movement, which he proclaimed at a national convention held on June 11 and 12, 1954 (Ben-Gurion came from Sdeh Boker especially for the occasion). Dayan thereby crossed into the proscribed domain of political activity.

The veteran Eshkol—who, as Jewish Agency treasurer and later finance minister, played a key role in fostering the immigrant settlements—was aghast at the creation of the "Sons of veteran settlements." The movement's quasi-military structure revived his childhood memories of pogroms in Ukraine; he perceived it as bands of galloping Cossacks headed by "Hetman" Dayan, not as a way of solving practical problems like the shortage of resources, instructors, irrigation water, education, and so on.

Early in June 1955, Dayan addressed a youth convention at Ein Harod, urging his audience "to storm the Knesset and other key redoubts; it is vital to replace the aging, defeatist leadership in the party, the Histadrut and the government." These remarks evoked no comment from Ben-Gurion.

The threat to the party old guard grew when chief of staff Dayan enacted pension regulations which, by providing a monthly pension equivalent to 40 percent of their last salary after twenty years, encouraged IDF officers to resign from the army at forty. Early retirement launched young officers—gifted, ambitious, and in their prime—into civilian life, to be pounced upon with lavish offers of senior jobs in business and services, closely followed by public and party organizations. Had the Mapai veterans consented to hold primaries, they would have confronted challenges by illustrious ex-officers: the results of the elections would have been easy to predict.

The veterans' fear of a "putsch" grew when Ben-Gurion nominated Lavon to succeed him as defense minister and peaked in response to reports about the plans he was said to be hatching at Sdeh Boker. Ben-Gurion was in fact repulsed by his party's clinging to the proportional representation system, which he blamed for the proliferation of parties and the system of government by coalition, whereby parties pursued their own interests at the expense of the state.

During his sojourn at Sdeh Boker, Ben-Gurion—as Sharett put it—"came up with a new notion" for electoral reform: creation of an *ad hoc* election slate which would draw support from different political camps, the common denominator being a wish for stable government. Led by Ben-Gurion, this "popular front" would contest the July 1955 Knesset elections on a platform of regional elections (that is, elections based on districts or constituencies); the "front" and Mapai would subsequently pool forces, forging a parliamentary majority to ram through a new electoral law that would allow for Mapai and no more than one rival party. At this point the "front" would disband and new elections would be called, in which Mapai would win an absolute majority. Ben-Gurion would then be able to form a strong and stable one-party government, which would impose laws, revive the economy, make the desert bloom, direct young people and immigrants to new settlements, and fortify Israel to discharge its historic tasks.

On May 8, 1954, Ben-Gurion outlined his plan to the Mapai leadership. The veterans suppressed their indignation; but behind his back, they pondered the precise connection between the "popular front" and Mapai. What guarantee was there that the front would voluntarily disband once it had completed its designated role? "Where [is the certainty] that Knesset members, newly elected and just beginning to taste prominence and fame, will consent . . . of their own free will to curtail their term of office?" Sharett inquired of his diary. The plan's vagueness in this respect made the Mapai veterans all the more apprehensive that—as Sharett wrote in his diary—"he isn't telling us all his secret thoughts."

In September, Ben-Gurion urged Mapai's central committee "to include regional elections in the party's platform." The "Bloc's" fear of single-candidate elections was still low-key; as Ben-Gurion noted in his diary: "To my surprise, there were few opponents. Altogether, 6 voted against . . . 53 voted for" the plan. Nehemia Argov (who hoped that this would be "a first step towards revolution" and "the beginning of the old man's return from Sdeh Boker") recorded in his own diary Lavon's interpretation of the central committee's unexpected approval: "There's nothing novel in the old man's proposal, and no hope of its realization. But we didn't want to vex him, and that's why we didn't tell him our unfavorable reactions." As the elections approached, the Mapai veterans discovered Ben-Gurion's "sensational scheme" of creating a "youth cabinet." Regional elections plus a revamped, youthful cabinet, constituted the "revolution" Ben-Gurion was concocting at Sdeh Boker.

The veterans' uneasiness grew still more when they detected growls of distant thunder emanating from Ben-Gurion and his circle of "young" confidants: first, Ben-Gurion threatened that, if his plan was not accepted, he would not resume office as prime minister. Even after returning to the cabinet as defense minister in February 1955, he told Sharett that only if "there is a majority for regional elections, to implement the matter immediately, will I be willing to enter harness for a further four years."

Other ominous rumbles from Sdeh Boker hinted of "a dictatorship on the way" and of secret plans for far-reaching structural and legislative reforms. Israel's most widely circulated paper noted that Ben-Gurion had become "active and enterprising" in his Negev retreat, and had furthermore "launched the 'annual political season' " by forming a shadow cabinet.

Had the "veterans" possessed during these events the wisdom of hindsight, they would not have worried: Ben-Gurion's political flirtation with "the young men"—the folly of an old man bedazzled by the charm of youth—proved short-lived. Nor did his revolutionary tendencies go beyond flashes of inspiration, unfulfilled slogans, and hollow talk. Had the veterans paid attention to what they saw and heard, they would have discovered neither "fronts" nor "revolts." What was more, when the July

1955 elections afforded Mapai only 32.2 percent of the vote—well short of the hoped-for 51 percent—Ben-Gurion did not quit the cabinet, and no revolution erupted. Everything remained as it had been.

Nevertheless, like some malignancy, the fear of a "putsch" was rooted deep in the veterans' hearts. Their apprehensions were quickened both covertly, by Katriel Shalmon and Ehud Avriel, and overtly, from a different quarter, by Isser Harel.

Shalmon, an immensely attractive, well-educated and accomplished man with a degree from the London School of Economics, had served as chief of staff Dori's acting financial adviser. In 1952, on Ben-Gurion's insistence in the face of opposition from chief of staff Yadin, Shalmon had drawn up "a survey of the state of the IDF's order of battle, from the viewpoint of its practical efficiency and the state's economic situation."

In 1951–1954 Shalmon was in London as military attache to the U.K. and the Scandinavian countries. Nehemia Argov, who liked him, kept Ben-Gurion briefed on his comments and insights. Shalmon fostered this three-way link with letters designed to make Ben-Gurion see him as an adviser and thinker. The letters expressed adulation of Ben-Gurion, whose published speeches Shalmon compared with the works of Plato, Aldous Huxley, and Winston Churchill, as well as Machiavelli's *Discourses*. Argov had the letters typed up, sending copies to Ben-Gurion, Dayan, and others.

In contrast with Machiavelli's *The Prince*, where the author portrays himself as a confirmed absolutist, his *Discourses* on the annals of the Roman republic represent him as a republican who nevertheless welcomes dictatorship under certain circumstances. There was an intriguing parallel between the *Discourses*, which had long fascinated Ben-Gurion, and his own *Mission and Dedication*. Probably in response to a request from Argov—who may have been egged on by Ben-Gurion—Shalmon elaborated upon the subject in a letter dated July 3, 1951. He drew analogies from Machiavelli with regard to the way Israel would fuse its massive influx of immigrants into a cohesive republic with a unified national will.

Pinpointing the source of evil in Israel's "multi-party regime," Shalmon proposed that the parties should give up their power in favor of a popular national movement centered in the IDF. This result was to be attained not by coercion but by shrewd, sophisticated propaganda. To create such a campaign Shalmon recommended Pinhas Lavon, the only Mapai leader who was "sufficiently realistic, gifted and clear of vision."

Shalmon may have been the first to make Ben-Gurion see Lavon as having the qualities required of a successor.

Shalmon again stressed the need for "the finest professional talents" to be led, in the manner of Italian Fascism, by persons with "the self-assurance of visionaries and *the cynicism* (italics added) of realistic perception." He concluded by pointing to Ben-Gurion as the only man capable of bringing about this transformation—making a flattering comparison with Churchill.

It is difficult to establish how much effect Shalmon's proposal had on Ben-Gurion's thinking. Ben-Gurion did prefer to achieve electoral reform by democratic means, but there are evident similarities between Shalmon's proposal for a popular national movement founded upon the IDF and Ben-Gurion's short-lived 1954 notion of forming a "popular front" and implementing a comprehensive, far-reaching transformation in a single term of office.

Ehud Avriel probably shared Shalmon's beliefs. Products of Western culture and close friends, both admired Ben-Gurion and advocated the same solution for the state's urgent problems. "We all believed," Avriel recalled, "that for the rapid creation of a new state, we needed a. slaves; b. dictatorship." Initially, he said, they presented to Yadin their proposal that the IDF, under Ben-Gurion's leadership, seize power. Yadin rejected it. Here, then, is the solution to the enigma mentioned earlier: the two men who urged Yadin to launch a putsch were Avriel and Shalmon. In 1955, the duo approached Ben-Gurion suggesting that he disperse the Knesset and lead a national emergency cabinet comprising young executives. Astounded, Ben-Gurion rejected the notion, as he later told Mapai's central committee.

In time, when their plan came to be regarded unfavorably, Avriel denied the story, trying to attribute the proposal to Shalmon, who had died in 1967. In January 1970, Avriel related that Shalmon had conducted some "idiotic conversation" with Ben-Gurion: "There's no time for all this Knesset nonsense, there has to be a shortcut." Asked by a journalist in 1974 whether he had urged Ben-Gurion to lead a putsch, Avriel replied: "That proposal, which was diametrically opposed to Ben-Gurion's philosophy, was put forward . . . by Katriel Shalmon. Ben-Gurion's response was: 'Get out of this room, and don't bother me with your nonsense.'"

However, Teddy Kollek had a different story. He told a journalist in 1983, three years after Avriel's death, that "I heard that there was once a conversation at Sdeh Boker between Katriel Shalmon and Avriel, and Ben-Gurion, and they said it was necessary to launch a revolution. The fact is that Ben-Gurion didn't pay them any attention."

It is doubtful, however, whether fear of a putsch would have reached such fantastic proportions, had not Isser Harel resorted to it as a weapon. By 1958, there were no grounds for attributing putschist notions to Shalmon, who had left government service, or to Avriel, who had become ambassador to Ghana. But Harel accused his perennial adversaries, Moshe Dayan and Shimon Peres, of harboring such intentions.

On January 18, 1968, Golda Meir, then secretary of Mapai, learned that Isser Harel—who had resigned in 1963 from Mossad and returned to civilian life—had joined Rafi, the party founded by Ben-Gurion's followers after their break with Mapai. She was appalled. "How can he?" she demanded. "How can he team up with Shimon Peres and Moshe Dayan?" It was, after all, Harel who, in 1958, "came and told us [Meir, Eshkol, Aran, and Sapir] that Moshe Dayan and Shimon Peres were preparing a military putsch; now he joins up with the same men he said were putschists?" Sapir confirmed that Harel had warned "of the terrible threat facing the state from a putsch Shimon Peres and Moshe Dayan are preparing." According to Meir, Eshkol "believed the story, just as I did."

The "Bloc" leaders' fears that Dayan and Peres were concocting a putsch were fanned by rumors that Elad had confessed under interrogation to being solicited by senior officers to give perjured testimony to the Olshan-Dori commission. Meir told the Mapai secretariat that she and her colleagues had "implored" Ben-Gurion to investigate the matter. "Among the greatest things Ben-Gurion did was the investigation into the Tubiansky affair," and she had urged him to do the same in the Lavon affair. "I profoundly regret that Ben-Gurion did not accept our view, and did not launch an inquiry."

Ben-Gurion appears to have refused because he suspected that the inquiry would be aimed at Dayan and Peres. A diary entry from late June 1958 records that leaders of "the Bloc" urged him to act against "the young men," and that Lavon "spoke bitterly of the young clique who want to conquer power." On learning that "of course the reference was to [Peres and Dayan]," Ben-Gurion publicly expressed his esteem "for those two persons and their loyal and effective labors."

Thus was a link established between two unfounded calumnies directed at Dayan and Peres: that they intended to seize power, and that they had tried to remove Lavon from the defense ministry by means of lies and forgeries. Many Mapai veterans held that if Dayan and Peres could contemplate a putsch, they were certainly capable of conspiring against Lavon. Lavon knew that Dayan and Peres had no part in the forgeries and false testimony, but he did not set the record straight. The two men thus bore Givly's guilt, and Lavon, who was intent on revenge, directed his vendetta against them, his longstanding personal, military, and political adversaries. The reason was simple: the party was not a suitable arena to pursue Givly, who in any case was no longer a threat to Lavon. Had it not been for the conspiracy between Dayan and Peres, Lavon claimed, the Olshan-Dori commission would have found him innocent in "the sorry business," he would have remained defense minister, Ben-Gurion would not have been recalled from Sdeh Boker, the threat of a putsch by Dayan and Peres would not have reared its head, and Mapai would have been spared the curse of the "biological debate" (see chapter 17).

The tempest that was to overtake Mapai brought Lavon and Sapir closer. However, Sapir's efforts to clear Lavon were undoubtedly motivated by more than the pursuit of justice. In the words of a Sapir intimate, "he wished to achieve a political objective, which he held most important and vital: to stop Dayan, Peres and their cronies from seizing power under Ben-Gurion's aegis."

The "Lavon affair" had yet to erupt, but its harbingers tainted the atmosphere at two Mapai conferences, held on November 22 and December 6, 1958, for the purpose of internal party reconciliation. In defiance of explicit requests from Ben-Gurion, Lavon refused to attend what he characterized as "the enthronement ceremony for Moshe Dayan and Shimon Peres."

After the first meeting, Eshkol told Ben-Gurion that he was overlooking the threat posed by "the young men," unlike numerous party members who were "fearful of Moshe Dayan launching a military coup."

"Who is fearful?" Ben-Gurion demanded.

"Lavon, Aran, others," Eshkol replied.

Ben-Gurion noted in his diary: "I could not believe my ears. I explained the absurdity of the notion. Even supposing someone should attempt it, the IDF would not be at his disposal."

The following day, November 27, Mapai's central committee deliberated Ben-Gurion's proposal for electoral reform (which he kept pushing, unsuccessfully, to his dying day). The system of proportional representation, Ben-Gurion asserted, gave rise to "a regime in which a small group can extort" and "make the cabinet a laughing stock." The public's revulsion toward its elected representatives was liable to provide the setting and motivation for a coup.

Suggesting that the coup threat might have materialized had he not been prime minister, Ben-Gurion added that "to destroy democracy, an army is needed." He "respects the IDF no less than anyone in Israel," but should the present system persist, and political fragmentation continue, the IDF would be in danger of political corruption, and he could not "swear" that it would not some day lend a hand to a putsch. To support his point, Ben-Gurion described how, before the July 1955 elections, he had been "approached by persons who said it is necessary to disperse the Knesset and establish a dictatorship. I was aghast because this was said by persons who are not Fascists, who really saw the ignominy of that regime. I cannot mention them by name."

Ben-Gurion was almost certainly referring to Avriel and Shalmon. His use of the term "Fascist" indicates his awareness of the ideological tincture of Shalmon's proposal. Unfortunately, seeking to show that regional elections were the only guarantee against a coup in the near or distant future, Ben-Gurion achieved the opposite: he convinced his hearers that their fears of a putsch were valid. The story was immediately leaked and published by the daily *Maariv* under the heading: "Ben-Gurion was urged to seize power." Taken up by other papers, the revelation spurred the Knesset to debate the possibility of a putsch.

At Knesset question time on January 7, 1959, a prominent member demanded to know whether those who had urged Ben-Gurion to seize power "were, or still are, government employees? If so, is the prime minister able to inform the Knesset of the termination of their employment?"

Ben-Gurion replied: "The person who leaked, or sold, this story to the paper, conveyed a lie. I did not say those things at the party central committee, and no one urged me to seize power, and I did not of course say I rejected that proposal because no such proposal was addressed to me."

The way he backed this denial, which was truthful only in the most literal sense—*Maariv* had used different terms from those Ben-Gurion used at the meeting—was by asserting that "there are no public figures more loyal to Israeli democracy than IDF officers, junior and senior, primarily the chiefs of staff . . . from the formation of the IDF . . . up to the present day."

At the second reconciliation conference, on December 6, 1958, the veterans still labored under the conviction that Ben-Gurion considered them expendable. Meir, the "Bloc's" senior leader, dropped "a mighty bombshell" when she announced that after the elections, she would eschew any position in the cabinet, the Knesset, or any other body. Her deliberately provocative statement carried a veiled threat that all the other veteran ministers would likewise shun Ben-Gurion's future cabinet. She hit her target, as shown by Ben-Gurion's diary entry that day: "I was incapable of thinking of anything. I was stunned." He could have been in no doubt as to the implications: the veterans were determined to fight back. If he ran for election in alliance with "the young men," he would forfeit their support, diminishing his chances of success.

On the surface, the two reconciliation meetings achieved their purpose by adopting a resolution calling for internal accord. On December 7, the headline "Harmony Achieved" in the Histadrut's paper *Davar* heralded the disbanding of the party's factions. But more discerning observers knew that the battle for future power raged on. The "Bloc" closed ranks around a hard core headed by the "troika": Meir, Sapir, and Aran. This triumvirate, which wielded enormous power—political, economic, and administrative—was ready to challenge Ben-Gurion. Another effect of the reconciliation meetings was a linkage between the veterans' fight to cling to power, and Lavon's efforts to prove his innocence; that linkage would spawn the tragedy that become known as "the Lavon affair."

The double standoff came to a climax in December 1958, on the eve of the elections for Mapai's Ninth Convention. Dayan—who had retired from active duty in the IDF in January 1958 and was finally released from military service that December—called for a pay freeze and efficiency layoffs of thousands of employees and for investing the money saved in state and public development projects; Lavon, now secretary of the Histadrut, objected, charging "the young men" with "a lack of political understanding." Dayan retorted: "Does Israeli youth, which has, over the past 15 years, crawled between thorns and rocks with rifle in hand . . . have less comprehension of the problem of the Jewish people than those who have been seated these past 20 years on the Histadrut building's fifth floor or elsewhere?"

The next day, a newspaper cartoon captioned "Rascal" depicted Dayan as an urchin lobbing a stone at the window of Lavon's fifth floor office at Histadrut headquarters. "The stone at the fifth floor" became the symbol of an unruly, impetuous Dayan, hinting at the danger he posed should he grow more powerful.

On December 31, a six-hour discussion at Ben-Gurion's office gave the Mapai veterans an opportunity to vent their fury at Dayan. Of all they had to say, Ben-Gurion's recorded just one quote, from Meir, who "attacked him harshly, giving a hostile interpretation to his words about 'those who crawled between the thorns and those seated in offices.' In her view, those words implied a military dictatorship."

Ben-Gurion took this opportunity to lecture Dayan on Histadrut ideals and values, urging him to curb his tongue. But that did not satisfy Lavon, who publicly accused Dayan of striving to destroy the Histadrut's solidarity by disregarding its values, depicting him as reckless and deficient in "serious human and public understanding." Mocking Ben-Gurion's insistence that because of his military record Dayan was esteemed as a public figure and politician, Lavon compared him to "another great general"—Douglas MacArthur, who had been fired by President Truman for meddling in policymaking. Dayan's remark about the antagonism between the soldier crawling between the thorns and civilian leaders "has strange and most worrying undertones," Lavon added, hinting at the lesson of Germany.

Mapai's slogan: "Say Yes to the old man" brought Ben-Gurion his greatest electoral triumph: his party won 47 of the Knesset's 120 seats, seven more than in the outgoing Knesset. Furthermore, Mapai's parliamentary faction was revitalized with eleven fresh faces—another record. With coalition partners eager to jump on Mapai's rolling bandwagon, Ben-Gurion seemed to face an easy task in putting together a government. But because of the "Bloc" troika's veto on the inclusion of "the young men," it took him six weeks to form his cabinet.

On Saturday November 21, 1959, a week after the elections, Ben Gurion convened "Our Colleagues" and confronted them with his intention to make Dayan agriculture minister, and Peres deputy defense minister. Convinced that the party's top echelons were their own exclusive preserve, the "veterans" were staggered equally by the nomination and by the fact that Dayan, not yet a minister, had been invited to the meeting. They interpreted this gambit as a warning of the far-ranging changes Ben-Gurion had in mind for the party leadership.

The obstacles the veterans placed in Ben-Gurion's path in putting together his cabinet were a reminder that the victory he had achieved with their aid far outweighed anything he could have hoped for had he allied himself with "the young men." They chose a well-tried tactic: as she had warned, Meir declined nomination as foreign minister, and Aran announced that he would not take the education portfolio. Ben-Gurion could have filled these posts with two "young" candidates he wanted in his cabinet: Dayan and Abba Eban. But he knew that appointing them would entail the resignation of other veterans, and it was doubtful whether any other party would join a coalition in which, except for himself, Mapai was represented only by "the young men."

Recognizing rules of the game that he had himself codified, Ben-Gurion interpreted the rebuffs from Meir and Aran as a sign of their willingness to deal. Sounding them out, he found that the "veterans" were resigned to swallowing Dayan as agriculture minister, though not in any more important position; but they vigorously opposed Peres's becoming deputy defense minister.

Ben-Gurion stood like a rock behind his proteges; and after six weeks, the "Bloc" leaders accepted Dayan as agriculture minister, with Eban as minister-without-portfolio. On December 17, 1959, the Knesset gave the new cabinet a vote of confidence; on the 21st, Ben-Gurion made Knesset member Shimon Peres deputy defense minister.

Ben-Gurion had thus prevailed against the veterans. But his triumph was short-lived: the stage was set and the actors were in the wings, awaiting the next act which would find the "Bloc" turning on its master.

17

Ups and Downs

In 1959, Ben-Gurion was at the pinnacle of his eminence, admired in Israel and among Diaspora Jews equally; the enlightened world saw him as a symbol of national resolve and courage. His glory rubbed off on his entourage, adding a notch or two to the public stature of his cabinet colleagues. Prominent among them were "veterans" born in the previous century: finance minister Levi Eshkol, foreign minister Golda Meir, and education minister Zalman Aran. An interim age group was represented by commerce-and-industry minister Pinhas Sapir, and the "young men" were agriculture minister Moshe Dayan and minister-without-portfolio Abba Eban. Deputy defense minister Shimon Peres was also brushed by Ben-Gurion's glow.

The way for the new appointments had been cleared when Ben-Gurion discarded some of the veteran ministers, particularly Sharett, whom he forced to resign as foreign minister in 1956, in favor of Meir. The November 1956 Sinai campaign, with its 100-hour lightning drive, had won Israel international renown, a strengthened military posture and, above all, acknowledgement that it was here to stay. That recognition facilitated renewal of an unprecedented level of immigration and economic growth. Held in the afterglow of these successes, the Fourth Knesset elections on November 3, 1959, gave Mapai 47 Knesset seats—a record unequaled before or since. The triumph enabled Ben-Gurion to form a government with a stable parliamentary base resting upon 86 Knesset votes out of a total of 120.

Was this cabinet the "youth cabinet" Ben-Gurion had contemplated? In fact, restoration to government office did not prompt him to launch his "revolution"; nor did the Sinai campaign. But he did decree the advance or decline of individuals. Dayan was among those in the ascendant, though not unrestrictedly. In an interview he gave later to a Parisian paper, Dayan recalled that when he stepped down as chief of staff in January 1958, he got a farewell letter from Ben-Gurion praising the diplomatic flair he had shown in dealing with Jordan's King Abdullah. Dayan could not suppress a wry comment: "If that was what he thought of me, well, after I resigned from the army, he invited me to join his cabinet, [but] didn't offer to make me foreign minister. If he thought I excelled in diplomacy, he didn't show me any sign." Dayan evidently had certain expectations of a senior portfolio; but those hopes were not fulfilled in Ben-Gurion's time.

The Sinai campaign revealed links with France in arms procurement and military cooperation, which had been fostered by Shimon Peres. He was appointed as Ben-Gurion's deputy defense minister in recognition of this achievement.

Thus, although the "young" Dayan and Peres did achieve advancement, it was only to a limited degree. If Ben-Gurion planned to have his "young Turks" leapfrog over the heads of the "veterans," he did not intend to put them ahead of Eshkol or Meir. But the veterans' apprehensions persisted: remaining on the alert for the battle to come, they dug in around their party redoubt, the Bloc.

Lavon's exile to the political wilderness had come to an end in May 1956, when, with Ben-Gurion's backing, he was elected Histadrut secretary, a post that would offer a powerful springboard for his campaign for rehabilitation. Lavon made Ephraim Evron the Histadrut's U.S. representative; on his return to Israel in 1960, Evron joined the board of the Histadrut's construction company. That year's revival of the "Lavon affair" found him taking a hand in efforts to clear his patron's name.

In July 1956, Benyamin Givly became OC of the Golani infantry brigade, which he went on to lead to good effect in the Sinai campaign. That experience in combat command prompted him to renew his demand for promotion to major general; however he was turned down by chief of staff Haim Laskov, who said that he must first clear his name of the suspicions of perjury and "destroying" documents. In January 1960, Givly became military attaché in Britain.

Ben-Zur, now redundant in the army, resigned in April 1958; a year later, a newspaper advertisement led him to a job with a chemical company near Haifa. His employers expressed total satisfaction with his work. Harkabi did very well as DMI, before and after the Sinai campaign; he too shared in the glory of that victory. In 1957, Dalia Carmel got a job as assistant secretary to finance minister Levi Eshkol; three months later, she became his principal secretary.

Those Israelis who had been directly involved in "the sorry business" thus had few grounds for complaint—except for Isser Harel, who was envious of Peres's success in arms procurement and the worldwide renown gained by Dayan in the Sinai campaign. When Ben-Gurion completed his cabinet appointments in 1959, he was astounded, he noted in his diary, to discover that Harel "is embittered over my making Eban and Moshe Dayan ministers, and Peres, deputy minister—and not [appointing] him." Harel demanded a post at Ben-Gurion's side as deputy prime minister. On being rebuffed, he approached the Mapai veterans, treating them to farfetched descriptions of the dangers Peres and Dayan posed for Israeli democracy. Since he was head of the secret services, his warnings invariably conveyed the impression that they were based on confidential intelligence, further heightening the Bloc leaders' dread of a putsch. Revival of the "Lavon affair" would see the strategy of the Mapai veterans dictated by this fear.

Initially, Ben-Gurion's 1959 cabinet promised to overshadow all its predecessors with a bold competence that held out the prospect of a four-year term replete with vision and achievement. In fact, his government held office only ten months. On October 4, 1960, 292 days into its tenure, Lavon addressed the Knesset foreign affairs and defense committee; it was the first blast of the storm long looming on the horizon—one that blew up almost simultaneously from four different quarters: Elad, Sharett, Lavon and the Bloc

As already related, Givly had renewed Elad's posting to Germany; but within less than a year, in January 1956, Elad was recalled to Israel at the demand of Isser Harel, who regarded him as a grave security risk. Although Elad once more managed to convince his new superiors, Yossi Harel and Harkabi, to send him back to Germany, in June 1957, Isser Harel received a report that he had contacts with Egypt's military attache in Germany. Lured to Israel by the offer of a job with El Al and an invitation to its Lod headquarters, Elad was held for interrogation from December 16, 1957 until his trial began on July 15, 1959. On March 1, 1958 he confessed to having perjured himself to the Olshan-Dori commission, at the behest of Givly and Ben-Zur.

Meanwhile, on February 17, 1958, chief of staff Haim Laskov appointed a commission to examine "the circumstances and causes of the collapse of the network in Egypt." The members were deputy JAG Lieutenant Colonel Meir Shamgar (subsequently president of Israel's Supreme Court); Zvi Aharoni, one of Elad's interrogators; and assistant Director of Operations Colonel Ariel Amiad, who presided over the commission and gave it its name.

The Amiad commission never completed its work, though an interim report it submitted showed that its members were convinced of Elad's perfidy. However, as long as the 131 operatives remained imprisoned in Egypt and unable to testify, there were no grounds for his indictment on treason and no evidence to prove that he was the traitor who turned in his subordinates. He was charged only with preparing to transmit intelligence secrets to Colonel Osman Nuri of Egyptian intelligence. A thirteen-month trial before the Jerusalem district court found him guilty of six offenses against the Official Secrets Act. On August 21, 1960, he was sentenced to twelve years' imprisonment (reduced on appeal to ten). The court's three judges, having heard Elad repeat his confession, appear to have been convinced that his perjury was solicited by Givly and Ben-Zur. If Ben-Gurion believed that his 1955 resolve to keep his hands off would put the Egyptian affair to rest, the court verdict demonstrated how wrong he had been.

Asked why Ben-Gurion had excluded him from his cabinet, Sharett replied: "Had I remained in the government, I would have opposed the Sinai campaign." It was indeed the prime minister's prerogative, which Sharett did not challenge, to replace him as foreign minister. But Ben-Gurion had no right to subject Sharett to a bruising and needless offense to honor and dignity—an unforgivable sin he committed on January 18, 1957, shortly after the Sinai campaign, in a public address.

Ben-Gurion spoke of "desperate efforts" to acquire the weapons that had been vital for the victory, asserting that Sharett, as foreign minister, had failed to accomplish this task, which had instead been achieved by

his successor Golda Meir. Thunderstruck to learn that he had been publicly labeled inept, Sharett never forgave Ben-Gurion for this "libel and
abuse"; till his dying day, he never spoke to him again.

Ben-Gurion's praise would have had more truth in it had he directed
it at Shimon Peres, the architect and executor of the arms deals, rather
than Meir. While still acting director-general at the defense ministry,
Peres had fostered "unorthodox" weapons procurement links with the
French government and armed forces. To Meir's indignation, he had
not kept the foreign ministry briefed about his deals; and she had objected to Ben-Gurion. His public praise of her may have been intended as a
sop; had he credited Peres with the arms deals, she would have resigned.

But in so doing, Ben-Gurion committed a gross error, for the main
French arms transactions predated Meir's appointment. He had in fact
no grounds for what he said. Be that as it may: as a result of this speech,
Ben-Gurion acquired a mortal enemy.

The great esteem Ben-Gurion had for Lavon since 1950, when Lavon
had been minister-without-portfolio in his cabinet, did not evaporate
after Lavon's failure as defense minister; it may in fact have influenced
Ben-Gurion's resolve to keep his hands off the Egyptian affair. In January 1956, Ben-Gurion "vigorously insisted" that Lavon head an emergency economic committee he had established. After they had a sharp
exchange at the first meeting, Ben-Gurion, sensing that he might have
slighted Lavon, hastened to write assuring him "that I had no intention
. . . reason or desire to offend you in any degree." In a rare gesture, he
complimented Lavon in writing: "You are among the few amongst us
blessed with a bold and independent mind, and a gift for perceiving
realities."

After Lavon had been, with his endorsement, elected Histadrut secretary, Ben-Gurion continued to court him, displaying concern for his
health. And before the 1959 elections, Ben-Gurion got Lavon elevated
from the twelfth to the fourth slot on Mapai's slate of candidates. At the
time, Lavon was already planning his rehabilitation campaign—a campaign that would maul Ben-Gurion beyond anything he had ever
endured from man or God.

During the run-up to the 1955 elections, the ranks of the Bloc had
been boosted by a doughty recruit: Pinhas Sapir. Like Dayan later, Sapir
had gone straight to the top, with no need to fight for promotion. While
serving as defense ministry director-general, he had caught Ben-Gurion's eye with his unique blend of traits: a flair for understanding and

processing data, an excellent memory, a capacity for hard work and hard decisions; a willingness to run risks, and leadership. Sapir went on to distinguish himself as director-general at the finance ministry under Eshkol. Ben-Gurion passed over more veteran leaders in order to include him in his 1959 cabinet.

As commerce-and-industry minister, Sapir displayed enormous boldness and drive. He had a gift for wheedling money out of the U.S. government; getting the Israeli economy's disparate sectors—Histadrut, kibbutz movement, and private business—to function in harmony; raising capital abroad; and coaxing contributions from Diaspora Jews to Israeli enterprises. In consequence, he developed enormous influence, which fostered an unblinking indifference to procedure and a habit of bypassing other ministries, in disregard of the government's budget as well as democratic decisionmaking. Sapir was incorruptible, his sole reward being his ability to offer quid pro quos, political or personal. He was lavish in bestowing economic or governmental benefits upon groups and individuals both within and outside his party. He disbursed his largesse by means of scribbled notes, or a tacit nod-and-wink—integral elements of a strategy which came to be named for him, and through which he accomplished an economic and industrial miracle that greatly enhanced Israel's growth and absorptive power. But its cost—to Mapai, and to Israeli society—turned out to be equally enormous.

In essence, Sapir's "system" was a sophisticated elaboration on the Bloc's tactics for controlling Mapai. Often referred to as Israel's "Tammany Hall," the "Bloc," consisting of a hard core of about a dozen party functionaries in Tel Aviv, with a wider circle embracing some sixty secretaries of major party branches and labor councils, was believed to have falsified election results in party branches, trade unions, and labor councils. Unlike Meir, Aran, and Namir, who left the dirty work to underlings, Sapir was adept in application of brute force and spoke the underlings' language. The Bloc progressively took on a new, "Sapir-like" hue.

Created by Ben-Gurion as his instrument in Mapai's internal struggles during the forties, the Bloc's initial purpose had been to preserve the hegemony of the veteran leadership he led over party and state. But as it became increasingly evident that Ben-Gurion was intent on promoting "the young men" over the heads of the veterans, the Bloc adopted a new objective: securing its own predominance, even at the price of Ben-Gurion's ouster. The change came about gradually, beginning in 1958 as the party prepared for the coming year's elections.

As a rule, Mapai's power struggles were waged behind the scenes, far from the eyes of press and public. But in the early months of 1958, *Maariv*, then Israel's leading newspaper, began publishing detailed leaks from confidential party deliberations—to the obvious benefit of the veterans. In response to a question from a party secretary, Ben-Gurion said he thought the leaks came from "a party member, an insider, who, for regular pay," supplied the paper with confidential reports.

Suspicion centered upon journalist Levi Yitzhak Hayerushalmi. An outsider from Jerusalem's long-established Orthodox community, Hayerushalmi adhered neither to the Bloc nor to "the young men," but was loyal to one man: Lavon. As Lavon's faithful spokesman and envoy to various party groups, he was a public relations wizard, with plenty to sell. Intimately familiar with the newspapers and the professional and personal tastes of their editors and reporters, he can be described as the secret weapon Lavon had honed for his campaign. Hayerushalmi deserves much of the credit for the overthrow of the Ben-Gurion cabinet.

It is now clear that the leaks from Mapai's inner councils also emanated from others, including Yona Kesseh, a former Sharett retainer who had switched to Lavon. Kesseh had served some years as the party's secretary, and was a perennial member of its governing organs. Another important source, who had close ties to Isser Harel and the Mapai veterans, was Israel Galili of the rival party Ahdut HaAvodah; he was a past master at planting untraceable information in the press. These men had one trait in common: opposition to Ben-Gurion's young men. In view of their access to internal sources, efforts to plug the leaks never stood a chance.

Dayan, who had resigned as chief of staff in late January 1958, supplemented his new pursuit of Middle Eastern studies at Jerusalem's Hebrew University with party activity. His speeches savaged the entire Mapai establishment: the Histadrut, the kibbutz movement, the bureaucratic apparatus, the economic leadership. But above all, he attacked the veteran leaders, "who look back in awe at what they accomplished" in the past, "before we were born." The men of the previous generation, he reiterated, "have reached an age when they can no longer perform revolutions" because "all energies run out." There were now "things that only the younger generation is capable of accomplishing." Small wonder that the veterans were convinced that he had embarked upon "a biological struggle" and was calling for "a youth revolt." The Histadrut daily

Davar published an article entitled: "The rumor is making the rounds in the land: the youth revolt is imminent."

It soon grew evident that Dayan was also taking on the bastion of Mapai-style socialism—the Histadrut—and its secretary, Lavon. Convinced that the former chief of staff was intent on destroying the Histadrut, Lavon became the moving spirit of the counter-offensive against him.

The agenda of Mapai's May 1958 convention included a proposal by Lavon to divide up the Histadrut's economic enterprises, endowing their employees with ownership and management rights and thus giving them a greater sense of participation. In response, Dayan—advocate of "a great Israel" with 4 million Jewish citizens by 1970—spoke out in favor of "efficiency layoffs," with the money saved being transferred to national development projects. However, this controversy did not produce clear lines of demarcation between the rival camps. Some veterans opposed Lavon's proposals, which, conversely, were espoused by some of the young men.

The issue of reform came up when the young men challenged the Bloc's sacrosanct selection committees, pressing instead for selection of the party's election candidates by internal primaries. The veterans countered that the young men's objective was "to elbow their way into [office] prematurely." To teach the young men what opposition they faced, a show of hands gave their proposal only 71 votes out of 1,200.

On June 7, 1958, an "ideological" meeting was held, attended by Ben-Gurion and the party secretary, to hear Dayan expound his considered and definitive political credo. Here again, his address was seen as seditious. Again he questioned the raison d'être of the party apparatus and claimed that the veterans' time had passed. They counterattacked so mercilessly that Ben-Gurion intervened, urging respect for the former chief of staff. "There are now few . . . generals glorified the world over" like Dayan, said Ben-Gurion, professing himself to be mystified at "the great anger" against him.

Still, Ben-Gurion disagreed with Dayan's notions, and demolished them one by one. Nevertheless, leaks from the debate led to descriptions in the press of Ben-Gurion coming out in support of Dayan. Not surprisingly, the veteran leaders were outraged. After many years spent in political skirmishes at Ben-Gurion's side, they could not recall when he had ever hastened to defend any of them; they took his words as clear proof that he intended to give Dayan a senior post. Nor was that impression dispelled when Ben-Gurion admitted that Dayan was politically ignorant, or when he directed Dayan "to cease the speeches" until he finally left the IDF.

Meanwhile General de Gaulle's military-backed rise to power in France only intensified the veterans' fear of being excluded from the government by a similar secret plan; the putsch Isser Harel had warned against seemed now to be taking shape before their eyes. Despite the economic boom and the rewards of the Sinai victory, which raised the prospects of electoral gains for Mapai, the party leaders realized that the unabated internal conflict was liable to destroy their hopes. With Ben-Gurion's blessing, Eshkol and Josephtal undertook to sponsor a reconciliation between the veterans and the young men. Closed meetings were held on two separate Saturdays, November 22 and December 6, 1958, offering the adversaries an opportunity to hammer out a compromise.

The veterans held that the young men should bide their time; if Dayan waited patiently, he too would finally make it—in another thirteen years, according to Sapir. Ben-Gurion argued, "There is no need to grant [the young men] any special privileges; but equally, they should not be given less than others." Interpreting that remark as an indication of Ben-Gurion's bias towards the young men, the fearful veterans attacked him for "becoming the advocate of one side before hearing all the comrades." Aran said: "I read that when Eskimos grow old and their teeth drop out, they are removed far away to the snow with a little food, [and left] to die. But we veterans still have teeth !"

The party's malady resisted the offered remedy; the veterans remained convinced that Ben-Gurion intended to promote his young protégés and that after the elections, he planned to embark on his "revolution."

18

Under Fire from the Press

Outwardly at least, the new government seemed to be functioning smoothly; but signs of its impending demise appeared with increasing frequency. Commerce-and-industry minister Pinhas Sapir told Mapai's central committee that, on learning of the charges hanging over Elad, he had reproached former 131 commander Yossi Harel for keeping him in the dark. After Harel's retirement from MI and the army, he had gone into business, making him dependent upon Sapir. He now confided to the all-powerful minister everything he had heard from Harkabi about the falsification of documents and coordination of testimony, pointing out that no investigation had been held.

Instead of sending Harel to Ben-Gurion, Sapir decreed: "You must go and tell it to Lavon." Harel's version is different: "Sapir said: 'Lavon is dying.'" Lavon had a heart condition, and Harel recalls being horrified: "The man was going to die, and he'd never know what happened." According to him, it was this noble sentiment—not political conviction, nor a wish to ingratiate himself with Sapir—that induced him to act.

On February 4, 1960, Harel visited Lavon at home where, with Evron present, he told Lavon all he knew. Lavon drew up a written summary of what he later described as "testimony on forgeries and concealment of documents at MI"; according to him, Harel "said it was roughly accurate." Lavon told the Knesset foreign affairs and defense committee that

Harel had signed the summary, but that claim turned out to be false; Harel charged that Lavon "added things I didn't say." He also recalled Lavon saying: "I gave the order after the Operation had already been carried out." The next day, the ailing Lavon received a visit from Ben-Gurion, but did not tell him what he had learned from Harel.

On May 5, 1960, while conferring with Lavon about a teachers' dispute, Ben-Gurion referred to the "event in Egypt," telling Lavon: "At the time, I decided not to touch it, because I was dubious about the possibility of getting to the truth of the matter," but he had heard that Lavon was "embittered." Lavon replied "that he had been embittered for several years, but had calmed down in the past two years"; however, he now had "important testimony from Col. Harel . . . that documents were forged." That same day, at Ben-Gurion's request, Lavon sent him the "Harel testimony." Ben-Gurion thereupon instructed his ADC, Colonel Haim Ben-David, to examine the charge "that MI personnel falsified documents relating to the Egyptian affair." In this manner, Ben-Gurion began—after a delay of five years—to "deal with . . . 'the sorry business.'"

At this juncture, a number of questions must be asked: Did Ben-Gurion and Lavon act in good faith? If not, what secret end did each pursue? Had Lavon already planned his rehabilitation campaign, and was the "Harel testimony" the opening round? Why did Ben-Gurion pretend to know nothing of "forgeries," when he had heard the same charge from Harkabi in May 1955? Did he ask for the "Harel testimony" to find out what Lavon did or did not know? If he genuinely wished to get to the bottom of the matter, why did he not entrust the task to the general security service, which was adept in such matters, and had already touched upon "the sorry business" in its interrogation of Elad? At their meeting he and Lavon had been sniffing at one another, each trying to discover what the other was up to.

Although Haim Ben-David was unswervingly loyal to Ben-Gurion, he was inexperienced in investigations, and lacked the traits needed to pursue them. He lost no time in interviewing Harel and four officers employed at the MI laboratory. On May 10, he submitted an interim report which noted that the testimony of another officer, abroad on an assignment, was "likely to be decisive in establishing the truth, and without it, I am unable to reach final conclusions regarding the question you posed to me."

That same day, out of the blue, Ephraim Evron showed up at Ben-David's office. Putting his trust in Evron's loyalty to Ben-Gurion—as one who had served as Ben-Gurion's former secretary—Ben-David told Evron of his investigation and its findings. Evron promptly told Lavon about it. In time, Yitzhak Navon, then Ben-Gurion's political secretary, would recall Evron "turning up, friendly, [feeling] at home as a former secretary to the prime minister . . . saying from time to time: the Egyptian matter has to be sorted out."

Ben-David flew to Europe and met with the fifth officer, writing to Ben-Gurion that his testimony "reinforces my conviction that alteration(s) were indeed made at MI after the setback in Egypt." But Ben-Zur denied having requested anyone at MI "to change anything in any document." With that—and without drawing any conclusion or recommending any further action—Ben-David ended his investigation.

The submission of Ben-David's report coincided with the end of Elad's trial, creating a kind of hiatus, since the announcement of the verdict was postponed for a month because the presiding judge was abroad. Ben-Gurion deferred a decision on the steps to be taken; meanwhile, Lavon was recuperating in Switzerland, where he received updates from Evron.

The Elad verdict was handed down on August 21, 1960. The following day, the court sent an excerpt to chief of staff Laskov, stating that Elad "has proved *prima facie*, to the degree of persuasion required of a defendant at a criminal trial" that he "rendered perjured testimony" to the Olshan-Dori commission, and "lied" to the chief of staff and the defense minister, "at the solicitation" of his superiors, Givly and Ben-Zur.

On August 25, the chief of staff wrote to Ben-Gurion requesting instructions. The same day, Ben-Gurion conferred with Isser Harel and adopted his proposal to appoint a military board of inquiry. On the 27th, he consulted further with Harel, and on the 28th sent Laskov the following directives:

On my instructions, Colonel H. Ben-David has examined whether "alterations" were effected in a document at MI. . . . His examination resulted in grounds for assuming that such alterations were indeed effected (by one account—on the instructions of Colonel Benyamin Givly; by another account—of Lieutenant Colonel Mordechai Ben-Zur).

One must add to this the excerpt [from the Elad verdict] mentioned in your letter . . . of 25.8.60.

These matters are connected to "the affair of the setback in Egypt."

You are therefore required to appoint a duly-authorized military board of inquiry to thoroughly investigate this affair, and it may be necessary to summon Colonel Benyamin Givly to testify.

Evron hastened to Ben-Gurion's office, where he learned from Yitzhak Navon that the inquiry board's president would be Supreme Court judge Haim Cohen. He took a plane to Switzerland, to bear the tidings to Lavon. On September 12 the members of the inquiry board were appointed. Presiding as a military reservist, Justice Haim Cohen was granted the ceremonial rank of colonel. The board was required to find out "whether . . . Colonel B. Givly, Lieutenant Colonel M. Ben-Zur, or any other MI officer, [acted] to induce witnesses, . . . Avraham Seiden-berg (Elad) in particular, to render perjured testimony to [the Olshan-Dori commission] . . . and to the defense minister and chief of staff; and whether such perjured testimony was indeed rendered."

In limiting the inquiry to perjured testimony and falsification of doc-uments—and excluding "the setback in Egypt"—Ben-Gurion was cling-ing, in the interest of political expedience, to his resolve of 1955 not to "deal with" the Egyptian affair. That misjudgment would enmesh him in the greatest political imbroglio he ever experienced.

On September 18, Evron, newly returned from Switzerland, advised Ben-Gurion that Lavon objected to the appointment of Haim Cohen, and demanded that the inquiry be called off. By his own account, Ben-Gurion retorted: "That's none of [Lavon's] business. The board was appointed on my instruction as defense minister when rumors reached me that called for an investigation." The next day, a leading daily report-ed that Lavon's 1955 resignation from the defense ministry "will appar-ently soon come up for review" as a result of "events which have recently occurred."

The objectives Ben-Gurion and Lavon had been pursuing at their May 5 meeting now began to emerge. Lavon had long propounded the following argument: if Givly had had to resort to lies and forgery to prove that Lavon gave the order, that in itself was clear evidence that he did not give it, and that Givly acted on his own. Lavon had therefore sub-mitted Harel's testimony to Ben-Gurion as evidence of his innocence, which, he claimed, had been further validated by Ben-David's findings and the Elad trial verdict. Thus elevating his deduction into decisive proof that he had been the victim of "a conspiracy" of MI officers, Lavon had little difficulty in propagating the notion that Peres and Dayan had had a hand in it.

This then was the arsenal Lavon had built up for his campaign, which he now threatened to unleash, unless Ben-Gurion promptly exonerated him. In his view, the inquiry board was nothing but a trick to deny him the acquittal he deserved; it proved that Ben-Gurion feared disclosure of the "conspiracy" and was sacrificing truth and justice to defend his young protégés. Lavon's evident readiness to use all the means at his disposal vindicated Ben-Gurion's prudence at their May encounter, when he concealed his long-standing knowledge of the substance of Harel's testimony.

When Ben-Gurion refused to call off the inquiry, Lavon brought his campaign out into the open, demanding immediate affirmation of his innocence. On September 19, Evron, at Lavon's request, met with Aryeh Dissentshik, editor of the daily *Maariv*, and his deputy Shalom Rosenfeld, to impart to them all the information he had gleaned at Ben-Gurion's office and enroll them into the Lavon camp.

The following day, September 20—one day before Lavon was to return to Israel—*Maariv* submitted to the military censor a news article full of sensational revelations and editorial comments. It started with the inaccurate claim that Ben-Gurion had appointed the Cohen inquiry to study "the testimony that caused Lavon's resignation from the government in 1955." The Cohen board had been instituted secretly, but the paper's scoop laid the groundwork for Lavon to make his campaign public. *Maariv* asserted that Lavon "is not interested in further inquiries, and will settle for a statement to the cabinet and the Knesset foreign affairs and defense committee that he suffered an injustice, and that the accusations leveled at him were unfounded . . . [as were] the demands for his resignation." Lavon claimed "that the Olshan-Dori commission's findings rested upon unreliable testimony and . . . on documents prepared . . . in advance of the inquiry" (the implication being that they had been doctored); those findings were refuted by "new testimony and evidence" that had come to light. "The decisive turn," wrote *Maariv*, came about when "one of those principally involved" in the Lavon affair "admitted . . . that he perverted his testimony to the Olshan-Dori commission so as to cast [suspicion] upon Mr. Lavon, and protect other persons implicated. . . ." The article concluded that "several Mapai ministers support Lavon's demand that the matter be brought to the cabinet's attention, and . . . his name . . . be cleared without further investigation or delay."

The censor stalled, and it was September 25 before a summary version of the article was published under a three-line headline spanning six front-page columns. That same day, deputy editor Rosenfeld, who had written the *Maariv* editorials with Dissentshik, warned Mapai's new secretary, Yosef Almogi, that he sensed "an enormous snowball beginning to roll, and who can foresee the outcome?"

Rosenfeld's prognostication, while apt, was due less to the prophetic spirit than to the briefing he had received from Evron. Without bothering to corroborate the claims of a man they trusted, *Maariv*'s editors allowed themselves to be convinced that Lavon had fallen victim to a "conspiracy." The other papers also ran front-page stories reiterating *Maariv*'s exclusives and daily reports about Lavon, supporting him both before and after a meeting between him and Ben-Gurion, scheduled for September 26.

At this point some details should be offered about the character and background of *Maariv*. The paper was closely linked with the Mapai establishment, which was both the source of its reports and the object of its loyalty. At the same time, possibly because most of its editorial staff were followers of the late Ze'ev Jabotinsky, the paper was eager to diminish the stature of Jabotinsky's historic adversary, David Ben-Gurion. The "Lavon affair" offered it a rare opportunity to serve the establishment, while simultaneously settling scores with the man at its head.

Ever since "the sorry business" had occurred, every paper had received leaks, from Lavon's camp and from Ben-Gurion's equally. During Lavon's first campaign, in 1955, his adversaries' leaks had proved more effective. But in the second round, the pro-Lavon sources had a decisive edge. Besides his own immediate followers, they also included Ben-Gurion's opponents.

Maariv was not alone in taking sides; but it was the paper with the largest circulation, and it backed Lavon without reservation. Arguably, *Maariv* was the decisive weapon in Lavon's assault on public opinion; its editors could not have been unaware that the campaign for Lavon soon escalated into a campaign against Ben-Gurion.

Lavon's meeting with Ben-Gurion on September 26, 1960, in Jerusalem, was that day's main story in *Maariv*, whose editors seemed familiar with every detail: the two were to confer after the cabinet meeting; Lavon would demand rehabilitation; Ben-Gurion would explain the circumstances surrounding the appointment of the Cohen board.

The article describing the meeting was matched by an editorial supporting Lavon's demand for rehabilitation: "*If* the Cohen board was appointed to establish the truth and the facts—and swiftly do justice, purge the air of rumor and elucidate accusations, including some of the gravest—*may blessings rain upon it* (italics added)." *Maariv* thus cast doubt upon the board's intentions. Riding roughshod over the truth in pursuit of their own ends, the editors knew the board had been created for the single purpose of discovering whether there had been solicitation to perjury and forgery within MI.

The editorial's final paragraph contained a veiled threat:

> Confidence is not acquired exclusively in elections and votes of confidence. It is acquired first and foremost through the public's perception that justice is done in the land, and that purity and good intentions predominate at the top echelons of government. That perception requires reinforcement.

The obvious implication: should Ben-Gurion defy *Maariv*'s dictate by declining to clear Lavon, it would prove that he was covering for his young protégés, and that he was not guided by the pure pursuit of justice.

At their meeting, Lavon urged Ben-Gurion to call off the Cohen board; when Ben-Gurion refused, he challenged Haim Cohen's appointment as presiding officer. Ben-Gurion expressed full confidence in Cohen. Lavon then urged Ben-Gurion to proclaim his lack of responsibility for "the sorry business." Again, Ben-Gurion refused. He wrote to his daughter Renana in London that he had told Lavon: "Pinhas, I didn't condemn you, but I'm no judge, and I can't acquit you because . . . I thereby condemn Givly. . . . Even if I were to proclaim your innocence, no one is bound to take my word for it because I am neither investigator nor judge."

Ben-Gurion's rendition of the exchange with Lavon was also featured in a press release published on October 2. Here too, Ben-Gurion specified that he saw "no need or obligation to exonerate him: a. because I did not condemn him; b. if someone condemned him, exonerating him is not within my power. I am neither investigator nor judge. I did not pass judgement upon anyone, least of all Lavon, nor will I take it upon myself to pass judgment." He stressed that "I did not counsel Lavon to appear before the inquiry commission, and such a thing did not occur to me."

On the 27th, *Maariv* cited "informed circles" to assert that "the two men did not reach agreement on termination of the affair." The paper deferred full publication of their exchange, clearly because immediate publication would reveal that Lavon, who had initiated the meeting, was also the source of information about it. In the days to come, *Maariv*'s main headlines and front-page editorials blazoned further exclusives.

The paper reported that Givly[1]—currently military attaché in London—had been summoned to Israel to testify to the Cohen board. "Lavon will not consent to appear as witness." Though aware that Lavon had invited himself before the Knesset foreign affairs and defense committee, *Maariv* attributed the initiative to the committee: "Demands are growing for an early meeting of the Knesset's foreign affairs and defense committee, to hear Lavon's own explanations of the affair."

In an editorial published on the 27th under the headline "The prime minister must speak out," *Maariv* challenged Ben-Gurion: "The findings at hand are certainly sufficient to put a public and statesmanlike end to this affair" by immediately exonerating Lavon. Everything now depended upon the prime minister: "The state will be tested by the degree of courage it shows in redressing the injustice and ridding itself of the *elements and public figures* (italics added) who maliciously embroiled him in this mess. We await word from the prime minister."

The term "elements" seemed to refer to Givly and his henchmen; but who were the "public figures"? Was *Maariv* not pursuing Lavon's demand of February 1955 by likewise calling for the dismissal of Peres and Dayan? The paper told its readers nothing of Lavon's reckless policies during his tenure as defense minister, nor his habit of flouting the prime minister, nor his faulty working procedures, nor his turbulent relationship with the chief of staff and defense ministry director-general. Nor did it do anything to dispel the false impression that Dayan and Peres had abetted the MI officers conspiring to overthrow Lavon. Furthermore, after denouncing the appointment of the Cohen inquiry board, *Maariv* made it the target of a demand for "a purge of the administration"—a reference to Dayan and Peres and other Ben-Gurion aides. Ben-Gurion got the point, as a later remark indicates: "Lavon may be aiming mainly at Peres, and perhaps, Dayan." With other papers reprinting its exclusives, *Maariv* became a newsmaker in its own right; its revelations convinced large portions of the Israeli public of the justice of Lavon's campaign.

After speaking with Ben-Gurion, Mapai secretary Yosef Almogi told a press conference that the party would not discuss the Lavon affair; he reassured the central committee that Lavon did not need rehabilitation, and was not slated to appear before the Cohen board. Lavon concurred: "The party has no forum to handle this matter" and "should not stick its

---

1. In deference to the censor, "the affair's" main protagonists, though widely known, were referred to by pseudonyms: Givly was "the senior officer"; Ben-Zur, "the reserve officer"; Elad, "the third man"; and so on. The pseudonyms have been replaced here by the actual names.

nose in." He was present when Mapai's secretariat similarly decided that "this affair will not be considered by [any] party forum."

But when Lavon took the floor at that same meeting, he spiced an implied attack on Dayan and Peres with the blunt warning: "This time, it won't be . . . someone talking and someone [else] holding his tongue. . . . For every statement, there will be a resounding reply, and there'll be no shutting of mouths, not even [on the pretext of] the sanctity of the IDF." In other words, in his battle for rehabilitation—including his statement to the Knesset foreign affairs and defence committee—he would stop at nothing.

Dining at Lavon's home on October 3, Almogi suggested that he conduct himself with moderation at the Knesset panel. As Almogi later recalled, Lavon paled, his features contorted with rage, and he gave vent to an explosive outburst: "I am prepared," he shouted, "to go one-on-one with anyone, even if it goes against the party, to uncover the conspiracy concocted against me !"

On October 4, Almogi drove to Sdeh Boker, where Ben-Gurion was spending the weekend, to alert him. But Ben-Gurion was unperturbed; that same day, he noted in his diary:

> Almogi came at 9:30. He is worried over "the Lavon affair." . . . He believes Lavon is possessed of a demon, and nothing exists in his world outside of "the affair." He is abetted by a whole bevy of journalists led by Levi Yitzhak [Hayerushalmi]. . . . Almogi fears that the psychosis which has seized the public is only beginning. I told him I do not share his alarm . . . No conspiracy, no incitement or molding of public opinion can long withstand the truth.

This passage contains two points worthy of note: it was the first time Ben-Gurion specified—if only by first name—the man responsible for the leaks to *Maariv*; and it shows him alert to the public outcry but secure in his statesmanlike course of bringing the Cohen inquiry's findings before the cabinet, which would then decide how to act.

The mistake Ben-Gurion made was with respect to the party. If he was aware that the veterans were closing ranks around Sapir and the Bloc, he failed to gauge their full potential; nor did he foresee their attack being directed at him, nor the transformation of support for Lavon into a weapon against himself. Confident of the loyalty of the old guard, Ben-Gurion felt secure in the power it granted him.

19

"Dreyfusiada"

Ben-Gurion's position regarding the Lavon affair, as set forth in his October 2 press release, was summarized in the oft-repeated statement that, not having condemned Lavon, he was not bound to exonerate him. Lavon should properly demand exculpation from Sharett. Having washed his hands of "the sorry business" in 1955, and having disregarded its aftermath on his return to the defense ministry, Ben-Gurion still refused to take sides in 1960.

On September 29, he wrote Sharett requesting the Olshan-Dori commission's terms of reference and asking whether Lavon or he himself had proposed appointing it. He also wondered about the connection between the commission's report and Lavon's resignation, for the Knesset record stated that "Lavon imparted the grounds for his resignation to the prime minister and the Knesset's foreign affairs and defense committee." In this manner Ben-Gurion was suggesting that anything that had occurred during Sharett's tenure in office that required elucidation or rectification was exclusively Sharett's responsibility.

Before Sharett could reply, Ben-Gurion sent him a second letter dated October 1: it had come to his notice that Lavon had demanded reforms in the defense establishment, and resigned when Sharett had rejected them. "If those proposals from Lavon are not a secret between you and him," Ben-Gurion wrote, "I would be grateful if you could notify me what was the program of radical reforms that Lavon proposed."

If Ben-Gurion expected Sharett to pull his chestnuts out of the fire by conceding accountability for the affair, he was in for a disappointment. No longer on speaking terms with Ben-Gurion, Sharett did not respond to the friendly tone of his letters, prefacing his reply with: "Greetings, prime minister!"

That same October 2, Sharett had a three-hour talk with Lavon during which time he probably showed Lavon the letters from Ben-Gurion. The influence of Lavon's responses appear manifest in his reply to Ben-Gurion.

Sharett detailed his dealings with Lavon in the wake of the affair. Lavon had advocated separating the defense ministry into three divisions, each of which would be accountable directly to the defense minister "after the post of director-general was abolished." Sharett's rejection of this plan was among the grounds for Lavon's resignation.

Sharett wrote that there seemed to be "some misunderstanding between you and Lavon; as I am given to understand . . . Lavon does not refer to the findings of the [Olshan-Dori] commission, but to some internal MI report [the Harel testimony] verifying the justice of his claim." Hence, Lavon's quarrel was not with the Olshan-Dori commission—for which Sharett was accountable—but with the officers who had conspired against him, and who came under Ben-Gurion's purview.

On October 10, Ben-Gurion, having been rebuffed by Sharett, invited to his office the five non-Mapai ministers who had served in Sharett's cabinet. He asked them whether Lavon's resignation had been brought about by the affair or by the rejection of his reform proposal and went on to suggest that it was up to Sharett to exonerate Lavon. He then inquired, "Why had they not demanded a cabinet discussion [of Lavon's resignation], instead of leaving [the] matter between the prime minister and minister of defense?" To Ben-Gurion's vexation, as he noted in his diary, "I received no satisfactory answer." His guests were more sympathetic to Sharett than to him.

On the same day this meeting was to take place, *Maariv* appeared with a banner headline that heralded "a new phase in the Lavon affair" and the escalation of the conflict. The following day, October 11, its main headline reported the Lavon affair taking "a turn for the worse," which "occurred yesterday, when Ben-Gurion openly sided with Peres and targeted Lavon for a fierce attack." Only much further into the unsigned report did the reader learn that Ben-Gurion had not assailed Lavon in public, but "at a meeting with the ministers of the minority factions in Sharett's cabinet." Under the byline of the paper's political correspondent, Moshe Meisels, the same issue published "a full report" of the meeting, with Ben-Gurion quoted as admitting his disappointment with Lavon as defense minister; he had "no idea what an army is" and was unaware that "an army isn't a construction company, and army officers are not clerks in uniform." Ben-Gurion accused Lavon of planning an onslaught upon Peres and Dayan, whose gifts and achievements, he said, were admirable, and likewise upon himself.

The paper received this detailed account from Yosef Serlin, who had been health minister under Sharett and was already known to have leaked confidential cabinet proceedings. To conceal Serlin's role, Dissentshik sent Meisels to Serlin to get his account of the meeting. Feigning surprise, Serlin assured Meisels that his word of honor to Ben-Gurion precluded such a breach of confidence. Consequently Meisels was astonished the following day to find himself identified as the author of the full published report. Serlin had delivered the minutes of the meeting directly to Dissentshik, and could therefore affirm on oath that he had revealed nothing to Meisels. Not for nothing did Ben-Gurion call Serlin "the villain." The "turn for the worse" was thus *Maariv*'s doing, and it was Dissentshik who manufactured the scoop that made Ben-Gurion a party to the Lavon affair.

During the three-week period between September 26 and October 18, the Lavon affair was taken up by the Knesset foreign affairs and defense committee, by the Cohen commission, and by Mapai. But the affair's ultimate effects were determined less by the actual events than by the way they were reported in the press. The coverage extended even to the proceedings of the foreign affairs and defense committee, whose publication was explicitly forbidden by law. Most of the leaks came from Lavon's camp, abetted by rival parties that leaped at the rare opportunity to settle accounts with the Mapai establishment and its leader. Ben-Gurion's side evened the score with leaks of its own. It was a media-fest without equal, which proceeded unabated even after the committee's members had sworn under oath to keep their deliberations confidential.

The Lavon affair resurfaced in 1960 because of Elad's confession to having perjured himself before the Olshan-Dori commission, on the instructions of his superiors. Accurate enough in itself, this fact was vastly inflated by the press, which depicted the scandal as tarring the entire "defense establishment"—a broad concept embracing the IDF, the defense ministry and the minister at their head. With military censorship keeping the public ignorant of the true details, rumors inflated the scandal to mythical dimensions. In this setting, the press portrayed Lavon as a saint waging a plucky defense against the false accusations that had forced his 1955 resignation. It was widely agreed that good guy Lavon had been the victim of attack from bad guy Ben-Gurion. The Cohen board was depicted as Ben-Gurion's tool for whitewashing the guilty and concealing a secret conspiracy. The Knesset foreign affairs and defense committee was presented as intending to conduct a full and unbiased investigation however painful the results might be to individuals and groups.

The press generated the impression that the affair was the fault of "Ben-Gurion's boys"—those army officers and government officials who took shelter under the prime minister's wings. With the principal protagonists cloaked by pseudonyms to bypass the military censor, public attention focused upon Dayan and Peres, and, of course, their patron, Ben-Gurion. When *Maariv* wrote that "representatives of all parties" on the Knesset foreign affairs and defense committee were resolved "not to permit the affair to be whitewashed," and to have "the guilty punished, whoever they were," everyone assumed it referred to Dayan and Peres.

To the uninitiated, the press reports led to a single conclusion: anyone who valued truth and justice was bound to side with Lavon's courageous campaign by demanding he be acquitted of the false charges against him, and that those who had conspired against him, however eminent, be punished. Accusing fingers pointed at Ben-Gurion.

As the Cohen inquiry had established that Elad's testimony to Olshan and Dori was perjured, Eshkol convinced Sharett and Lavon to adopt the course Ben-Gurion had originally proposed. In an interview granted at his own prompting, Sharett declared himself "certain that, had the facts established by the Cohen board been known at the time, they would have offered substantial proof that the accusations then leveled at Pinhas Lavon regarding direct responsibility [for the Egyptian operation] were false." On October 2, the day the interview was published, Lavon commented: "Insofar as I am concerned, I consider the affair closed [in view of] Sharett's statement published today." The next day Eshkol declared he was "gratified by Lavon's statement."

But Ben-Gurion was no longer prepared to rest content with this solution. Mortally offended by the statements Lavon made to the Knesset foreign affairs and defense committee, and the campaign of incitement he and his allies conducted in the press, Ben-Gurion refused to stomach the insult.

Lavon chose to address the Knesset foreign affairs and defense committee because of the prospect of political profit this offered. He knew that Mapai's adversaries, seizing upon this rare opportunity to make hay at the expense of the ruling party, would be supported by Ben-Gurion's rivals within Mapai, swinging a majority of the committee behind him.

Lavon appeared four times before the committee, on October 4, 11, 17, and 20, creating consternation in Mapai; he was widely accused of "exceeding all bounds." Aran, who supported him, told the Mapai secretariat of his "horror" at Lavon's statements; Sharett characterized them as "a weave of atrocities." Another party member portrayed Lavon as "picking up an axe and embarking upon mayhem."

Lavon depicted the defense establishment under chief of staff Dayan and director-general Peres as irresponsible and out of control. Confronting "a defense minister who spends the entire day and all his time at the ministry," preoccupied exclusively with defense affairs and "unwilling to be a mere figurehead," the two men had begun to act without his knowledge or approval. In view of their indifference to his directives, "the question arose: does the defense minister possess any powers?"

In his first address to the Knesset committee, in which he unraveled the mystery of the affair and the lies and forgeries that brought about his overthrow, Lavon revealed that he had demanded Peres's removal as far back as 1955. *Maariv* reported that "The committee listened astounded, and resolved to proceed with the inquiry," adding that Lavon's testimony had "stunned even those members familiar with the affair." It was easily deduced that Peres was among the leading conspirators.

Lavon's third appearance before the committee was prefaced in *Maariv*'s October 14 issue with an article by Shalom Rosenfeld entitled: "The business—sorry indeed," which implied that Ben-Gurion helped cover up the falsification of testimony and documents. Even within Mapai, the impression was growing that Ben-Gurion was unjustly persecuting Lavon and publicly slandering him. This impression was reflected in "an open letter to the prime minister" signed by seventy-four members of Kibbutz Hulda, graduates of the "Gordoniya" youth movement Lavon had once headed. Published October 17 in *Maariv* and the Histadrut daily *Davar*, the letter said, "We fail to comprehend why you had to proclaim that, were you to face a choice between Pinhas Lavon and Shimon Peres, you would choose the latter." The letter concluded by asking Ben-Gurion whether he did not think that, "precisely at this time," when the affair was being deliberated by the Knesset foreign affairs and defense committee, "it was the prime minister's obligation to withhold any utterance showing partiality, or open to interpretation as such?" Accordingly, "not only we, loyal followers of Pinhas Lavon, but many thousands of Mapai members, are amazed at your conduct, as prime minister and leader of Mapai."

Ben-Gurion was "offended" by the letter, but above all he was hurt by analogies that were being drawn between the Lavon affair and the Dreyfus affair in France. Newspaper articles that made the comparison cast Lavon in the role of Dreyfus, the innocent victim of a smear; Ben-Gurion was depicted standing behind the conspiracy allegedly hatched in 1955 to overthrow Lavon.

The term "Dreyfusiada"(a sardonic neologism that can be translated as "Dreyfus festival") was first used by an Ahdut HaAvodah paper, followed by *Maariv*. In an interview published on October 14 under the heading: "There is a danger of military dictatorship in the country!" Mapam leader Meir Ya'ari warned that Ben-Gurion posed a serious threat. Recalling the latter's account of "persons" who told him "that it is vital to disperse the Knesset and establish a dictatorship," Ya'ari said he had "no doubt that such a group exists"; "it is the group surrounding Ben-Gurion. I refer to the persons involved in all this 'Dreyfusiada.' . . . We are all at risk—all of us, even Mapai itself!" Other papers took a similar tone.

Ben-Gurion criticized the Knesset foreign affairs and defense committee in scathing terms. It was not objective, he asserted, and therefore had no right to sit in judgment. He accused the press, *Maariv* in particular, of misrepresenting him and setting him up to be blamed for the "Dreyfusiada." And in fact, the use of that term revealed *Maariv* as the axis of the broadest and most comprehensive coalition ever forged against Ben-Gurion. It embraced left and right, extending from street-corner demagogues to philosophers, from pioneer farmers to Mapai party officials.

Ben-Gurion directed particularly bitter attacks at Mapai's representatives on the Knesset committee. At a secretariat meeting on October 18 and at the following day's session of the party central committee, he condemned their silence in the face of lies and slanders. Some were eager "to conduct a 'Dreyfusiada', and those capable of silencing them, don't," he said, alluding to Sharett. After all, "silence implies consent." Did his colleagues agree that he had gone along with a conspiracy of lies and forgery against Lavon? The party's representatives on the committee "did not deny it" during the three meetings devoted to the Lavon affair.

Maariv, fully briefed on party secrets, reported on the 18th that the secretariat had been "convened at the demand of several members who argued" that the party could no longer sit by inactive. In this fashion, without rescinding its earlier decision not to discuss the matter, Mapai entered into the complexities of the Lavon affair.

The Cohen board's report, submitted on October 15, 1960, gave Ben-Gurion clear grounds for claiming that Lavon's demand for rehabilitation was unsupported by its conclusions. Cohen and his colleagues found that it had not been established—either by Elad's testimony at his trial, the "Harel testimony," or the Ben-David report—that Lavon's resignation was the result of perjury and forgery. The board also "concluded that those alleged forgeries . . . have not been proved," for "there is before us no scrap of evidence" that any documents were prepared at the MI documentation department laboratory in order "to serve as evidence at any proceedings." Based on testimony by a police forensic expert, the report also asserted that "Givly's letter was sent to the chief of staff on July 19, 1954, and contained the same two pages of which a copy is now in our hands, without any alteration being made."

Ben-Gurion could feel pleased that the forgery charges leveled at his officers had been dismissed by the board. But he was dissatisfied that it stopped short of unequivocally vindicating the IDF, the crowning glory of his life's work. The board linked Ben-Zur's October 5, 1954, report and Almog's meeting with Elad in Paris on January 2, 1955, noting that "in the letter sent to Elad via Almog, Ben-Zur, with Givly's approval, took steps to induce Elad to submit to the Olshan-Dori commission testimony of one kind, and not another." The report rejected Almog's professed ignorance of the contents of the letter he delivered to Elad in Paris:

> We do not believe Almog's [claim] that the purpose of his mission was not known to him, and we think that Almog did not tell us the whole truth . . . concealing from us matters he knows and remembers well. . . . We have expressed to him our concerns . . . that he is unfit to serve in a responsible capacity in the state's security services.

The board believed that Almog had been sent to Paris to make sure Elad's testimony to the Olshan-Dori commission refuted Ben-Zur's

October 5 report to Dayan and its assertion that 131 had carried out the July 2 and 14, 1954, operations. The board also rejected attempts by Ben-Zur and Givly to explain away the discrepancies between their story and the Ben-Zur report, asserting that the report had been brought to Givly's attention when he returned to Israel on October 20:

> Had it contained a flaw or error or inaccuracy—doubly so if there were willful falsification—for whatever reason, it would not have been left in its extant wording. Having been left as it was on the day of its submission, no wonder it offers evidence to refute a conflicting version first related much later.

The board accordingly deduced that "the instructions Ben-Zur gave Elad in late May 1954 were not just communications instructions, and the operations referred to therein were indeed carried out by our people" in keeping with those instructions. In putting words into Elad's mouth, Givly and Ben-Zur knowingly "solicited perjury," which is why "Givly delegated the task to a man like Almog, and all the aforementioned steps were taken to ensure its success." The board did not doubt that the subornation of Elad also extended to his conversations with the chief of staff and defense minister.

While discovering no evidence of documents being tampered with, the Cohen board did find that some had been spirited away, including a report Ben-Zur claimed to have submitted immediately after his Paris meeting with Elad in late May 1954, and the record of a meeting concerning the Egyptian episode attended by Givly, Ben-Zur, Avraham Dar, Yossi Harel, and Elad. The board commented: "Were there anything in that record to refute the October 5, 1954, report, it should have been brought up before us; but all the searches for it have been fruitless."

Documents relating to Elad's instructions, which should have been housed in the unit's archive, had "vanished, apparently as far back as early 1955." Ben-Zur denied complicity,

> but it cannot be overlooked that he and Givly alone could have had an interest in the disappearance of those documents. . . . We are in no doubt that they did not vanish fortuitously, but were purposely spirited away—although we have before us no adequate evidence pointing to the responsibility of any particular individual.

With respect to Ben-Zur the board concluded:

We regret to affirm that Ben-Zur perjured himself under oath, before us and before the Jerusalem district court; but we incline to believe that it was his stupidity, not his malice, that motivated him.

About Givly, the conclusion was:

We are in no doubt but that he knew and remembered more than he was prepared to testify before us, and we regret not having received from him that full and frank testimony we could have expected of him. We also noted with regret that he found fit, in his testimony before us, to shrug off responsibility for his subordinates' deeds, which were unquestionably carried out in coordination with him, if not on his specific instructions.

The Cohen report concluded that further questioning of Harkabi, Yossi Harel, Shalom Weiss (of MI's documentation department), and Dalia Carmel was likely to shed light on "the one matter still calling for examination"—namely, whether the documents Givly submitted to the Olshan-Dori commission were forged; and whether Dalia Carmel, acting "on Givly's instructions," altered entries in the "notebook."

The Cohen board's characterization of Givly, Ben-Zur and Almog indicated that Ben-Gurion's IDF was not as pure as the driven snow. This made it increasingly hard for Ben-Gurion to claim that exonerating Lavon would entail condemnation of an honorable officer, for Givly could no longer be depicted as the embodiment of innocence.

In addition, the finding that Ben-Zur had met with Elad in late May 1954 to give him operational instructions undermined Ben-Gurion's contention that Givly's resort to lies was not decisive proof that he gave the order for the operation in Egypt. The Cohen report established that Elad's perjured testimony was to conceal that he had in fact given the order.

Ben-Gurion found the board's report hard to take. He forbade its release, approving publication only of the fact that it had been submitted to him, and that he had referred it—on October 18, 1960, the day of his embittered address to the Mapai secretariat—to Attorney-General Gideon Hausner for a studied opinion.

Between the lines of Ben-Gurion's letter to Hausner appear signs of his efforts to control the damage inflicted by the Cohen report. He put three questions to the Attorney-General, worded so as to elicit negative answers which he could make public to validate his position. (The questions are listed out of sequence for the logic of the argumentation.)

1. In the board's findings, or in the testimony submitted to it, are there grounds for any person to be put on trial on charges of forgery, perjury or any other offense . . . ?

3. Has it emerged from this investigation that any forgery was perpetrated in relation to "the sorry business"?

Ben-Gurion knew that a combination of legal quibbles, inapplicability, and the statute of limitations would dictate negative answers to these two questions. But they were both overshadowed by the intervening second question:

2. Does any conclusion arise from the inquiry board's investigation and findings to the question: who gave the order for "the sorry business"? Or did the entire inquiry . . . not relate in any way to "the sorry business"?

Having personally drafted the Cohen board's terms of reference, Ben-Gurion knew that this question too would elicit a negative reply. The last part of his letter betrays his intention:

If you find no grounds, based on the findings, to place any person on trial, return the file to me, and it will be preserved in confidentiality until the chief of staff decides what is to be done with it.

Ben-Gurion then went on to protect his flanks:

With the concurrence of the chief of staff, I have decided that, pending your replies, Col. B. Givly will not be permitted to occupy any post in the army.

Hausner's reply, dated October 21, concluded that "there is no scope for embarking upon investigation, or placing anyone on trial" on the strength of the board's findings, "with the possible exception of the indictment of Mordechai Ben-Zur" (on charges of a coverup). As to the crucial second question,

the answer lies in the Cohen board's terms of reference. The board was not appointed to investigate or establish who gave the orders for "the sorry business," and its inquiries therefore did not relate thereto. Accordingly, my answer to Question 2. . . . is that the Cohen board did not touch upon this matter directly.

This was the answer Ben-Gurion wanted. He approved the release of Hausner's opinion, and it was published in all the papers, although Hausner concluded his letter by noting that "the Cohen board's investigations did not establish whether or not any forgery was committed in relation to 'the sorry business,' but investigation of that matter should be completed."

Hausner came to Ben-Gurion's Tel Aviv home to present his opinion; in the course of their talk, he said that "the Cohen board findings per se . . . can resolve the stalemate arrived at by the Olshan-Dori commission" and lead to "a certain clearcut conclusion." In other words, however inconclusive the findings were, they still provided sufficient grounds to exonerate Lavon "with no need for further investigation."

Now that all parties had welcomed Sharett's public statement releasing Lavon from responsibility for "the sorry business," Ben-Gurion spurned it—due in no small measure to his wounded vanity. He may now have realized how misguided he had been when he failed to order a thorough investigation to establish responsibility for the Egyptian calamity in 1955. But there was no turning back the clock, and he now faced a choice: he could either follow the recommendations of Gideon Hausner and the Cohen board by appointing a new inquiry to complete the investigation of the forgeries; or, he could appoint a full-fledged state inquiry commission to determine who was to blame.

Ben-Gurion opted for the second alternative, insisting that only a "judicial inquiry" could have the authority to make a judgment and lay the affair finally to rest. By this he meant a state inquiry commission duly constituted under the 1921 Commissions of Inquiry ordinance, empowered to question witnesses under oath; he envisaged the commission chaired by a judge, and its members, unlike the partisan politicians on the Knesset foreign affairs and defense committee, would be "objective."

From the perspective of the national interest, he was doubtless right, as indicated by the fact that Israel's 1968 law on inquiry commissions, "in essence reflecting the views of David Ben-Gurion," remains in force to this day. But history rarely grants a second chance. What had been feasible in 1955 was out of the question in 1960, with the press, public opinion, and the parties—including considerable portions of Mapai—now supporting Lavon and opposing a further inquiry. Politically, Ben-Gurion was utterly misguided; an unswerving adherence to a hopeless cause was one of the worst mistakes a politician could make, and he made it.

20

Eshkol the Healer

Ben-Gurion's unrelenting demand for a "judicial inquiry" to investigate "the sorry business" and Lavon's resignation came into conflict with the equally vigorous opposition of Lavon and his numerous supporters, who demanded his immediate rehabilitation or, failing that, resumption of the Knesset panel's hearings. One grievance both sides shared, however, was that the party's three senior leaders—Eshkol, Meir and Sapir—had been abroad ever since the affair's re-emergence had rocked party and country.

On October 11, 1960, even before the Cohen board had completed its work, Ephraim Evron had flown to New York. Dalia Carmel, who was staying with Eshkol at the Essex hotel, recalls being highly offended when Evron entered their room in the afternoon, and "requested me to leave."

Let us return to Carmel. In May 1957, while returning to Israel by sea, she had run into "Palmoni" (a pseudonym; the man is now a prominent businessman), an acquaintance from the London embassy. A senior finance ministry department chief fourteen years her senior, he was married, with children. On this voyage they had a shipboard romance which unfolded into a years-long love affair.

According to Palmoni, Carmel had "much personal charm, affection, and a flair for culture." But he found her weak in character, and still devoted to Givly. Although never romantically intimate with him, she remained under his influence even after her resignation from the army. She confided to Palmoni her account of altering the copy of Givly's July 19, 1954, letter to Dayan. Palmoni recalled that she had shared the story "with everyone close to her," and judged this to be an effort "to break away from Givly."

Palmoni told Carmel of a vacancy at the finance minister's office. In November 1957, she became Eshkol's principal secretary; soon, she says, "we were very good friends." She, "so loving, loyal, open"; he, in need of support and understanding outside the office. Elisheva, Eshkol's wife and the mother of his children, had died of a malignant illness in 1959, whereupon Carmel shouldered part of his domestic burdens: "I ran errands and looked after things and did his packing and tidied up—far beyond what a secretary should do." A growing portion of her day was spent at work with Eshkol, and in the company of his family and himself.

Eshkol's personal interest in Carmel also grew, bridging the forty-year age difference between them. Learning of her affair with Palmoni, he grew jealous and treated her with marked coolness. Whenever she was not with him, Eshkol suspected her of cavorting with Palmoni. At the same time, the long hours she spent with Eshkol convinced Palmoni that they were lovers. As a result, "Eshkol would detain me as long as possible so I wouldn't get to Palmoni," while the latter, "terribly jealous," would spy on her "and snoop among my neighbors to find out if there was anyone" at her home.

Eshkol knew of Carmel's past service with MI, and her conviction that "Lavon is a pathological liar." He also became aware of her adulation of Givly. In January 1960, the finance minister's office received a list of colonels due for promotion to Major general. Carmel demanded to know why Givly's name was not on it. She says Eshkol explained that this was because of suspicions of "forgeries at the time of 'the affair.' Givly will never make Major general, he has nothing at all to look forward to." Eshkol's words left Carmel dazed. "I concluded that I had committed a forgery. And I hadn't forgotten it. It can hardly be said that I passed it over, or forgot it."

Shortly afterwards, when Ben-Zur visited—"he would come around and see me at the office regularly once a month"—she asked: "I'm curious to know whether we did the forgeries at Givly's bidding, or was it your idea?"

To which Ben-Zur replied, "Why, do you want to go to the police?"

Carmel, replying, "I don't want to go to the police. I want to know," made Ben-Zur promise not to tell Givly about this exchange.

A few days later, Givly's nomination as military attaché in London became public. Calling him to congratulate him, Carmel was startled to discover that Ben-Zur had not kept his pledge. Promising to answer her question, Givly invited her to lunch. But their get-together was cut short by a phone call summoning Givly to return immediately to his Central Command office, and Carmel lost her chance to learn whether he had instigated the forgery.

After she had worked for Eshkol for three years, he got her a job at the New York office of the Israel Development Bonds. She flew to New York on September 4, 1960. On September 1—three weeks before the eruption of "the Lavon affair"—Eshkol had embarked on a tour of the capitals of Europe and the United States. He arrived in New York on the 8th, to attend a Bonds convention, World Bank meetings, and other engagements.

A new chapter commenced in Carmel's life. As they worked side-by-side at the Essex hotel, their friendship flowered into love. Despite the great age difference, the attraction was not hard to understand: the towering Eshkol was an attractive man, sagacious and charming, with laughing eyes and cheerful features. He exuded avuncular warmth and affection, and his sense of humor was second to none.

Evron's trip to the United States was confidential. Only much later did he reveal that its purpose was to update Eshkol on the affair, and alert him "that a major crisis was about to erupt, and he had better return as soon as possible to quell the tempest and find a way to douse the conflagration before it spread."

However, Eshkol did not leave New York until October 17, his scheduled date of return. Meanwhile, on October 14, *Maariv* reported growing pressure within Mapai to set aside the secretariat's previous decision and discuss the affair, with proposals for "a select body" of leaders, including Eshkol, to "end public controversy among the heads of the party" through mediation. With Eshkol designated as a mediator, Evron's journey was evidently designed to sell him on the merits of Lavon's case, before the other side could convince him that justice lay with Ben-Gurion.

After talking with Evron, Carmel recalls, Eshkol "set about squeezing me dry: were there, or weren't there, forgeries?" Or, to be precise: had she altered the copy of Givly's letter to Dayan? Eshkol could only have learned of this from Evron, who apparently had not confined himself to depicting the crisis looming over Mapai but had also described "the conspiracy" against Lavon, and Carmel's alleged role in the forgeries. According to Carmel, she now found herself "in an awful fix." On the one hand, she still felt "loyalty to Givly and Ben-Zur and their bunch." On the other hand she felt a commitment to Eshkol, "my boss, and I had never lied to him," which was now reinforced by their love. She opted for silence. "I didn't reply. Whenever he asked, I'd find some pretext."

In fact, Eshkol's barrage of questions did not find Carmel unprepared. When news of the Cohen board's appointment reached Givly in London he went on high alert; his precautions included a letter to Carmel dated September 26—the first of a series of written briefings to put her on her guard against an eventual interrogation regarding the forgeries. Informing her of "the decision to renew the investigation of the Lavon affair," he updated her on the latest details:

> The inquiry board will try to find out whether Lavon's claims are indeed correct; having been alongside me all those years, you are liable to be summoned to Israel. Remember our talk in Jerusalem.
> I hope we come out of the affair without allowing Lavon to be rehabilitated. I will certainly not consent to be a sacrificial offering. . . .
> Yours, *Benyamin*.

Givly's resort to the first person plural to hope that "we" would come out all right—implying that they were both guilty to the same degree and faced an identical risk—was designed to induce Carmel to take part in a joint salvage effort. The "talk in Jerusalem" referred to their conversation in the restaurant, about which Carmel's recollection appears to be faulty; Givly must have taken the opportunity to ease her misgivings.

There was no let-up in Eshkol's questions right up to the final moments before his departure for Israel on October 17. As Carmel escorted him to his plane, he flung at her: "It's a pity you didn't talk. I assure you, I wouldn't have told a soul." She burst into tears; as they took their leave, he said: "I asked and you didn't reply; there seems to have been more than the things I asked, am I right?" Carmel remained silent, "and then he said: Silence implies admission." "With that," she recalled, "he left for Israel."

Over the years, Carmel adhered to the story that she maintained a silence which Eshkol, in his wisdom, took as an admission. However,

without detracting from Eshkol's wisdom, it appears to have been supplemented with full and precise information furnished by her. After all,
her forgery was no "closely-guarded secret"; if she had recounted it to
Harkabi, Hareven, and Palmoni, she probably shared it with Eshkol too.
Clues can be found in three letters from Eshkol. On November 5, 1960,
he wrote: "I shall keep my promise. Don't worry." In another, dated
November 12/13: "Don't worry. I'll watch my mouth." Clearly, Eshkol's
promise related to a secret she had confided to him, not something he
had deduced from her silence.

This conclusion is borne out by another letter, dated November 24,
sent double-sealed by diplomatic mail: "As I wrote you, I will keep my
promise to you most faithfully. But you will be interrogated under oath,
and you have no way out [other than] telling the truth as you know it."

For as long as the Lavon affair raged on, Eshkol remained true to his
word; but on his marriage to Miriam Zelikovitch on March 3, 1964, his
pledge appears to have lapsed. He told Zelikovitch that Carmel had
committed the forgery of which she was suspected, adding that she had
confided her secret to him at the Essex in October 1960, when they were
in bed, "and people don't lie at such moments." Zelikovitch repeated the
story to a journalist friend.

Asked subsequently whether she whispered her secret to Eshkol as
"pillow talk," Carmel replied: "Was it pillow talk? I don't know. He asked
me very many questions on the matter, and I didn't answer them. I managed to evade them. But he gave me no rest."

Efforts to win Eshkol over were renewed the moment he set foot in Israel
on October 18. First, he met with the "troika"; then, he spent the night
in his Tel Aviv hotel room conferring with his colleagues of the Mapai
leadership and "the young men." After that sleepless night, according to
Maariv, "he renewed his mediation efforts this morning" as "sole arbi-
trator," having been chosen by the secretariat "to deal with intermural
and collegial relations in connection with the affair."

During October 18 and 19, Mapai's secretariat and central committee met in almost continual session, in a desperate effort to extricate the
party from the crisis. Tension was heightened by the certainty that the
proceedings would be leaked to *Maariv*. Some suspected a listening
device planted in the conference room, and Aran "proposed that future
secretariat meetings do not take place in this room, but in one without
windows."

The party's masters of adroitly worded compromise put forward all manner of proposals, but in vain. Henceforth, the term "judicial" became the buzzword for Ben-Gurion's supporters; while those who wanted to see the matter cleared up by "a proper body" were followers of Lavon. Mapai was in uproar, and the entire country with it.

Eshkol found himself between a rock and a hard place. A man of compromise, averse to controversy, he was probably disinclined by nature toward a Ben-Gurion-style judicial inquiry. But he had additional grounds to oppose it; he was alone in knowing that the forgery would be proved, and that a judicial inquiry would fully exonerate Lavon. Evron must be given the credit for this: had he not shown up in New York, Carmel would not have owned up to the forgery, and Eshkol would not have been in possession of exclusive information yet to be confided to any commission.

However, Eshkol was obliged to play down his own motives and calculations: should he reveal who had made the forgery known to him, he would not only break faith with Carmel and incriminate her but also have to explain what had induced her to choose him as her confidant. Eshkol finally disclosed the secret to Ben-Gurion in 1965, though without naming Carmel (see chapter 24). Having resolved to keep all this confidential, he had to be careful not to disclose his own preference: delegating a ministerial committee to solve a riddle whose solution he in fact knew. The responsibility Eshkol had undertaken, and his fear of the censure he would face should the truth emerge, combined to condemn him to total isolation. Eshkol kept his mouth shut.

Eshkol's mode of operation involved interminable "rounds of consultation": with followers of Ben-Gurion, followers of Lavon, and the waverers. Searching for a way to break the impasse, he sought to address Ben-Gurion's demand with a body that would be state-appointed, while reassuring Lavon that it would not be "judicial." At the secretariat's evening session on October 19, he put forward a formula that seemed advantageous to both parties: the affair would be deliberated by "authorized state-appointed institutions." The term "authorized" lay midway between "judicial" and "proper." It was the first indication that Eshkol would attempt to resolve the affair once-and-for-all by submitting it to a ministerial committee which alone had the power, he believed, to pursue the investigation without being explicitly designated as a state commission of inquiry.

Ultimately, he selected justice minister Pinhas Rosen, head of the Progressive party, as his stalking-horse. It was Rosen, he would insist, who came up with the idea of an investigation by ministerial committee. But Sapir wrote Ben-Gurion that Eshkol "was among the first to promote the idea of a ministerial committee, rather than a judicial inquiry commission."

It seems that Eshkol hit upon this idea no earlier than October 24, and the cabinet approved the establishment of the committee within a week—an impressive achievement, particularly in view of the obstacles he had to surmount: most of the other parties were opposed to having the investigation snatched from the Knesset foreign affairs and defense committee, and Ben-Gurion maintained his insistence that the truth could be revealed only in a judicial inquiry.

Why did Ben-Gurion not exercise his prerogative as prime minister to appoint a judicial inquiry? It seems he hankered after the role of the righteous man of Jewish tradition, whose "labor is done by others": rather than do it himself, he wanted someone else to set up the inquiry commission, preferably through a show of hands in party or cabinet. But that avenue was blocked when Lavon warned he would respond to the constitution of an inquiry commission by publishing "a secret file" containing "material even graver" than what he had already revealed. This threat threw the party into a panic: "It would be a terrible Pandora's box," said Eshkol, and Sharett warned that an inquiry commission would be "a mass grave."

In addition, newspaper commentators swayed public opinion against an inquiry commission. Ben-Gurion may have refrained from appointing a commission because he knew that he did not have a majority in the cabinet, the Knesset, or the party. "I am not sole arbiter," he wrote on the 28th, "and I am not empowered on my own authority to establish such a commission."

As Rosen later pointed out, Ben-Gurion never took any of the opportunities offered him—in May 1955, May 1958, September 1960 (when he appointed the Cohen board), nor finally, at the September 30 cabinet meeting–to institute a judicial inquiry. "Throughout his tenure as prime minister," Rosen wrote, "Ben-Gurion did not lift a finger to constitute a judicial inquiry"; and moreover, he ultimately accepted the ministerial committee in order "to reserve his freedom of manoeuvre and tactical action" in case the committee's findings "were to his satisfaction, with no need to query" its appointment or status. "There can be no doubt that, had he stated then [October 30] that he regarded the appointment specifically of a 'judicial' inquiry commission as a question of principle as far as [to warrant] a cabinet crisis—the 12 ministers who voted for my proposal [Rosen himself included] . . . would have reconsidered the matter.

Meir returned to Israel on October 27 and joined the opponents of a judicial inquiry. The moment she did so, as was her wont, she became convinced of the justice of her opinion and defended tenaciously, giving Eshkol powerful support. According to *Maariv*, Eshkol now told Ben-Gurion that the proposed ministerial committee was assured of a majority, and asked him not to submit to the cabinet his proposal for a judicial inquiry, for with Sapir and Meir virtually certain to vote against it, it was "liable to divide the Mapai ministers into two camps."

On Sunday October 30, in what *Maariv* termed "a last-minute effort" before the weekly cabinet meeting, Eshkol convened the Mapai ministers at his Jerusalem office to ensure a united vote in favor of a ministerial committee. Ultimately, he got seven ministers on his side; only Ben-Gurion and Dayan opposed the committee. It was the first time ever that virtually all the Mapai ministers voted against Ben-Gurion; they would certainly not have done so without the moral authority wielded by Eshkol and Meir.

Meir told Ben-Gurion that while she had formerly leaned toward a judicial inquiry she was reluctant to be on the same side as Shimon Peres, with whom she had accounts to settle. She had no difficulty believing stories about "threats to Evron to 'take care' of his wife and children," and was sure Peres was behind them. In her political and social views, she was, as Almogi put it, "a Ben-Gurionist *par excellence*. . . . She could not tolerate Lavon and invested all her energies into . . . his removal" in 1955. However she now sided with Lavon against Ben-Gurion, apparently because she was convinced that there had been a "conspiracy" against Lavon, with the connivance of Dayan, and, principally, Peres, who still had the support of Ben-Gurion.

This belief also seems to explain why the veterans did not defend Ben-Gurion against the "Dreyfusiada" charges, instead opting for the silence he condemned. Fear of the young men blinded them to the fact that they were indirectly endorsing a calumny against Ben-Gurion which was far more defamatory than the slander they had allegedly concocted against Lavon.

The cabinet devoted its sessions of October 30 and 31 to the affair. At the first one, Ben-Gurion announced that he was confining himself to an exposition of his position in favor of a judicial inquiry, and would not take part in the deliberations or voting. With twelve votes in favor and two abstentions, the meeting resolved to appoint a committee of five ministers, "which shall study all the evidence relating to the affair, and submit its findings to the cabinet." At the second meeting, Eshkol proposed to enlarge the committee with one representative each from Mapam and Poalei Agudath Israel. This resolution was adopted by twelve votes, with Dayan alone abstaining.[1] Ben-Gurion did not attend the meeting, on the pretext that he was "preoccupied with preparing a reply to the debate in the Knesset." According to Rosen, he sat in his office "petulant, refusing to enter the cabinet chamber to consider the appointment of two additional members" to the ministerial committee.

Eshkol, acting as courier between Ben-Gurion and the cabinet, finally returned to the cabinet saying that Ben-Gurion had accepted the institution of the committee, and the discussion ended with the selection of its members.

Both sides were playing a perilous game. Rosen and the other ministers appear to have been motivated by fear of an eventual dissolution of the government. Eshkol, for his part, apparently deliberately misled the cabinet, for it is unimaginable that he got Ben-Gurion's to consent outright to the seven-member committee.

Subsequently, indeed, Ben-Gurion blamed Eshkol. Having read and reread the minutes of that meeting, he wrote: "I had no idea of the 'inducements'" exercised upon several ministers by Eshkol. He also spoke with Rosen, who said he had voted for the ministerial committee only after "Eshkol assured him that I had come to terms with its creation." Ben-Gurion later wrote to Rosen that "others may be accountable more than you" for rejecting a judicial inquiry and appointing the ministerial committee, because "behind-the-scenes activities influenced you." In short, Rosen had been "misled" and "drawn on" by Eshkol. In a 1967 diary entry, Ben-Gurion remarked that the committee's "architect was Eshkol [who] misled the [cabinet] members into thinking I was in favor."

What also emerged at that meeting was that, as Josephthal (who among others thought the meeting would be a "procedural discussion"

---

1. The committee consisted of: Rosen (Progressives), chairman; Eshkol and Shitrit (Mapai); Yitzhak Ben-Aharon (Ahdut HaAvodah); Israel Barzilai (Mapam); Benyamin Mintz (Poalei Agudath Israel); Moshe Haim Shapira (National Religious Party).

about the ministerial committee's powers and mode of action), noted, "many already have . . . their minds made up—before seeing the evidence." Yitzhak Ben-Aharon, for example, declared that the information already divulged to the Knesset foreign affairs and defense committee "suffices for me to know that Lavon did not issue the order." Eshkol remarked that "On the whole, I concur with Ben-Aharon's interpretation of the matter."

Before the committee's first meeting, then, before its members set eyes on any documents, some—including the most prominent—knew what its findings would be. Echoing Josephtal, *Maariv* of October 25 offered an accurate prediction of the flaws and discrepancies that would mark the work of the ministerial committee; its bias was thus no secret.

There is no doubt that, in having the judicial inquiry struck from the agenda in favor of the ministerial committee, Eshkol was pursuing Ben-Gurion's best interests, and the welfare of the party. However, he must have known that the exoneration of Lavon would diminish the prospects for the young men—mainly Dayan and Peres—to leap directly into the leadership. Furthermore, he can hardly have been unaware that he himself was likely to ascend. Though he did it unintentionally, it was Eshkol who demolished Ben-Gurion's unique status.

21

Givly Demands an Inquiry

When Givly returned to Israel from London in October 1960 to testify
to the Cohen inquiry, the mood he encountered was totally unlike anything he had experienced at the time of the Olshan-Dori commission, as
is clear from a November 3 letter to Dalia Carmel: "I found myself for
the first time so isolated, so lonely. No one will talk to you or say hello."
Worst of all was his "disappointment in people."

It was now evident that his former subordinates were no longer willing to lie on his behalf, and "the fraternity of the [intelligence] corps"
could no longer be invoked to that end. However, the vacillation displayed by Aluf Hareven, his former aide-de-camp and now a major at
MI's research department, showed that he did hesitate to give truthful
testimony, out of unwillingness to incriminate Givly.

Testifying before the Cohen board on October 13, Hareven revealed
that Carmel had told him of her alterations to the "notebook" registry of
documents sent to Lavon; that she had told Harkabi in London of having made changes on the copy of Givly's July 19, 1954, letter to Dayan;
that Givly had deliberately delayed bringing Elad to Israel to testify
before the Olshan-Dori commission; and that "Almog traveled [to Paris]
to deliver Ben-Zur's letter to Elad." The Cohen board relied on his deposition to find that Elad had been solicited to commit perjury.

Afterward, Hareven was uneasy. On the 18th, after a few days' hesitation, he wrote to Givly: "The question facing me . . . was: should I evade

telling what I know—and there were good reasons for evasion," namely: his preference for Givly over Lavon and his standing in the army when the contents of his testimony became known. All in all, "Why should I get mixed up in a business to which I have no connection other than chancing to hear of it?" He also felt "a debt of gratitude" toward the person who "advanced me in the [intelligence] corps, and profound esteem . . . to this day for a man whose flaws, however great, are still only part of a great and positive personality." Nevertheless, "I chose ultimately to give truthful answers to every question I was asked," just as he would have done had his son "fallen into some transgression calling for justice to be done."

The Cohen board granted Givly the right to interrogate witnesses, but he waived it. However, on reading the testimony of his subordinates and henchmen, he realized that their opinions of him had changed. Indeed, Almog later said that Lavon and Givly were "two crooks." Avraham Dar, Ya'akov Hefetz, and Carmel too had expressed similar sentiments over the years. Even Ben-Zur, who until now had surpassed all the others in his loyalty, finally realized that Givly had tried to frame him. Small wonder that Givly felt "so isolated, so lonely." True, he also boasted to Carmel of "a very few friends who have not deserted me for a single moment, heartening and supporting me"; but that claim seemed designed to strengthen her own loyalty to him, lest she follow in Hareven's footsteps when called to testify.

To Ben-Gurion, "the fact that after 'the sorry business' . . . Givly lied or tried to falsify a document, or solicit someone to perjury, proves nothing." It showed only that Givly "was dragged into the mire by the defense minister, and wished to cleanse himself by any means." Even though he never said so in public, Ben-Gurion thus agreed with the notion of "lie for lie." Outwardly, he persisted to his dying day in believing Givly's claims, which seemed verified by the Cohen inquiry findings that the copy of his letter to Dayan had not been falsified.

Even though the board's findings obliged Ben-Gurion to discharge Givly from the army, Givly continued to regard Ben-Gurion as his sole salvation. When accused of "shedding Lavon's blood," Ben-Gurion would retort: "I shed Givly's blood when I dismissed him from all military service; is Lavon's blood a deeper crimson?" Carried away by gratitude toward his protector, Givly "swore by his only daughter that the order for the operation in Egypt was given him by Lavon." Ben-Gurion counseled him to "demand an inquiry commission," whereupon Givly responded: "I'll mortgage my home to establish my innocence." This account of their exchange comes from *Maariv*'s military correspondent, who was in touch with Givly. Ben-Gurion's diary entry is different: Givly had "told his father he did not tell a lie, did not steal, did not cheat." Ben-Gurion advised him to "consult an attorney on how to bring the matter to a judicial hearing." A kind of alliance seems to have been struck: Givly would demand an inquiry commission, and Ben-Gurion, pursuing the same end, would prevent Lavon from being exonerated except by such a commission.

Givly took the first step by hiring attorney Ya'akov Salomon. On October 22, he petitioned the chief of staff "to submit to the duly-constituted authority" his request to enable him "to clear my name in the only way available to me . . . an inquiry commission in accordance with the Commissions of Inquiry Ordinance, 1921" to establish who issued the order. The chief of staff transmitted the request to Ben-Gurion, who passed it on to justice minister Rosen at the cabinet's October 23 meeting. Rosen rejected the request.

At the following week's meeting, which convened to appoint the ministerial committee, Rosen expounded his position, probably adopted in consultation with Eshkol: "If I have no new evidence, I see no point in fulfilling Givly's request. But this entire matter will be a subject for the ministerial committee which I am about to propose. . . . It has to see whether there is ground for an inquiry commission."

The ministerial committee held its first meeting on November 3. *Maariv* published an interview with Rosen, its chairman. When asked if the seven-member committee would go into the question of who gave the order, Rosen replied, "Yes indeed. . . . we shall study all the evidence; depending on what we turn up, we may propose constitution of an inquiry commission, or transformation of the ministerial committee into an inquiry commission with all the [attendant] legal powers." Rosen added, "Givly's . . . appeal against the Cohen board's findings will also be brought before the seven-member committee," which "will also study his claims."

Was Givly's demand for an inquiry commission genuine or feigned? He declared repeatedly that he "wished to exhaust all the judicial paths open to him in his demand that justice be done," and pinned his "hopes on the institution of a commission . . . to find out who gave the order." But the letter attorney Salomon delivered to Rosen on November 3—coinciding with the first meeting of the ministerial commit-

tee—contained no firm demand for an inquiry commission; on the
contrary, Salomon seemed to be signaling Rosen that—public declara-
tions notwithstanding—he and his client were not pressing for such a
commission.

Rosen seemed to have got the message, for his reply, not sent until
November 15, stated: "I have taken note of your request." Going strictly
by the book, he added that the seven-member committee had not been
assigned to discover who gave the order but only to study the evidence
and advise the cabinet what to do; and that, unless the cabinet decided
to change its terms of reference, it was not an inquiry commission.
Nonetheless, neither Salomon nor Givly protested, and not a word was
leaked to *Maariv* or any other paper. The attorney and his client—who
had recently sworn by his daughter's life, and vowed to mortgage his
home to support his quest for justice—simply waited for the ministerial
committee to reach a decision.

It seems, then, that Givly's demand was only a pose. A similar impression emerges from a confidential meeting he had with Eshkol. Givly
began by approaching Kfar Saba Mayor Mordechai Surkiss, a member of
Mapai's secretariat and central committee. Honest, independent and
boisterous, an intimate of Eshkol but also a loyal admirer of Ben-Gurion,
Surkiss could afford to differ with the latter. Considering the campaign
against Lavon beneficial neither to the party nor Ben-Gurion, he
opposed a judicial inquiry.

Disguised behind dark glasses, Givly arrived at Surkiss' home the
evening of Friday November 18, and declared: "You are the only person
who can fix me up with a meeting with Eshkol, for tomorrow."

Surkiss called Eshkol: "Eshkol, that charming character Givly has
arrived from London, he wants to see you."

Eshkol: "Not without you! I won't talk to him without you."

Surkiss explained, years later, that Eshkol wanted the meeting attended by a witness he could trust, "so afterwards it didn't produce some yarn
about Eshkol doing something to Givly."

Givly: "All the better, I'm ready and willing." Surkiss then accompanied Givly to his meeting with Eshkol in Jerusalem.

Surkiss kept silent after the meeting; only much later did he reveal
that, when Givly complained of having been wronged, "Eshkol listened
but promised nothing." Surkiss denied rumors that "Eshkol promised
Givly something if he would abandon the business, or threatened him if
he insisted on a state inquiry commission."

This denial shows that Givly requested the meeting to find out what he could gain by withdrawing his demand, and that Eshkol showed an interest in this. Indeed, on their drive back from Jerusalem, Givly remarked to Surkiss: "You know what? I'd do anything to dispense with trials and all that."

Surkiss welcomed the notion, waiting to hear Givly's price.

Givly replied, "I've come out of the affair humiliated. I want to go back to being military attaché. That's my condition. I don't demand anything, no job, nothing."

They halted at the home of Givly's parents in Petah Tikva, and Surkiss called Eshkol: "That's the condition this character is setting."

Eshkol, however, balked: "Do I decide? It's Ben-Gurion's business, not mine, I don't want to get involved."

Later Surkiss claimed the credit for Givly's decision to drop his demand for an inquiry commission: "I saved him in the matter of the trial"; but he also conceded that, in fact, "Benyamin didn't want an inquiry commission." It may be surmised that Eshkol too was aware of this, and he appears to have told Rosen that Givly would not insist.

But Givly was acting on two levels, for even if he withdrew his demand, he had no guarantee that the seven-member committee would drop its investigation. Aware that Carmel might be called to testify, he followed the now well-trodden path of preparing her deposition. He wrote her by way of his friend Avigdor Slutzky, formerly of the intelligence corps, now a businessman in Switzerland; his letter bore a Zurich postmark dated November 3, 1960, and a New York postmark from the 5th.

The letter begins "Dear one" and expresses the "profound conviction" that, unlike others, Carmel has not turned her back on him, and that she is "perhaps" closer to him than any of his friends.

> If there is no truth in that assumption of mine, do not go on to read the following lines. Throw the letter into the garbage, and henceforth do whatever your heart desires. But as I said, I will continue writing because I am sure that, in this instance, my instincts have not betrayed me, I have been betrayed sufficiently by others.
>
> Israel today is a jungle of two-legged [beasts], all pursuing one another, lies and falsehood are on every lip, and "the truth is but in their mouths," not in their hearts.

Under the circumstances, small wonder he felt that he had been "badly maligned" by the Cohen board:

> I have become the personification of moral depravity, and head of a
> den of iniquity. You who knew me so well, am I really like that? What
> don't they say about me here nowadays? And impotence everywhere,
> no one stands up to fight back.
>
> I imagine that the foregoing lines and words are enough to let you
> know what hell I am enduring here. Now that I have already emerged
> beaten and shattered, smeared and tarnished, there are those still pre-
> pared to malign and condemn, and drag us both into new mire.

Carmel, he implied, was equally liable to fall victim to the same injustice;
by defending him, she would also be saving herself. It was therefore necessary to tell her what she was likely to be confronted with in an interrogation:

> Aluf Hareven has testified to having heard from Harkabi, who heard
> from you—and he too heard from you—that you, acting on my
> instructions, effected alterations in some "notebook." By his account,
> this notebook listed the documents going to the defense minister. . . .
> And if that isn't enough for you, they go on and on about instances of
> forgeries which, thank God, have so far not been proved.
>
> I don't know what you said to Harkabi and Hareven in this con-
> nection, or if you said anything to anyone else . . . [about] all kinds of
> dirty work committed in Ben-Zur's unit at that time.

To clear up that point, Slutzky:

> will contact you to find out . . . what you really said . . . if this letter of
> mine is not too late, because it may all be behind us, and it remains
> only to prepare a gallows for me.

Now Givly came to the essence: prevailing upon Carmel to commit
perjury.

> My dear, you know what I feel for you, and more than that, I know what
> you feel for me. I do not know whether it lies at all within your power
> to save me, but perhaps after all—and then only if you are clear on hav-
> ing no part in this affair, no hand in "alterations" or falsifications,
> whether or not there were any—I am convinced once more that there
> is a slander of the foulest kind against us, and I have no doubt who
> concocted it.[1] You should be doubly wary of all those "friends" who
> always seem congenial, but wield a sharp knife behind your back.

---

1. An apparent reference to Harkabi.

I imagine they are liable to ask you a number of questions:

a) Did you, on instructions from any of us, make any alterations in a notebook or journal?

b) Did you in any particular way help in the work of Ben-Zur's unit?

You will understand from these questions what their intent is, and tell me just one thing: that you are ready to answer them all with *No*. As to the tally of morals and conscience, I am prepared to reckon it between ourselves, only after we can meet face-to-face and talk as we knew and enjoyed.

It will not surprise me if they try to cajole you, to force you, to exert pressure upon you, to extract an admission of all these things. But as I told you, I would not appeal to you unless I were convinced of the justice of my deeds. My conscience does not trouble me. In this whole dismal affair, I personally will assuredly be victim and scapegoat, and my plea to you comes at a moment which may be the worst moment I have ever endured; will you turn me down?

Anxious to impress upon Carmel that his interest in her, and his feelings toward her, were not necessarily connected with this appeal, Givly concluded his letter with reminiscences of better times:

I was in Jerusalem, and I dropped by that little cafe; the first question the waitress asked was how you are? Isn't that strange? Two days ago I visited your family and found only your mother. We spent some time in a long conversation, and of course, we also mentioned you. She wishes, is interested, that you study something general to extend your horizons and education.

If you have to come to Israel . . . please promise you will pass through London on your way and see my family. They will certainly be pleased to see you, and hear a kind word from you. . . .

Finally, he asked her to write him—"so I know whether you are with me"—at the address of a former subordinate. Promising to visit her in the United States "if everything passes away and works out," and adding an enigmatic remark—"Don't be surprised at how this letter reaches you, a man's paths are always open"—he closed with: "Yours in friendship, Benyamin."

Two days later, on November 5, Eshkol too wrote to "Dear Dalika" in reply to two letters of hers. Hinting that she was likely to be called to testify before the seven-member committee, and reassuring her that he would not reveal her secret, he noted that "the affair" has abated somewhat. But it is not buried totally. It will keep us busy. We have somewhat gained control. I had a part in that. . . . About the affair itself, I will not say a word here. There are several reasons. You will surely understand. I assume that you are likely to pass this way in the coming days or weeks, if not at some other [time], at all events, at some opportunity for a face-to-face. Meanwhile, I will keep my promise. Don't worry.

In another letter dated November 12/13, Eshkol again alerted Carmel to the possibility of interrogation, and again vowed to keep her secret:

Meanwhile, you probably received my letter [of November 5]. I do not write about "the affair," its effects etc. for several reasons, I am not certain that letters to you won't be read by others. On some occasion sometime, if you wish to explain your misgivings and complaints about what has been done, perhaps we'll have an opportunity to clear it up. . . . Don't worry. I will watch my mouth. But after all, you are likely to be interrogated or questioned *under oath.*

Three days after that, on November 16, Givly again wrote. His double-sealed letter was sent to New York by Givly's wife Esther in London:

Dear Dalia, Shalom!
It is superfluous to tell you how moved I was by your letters. I have never had a shadow of doubt as to your loyalty to me. I have admired and respected the relations between us, and above all, yourself. . . . My dear, I want to say a few words on the matter, please do not be angry. "Respectability" will not take a favorable view [of the fact] that we are corresponding under present circumstances. On the contrary: should it become known, it will boomerang on me and against me. Accordingly, except for the letter you sent me by way of Kollek, there has been no correspondence between us whatsoever. The only way to send me letters is not by friends or relatives of either of us, but by [means of] just plain Jews, preferably not Israelis, who will drop the letter into a mailbox in Israel addressed to my friend in Herzlia. What I am about to tell you may sound grave, but it's reality, and in these crazy times one must not toy with illusions, and things have to be seen for what they are.
    . . . Here everyone is expectantly waiting for "the ministerial committee" to finish its work, seemingly not before the end of the month. Meanwhile, there are numerous conjectures as to its recommendations, but in truth, no one knows, everyone is guessing. There is an

inclination to complete the testimony mentioned in the Attorney-General's opinion, yours included. It is unclear how they will go about it. It is of course possible that you will be summoned to come to Israel. Possibly, someone there will be appointed interrogator to take your deposition on oath.

. . . Should you be called to return, arrive discreetly, without notifying friends and colleagues, and contact me immediately. Bear in mind that a meeting between us before you testify is almost totally proscribed, therefore prudence is a good and important thing. In any case of questioning or giving a deposition, I think you know very well what is in store for you. You will be asked about alterations to some notebook or journal, about deliberate destruction of evidence, or "special typing." I tell you all this because these are the questions upon which everything hinges. To all of these, just one answer, no other: "Nothing of the kind!"—not 'you don't remember.' As in any interrogation, the questions may be indirect, but it is important you remember their purpose.

Now, my dear, it is important you bear in mind something further. The Cohen report linked me with the fat dummy [Ben-Zur]; an excellent characterization. Accordingly, whatever our attitude toward him, I myself won't get clear of this business if I or you attribute to him any act [related to the forgeries].

Accordingly, I have the greatest interest in knowing, in precise detail, what you said about the fat dummy to your big boss [Eshkol] when he saw you recently,[2] and what you said years ago to the little Sepharadi[3] and the skinny author [Hareven] because, as I have already told you, both of them quote you and everyone attaches considerable weight to these quotes. . . . Of course, you will have no difficulty now in denying everything attributed to you, and whatever you say today will be accepted.

I must get an early answer from you on these points, but that must be within the restrictions on writing as noted at the beginning of my letter, do not make light of them.

---

2. This indicates that Carmel had written Givly about her conversation with Eshkol before his return to Israel. It is further proof that, far from maintaining a silence that Eshkol construed as admission, she told him her story, including the "alterations" she made at Ben-Zur's direction.

3. Here Givly used a derogatory term for a Sephardic Jew to refer to Harkabi—who, however, is not Sephardic; his parents came from Russia.

Finally, Givly inserting a personal touch, expressed the hope that "despite everything, you find a free moment to yourself, and manage to enjoy the milieu in which you find yourself." He told Carmel that Palmoni (of whose relations with her he was aware) "gave my attorney [your] regards to me, and I was overjoyed. All the best, my dear. Look after yourself, and my full esteem to you for everything. The day will yet come, and not only will justice emerge into the light—but I will repay you your just due."

Givly's November 19 visit to Eshkol's home must have given the latter an idea that he would try to work on Carmel's feelings for him. On November 24, Eshkol sent her—in his own handwriting, also double-sealed— the following lines, some of which have already been cited in chapter 20. His style—the letter opens "Dalia, Shalom," and concludes "with collegial felicitations, L. Eshkol"—is excessively circumspect, reflecting his membership on the ministerial committee, as well as the risk he was taking in breaching confidentiality:

> I have received your long letter. I was greatly pleased with it. When I find a little time, I shall write. I am in Tel Aviv. I have plunged into reading and studying the evidence of "the affair," along with the committee. Your name is mentioned [in the Cohen board report] several times, i.e. in the testimony of several persons. No doubt you will soon be invited to a formal interrogation on oath, etc.
>
> The purpose of this note to you: to beg you, and advise you for your own good, to tell the whole truth as known to you.
>
> Please, *for heaven's sake*, and *for your honor*, don't get implicated. You are just at the beginning of your course in life and society. I am apprehensive lest certain emotional promises [to Givly—S.T.] burden you in telling all you know. . . .
>
> . . . I will keep my promise to you most faithfully. But you will be interrogated on oath, and you have no way out [other than] telling the whole truth as known to you.
>
> Dalika, forgive me for the slightly harsh and somber style.
>
> You will certainly understand the reason for the despatch of this letter double-sealed. . . . I think you will be interrogated in New York.
>
> . . . I apologize, I thought the bonds of friendship command me to advise you faithfully. It is of course possible that [you would have testified thus] anyway in keeping with conscience and truth. That is how I know you. I merely wished to give you support in a possible conflict.

In this fashion, Carmel's impending testimony became the object of a duel-by-correspondence between the two most important men in her life, whom she adulated to an almost equal degree. But whereas one drew her toward the past, seeking to rekindle old memories and revive comradeship, the other addressed the future, urging her, at the threshold of her independent life, to plot her course well, for her own self-respect and her honor in the eyes of others. Both appealed to her conscience: one, invoking MI *esprit de corps*; the other citing civic duty.

Unlike Givly, whose ploys were aimed at inducing Carmel to lie, Eshkol was working to uncover the truth. However, precluded from sharing Carmel's revelations with his colleagues of the cabinet or the seven-member committee, he also sinned against the law and proper procedure. He was convinced that Givly had given the order, without instructions from Lavon, and was thus to blame for "the sorry business." When that was established, Eshkol was sure the seven-member committee would be persuaded of Givly's guilt and would draw the inescapable conclusion that Lavon must be exonerated; Ben-Gurion too would be forced to concur. With that, "the Lavon affair" would come to an end, and life would revert to normal.

Everything thus depended upon Eshkol's ability to convince Carmel to offer honest testimony against her idol Givly. Eshkol's letters reveal him as a pilot covertly steering the seven-member committee toward a verdict known to him in advance—and in the process trampling upon every procedure and regulation underlying sound government. Beyond this, his letters made Carmel privy to details from the committee's deliberations, which had been placed under "total blackout."

The cabinet had instructed the seven-member committee to "study all the material relating to the affair, and submit its findings to the cabinet." The cabinet probably never had a committee whose members attended meetings—a total of 19, twice weekly—with equal dedication. It is hard to suppress a smile at the spectacle of seven ministers riveted to the minutes and reports of the Olshan-Dori and Cohen inquiries, as well as other testimony, documents, and memoranda, which they took turns reading out to one another—extending to Givly's relations with Carmel. Except for police minister Bekhor Shitrit, formerly an assistant superintendent with the British mandatory police, none of them had any experience in investigations, and they themselves were critical of their own attempts to grope their way by means of deductions and reasoning based on their political experience.

Much of the committee's deliberations concerned the question of witnesses. Eshkol was anxious to interrogate Carmel, Harkabi, Yossi Harel, and an officer from MI's documentation department, and others felt it would be impossible to draw conclusions without hearing Sharett, Lavon, and Dayan; but if they did that, they would clearly have to hear Givly. Rosen asserted that the committee was "a study commission" and could not hear witnesses without authorization from the cabinet.

Finally the committee agreed to a proposal by Ben-Aharon that the four witnesses specified by the Cohen board should be questioned by the Attorney-General. It was only then, on December 5, that Rosen informed the committee that—since he believed that interrogating these four witnesses would not constitute a breach of the committee's terms of reference—he had already empowered Hausner to question three of them, and Hausner had already left for Paris.

But Eshkol's letters to Carmel indicate that he already knew on November 5 that she would be asked to testify, and that her interrogation would be conducted outside Israel. During its deliberations, Eshkol played a decisive role in making the decision to hear witnesses, in which process the committee overstepped its terms of reference and transformed itself into an investigative committee drawing substantive, final conclusions. Clearly he was motivated by Carmel's revelations and by Givly's willingness, in return for certain concessions, to waive his demand for a state inquiry commission.

In addition to being the "architect" of the seven-member committee, as Ben-Gurion was to depict him, Eshkol in effect controlled every phase of its work from behind the scenes. All his assumptions proved correct—except that Ben-Gurion did not live up to his predictions. To his dying day, Ben-Gurion insisted that a judicial (state) inquiry commission would have been the only way of resolving the affair.

22

Carmel's Confessions

When chairman Pinhas Rosen notified the seven-member committee on December 5, 1960, that Attorney-General Gideon Hausner had flown to Paris early that morning, he urged the committee members not to reveal that the Attorney-General had gone there in connection with the investigation: "I do not wish there to be any contact between Givly and Dalia Carmel. Admittedly, wiser persons say there has already been [such contact and] she has been forewarned."

If by "wiser persons" he meant Eshkol, Rosen was right. Carmel had indeed been alerted by Givly: as promised in his November 3 letter, his friend Slutzky lost no time in contacting her. Slutzky's letter, sent from his Geneva residence on November 10, was a paean to those who stand by friends in their hour of need. He invited Carmel to pass through Geneva on her way to testify.

Was this letter designed to induce Carmel to render perjured testimony? Slutzky wrote, "you will have to act according to your own conscience and feelings." But then he appealed to that conscience: "A friend of mine, in this case B. [Givly], is in distress. He needs support. From me he will have it without asking for it. The trouble is that in reality I can help so little as I happen to be a complete stranger to the 'issue' in question."

Carmel, of course, could be of great assistance. While the word "truth" appears several times in Slutzky's letter, it is used only as a modifier, as in "true friendship" and "true loyalty." An obligation to true testimony is not mentioned.

On Thursday December 1, 1960, Israel's consul-general in New York notified her that she was to fly to Paris to be interrogated by the Attorney-General; a round-trip ticket awaited her at the El Al offices. Before boarding the plane, she sent a letter to Eshkol, asking him to arrange for an additional ticket so she could fly on to Israel and tell her parents of her interrogation before they read about it in the papers; she also requested that Givly's attorney be notified.

En route, Carmel used the airliner's air-to-ground phone link to call Slutzky in Geneva, telling him she was on her way to Paris. He warned that the hotel room the Israeli embassy had prepared for her might be bugged, and asked her to contact him when she arrived.

Landing at Orly airport in the early morning of Sunday December 4, Carmel ran into an Israeli embassy chauffeur who claimed to be meeting someone else, but offered to drive her to the hotel chosen for her. Obsessively suspicious, she sent him packing and took a bus to the air terminal, from where she called Slutzky. He gave her the address of a hotel near the Cafe de la Paix, on the Boulevard d'Opera. The next morning she flew to Geneva and returned to Paris that same day.

Why did Carmel undertake this extra effort, which also entailed an expense she could ill afford? She would say later: "I went to Geneva because of my conscience, to ask what to do. . . . I had a terrible inner conflict." She was indeed torn between her loyalties to Givly and to Eshkol, to friendship and to truth. But she had a further reason for distress. Givly's November 3 letter had urged her to deny she had made any alterations to the notebook, but she had completely forgotten about it. She said later that she did not recall it until the late sixties, explaining that this task had been done in the course of her "routine work," not as "part of alterations or falsifications." Thus "the notebook didn't trouble me because I remembered nothing. What troubled me was what would happen if they brought the letter [to Paris]." But neither Givly's letter nor his message via Slutzky mentioned this issue. Unsure what to say should Hausner question her about the notebook or the letter, she looked to Slutzky for answers.

Had Carmel read the testimony and conclusions of the Cohen board as Givly had, she would not have been uncertain. Based on expert testimony from Captain Avraham (Albert) Hagag of the police laboratories, the board concluded that the copy of Givly's letter had not been tampered with. Feeling quite secure on that point, he did not need Carmel's assistance. But the board had taken note of Hareven's testimony about "alterations" inserted into the notebook.

Carmel later portrayed her talks with Slutzky in Geneva as an "intellectual exercise." When she asked him what she should do, he only reiterated, "You have to follow your conscience." She took that to mean she had to cover for Givly: "That means I have to carry [on my conscience] the story of the forgery, and then also . . . lying under oath." "We'll cross that bridge when we come to it," he responded, and advised her, for the time being, to volunteer no information. After presenting her with a large box of chocolates as a token of his gratitude and taking leave of her, he probably contacted Givly to reassure him that her loyalty was unquestioned.

Slutzky died in 1987; his widow Rachel clearly recalls Carmel's visit. She remembers Slutzky "in great indecision at the time, he was in a very awkward fix, and it's highly probable that he spoke ambiguously at first, because he was prepared to help Givly in everything." But "in time, he realized that Givly had wronged Carmel, and that angered him. Recognizing Givly's character, he broke off his friendship with him."

Arriving at the Israeli embassy in Paris on the morning of December 6, Carmel was summoned to the ambassador, who handed her a small white envelope marked: "Dalia Carmel, to addressee alone." It had been sent by diplomatic mail to New York, but missed her and was sent on to Paris. It was Eshkol's letter of November 24, imploring her "*for heaven's sake* and for *your honor*" to tell the whole truth.

Gideon Hausner, pallid, balding, and with a distracted air, was distinguished for the earnest diligence to which he owed his high office. Before leaving for Paris, he had planned a confrontation between Carmel and Harkabi. Reaching the Paris embassy on December 5, Hausner set the stage for this confrontation: the scene was the military attaché's office, the props included a telephone with listening device installed, and he drew up the cast list in order of appearance.

He began on December 6 by interrogating Harkabi, whose story— made public in 1960 as "the Harel testimony"—rested principally upon Carmel's 1955 account in London. Having concluded this portion of his deposition, Harkabi left the room. Carmel then entered; not having seen him, she thought she was the first to be interrogated.

"Before commencing her account, she asked to be permitted to phone Salomon in Haifa," Hausner would tell the seven-member committee. He believed she did so "as the result of a letter she received from Israel, not from Givly, she did not tell me who it was from. . . . I do not know what was in the letter." No one could have imagined that it was from Eshkol, who listened pokerfaced to Hausner's account.

Salomon "instructed her to tell everything she knew," for "I assume Salomon understood that such conversations are monitored and that he was not at liberty to coach her." Hausner now offered her immunity, formally pledging "that she would not be placed on trial with regard to any of the details she would reveal" and requesting her "to tell all she knew."

Carmel recalled the exchange differently. She said that Hausner asked initially whether she desired written assurance that her testimony would not incriminate her. She said she did, adding that she wished to consult Salomon, claiming she had read in the papers that Givly had retained him. She was allowed to call, and Salomon told her "to tell the truth."

Carmel recalled Hausner beginning the questioning with the words: "I know of your intimate relations with Givly, and I hope you will nevertheless tell me the truth, the whole truth." The questioning turned to the men in her life. Hausner reported on it in a cable to Rosen, who told the committee: "Dalia is full of admiration for Givly, but she denies all the gossip about her. . . . She has never encountered such men as Eshkol and Givly; Givly is a truly amazing man, one hundred percent honest, but she decided—being convinced that Lavon lied—to fight the lie with a lie."

According to Carmel, that day's interrogation went on for "rather many hours." Hausner questioned her "about meetings, telephone calls, typing, and so on," and about her feelings toward Lavon, whom she detested, among other reasons because of the cavalier way he treated her. Whenever she came to his home to deliver documents, he had her wait on the stairway or in the corridor, never offering her a chair. "I am prepared [to commit] any crime" against Lavon, she told Hausner. "He is a pathological liar." She subsequently asked him to delete the word "crime" and substitute that "she was ready to do almost anything" against him, for "she is sure that Lavon gave the order. When I asked how she knew, she said: Lavon is capable of any lie, Givly is incapable of lying, but it needs to be proved, it does not emerge adequately from the documents."

Hausner questioned her on her work with Ben-Zur, and about Givly's July 19 letter to Dayan. He recorded her reply:

True, Ben-Zur asked me . . . to do additional work for him or for the unit. . . . the work included typing out translations from the Arab press, typing letters, reports and cables. Everything to do with the Egyptian affair. Among these was something Ben-Zur asked me to alter, in a document or certain documents, such that the alterations were meant to stress that it was Lavon who gave the operational order. . . .

In this way Carmel kept faith with Eshkol. But when Hausner produced the copy of Givly's letter to Dayan, she shifted the balance to the opposite side, maintaining faith with Givly:

I see the letter dated 19.7.54 that you are showing me, it is the copy of Benyamin's letter to the chief of staff. In response to your question whether the paragraph commencing with the words "On Lavon's instructions . . . " may have been the one I was asked to alter or supplement, I say: "I do not remember."

Years later, Carmel clearly recalled Hausner producing the copy of the letter: "We got to the documents, and Hausner gave me Givly's letter of July 19 to read. I began to read and got a fit of giddiness." What she feared had materialized. But at this crucial moment, salvation appeared from an unexpected quarter: suddenly—as scheduled—Harkabi knocked at the door. Announcing that he had to return to Boston to take his Harvard examinations, he asked to be interrogated without further delay. Hausner asked if Carmel minded the interruption, and she agreed to it gladly. As she put it, "I kicked up my feet and ran for dear life, to call Slutzky in Geneva."

But before she left, Hausner reported, he ordered Harkabi to "say in her presence what you told me," and Harkabi repeated what he had heard from Carmel in London in May 1955. But instead of shaking her confidence, as Hausner had expected, the confrontation awakened doubts in Harkabi, for Carmel's recollection of the precise date and many other details of their meeting was far more accurate than his own. "Perhaps he himself was making mountains out of molehills, and attributing too much importance to rumor and gossip," for when he had first heard Carmel's story, it "did not strike him as requiring investigation." Hausner told the committee that he himself trusted Carmel's memory far more than Harkabi's.

Harkabi's unexpected entry, and the staged confrontation, had failed to throw Carmel off balance; on the contrary, it offered her an escape. As she recalled: "Harkabi entered with excellent timing, for which I was very grateful." She gained the breathing space she had desperately needed.

Outside, she rushed to call Slutzky: "Mister, the letter is here! What do I tell Hausner?"

Slutzky told her "There's nothing for it but to tell the truth."

Carmel recalled: "I decided I'd go along the following morning and say it was that letter"; which was just what she did. That evening, Hausner, who knew her parents, invited her to an excellent Left Bank restaurant; from there, they strolled across the Alexander III bridge, the finest in Paris, to their respective hotels.

In his report, Hausner gave Carmel no credit for her decision to confess. At the restaurant, he said, he explained that "Israel is in an uproar" over the Lavon affair, which could quickly be ended with her help. He reinforced this appeal to patriotism with a personal caution. "Why should she, a young girl, enmesh herself in a tissue of lies," and so on. "After a long, informal conversation, she said: Good, I'll come to the embassy tomorrow and fill in the holes in my testimony." In Hausner's version, the dinner and the stroll on the bridge not only preceded her confession, but perhaps even prompted it.

One point is certain: Carmel's testimony on December 7 was totally unlike her previous day's deposition. Again exhibiting the copy of Givly's letter to Dayan, Hausner noted her reply as follows:

> I say now, with 99% certainty, that in the relevant passage in the letter of 19.7.54, there was a reference to something previous, like: "In accordance with instructions issued" or "In accordance with conversations which were held" or something similar; and Ben-Zur told me to put in . . . the words "On Lavon's instructions." . . . in place of the previous wording which did not specify Lavon.

Hausner swiftly cabled Rosen, who hastened to tell the committee: "Dalia Carmel has confessed."

Carmel hoped that her confession would rid her of the burden afflicting her conscience those past six years, and afford her expiation and relief. But instead she burst into tears. "At the termination of the examination, she was so distraught that, when the military attaché entered the room . . . he asked whether he should call a doctor." When she pulled herself together, Carmel asked repeatedly: "What will you do to Benyamin now, what will happen to Benyamin?"

The next morning, Carmel learned that the ambassador had received a cable from Eshkol, approving an El Al ticket to Israel at official expense. She landed at Lod at midnight; but, delayed by lengthy customs inspections, she did not get out of the terminal until 2 in the morning; her purse contained $30 and no Israeli currency. Calling from the El Al desk, she contacted Eshkol at his Tel Aviv hotel. He awoke easily and said, "Come over right away," offering to send his own driver. It was plain to Carmel that he wished to see her before Givly did.

Scanning the phone directory, she found the number of Givly's parents. He was slow to wake; it was several minutes "before he realized who was speaking." They arranged a rendezvous for 4 in the morning in downtown Tel Aviv. A former MI officer who had landed after Carmel drove her there.

Givly arrived, and they drove through the darkness to the beach. In Carmel's account,

> he knew I had been interrogated, but not on what points; when I told him I had confessed to Hausner about forging the letter, he raved. He said he never knew of any forgeries, nor of the falsification of the letter. He asked if I wanted to meet Salomon. I said one of the reasons I was there was because I wanted to meet Salomon. We arranged for him to await me at the Dalia café on Hayarkon street at 3 in the afternoon, and we would drive to Haifa to see Salomon.

At 5 in the morning, before daylight, Carmel—"by now out of my mind," as she put it—alighted from Givly's car alongside the Dan hotel. Recognizing her, the receptionist allowed her to go up to Eshkol's room. These were not the circumstances of a lovers' reunion. Carmel recalled that she went to see Eshkol "to brief him on exactly what I had told Hausner, because he was on the ministerial committee," and to tell him she intended to see Salomon. Carmel recalled that Eshkol "didn't think it would be proper for me to see Salomon. I told him I had to. Since Hausner had behaved like a vulture, and I didn't believe anyone, I wanted to tell Salomon in person what I said. He had a client to defend, and I wanted him to know from me what I had said." She did not tell Eshkol that she had already seen Givly, and was driving to Haifa with him.

Eshkol, she said, "tried to persuade me not to go to Salomon." He delayed her until 3 in the afternoon, when public transport had shut down for the impending Sabbath. Then "Eshkol left for Jerusalem, and I headed for the Dalia café to meet Givly."

When Carmel told Salomon of her Paris interrogation and confession, he called her "ass, camel, and monkey's-head" and other flattering epithets. Even when she reminded him of his instructions over the phone to tell the truth, "he said I was an ass for owning up to the forgery."

On Saturday night, she was startled to receive a call from the head of the general security service, requesting her to put off her departure from Israel. On Sunday or Monday, "Givly requested that we go again to see Salomon." Her second and final meeting with the attorney, also with Givly present, was on December 11 or 12, 1960, "and Salomon asked whether there was a way of modifying" her Paris confession, "whether I could back down."

Carmel claims that she replied she could not. But Salomon may have warned her that if she did not, she would be responsible for the severe penalties Givly and Ben-Zur would receive. She recalled: "I sensed in my conscience that Givly might be sent to prison on my account, or . . . that he could get into trouble. That was what I feared."

On Tuesday, Superintendent Ze'ev Margalit summoned her to a police interrogation on Thursday December 15. Faced with a choice between rescuing Givly with false testimony and incriminating him by telling the truth, Carmel felt she was in the middle of a "witches' caper," with Givly and Eshkol each trying to get her on his side. Eshkol's purpose was to quickly resolve the Lavon affair. When Carmel begged him to look after Givly, "not financially, but to help him so he isn't thrown to the dogs," Eshkol felt reassured that he had achieved this.

Eshkol worried that the police expert, Captain Hagag, would testify again, as he had for the Cohen board, that the copy of the letter to Dayan had not been falsified; he was also concerned that the findings of the police would be influenced by the fact that their Inspector-General was a close friend of Peres. Eshkol therefore urged the seven-member committee to reach a conclusion without waiting for the police to finish their investigation. Furthermore, hearing Carmel's almost daily reports on her police interrogation and on her talks with Givly and Salomon, Eshkol feared that she would wind up retracting her Paris confession. He soon discovered that his apprehensions were justified, for Carmel attempted the impossible task of satisfying everyone, trying to keep faith simultaneously with Givly, Eshkol, and the law as embodied in the Attorney-General. Hausner too told the seven-member committee he was afraid Carmel would retract her confession.

The police interrogation proceeded at a snail's pace. Carmel was questioned on December 15, 18, and 21. On the 18th, at Hausner's recommendation, she was confronted with Ben-Zur, but he "continued to insist that he had not asked her to amend any document." Despite his denial and Givly's (who was interrogated on December 19 and 23), she did not budge from her statement as recorded by Margalit at her first interrogation on the 15th: "Miss Dalia Carmel reiterated her version that, on the instructions of Ben-Zur, she made a change in the document, whose substance was to stress that the operation was carried out on Lavon's instructions." However, when she was actually shown the copy of the July 19, 1954, letter and asked whether she had altered it, she replied:

> It may be the letter, but I do have doubts as to whether it is indeed the letter. . . . When Hausner showed me in Paris the typed copy of the DMI's letter of 19.7.54 to the chief of staff, I studied it several times; I tried to recall, and it appeared to me, to a degree of 99%, that it was indeed the letter wherein the alteration was made. Subsequently, I again delved into my memory and came up with a doubt whether I had indeed been accurate in saying that that was the document. Now that you show me the copy of the letter, and I study it, that doubt lingers.

She also failed to recall "precisely how she received the order to amend the document, i.e. whether by word of mouth, in writing, or otherwise," for "at that time, she processed much material for Ben-Zur, and the alteration she made was to one of those documents."

The police also pursued the suspicion that Carmel had made alterations in the notebook recording the documents delivered to Lavon. In a confrontation with Hareven, she denied his statement to his interrogators "that he had heard from Dalia that she was asked to replace two pages of the notebook":

"As far as I remember, I inserted no alterations into that notebook. . . . I have no recollection of any such conversation [with Hareven], nor was there any setting for such a conversation. I don't know where he gets those things."

Incidentally, the notebook—like other important documents—had vanished, and vigorous searches failed to locate it.

The police investigation had reached a dead end. Margalit claimed that the only way out would be a polygraph test; but Givly refused. He argued that, as an IDF colonel, his word of honor was "adequate and worthy of respect"; Ben-Zur, after consenting initially, announced that "in the light of developments, he does not wish to be examined by polygraph." Carmel, having meanwhile retained attorney Erwin Shimron, on his counsel agreed "only on condition that Givly and Ben-Zur also consent."

But, following Eshkol's lead, the seven-member committee did not wait for the police to finish. Carmel's Paris confession convinced it that Lavon did not give the order, and on the 13th, despite—or perhaps because of—their awareness that her police interrogation would begin on the 15th, all seven agreed to exonerate Lavon. But at the insistence of Rosen—who was still weighing the possibility of hearing Dayan, if not Lavon and Givly as well—a further meeting was scheduled; and in fact the committee held three more sessions, on December 15, 19, and 21.

Rosen, who bore "the same heavy responsibility . . . as each one [of the committee's members] plus one percent . . . because I am justice minister," sought to reconcile the committee's conclusions with the requirements of procedure, law, and justice. In his view, the decision to exonerate Lavon raised unanswerable questions: if Lavon did not issue the order for the Egyptian operation, who did? Would it be proper to assert that Lavon did not give the order, without saying who did? If the committee simply asserted that Lavon did not issue the order, would it not be saying that Givly did, on his own authority? But the committee had no evidence for that. Rosen's conscience was also troubled because Givly's demand to state his case before the committee had been rejected. Being justice minister, he was sensitive to possible criticism from jurists, which might be heard in court.

Eshkol was not burdened with any such agonizings. By summoning witnesses, he said, "we turn ourselves into an inquiry commission," whereupon "dozens will have to be summoned"; the findings should be brief. Nor did it bother him that exonerating Lavon implied condemning Givly: "We have reached the conclusion that the claim that Lavon gave Givly the order has nothing to stand upon"; likewise, "we have to say that [the copy of] this letter, upon which very much rests . . . has been shown up as a forgery." Thus he gained a majority to exonerate Lavon.

In order to forestall the possible refutation of its principal finding, the committee prefaced its statement with a statement that regardless of what Carmel might tell the police, it was accepting her Paris confession as the truth.

Rosen stated: "I believe in Dalia's examination in Paris; I will not believe in what she is now telling the police." Thus, on December 15, the first day of her testimony, the committee confirmed its final position regarding the falsification of the July 19, 1954, letter. The eighth section of its conclusions asserted: "There are reasonable grounds to assume that . . . Givly submitted the forged copy to the Olshan-Dori commission as evidence that he received an operational order from Lavon."

The committee devoted its two last meetings, on December 19 and 21, to drafting its findings, although the December 21 meeting began with Rosen's report on Carmel's police testimony. He read out portions of her deposition, concluding: "The main thing for us is that she says . . . she does not remember these matters exactly." He also recounted Givly's testimony to the police: "He submitted the [July 19, 1954] letter . . . to the Olshan-Dori commission, but did not know someone had inserted an alteration . . . [and thought] whatever was written there was correct." But Rosen still had his doubts: "If a lawsuit is filed, I do not know how a court will find its way out of the matter." Should Carmel testify in court as she had to the police, "I do not know if it will stand up in court." In other words: there was insufficient evidence to indict Givly for falsifying the copy of the letter.

At length the committee submitted its findings to the cabinet on Sunday December 25, 1960, although Ben-Gurion received them on Friday the 23rd. After much debate arising from conflicting party interests, it agreed to consider the matter closed, thus ruling out a judicial inquiry. The main conclusions were as follows:

"A majority of the committee expressed the opinion that hearing witnesses is not within its powers"; that "Givly submitted the falsified copy [of the July 19, 1954, letter] to the Olshan-Dori commission as evidence that he received the operational instructions from Lavon" [a formulation that avoided the question of whether Givly himself falsified it while serving to exonerate Lavon]; that the instructions Elad received from Ben-Zur in late May 1954 "were not just communications instructions, and that the operations referred to therein were indeed carried out"; that "Lavon did not give the instructions Givly mentions, and that the 'sorry business' was carried out without his knowledge"; that "there are no grounds for the claim that the order to Givly was issued by someone else, whether within the security establishment or outside it"; and finally, that the committee had focused

upon one question principally, [namely] whether Givly received the instructions . . . from Lavon. We did not engage in, nor establish hard-and-fast facts on other questions which the Olshan-Dori and Cohen inquiries occasionally touched upon, such as . . . overall defense poli-

cy in the relevant year, or . . . the administration, organization, and
staff which were faulty in a certain unit that year (including the question of the forgeries and spiriting away of documents) and . . . certain
other defects existing at that period, and whose source was *inter alia* an
absence of clear delineation of authority and responsibility at the
senior echelon. These are subjects whose elucidation is not likely to
entail a change in our conclusion regarding the affair. . . . we are therefore of the opinion that the examination of the affair should be
regarded as closed and sealed.

On December 27, 1960—two days after the cabinet approved the seven-
member committee's findings—Margalit submitted a summary of his
investigations to the police Inspector-General, the Attorney-General,
and the military police investigation department. After studying the
summary, which was based on Hagag's renewed assertion that the copy
of the letter Givly had submitted to the Olshan-Dori commission was the
original, with no alteration or falsification, the acting commander of the
MP investigation department pronounced: "No case." Hausner wrote to
Salomon:

I hereby inform you that I have terminated my study of the investigation material in relation to the charge of forgery, or disseminating a
forged document, against your client Col. B. Givly.
   My conclusion is that the body of evidence in my possession is insufficient for filing an indictment against your client for forgery, or dis-
semination of a forged document, in matters relating to "the affair."

Hagag—who seemed to be living on another planet—submitted a seventh and final investigative report that reiterated his earlier assertions.
He and Ben-Gurion were alone in maintaining that Givly was innocent
of forging the letter. Ben-Gurion went through the rest of his life with
that conviction unshaken. Had he lived longer, to early 1995, he would
have heard Ben-Zur, too, admitting to forgeries, at Givly's instigation.
Interviewed by ex-MI peers, for a TV documentary, he was taped saying:
"Givly put me up to the choice, 'either you are with us or with them,' and
I chose the way of lies."

23

Down Hill

Apparently aware of the ministerial committee's inclination to exonerate him, Lavon must have seen a decisive victory over Ben-Gurion virtually within his grasp; otherwise, there is no accounting for his conduct during the two weeks before the findings were submitted for cabinet approval on December 25, 1960. A sensible man would have avoided becoming intoxicated with victory and tried instead to increase his prestige and public sympathy through graciousness, treating Ben-Gurion with courtesy. But Lavon chose otherwise.

On December 14, the Histadrut marked its fortieth anniversary with a large rally, preceded by a press conference with Secretary-General Lavon. Ben-Gurion attended neither event, but his presence was nevertheless felt. At the rally, references to him drew applause, and many were irked because Lavon had not extended to him the special invitation he deserved as one of the Histadrut's charter members and its leader for its first fourteen years. Ben-Gurion's name was not mentioned at the press conference, but he was the main target of virulent criticism from Lavon—an onslaught that caused widespread indignation, as had Lavon's statements before the Knesset foreign affairs and defense committee.

Lavon's conduct was debated extensively at angry sessions of the Mapai secretariat on December 16 and 31. Coinciding with the final deliberations of the ministerial committee, this debate provided the backdrop against which its findings were adopted and submitted for cabinet approval, and set the scene for the fateful developments that ensued.

Ben-Gurion attended neither secretariat meeting, but two letters from him were read out at the first. In one, Ben-Gurion declined to be interviewed, making his distaste for Lavon clear: "To my great regret, I cannot take part in *Davar* as long as it is subject to the present regime ." Lavon had cited this "slap in the face" as the reason why he had not invited Ben-Gurion to the rally.

Ben-Gurion's second letter said he would explain his absence from the rally after hearing the ministerial committee's findings, at which time he would elaborate on "what I know about the antics of Pinhas Lavon over the past two months, and during his tenure as defense minister."

It was now clear that Ben-Gurion was refusing to accept Lavon's rehabilitation, unless it was granted by a judicial inquiry. With coexistence between the two no longer feasible, Mapai's leaders confronted a painful choice: Ben-Gurion or Lavon. They feared that the now unavoidable clash would be the ruin of Mapai.

As long as it seemed possible to placate Ben-Gurion by condemning Lavon, most of those who spoke at the meeting thought Mapai's survival depended on doing so. Even those who had sided with Lavon unleashed an onslaught of criticism at him. Aran, a leading Lavon supporter who alleged that "a large portion" of the secretariat's members were "secretly organizing to put [Lavon] to the stake," confessed himself "horrified by Lavon's statements."

The secretariat resolved to condemn Lavon's statements at the press conference; Lavon himself "voiced regret over some of the expressions he had used."

Evidently convinced that Ben-Gurion was about to resign as prime minister, the anxious Bloc leaders considered how to uphold the ministerial committee's findings and still prevent the resignation. Meir worried that a secretariat debate would turn into a duel, and that—as Ben-Gurion had hinted—he would accept the committee's findings only at the price of Lavon's head. Eshkol agreed to pay it; he was, however, unanimously elected the "peacemaker."

Supporters of the committee's findings held all the trumps—party discipline, the committee's unanimity, its guaranteed cabinet majority. Ben-Gurion retained a single card: justice. He reiterated that the power to acquit or condemn belonged exclusively to a court of law—not a political body. But to make that contention powerful enough to undermine the committee's findings, Ben-Gurion needed Givly to demand a judicial inquiry. He had a bitter disappointment in store.

Apparently at Salomon's urging, Givly had concluded that he would gain nothing from a judicial inquiry. Aware that such a stance implied an admission of guilt, they decided on a gradual retreat, behind a smokescreen of doubletalk. In the columns of *Maariv*, Givly continued to display determination: "I will fight to prove the justice of my case, I won't give in." Giving the false impression that such a battle would impoverish him, he maintained, "I'll hock my home to pay for my defense . . . even if I have to raise corn, I won't give up the fight." But in private, his demand dwindled. In a letter to Ben-Gurion dated December 23 1960, two days before the committee's findings received cabinet approval, the shrill note resounding from the pages of *Maariv* had been softened:

> I know how greatly you desire to enable me to bring the matter to a hearing before the proper body. But I do not know whether the aforementioned circumstances have not put an end to the possibility of establishing the truth as I claim to clear my name. Under such conditions, and in the perplexity wherein I find myself now, I entrust the matter to your consideration.

Eshkol now had reason to expect Givly to drop his demand as well as grounds to hope that, when the cabinet approved the findings, the wolf would be sated while the lamb emerged unscathed. All would cry good riddance to the affair: Lavon would be rehabilitated; harmony would be restored to Mapai; Ben-Gurion would be free to devote himself to defense matters; the cabinet would revert with renewed vigor to its normal tasks; the Knesset, its foreign affairs and defense committee, and the people of Israel, would heave a collective sigh of relief.

Dalia Carmel would no longer need to wrestle with her conscience and would be rid of her emotional commitment to Givly. Eshkol was convinced that Carmel was satisfied, because he was satisfied with her, and, as people do, he projected his own feelings onto her. He bore her no grudge for her testimony to the police; on the contrary, he was proud that "she did not backtrack on the principal points of her [Paris] testimony," in spite of the pressure exerted on her. Everything paled against the fact that she had confided the secret which had enabled him to constitute the ministerial committee and guide it to its conclusions. Like all lovers, he saw nothing but her good and attractive qualities. When she returned to New York in January 1961, they renewed their correspondence; his arrival in the United States in January 1962 for a two-month tour rekindled their love affair.

When he visited New York again in September, they vacationed at a resort in the Catskills. Carmel painted and Eshkol rode horses, commiserating with them "for not having the privilege of bearing you on their backs." They appear to have harbored tentative thoughts of marriage. Carmel told him her parents "worry about gossip"; on his return to Jerusalem, he wrote: "Dalik, your place is here with us." But he understood that she found the notion of marriage hard to contemplate.

Ultimately, Carmel appears to have declined his proposal; and Eshkol, who became prime minister on June 26, 1963, married Miriam Zelikovitch in March 1964. He then wrote to Carmel: "I gave you 'first priority' at the time, and even understood and accepted your tender, puzzling refusal, I did not even take offense. Gracefully, I swallowed virtually everything." Their letters became less frequent until they stopped corresponding in 1965.

Last but not least, even Givly wound up satisfied. He was spared a debilitating investigation that threatened to incriminate him and tarnish his reputation; equally, he avoided impoverishment, for in a land whose financial faucets were largely monopolized by state and party, he would have found no way of rehabilitating himself and making a respectable living. By giving up his demand for a judicial inquiry, he could preen himself as a righteous man wronged, while simultaneously getting lavish assistance in feathering his own nest.

On December 15, 1960, during Carmel's police interrogations, Eshkol—recalling Givly's visit in the company of Surkiss—asked her to convey on his behalf "a request that Givly drop his demand for an inquiry commission"; her letters testify that she did meet with Givly, and that Eshkol backed his request with a pledge of assistance.

In February 1961—to leap ahead in our narrative—Eshkol sent an aide to Ephraim Ilin, owner of the large Kaiser-Fraser vehicle works in Haifa, asking him to offer Givly a job; Ilin consented. On March 12, 1961, the press reported Givly's appointment as a senior executive with Kaiser-Fraser—whereupon Sapir, apparently after a word from Eshkol, also became a devoted Givly fan.

On the eve of the December 25, 1960, cabinet meeting, Eshkol had
every reason to believe that everyone involved in the affair was satisfied
with his or her lot. This assumption was shattered at the cabinet meeting
by Ben-Gurion, who subjected the ministerial committee's findings to a
vituperative attack; although Givly had pulled the rug out from under
him, he continued to insist on a judicial inquiry, even threatening resignation explicitly this time. Nevertheless, a majority approved the findings, with only three abstentions—Ben-Gurion, Dayan, and Eban.

Although Ben-Gurion intended to remain calm, his voice grew angry
as he read out his written statement. His first point concerned the committee's mandate. Its task was to study the material relating to the affair,
and advise the cabinet "what it thought should be done in future." On
November 11, its chairman had written Ben-Gurion, affirming that its
conclusions would be "merely procedural." But now, the committee was
submitting conclusions both substantive and judicial. Moreover, it condemned Givly without trial or due process, which was "a harsh blow at
the fundamentals of a democratic state and the basic rights of its citizens." Its conclusions were accordingly void.

Second, Ben-Gurion sharply criticized the committee's procedures. It
had declined to summon witnesses supposedly because of the frailty of
human memory; but it did call those witnesses it wanted: Carmel, Harkabi, and Ben-Zur. The committee based its conclusions upon "new testimony," yet had disregarded any evidence that might have been submitted by the witnesses it did not call.

The seven ministers had taken into account "Lavon's appeal" against
the findings of the Olshan-Dori commission, but not "Givly's appeal"
against the findings of the Cohen board. In adopting the latter, the committee affirmed the assertion that Givly had lied; but it conducted no
examination of Lavon's countless lies. For example, Lavon had told the
Knesset foreign affairs and defense committee that "he has additional
material, and will willingly disclose it to an authorized body"; but when
Rosen approached him, it turned out "that he has no documents which
were not before the commissions that investigated the affair." Lavon
alleged that the IDF detachment captured by the Syrians in December
1954 had acted without authorization from senior command; but the
committee had refused to hear Dayan, who denied this charge.

Ben-Gurion then pointed out that the ministers of justice, interior,
police, and finance, who had all been members of the 1954 cabinet,

were aware of the facts, yet had refrained from condemning "Lavon's lies." This "voids your grounds for condemning Givly."

Finally: the committee based its conclusions upon the falsification of the copy of Givly's letter, knowingly ignoring the fact that the police were still investigating that question.

His first two points enabled Ben-Gurion to make the third: only a judicial commission—free to resort to attorneys and empowered to interrogate witnesses—was both authorized and competent to uncover the truth. In its refusal to constitute such an inquiry, the cabinet denied Givly's right to demand judicial scrutiny of Lavon's crimes.

Fourth, while not accusing Lavon of giving the order for the Egyptian operation, Ben-Gurion refused to embrace the committee's assertion that it was carried out solely on Givly's authority. It was unimaginable that an officer—however senior—would order such an operation on his own authority.

The cabinet, brushing aside these comments, approved the committee's conclusions. Whereupon Ben-Gurion announced: "The sole conclusion I have to draw is—I am departing." Gathering up his papers, he left.

It was Ben-Gurion the warrior at his finest. Formerly, such words would have inspired dread in friend and foe alike; but he now faced an equally dauntless warrior: Meir. Before Ben-Gurion could finish his sentence, she rose and stalked out; she then wrote a letter of resignation and entrusted it to the cabinet secretary for submission to the cabinet meeting of January 1, 1961. Ben-Gurion was not unprepared for this. According to his secretary, Yitzhak Navon, Meir had warned beforehand that, if Ben-Gurion threatened resignation, "I'm getting up and leaving the cabinet." According to the mores of Mapai at the time, this bold pitting of threat against threat was a challenge to Ben-Gurion: she had summoned him to a duel.

In January 1961, in a letter to Ben-Gurion, Givly announced total retreat from his demand: "I have decided not to take any further initiative for the present in relation to the appointment of an inquiry commission." Of all the pretexts he enumerated—his unwillingness "to be a kind of sacrificial offering for regulating inter-party or intra-party matters," the arduous years he had endured, and, ironically, the lesson he drew from Be'eri's ordeal—only one contains an evident truth: "My family and I are in need of rest and respite, I have to reach early decisions regarding my future."

When Eshkol realized that Givly set greater store by his financial prospects than his good name, he took a number of steps, the most important being Hausner's January 10, 1961, letter notifying Salomon that "the body of evidence in my possession is insufficient to submit an indictment against Givly." He also arranged to provide Givly with a respectable job and adequate income.

Relieved of the threat of criminal prosecution and assured of a comfortable future, Givly could breathe freely. He and his attorney announced that "as far as we are concerned, the question has been effectively resolved by the Olshan-Dori and Cohen inquiries, and by the police investigators' findings refuting the forgery charges." As Eshkol had foreseen, Givly was now free to pursue his own interests, while simultaneously claiming to be innocent of the charges made against him by the seven-member committee, and accusing others—absurd as it may seem, Ben-Gurion above all—of obstructing investigation of the affair by an inquiry commission.

Severely disappointed to find his tried and true weapon of threatened resignation less effective than it had been, Ben-Gurion did not resign immediately after the December 25 cabinet meeting. The following evening, he conferred with Eshkol, who argued that the government could not exist without him. "I was surprised," Ben-Gurion later wrote Eshkol, "by the extent to which you do not attempt to understand me, or see the impossibility of me going on. . . . You were well aware of my opinion right from the onset of the affair, you were not bound to consider my opinion (I say that in all collegiality and good will) but you cannot ask me to bow to your verdict." He added: "I utterly reject . . . your view that the state supposedly stands or falls with me."

Ben-Gurion proceeded to draft a letter of resignation; on December 29, 1960, before sending it to the party secretariat, he gave a handwritten, unsigned copy to Almogi. Predictably startled, Almogi begged him to delay a few days, and Ben-Gurion consented, hoping that the breathing-space would, as before, render the letter unnecessary.

Afraid that the resignation would be submitted at the January 1, 1961, cabinet meeting, Mapai's secretariat convened the previous day, along with the party's Knesset faction. Almogi read out the letter, "which has already gone for typing and signature," warning that it was "liable to be sent to the press."

Like the letter to Eshkol, the resignation letter maintained that "The state and government do not depend upon any single individual, whoever he may be." Ben-Gurion's resolve to resign was "final and firm," for he was unable, "by decree of my conscience," to "share responsibility" for a government which had approved the findings of the seven-member committee, flouting his principles of statehood, which "outweigh all other considerations in my eyes. And the supreme principle of statehood, as I perceive it, is the security of the state, and its leaders' unsullied conscience."

Just as he did not demand that Eshkol and his colleagues relinquish their course of action, they had no right to demand that he "be true to something which affronts my very being as defense minister." Nevertheless, "I leave the government without any resentment or anger or indignation. I disagreed with colleagues' views, but continue to hold them in esteem and believe in them as ever. It is permissible for them to think differently from the way I think, and to act on their own opinions. No individual is entitled to use pressure to impose his view upon his colleagues."

As "a citizen," Ben-Gurion said, he intended "to assist . . . in developing and repopulating the Negev, and in attracting pioneering youth, scientists and intellectuals from the Diaspora to Israel." But his veteran colleagues, familiar with his ways, took that pledge as a subtle stratagem, a kind of "Sdeh Boker II" indicating that he was prepared, on certain conditions, to return to his office. They perceived the letter as a calculated step in his strategy.

That strategy was related to two aspects of Lavon's triumph. The personal side was overt and public. As David Giladi had noted in *Maariv* back in November, Lavon's intention was "to undermine Ben-Gurion's prestige," and the sense of "utter security" every citizen felt thanks to him. The committee's findings had shattered the Ben-Gurion myth. From now on all would know that "there were and are irregularities within the defense ministry and establishment . . . and machinations and personal jealousies and mutual intrigues and slanders in that holy of holies, and . . . a lack of adequate control and a lack of subordination." Accordingly, "Mr. Ben-Gurion had better withdraw to Sdeh Boker."

The second aspect, veiled and unstated, had to do with Dayan and Peres. Eshkol had insisted that the committee find Ben-Gurion innocent of any involvement in the Egyptian affair: "There are no grounds for the charge that the instruction to Givly was issued by any other person, whether within or without the defense establishment," it wrote. But he did nothing to clear "the young men"—a term that clearly referred to Dayan and Peres—of the false charge of complicity in the "conspiracy" to overthrow Lavon.

Meir had made an analogy between the Tubiansky affair and the Lavon affair. "Among the great things Ben-Gurion did," she said, "was the investigation with respect to Tubiansky. It was not a political matter, and the investigation had a single purpose: ridding [Tubiansky's] wife and child of a terrible stigma." She seemed to be asking why Ben-Gurion balked at an investigation when the terrible stigma attached to Lavon. Was it because "the young men" who were his intimates had connived in Givly's "conspiracy" against Lavon ?

Those "young men" were thus the reason why the veteran leaders, who had resented Lavon's appointment as defense minister in December 1953, and pressed for his resignation in 1955, switched sides in 1960 to become his allies. Without this conflict the veterans would doubtless have lined up with Ben-Gurion, and the seven-member committee would never have come into being. Lavon's triumph over Ben-Gurion was thus transmuted into the veterans' victory.

It seems now that Meir foresaw Ben-Gurion's next move: his resignation would entail the resignation of the cabinet, whereupon he would form a new government that would disown the ministerial committee's conclusions. Indeed, in February 1961, when journalists asked Ben-Gurion whether the new government soon to arise would adhere to the findings of the seven-member committee, he replied: "No, it is not a matter of the new government. The [former] government broke up over [the findings and they] are nonexistent."

Meir, however, was determined to forestall such a development. Her December 25, 1960, resignation threat was a signal to Ben-Gurion that, if he wanted a new government, he would have to form it without the Bloc, without the "troika," and possibly, without Eshkol. A time-bomb set to go off the moment Ben-Gurion submitted his own resignation, the resignation letter Meir deposited with the cabinet secretary was also the trigger of a chain reaction.

The secretariat meeting of December 31, 1960, witnessed an unprecedented face-to-face confrontation between Ben-Gurion and the Bloc. It was a form of palace coup aimed at designating a crown prince without toppling the king from his throne. Gone were the days when Ben-Gurion would make decisions, or alternately, draw the Bloc into what Dayan called "an understanding agreeable to all, on the course the government should take." The "troika" had its foot wedged in the door of the throne room, and there was no way of dislodging it. The trio's grit and mettle appeared to draw upon two sources. One was honor and principle. Eshkol was jealous of his honor and attentive to his principles. In his view, both would be eroded by annulment of the committee's conclusions.

Meir told the secretariat:

> We want the people to respect the government as it is, collectively. We want the world to know that the government exists, and that we are not licentious nor are we of the underworld. Seven cabinet members . . . examine a fundamental matter, important and grave, and produce a unanimous decision. After that, must we go to the people and the world and say: "Nonsense, it's improper procedure"? . . . If the committee's seven members, 50% of the cabinet, are capable of [such nonsense] . . . why trust them on other matters ?

The "troika's" other—and arguably main—source of power was Ben-Gurion's inability to put together a government without it. The question now posed was: a government without Mapai, or without Ben-Gurion? Horrified at the mere thought, his followers hastened to submit various draft resolutions expressing one theme: there could be no government without Ben-Gurion. It was the first time in the annals of the state of Israel that the secretariat of the ruling party had considered this issue, and there could be no clearer sign of Ben-Gurion's decline.

The veterans opposed such a resolution. "Stating that no party member [but Ben-Gurion] shall be prime minister," said Meir, "has a discordant ring." She asked: "Is it permissible to surmise that a man—even the most revered amongst us—is capable of error, or is it sacrilegious to think it? If it is permissible to think it, our colleagues are permitted to think that Ben-Gurion is proposing something on which he errs, and they differ."

It soon became evident that the "troika's" warning of a series of resignations posed a threat—aimed at Ben-Gurion—that Mapai would lose power, and that the debate in effect turned upon confidence in Ben-Gurion. In addition to the resignations already in the offing, Ben-Gurion had to anticipate being unable to form a new government. That would mean an end to Mapai's hegemony, and the ascendancy of other parties.

Understanding this, Dayan, a master of the art of fence-straddling, startled the secretariat: "These past three months, Mapai's policy . . . has been conducted and expressed by Eshkol, not Ben-Gurion; and Ben-Gurion cannot get over the fact that Mapai's policy [as conveyed] by its representatives, was not his policy."

Nevertheless, "Ben-Gurion will not form a government with Peres and Dayan, nor even with Abba Eban and Josephthal," Dayan asserted, but would aim for a cabinet with Meir, Eshkol, and Sapir, and "had Aran not resigned, Aran too." Therefore, "either . . . Aran, Golda, Eshkol, and Sapir reach an understanding with Ben-Gurion on . . . the course the government should follow," or "Ben-Gurion resigns, and Mapai forms a different government."

Evidently Dayan saw how the balance was tilting:

> Should it happen that Ben-Gurion resigns, and I thought it would be to the state's benefit that a Mapai government emerge, and should I be invited, heaven forbid, to join that government as agriculture minister—I'd join. . . . The state comes before all else, Ben-Gurion included. When Mapai's secretariat decides it will not form a government without Ben-Gurion, [then] unless Ben-Gurion backs down, that means a different party will form a government.

This willingness to join a government without Ben-Gurion was not what the secretariat expected to hear from Dayan, who was now revealed as a vane veering with the wind.

The willingness of Dayan, the leader of "the young men," to cross over to the camp of the "veterans" marked the end of the generational confrontation which had accompanied the Lavon affair, for it demonstrated that the veterans were in no danger, and that their apprehensions had been groundless. On the other hand, the counter-putsch engineered by the veterans under Meir had been successful. The "old man" had fallen between two stools; at seventy-four, his future was all downhill.

24

The Banana Peel

On January 4, 1961, Pinhas Sapir sent the cabinet secretary his letter of resignation; the promised mutiny was in full swing. Besides trying to mollify Ben-Gurion, Mapai now had to woo two of the leading apostles of Lavon's exoneration. Lavon, feeling heartened, called for "a halt to the pursuit of the affair"; but Ben-Gurion, brandishing the banner of truth-and-justice-above-all, continued to insist on invalidation of the ministerial committee's findings and the institution of a judicial inquiry.

A decision to create an "examining committee" to probe the conduct of Lavon and others seemed briefly to offer a way out. But Meir refused to join it, and it was dissolved. The Knesset foreign affairs and defense committee and then the plenary Knesset endorsed the findings of the seven-member committee, whereupon Ben-Gurion handed his resignation to the president on January 31.

Mapai faced total rupture. Eshkol the peacemaker, having completed the first phase of his task with the rehabilitation that appeased Lavon, now proceeded to the second phase: appeasing Ben-Gurion by unseating Lavon from his position as Histadrut secretary. This seemed the only hope of avoiding a split in the party. On February 4, a closed meeting of Mapai's central committee voted by 150 to 96 with 5 abstentions for a proposal by Eshkol, approved the previous day by the party secretariat, which stated: "In the existing circumstances, Lavon cannot represent the party as Histadrut secretary." The broad support that Lavon retained reflected the irony that those who had helped engineer his ouster from the government in 1955 now opposed his dismissal from the Histadrut.

Only Eshkol, hoping to bury the affair once and for all, in a calculated move supported Lavon's dismissal in this case as well as the previous one. He hoped that, once Ben-Gurion had settled the score with his adversary, he would withdraw his resignation and that Meir and Sapir would then do the same, so that the government, the party, and the country at large could return to normal. But the opposite happened: Lavon's dismissal, masterminded by Eshkol, was blamed on Ben-Gurion, and the storm erupted anew.

Lavon's supporters in the central committee, comprising the entire leadership except for Eshkol, refused to buy Ben-Gurion's leadership at the price Eshkol had set. Before long Ben-Gurion faced a wall-to-wall coalition embracing left and right, within Mapai and beyond it, which rallied behind "intellectual" standard-bearers—academics, poets, writers, and journalists. For the first time, Mapai's internal affairs were encroached upon by circles hitherto indifferent toward the party and aloof from political activity in general.

A case in point was a petition calling "for cleansing of the air and restoration of confidence." Published on December 30, 1960—before Lavon's dismissal—it was signed by fifty intellectuals, headed by four renowned professors from Jerusalem's Hebrew University: philosopher Nathan Rotenschtreich, Judaica scholar Ephraim Orbach, and historians Ya'akov Talmon and Yehoshua Praver. While appearing initially to favor neither side, they soon gave Lavon unqualified support. On January 11, a heavily attended rally under their sponsorship affirmed that Israeli democracy faced a threat from Ben-Gurion, who had engineered Lavon's dismissal.

It was a striking illustration of how academics, however illustrious, can be misguided by politics. In exceeding the bounds of their expertise, academics distinguished for intellectual honesty and impartiality sometimes adopt intransigent positions on the strength of untested data. There is no other way to explain how these "intellectuals" fell for the slanted leaks inundating the press, taking it upon themselves, without thorough study, to guide public opinion by means of proclamations and protests.

The rift within Mapai was an open invitation to adversaries from right and left, from opposition and coalition equally, who had never seen a better opportunity to draw voters away from the ruling party, perhaps even overthrow it. Calling for the ministerial committee's findings to be upheld, they united in demanding general elections, which the Knesset approved on March 28, 1961.

The elections, held August 8, did not fully meet their expectations. Mapai lost five of its forty-seven seats, but remained stronger than any of its rivals, and was still the only party able to put together a coalition cabinet. All the same, the elections ushered in the beginning of a new political era. The new Liberal party—a fusion of the former General Zionists and Progressives, which won three seats more than the combined number previously held by its two components—would later unite with Herut, ultimately forming the Likud; this process would, for the first time, produce a genuine alternative to Mapai.

As the representative of the Knesset's largest faction, Ben-Gurion was twice called upon by the state president, Yitzhak Ben-Zvi, to form a government. But Mapai's outgoing coalition partners refused to deal with him as long as he continued to insist on invalidating the ministerial committee's findings and setting up a judicial inquiry. Ben-Gurion was therefore forced to notify the president that, "under present circumstances," he could not form a government. Hailed initially as the most formidable administration Ben-Gurion had headed, the cabinet from which he had resigned, and which resigned along with him, was also the last he ever put together.

The president now called on Eshkol to take up the task. But such was the resistance to Ben-Gurion becoming prime minister that coalition talks dragged on for nine months; it was December 2, 1961 before Ben-Gurion could present to the Knesset the cabinet Eshkol had constructed for him. There was no precedent for a cabinet headed by anyone other than the man who had put it together. Its narrow parliamentary majority—63 out of 120—reflected its parlous state.

Ben-Gurion consented to lead this cabinet for the single purpose of annulling the ministerial committee's findings and instituting a judicial inquiry. When he failed to do this, he resigned. The 601-day tenure of Ben Gurion's last government was the cruelest period of his life. But he persisted, pursuing his campaign even after his resignation. His enemies multiplied, and he was increasingly isolated. To Ben-Gurion, Eshkol was now his greatest adversary, overshadowing even Lavon.

The gloom of Ben-Gurion's solitude was lit up briefly when the veterans who now dominated Mapai, eager to win his sanction for a projected

alliance with Ahdut HaAvodah (which had enlarged its Knesset representation from seven to eight), seemed willing to reconsider his demand
for a judicial inquiry. But this proposed "alignment" of the parties, entail-
ing the return of the interim generation which had quit Mapai with the
1944 schism (Ahdut HaAvodah leaders Yitzhak Ben-Aharon, Yigal Alon,
and Israel Galili), ran into opposition from the young men, who saw it as
a further move aimed at shunting them aside, buttressing the rule of the
veterans and reinforcing the party's anti-Ben-Gurionist stance.

Eshkol, who more than any of his colleagues agonized over the rift
with Ben-Gurion, drove on October 22, 1964, to Sdeh Boker to solicit
his blessing for the alignment. But instead of a blessing, Eshkol was
regaled with an account of Ben-Gurion's most recent moves: he had presented a demand to the justice minister and Attorney-General for
"appointment of an inquiry commission composed of Supreme Court
judges, to consider whether the cabinet's refusal to appoint a judicial
inquiry commission as demanded by Givly, and its appointment instead
of a seven-member committee of ministers, and whether the procedures
of that committee and its conclusions, are consistent with truth, justice,
and the laws of the state." The conversation revolved around "the errors
of the seven-member committee," and Ben-Gurion's diary recorded
Eshkol's explanation of his conviction that Lavon deserved rehabilitation: "Someone told him a secret which changes everything, but he
never told anyone that he has a secret, and that secret justifies his conclusion and his conduct."

Ben-Gurion commented: "If he alone heard the secret, it does not
exist for the world, and all will draw the conclusion that each of us drew
[our conclusion] according to the information in our possession."

Eshkol had revealed "the secret"—or rather hinted at it—in order "to
win Ben-Gurion over" for the alignment. Perhaps he calculated that if he
gave in to Ben-Gurion about the judicial inquiry—of whose verdict he
was confident–in exchange Ben-Gurion would moderate his objections
to the alignment, rescuing Mapai from a fresh split.

Briefly, Ben-Gurion seemed close to attaining his objective. On
December 6, 1964, Eshkol's cabinet deliberated a proposal by the justice
minister, supported by the Attorney-General's recommendation, to
appoint a state inquiry commission. At long last, Ben-Gurion could look
forward to a measure of satisfaction. He must have told himself: Better
ten years late than never.

More than anyone, Givly was dismayed at this prospect. He had hoped
that the threat of a renewed probe had passed forever; but here he was,

again threatened with an inquiry commission. "We all thought," he
wrote Carmel on November 29,

> that the matter is finished, or, in the Knesset's terms, "closed and
> sealed." Everyone has suffered, you, and I, and other friends of ours.
> After two years, Ben-Gurion unexpectedly comes out "in my defense
> and yours"—no-one asked him to, but his conscience seems to trouble
> him for not having thought up in the course of two years a way to
> appoint an inquiry commission, and for not having then granted me
> and my attorney all we demanded in order to prove the justice of our
> case.

It was now late 1964, and Carmel was no longer a girl-soldier, bedazzled
and adoring; but, failing to sense the change, Givly tried to impress on
her his notion of the injustice visited upon him. The "bad guys," however, were no longer Lavon and his followers, but "the circle standing
behind Ben-Gurion and abetting him in the forcible demand to establish a judicial inquiry commission, without anyone knowing what it is or
what it's good for." He added: "Everyone—myself included—is sure
there is no further need for all that."

As before, Givly proceeded to prepare Carmel's deposition:

> The main problem is accordingly the matter of your testimony in rela-
> tion to the letter; hence, my girl, you must not say a word, or disclose
> anything, in this matter. Should you be summoned to Israel, you must
> first notify me by cable when you are arriving, and immediately make
> discreet contact with Attorney Ya'akov Salomon, as it will be up to him
> to set out our line of defense, perhaps even appear on behalf of us all.
> . . . First and foremost, what I have just said: say nothing. If . . . your
> deposition is taken abroad, you must reiterate your most recent testi-
> mony in Israel, wherein you claimed (unlike what you claimed in Paris,
> that you added something or other to the letter to the chief of staff)
> that you remember no such thing. . . . The letter sent by me to the
> chief of staff is the decisive element in establishing the issuing of the
> order by Lavon, and on that point matters must be clear.

As in 1960, Givly urged Carmel to send her letters "double-sealed" to a
Haifa address. "It is vital to maintain composure and a good mood"; he
was convinced Carmel would not let him down because "we have already
been through this once. I hope we withstand it all again." Finally—as a
reward for her loyalty?—"I promise I will come to the United States." He
signed himself "yours as ever."

Within 24 hours Givly sent a second letter:

And so, my dear, we have both been sucked into a tempest whose outcome is unpredictable. . . . We are liable to find ourselves "in the cart" again. . . . My heart goes out to Eshkol, who is attempting to extricate the government, the country, and himself from the labyrinth into which all have been drawn entirely to the demand of one person, Ben-Gurion. The "old man" has totally lost all factual and rational judgement, and acts on the most dangerous of impulses . . . to try and regain a position of influence and power.

More than six weeks elapsed without a reply from Carmel. Evidently fearful that she had joined the "witches' caper," Givly wrote again on January 25, 1965: "If you do not wish to write me, for your own good reasons, please reassure me, if only in one sentence, that the letters arrived, whatever you did with them."

Reiterating his pledge "to get to the United States and be with you," he added: "The only question now is whether you will wish to see me, will rejoice at my arrival as I knew you would have in the past, have matters really changed to that extent??"

He answered that question himself: "No, no, that can never be. If I am obligated in any way, I will be ready, even at the price of my life, to [repay the debt] so as to [retain your] respect for my person."

On February 17, 1965, Carmel replied with a lengthy letter typed single-spaced in English. She began by noting that the eleven years gone by since the end of her obligatory military service "show on my calendar too." However, "On listening to the tone of your letters, one can hear the intonation of a grown-up talking to an immature girl." Givly had to realize that "Times have changed. I have learned my lessons during my short life, and the experience I have gained is a guide to my actions and behavior."

She would be glad to see him in New York, for she wished "to lay the cards, face up, on the table, once and for all, and discuss . . . with you face to face things that have been hampering your life and mine for the last 10 years." It was time for a reckoning. Regarding his motives in writing her,

alas, they are neither just, honorable or moral, especially for a person who keeps harping on the question of morals all the time. Weren't you already blamed once before for having done the same thing when Avry [Elad] was on trial? Wasn't that already confirmed—what we call, in simple language, perjury???

As for Ben-Gurion:

> Whatever prompted B.G. to start a one-man fight . . . the fact is that he opened a fight, which . . . could have been your fight to clear your name and conscience regarding this whole affair . . . to prove your contentions. Instead, you were the least interested party in this second round . . . If it was because of financial reasons (L.E. [Eshkol] promised to help you out) or lack of access to documentation . . . of 1954–5, or the inconvenience of having this affair reopened . . . is of less importance. The fact is that you declined the opportunity you had, to have your case aired and reviewed. . . . However, there is only one thing I want you to understand . . . thoroughly. I was not an accomplice. I was not a partner, nor an equal colleague. I was a soldier in compulsory service, who complied with another officer's request—Motke [Ben-Zur]—to do the thing which I subsequently admitted both to Hausner and the police. No, sir, . . . WE DO NOT BELONG IN THE SAME BOAT. . . . But on the other hand, while Ben-Gurion is trying vehemently to prove that his men in the army couldn't perjure or forge, that all this was a mistake, you go ahead and compound the satire by trying to "prepare" the witnesses all over again. In your two letters you made me . . . a fool. . . .
>
> Your suggestions were all understood, from a simple human point of view . . . of the cowardly feeble human being. They were not understood from any other just, fair or moral point of view. . . . I am saying this to you unequivocally—I am not denying [the testimony I gave in Paris].
>
> I wish you were a man; and if and when those proceedings would have started you would have gotten up to pound on the table in an honest, clear-cut way, and not "conspire" in this fishy . . . manner. Frankly speaking, I think that truth, honestly stated by someone who has his weaknesses, can be more powerful and carry greater weight than a set of phony facts he arranges to try to create the impression of being honest, strong and incapable of human errors. Alas, isn't that too late.

The Givly chapter in Carmel's biography was over—but not the affair. Her future life was shaped by her alterations and forgeries of 1954. Instructions from foreign minister Golda Meir probably lay behind the rejection of her applications for a job at Israel's New York consulate, and for extension of her diplomatic passport. Even when she got a job with

Israel's commercial delegation in 1962, she soon became aware of her low status and felt "under social siege," "deprived and offended." Her cries of distress reached Eshkol, who hastened to her assistance. In a striking illustration of love's potency, Israel's "Number 2," shortly to replace Ben-Gurion, secretly sent handwritten letters to a middle-level government employee, whom he directed to destroy them after reading them and to find Carmel "a suitable and honorable position in our empire."

Eshkol was also operating out of political expediency: as he wrote candidly, he found it convenient for Carmel to remain outside Israel. Thus, when Meir's long arm foiled his attempt to get her "a suitable position," he enlisted the aid of senior officials, including El Al's chief executive, who gave Carmel a job in the airline's claims department in New York.

Eshkol's marriage to Miriam Zelikovitch in March 1964 was a further reason for deferring Carmel's return to Israel. This enforced postponement, reinforced by a wish to keep her distance from a country where her name was linked with a painful episode, transformed her temporary stay into a permanent one; she would always feel as if she had been forced out of Israel. In 1978, she married Herbert Goldstein, an admirer of Eshkol and a longtime executive in Israel's fuel industry; she now lives with him in New York.

For ten years, Israel lived in the shadow of the question: who gave the order?—as though the answer had not been obvious ever since the Olshan-Dori commission submitted its inconclusive report to Sharett. That commission assigned Lavon and Givly equal responsibility for the Egyptian operation. Olshan and Dori, Moshe Dayan, Isser Harel, Yehoshafat Harkabi, Yossi Harel, and, ultimately, Ben-Gurion—all in their own fashion concluded that the key to the riddle lay in the famous conversation in which the two men agreed on the desirability of sabotage operations in Egypt. Each, however put a different construction on the conversation and its implications: Lavon maintained that he gave orders for planning, whereas Givly saw a green light for action. Dayan's journal for May 12, 1955, records Harkabi telling him that, in his opinion, "Lavon granted Benyamin overall authorization, implicit or outright. Each echelon gave those below clearer instructions."

The present writer agrees with this view, being convinced that there was a firm understanding between Givly and Lavon, which they maintained for two to three months, that operations by 131 in Egypt were possible and desirable, and that from then on each echelon upgraded the scheme, turning the understanding into policy and preparatory planning into actual operations.

At the end of May, 1954, Givly sent Ben-Zur to Paris for the fateful meeting with Elad. There can be no question that Ben-Zur gave Elad operational orders at that time—to send the "Shipment Possible" cable to confirm that the team was ready, then await the agreed-upon signal to start operations—and that on July 16 Givly gave Ben-Zur the order to commence operations. The Cohen board affirmed,

> The inescapable conclusion is that the instructions Ben-Zur gave Elad . . . were not just communications instructions, and that the operations referred to therein were indeed carried out by our people. Making the utmost effort to judge Ben-Zur leniently, it can be claimed that the instructions he gave Elad were ambiguous. . . . And Elad could—or perhaps should—understand that he had been given freedom of action, tacit if not explicit. . . . Ben-Zur . . . regarded the operations actually carried out as the natural and self-evident outcome of those orders.

This conclusion supported Dayan's claim that Givly extracted Lavon's "retroactive approval"; for Lavon did not say he did not give the order; he said he gave it retroactively. Why should he say this if he never gave it? The implication of Lavon's "retroactive approval" is that even if he did not give Givly the specific order on the 16th, this order was not contrary to his wish or policy.

How, then, to explain the operations on July 2 and 14? At the time these operations baffled Givly and Ben-Zur, who initially explained them as the handiwork of Egyptian malcontents, communists, and others, then accepted and endorsed Elad's explanation that his boys were itching for action and got out of control.

Only in 1958 did it become clear, thanks to Zvi Aharoni and Victor Cohen, that Elad, whose cover had been blown by Egyptian counterintelligence, had been made to play the role of a double agent. When the Cairo defendants were freed and came to Israel in 1968, they confirmed this as fact. Therefore the operations on July 2 and 14 were carried out according to a scenario supplied by Egyptian counterintelligence.

Had Givly told the truth, suspicions against Elad would have been aroused much earlier. But, taken by surprise when Lavon, who after nearly four months of solidarity and harmony suddenly turned against

him, Givly resorted to falsification and perjury. Had he told the truth—
that there was an understanding between him and Lavon, and that
Lavon gave him the order retroactively on July 30, because for some reason or other he did not get it in time to issue his own order on July 16—
history would have taken another course. Lavon's admission that he did
issue a retroactive order would have been taken as an admission that the
July 16 order did not displease him.

Why did Givly and Lavon behave as they did? One answer offers itself
readily, based on the adage that victory has many fathers while defeat is
an orphan: they both waited to see how things would turn out. Givly,
being closer to the sources of information, knew first that the operation
was a complete debacle, and hastened to obtain the retroactive order
from Lavon. Then, when the Egyptians imposed a news blackout, leaving Givly and Lavon in the dark, they found security in an alliance. It was
Dayan who, by forcing their hands, shattered this silence of solidarity.
From November 1 on it was everyone for himself.

Finally, was Givly stupid enough to act on his own authority without
notifying the minister in charge? If he had failed, his head would be on
the block. The answer to that question was best expressed by another former chief of staff, Lieutenant General Zvi Zur:

> In my opinion, Givly reported to Lavon, but I don't know how he
> reported, or what he said. I'm not sure he didn't present the picture
> imprecisely. There are people I rely upon to report accurately. When
> Benyamin Givly reports, I permit myself a little disquiet. In other
> words, I'm sure Givly spoke with Lavon about the Egyptian operation,
> but I don't know exactly what he said. Somehow, that doubt will always
> be with us.

Everyone seemed to have come to terms with "that doubt"; the renewed
proposal to set up an inquiry commission was dropped, leaving Givly
free to resume his upward course. A letter to Carmel in January 1965
mentions his friendly relations with Pinhas Sapir. After six years with Ilin,
Israel's economic czar got him a job with the Histadrut's major consumer network. With Sapir's backing, Givly continued to climb, reaching
the pinnacle of his success as chairman of the board of directors of the
Electricity Corporation (isn't it where our story started?). He also
became a "society figure" who crowned beauty queens and opened art
exhibitions. In 1968, he divorced Esther to marry Elisheva Ahituv, with
whom he had lived since 1966.

In February 1965, Israel's former consul-general in New York, Benyamin Eliav, came back on a visit and saw Dalia Carmel. They talked about the affair, and Carmel showed him Givly's letters. Eliav was overwhelmed: the letters might yet convince Ben-Gurion that the seven-member committee's findings were correct and avert a split in Mapai. At his request, Carmel gave him copies.

On his return to Israel, Eliav showed the letters to Shaul Avigur. Suspecting Carmel of seeking vengeance and publicity, Avigur resolved to question her in person. Meanwhile, Eshkol had backed away from his previous readiness to reconsider an inquiry commission; and in May 1965, Mapai was sundered on that rock of contention.

That same month, Avigur gave Ben-Gurion an account of Givly's letters to Carmel, and received approval for his meeting with her; but due to the split in Mapai and other reasons, it was deferred for several weeks. For the sake of confidentiality Carmel and Avigur met in Vienna for ten days of questioning.

The schism and its consequences—the emergence of Rafi and Ben-Gurion's expulsion from Mapai—apparently left no one interested in trying to enlist Carmel to convince Ben-Gurion of his error. Nevertheless Avigur insisted that she tell Ben-Gurion her story in person.

Avigur brought Carmel, unannounced, to Ben-Gurion's home at 9 in the evening of October 17, 1966. It is unclear what Avigur hoped to gain, other than further humiliating Ben-Gurion. Avigur was present in Ben-Gurion's library throughout his talk with Carmel; but if he hoped to see Ben-Gurion put to shame by discovering his error, Avigur was disappointed. Ben-Gurion refused to be convinced that the copy of Givly's letter submitted to the Olshan-Dori commission was forged. He elected to believe the findings of police captain Hagag, rather than Carmel's explicit admission.

Having left us no explanation for this choice, Ben-Gurion has left it open to interpretation. First, no man—particularly one who has reached a ripe old age—likes to confess his errors. Second, everyone finds it hard to admit that an important, fateful action was erroneous and misguided: it is doubly difficult for a prime minister when such an error sealed his fate toward the end of his days, robbing him of popular sympathy.

Ben-Gurion was aware, furthermore, that the affair was a political struggle *par excellence*; no one involved could claim to be objective. He may have realized that Carmel's account represented the "secret which changes everything" of which Eshkol had told him on October 22, 1964. He probably fathomed Eshkol's own secret, and realized that he had been right in surmising that her confession would most benefit Eshkol, who had become his principal adversary. In Ben-Gurion's standoff with his opponents, an admission of his error in this instance would have been self-defeating.

What was more, Carmel's confession, having come to his attention late, could neither change the past nor turn back the clock. Acknowledging that confession could only expose the fact that his senseless obstinacy had inflicted much harm upon his party, his government, and his people. Continuing to cling to his own truth was thus preferable to admitting an error which it was anyway too late to rectify.

Finally, Ben-Gurion did not, and could not, embrace a truth uncovered in such a manner—whether in his library, or in a New York hotel bed, or in another hotel in Vienna. He would have acknowledged the validity of Carmel's confession had it been deposed in a manner befitting national and legal propriety: before a duly constituted inquiry commission. But such a commission was prevented precisely by those, like Eshkol, who upheld the truth of Carmel's account.

That said, Ben-Gurion's response must be traced to its principal source, arguably the fundamental motivation dictating his conduct throughout "the Lavon affair": his view of the IDF. Regarding Israel's security as sacrosanct, Ben-Gurion saw the IDF as flesh of his flesh, his most cherished brainchild. In his eyes, the allegation that Lavon's forced resignation in 1955 arose from a conspiracy hatched by MI officers under Givly—with or without the connivance of Dayan and Peres—was an ugly smear on the immaculate tunics of his soldiers. Recall Ben-Gurion's comment, often repeated subsequently, at the cabinet meeting that approved the findings of the seven-member committee: before and after Lavon's tenure as defense minister, the IDF was free of false testimony and forgeries. Was it conceivable that, within a few months of Ben-Gurion's resignation and his withdrawal to Sdeh Boker, the IDF had changed beyond recognition, filling its ranks with liars and forgers? Whoever charged the IDF with "conspiracy," false testimony, and forgery was clearly accusing Ben-Gurion of raising and fostering a corrupt army. He found that unacceptable. By his own account, he was no admirer of Givly; but his support of Givly the individual, even when Givly no longer wanted it, really signified support of his own internal ideal of an IDF officer. Ben-Gurion seamed to be saying: my IDF never lies.

It sometimes happens that an individual meets his doom through some marginal error or trivial oversight, rather than from a setback in his principal endeavor—as when a boxing champion who trounces all his adversaries in the ring goes out and slips on a banana peel in an alleyway. Anyone—an individual or entire nation—is liable to slip up in this manner; and if that is so, it seems that David Ben-Gurion's own private banana peel was Benyamin Givly.

Epilogue: A View from the Present

We have seen how Lavon's accusations had particular impact because they dovetailed with fears being nurtured by the veteran leaders of Mapai, who strongly suspected that Ben-Gurion was in fact planning to discard them in favor of the younger men. They supported Lavon in part because they believed his accusations about Dayan and Peres, but still more because they believed that doing so was their only way to influence Ben-Gurion to support them as his successors.

In fact, Ben-Gurion never intended to advance Dayan and Peres over Eshkol, Meir, or Sapir, but in any case, they were ready to fight for what they considered their inalienable right even at the cost of Ben-Gurion's political head. In their eyes, too, long-cherished Israeli values—and consequently Israel itself—were in mortal danger. They feared that the armed forces and the defense establishment would come to dictate the electoral process and render it, the party system, and the Knesset redundant and useless. The military would become the principal social, cultural, and political force, and the defense establishment the leading economic and industrial factor.

Their argument went beyond an ordinary defense of democracy. For in their eyes, the military and the defense establishment had proved themselves unworthy of public trust, revealing an uninhibited, unrestrained lust for power, a lust that would stop at nothing, not even the use of lies and deceit to remove a minister who stood in their way. In their boundless self-righteousness they were likely to wage disastrous campaigns and entangle Israel in endless wars for their own satisfaction. Such behavior was a flagrant violation of a generally accepted axiom of Ben-Gurion's, which he had made part of Mapai's political credo: that Israel could survive only on a foundation of justice, truth, and exalted morality.

If Lavon's accusations turned out to be true, the veterans' fears would be justified. In any case, the accusations furnished the veterans with powerful political weapons and ammunition to fight the "Whiz Kids" and, if necessary, Ben-Gurion himself. At the same time, however, these Mapai leaders, though claiming to be the real defenders of Israel's democracy and moral values, objected to Ben-Gurion's insistence on examining Lavon's accusation by the only appropriate democratic tool, a state committee of inquiry presided over by a member of Israel's supreme court. They demanded instead that Lavon be peremptorily rehabilitated—that is, that the government, a political body, exonerate him, in violation of democratic procedure.

Ben-Gurion's camp painted just as grim a picture of Israel's future. The veterans, they claimed, wanted to avoid examination of the accusations by a committee of inquiry only to assure their own political ascendancy at the expense of Ben-Gurion and the younger leaders, even if this meant ruining them. They were not protecting the democratic process and the party system by supporting Lavon's unproven, false and malicious accusations, and were in fact entirely unworthy of trust. It was they who were using lies and deceit to further their cause. By weakening Israel's moral values, by placing their craving for power above truth, above Israel's critical need for a strong defensive force, they were the ones who were demoralizing Israel's citizenry, polity, and military, thus undermining the nation's existence.

Here, then, were volcanic fratricidal forces erupting within Mapai. In so doing they bequeathed their credo to future political practitioners: a politician is a Samason, in ego if in no other wise, entitled as such, in fighting opponents and rivals to bring the temple down.—"Let me die with the Philistines"-like—no holds barred. These internal forces were intensified by outside militants and their followers. Mapai's rival parties taking the opportunity to turn its disintegration to their advantage, eagerly joined the fray, on the veterans' side. Not satisfied with drawing strength from sympathizers and followers, the two camps pressured the undecided to stand up and be counted—a process that did not end until

Israel's entire citizenry was enlisted on one side or the other. Little wonder that when the collision took place it was, politically and socially, as catastrophic as an earthquake measuring 10 on the Richter scale, and it brought to an end forty-four years of Labor rule.

Thorough changes take time. Many forces were at work to bring about this spectacular transformation. Ben-Gurion's fall and the intramural quarrels that beset Labor in the wake of the Lavon Affair enabled the party's rivals to present a realistic alternative to Labor for the first time in two generations. Only a nudge was needed to push Labor out of office, and the discontent with this party created by the conduct of the Yom Kippur war of 1973 answered its opponents' prayers.

Indeed, the Yom Kippur war—which the Israeli public saw as a debacle—and the recriminations in its wake against Labor prime minister Golda Meir and her defense minister, Dayan, are conventionally believed to be the cause of Labor's undoing. However, there is enough evidence to prove that without the Lavon Affair, Menahem Begin's Likud Party would not have come to power.

This shift in government had profound implications. Begin radically transformed Israel's political makeup and outlook, bringing the entire nation to the brink of an abyss whose first fissure the Lavon Affair had opened with its revelation of serious flaws in the ethics and principles of senior figures in the government and army. In fact, Lavon's actions as defense minister, the ethical lapses of Mapai's political leaders, and the violent, expansionist nature of the Begin government are all related. The moment Labor lost its dedication to its original principles, the way was paved for Likud to take over.

The process began with Lavon. A leading dove all his life, he underwent a sudden, stunning transformation into a fierce hawk upon becoming minister of defense. There has never been, either before or since Lavon, a cabinet minister so reckless, so unmindful of and indifferent to international law, the UN, and foreign public opinion. Some of his initiatives—all fortunately aborted by Chiefs of Staff Maklef and Dayan—are heavily censored to this day. Had they been carried out, Israel's membership in the family of nations would have been brought into serious question.

The question of what brought about this change in the low-keyed, soft-spoken, book loving, philosophical Lavon long bedeviled friends and foes alike. One widely held explanation was that his "hyper-activism" was a calculated stance, meant to win the support of the armed forces, the young and the masses of Israelis newly arrived from Arab and Muslim countries, all a major source of votes. This explanation accepts the view, held in 1954 by both Mapai factions, that in nominating him as minister of defense Ben-Gurion was signaling that Lavon was his choice for the next prime minister as well. If so, Lavon's aggressive political stance—completely at odds with Prime Minister Sharett's—was assumed in preparation for an electoral showdown with Sharett. In any case, it is clear that on assuming office Lavon did his best to out-military the military, being ready and willing to challenge even Western powers in the name of Israel's security. This political excess was a pattern for the excess in his behavior as a party leader. Once he fell out of power and public grace, he was in a rage to both erase the blemish cast on him and avenge himself. He made it clear that unless he was mollified and satisfactorily rehabilitated, he was willing and ready, Samson-like, to bring Mapai's, and even Israel's, temple down.

Lavon's tendency toward violence is in turn related to the ethical lapses of other Labor officials. He broke every rule in Mapai's book, the most important being that the good of the party, and even more the good of the country, was paramount, to the exclusion of personal wrongs and injustice. Mapai, long a serious, responsible servant of Labor Zionism, depended on this code of ethics, and not only for electoral reasons. An act like Lavon's—openly accusing his colleagues in leadership of grave crimes—was bound to wound the party and usher it out of power. This would usher in Herut, and that, from Mapai's point of view, was tantamount to Israel's demise. Time and again Ben-Gurion repeated that Begin's ascendancy would destroy Israel. "I have no doubt," he wrote Sharett on March 21, 1963, "that Begin's government (if it ever comes about) will bring the ruination of the State. In any case his government will turn Israel into a monster"—a clairvoyant vision traditionally subscribed to by all Mapai's veterans, including Lavon.

After the Lavon Affair, Labor and its bastion, the Histadrut (Israel's Federation of Trade Unions) were no longer trusted as bearers and practitioners of a lofty social and national mission. The Affair showed their leaders up as party hacks who put their own good above everything else. The same was true of the regular army. No longer was it revered as the nation's sacred savior, as it had been during Ben-Gurion's tenure. To many the regular army, after 1960, had become just another venue for self-serving careerism. Worst of all, political leaders once believed to be the public's humble servants, working exclusively for the good of the people, suddenly appeared as cutthroats motivated by an insatiable lust for power and domination.

The Lavon Affair, like all severe trauma, was complex and multi-faceted. To some it appeared, at least initially, to be one of Israel's childhood diseases: the nation was not quite six years old when Lavon and Givly decided that they could prevent Britain's final withdrawal from the Suez by some minor sabotage operations. They felt it was incumbent upon them to do so because this withdrawal would remove a buffer between Egypt and Israel and make it easier for Egypt to launch a surprise attack on Israel. Such a possibility would require Israel to constantly maintain stronger border fortifications and larger border garrisons—necessitating the mobilization of more and more reserves—at a great, perhaps even unsupportable cost.

Lavon and Givly were quite blind to the likelihood that such operations would boomerang back at them. Not only is it impossible to reverse the course of history; but if their initiative succeeded, it would have impeded Egypt's long, drawn-out liberation from imperialism. That is, it would, on the one hand, gain Egypt the world's sympathy, and on the other, deepen its enmity to Israel. Even at the time the initiative was regarded as the worst form of political folly by the wiser but unconsulted statesmen Sharett and Ben-Gurion in retirement. In retrospect it was commonly accepted as unmatched idiocy. But since neither Lavon nor Givly can be considered feeble-minded, some allowance must be made for their lack of experience.

Such folly should, however, have been unimaginable in a more mature Israel. And, had Israel learned from experience, the attempt to stop the progress of history should never have been repeated. But Likud chose to regard Lavon and Givly's initiative not as folly but as a failed operation which, with better planning and execution, could have succeeded. In other words, Likud saw in the 1954 sabotage operations in Egypt license given by a Mapai Cabinet—by implication, that is, by Ben-Gurion or Sharett—to a similar attempt to arrest the process of Palestinian self-determination.

The connection between Lavon's and Givly's behavior and the later policies of Likud cannot be understood literally. As explained above, Lavon set a precedent, and there is nothing as bad as a bad example. If rebuked in public by Labor, Likud could always retort that it was using Labor's own methods.

Thus under Begin, twenty-eight years later, the same folly was repeated, but with artillery and tanks: a war in Lebanon, based on the false notion that by sheer force Israel could impose a friendly Maronite rule against the will of a Muslim majority. This stupid tactic was chosen only because, adhering to its ideology with a willful disregard of historical reality, the Begin government refused to recognize the Palestinians, overwhelmingly Muslim, as the rightful owners of part of Palestine.

With the advent of Begin, a new Israel was born in world public opinion. From a peace-loving nation, which realized its dream of nationhood by hard labor and self-sacrifice and took up arms to defend itself only in no-choice situations, Israel was transformed into a society bent on conquest and domination, ready to shed its own and its enemies' blood in the service of ideological aims set by its government.

Labor, returning to power in 1992, after fifteen years in political exile, is now trying hard to save Israel from falling into the abyss to whose edge Likud brought it. But Labor has been unable to rid itself of the effects of the Lavon affair, whose specter still hovers over much of Israeli politics. Lavon's turning against the party leadership, and this veteran leadership's turning against Ben-Gurion, its own leader, benefactor, and mentor, gave the green light to many an upstart and opportunist to do the same, causing great disarray in Israel's political system.

The long and fierce (though veiled at times) rivalry between Prime Minister Yitzhak Rabin, political "favorite son" of pro-Lavon ministers Golda Meir and Pinhas Sapir, and Foreign Minister Shimon Peres, Ben-Gurion's anti-Lavon protegé, had its roots in 1960, when the Lavon Affair cleaved Israel into two uncompromising camps. However, their unreserved cooperation in the pursuit of peace gives rise to the hope that old wounds might heal and the true spirit of Zionism be revived. With Rabin's assassination on November 4, 1995, this hope now entirely hangs on Prime Minister Peres, who would not be where he is today had Lavon, Meir, and Sapir had their way in 1960.

Biographical Notes

Aharoni, Zvi (1921–):   German born, senior Shin Beth and Mossad officer, outstanding investigator and interrogator. As member of Amiad Committee, conducted investigation and wrote report concluding that Elad had betrayed Unit 131 to the Egyptians.

Almog (Wuerzmann), Mordechai (Sam) (1917–):   Lieutenant Colonel, born in Bessarabia, head of intelligence gathering at MI, and Givly's second in command.

Alon (Paicovitch), Yigal (1918–1980):   Major General, Palestine born, Palmach commander in chief (1945–1948), prominent member of Ahdut HaAvodah; put at Be'eri's disposal the firing squad that executed Tubiansky. Later minister of labor (1961–1968), deputy prime minister (1968), minister of education (1969–1974), and minister for foreign affairs (1974–1977).

Amiad (Klibaner), Ariel (1924–):   Colonel, Palestine born, head of IDF signal corps, deputy head of general staff branch of IDF (1958), head of a committee named after him to investigate Elad's treason (1958). Later Director General of the ministry of agriculture (1960–1965).

Argov (Niemoitin), Nehemia (1914–1957):   Lieutenant Colonel, Latvian born, aide de camp to Ben-Gurion as minister of defense and military secretary to Ben-Gurion as prime minister (1948–1953, 1955–1957). Succeeded in both these roles by Colonel Haim Ben-David.

Avidar (Rokhel), Yosef (1906–1995): Major-General, Ukrainian born, Haganah functionary, head of its Instruction Branch, IDF's first Quarter Master General (1948), GOC Northern Command (1949–1952), GOC Central Command (1952–1954), head of General Staff Branch at IDF's GHQ (1954–1955) and acting COS in July 1954, Israel's Ambassador to the Soviet Union (1955–1958).

Avigur (Meirov), Shaul (1899–1978):   Russian born, Sharett's brother-in-law, prominent Mapai member, Haganah chief, head of Mossad leAliya Beth. Ben-Gurion's right-hand man in the ministry of defense during Israel's war of independence, and his advisor for special affairs.

Avriel (Ueberall), Ehud (1917–1980):   born in Vienna, Mapai member, important activist of Mossad leAliya Beth, outstanding arms procurer before and during the war of independence, Ben-Gurion's close aide, director general of the prime minister's office (1950–1952), director of ministry of finance, deputy director of ministry for foreign affairs (1952), outstanding diplomat (1948–1950, and intermittently 1957–1977).

Azar, Shmuel (1930–1955):   leader of Alexandria's Unit 131, teacher of mathematics and physics. Sentenced to death in Cairo trial and executed in January 1955. Disinterred and buried in April 1977 in the central military cemetery at Mount Herzl, Jerusalem.

Be'eri (Birenzweig), Isser (Ittai) (1901–1958):   Lieutenant Colonel, Polish born, head of SHAI Haifa (1947), deputy chief of SHAI (1948), chief of SHAI (1948), MI chief (1948–1949). It was under his authority that Tubiansky was tried and sentenced.

Ben-Gurion (Gruen), David (1886–1973):   Polish born, leader of Mapai, commonly regarded as founder of Israel, its first prime minister and minister of defense (1948–1953, 1955–1963), resigned from both portfolios and from the Knesset on June 6 1963, reelected to Knesset as member of Rafi (1965), resigned from Rafi and political life on May 19, 1970.

Ben-Zur (Bentchevsky), Mordechai (1921–):   Lieutenant Colonel, Polish born, MI, commander of Unit 131 (April 1951–December 1954).

Binnet, Meir (Max) (1917–1954): Lieutenant Colonel, Israel's crack secret agent in Egypt. Committed suicide in Cairo jail in December 1954 in order to avoid testifying in Cairo trial.

Carmel (Wieser), Dalia (1935–): Sergeant Major, Palestine born, conscripted to IDF's intelligence branch 1953, Harkabi's secretary (1953–1954), Givly's secretary (1954–1955), secretary in military attaché office in London (1955–1956), Eshkol's secretary (1957–1960).

Cohen, Haim (Herman) (1911–): Born in Luebeck, Germany, Israel's first solicitor general and director of public prosecution (1948–1950), Attorney General (1950–1960), Justice, supreme court (1960–1981).

Cohen, Victor (1925–): Damascus born, senior Shin Beth and Mossad officer, Aharoni's deputy.

Dar (Darling), Avraham (John) (1921–): Major, MI, Palestine born, founder of Unit 131 in Egypt (1952–1953), sentenced to death in absentia in Cairo trial.

Dassa, Nissim Robert (1933–): Egyptian born, member of Unit 131 Alexandria, sentenced in Cairo trial to 15 years imprisonment, freed 1968, television journalist in Israel.

Dayan, Moshe (1915–1981): Lieutenant General, Palestine born, IDF's fourth chief of staff (1953–1958), minister of agriculture (1959–1964), minister of defense (1967–1974), minister of foreign affairs (1977–1979).

Dori (Dostrovsky), Ya'akov (1899–1973): Lieutenant General, Polish born, IDF's first Chief of Staff (1948–1949).

Elad (Seidenberg), Avraham, Avri (Paul Frank, Robert, The Third Man) (1925–1994): born in Vienna, served in Palmach during war of independence, deputy battalion commander after the war, busted from major to private after being found guilty of theft, drafted by MI in 1953, appointed head of Unit 131 in Egypt May 1954, sentenced to death in absentia in Cairo trial, found guilty by Jerusalem court in 1960 of preparing to pass military secrets to Egypt and sentenced to 10 years imprisonment.

Eshkol (Shkolnik), Levi (1895–1969): Russian born, prominent member of Mapai, assistant minister of defense (1950), minister of agriculture (1951), minister of finance (1952–1963), minister of defense (1963–1967), prime minister (1963–1969).

Evron (Epstein), Efraim (Eppy) (1921–1995): Palestine born; graduate of Israel's first school for diplomats (1948), Mapai member, private secretary to Sharett (1949–1950), private secretary to Ben-Gurion (1950–1952), private secretary to minister of defense Lavon and his chief aide (1954–1955), senior Histadrut official (1955–1961), minister in Israel's embassy to the UK (1962–1965), minister in Israel's embassy to the U.S. (1965–1968), deputy director general (1969–1977) and director general, ministry for foreign affairs (1977–1978), Ambassador to the U.S. (1978–1982).

Givly, Benyamin (1919–) Colonel, Palestine born, senior SHAI officer (1946–1948), head of MI-1 (1948–1949), MI deputy chief (1949–1952), DMI (1952–1953), head of Intelligence branch of IDF (1954–1955), brigade commander (1956), chief of staff, central command (1957–1960), military attaché to the United Kingdom and Scandinavia (1960).

Gorali (Goralnik), Avraham (1911–1954): Major, Polish born, first JAG of Haganah and IDF.

Harel (Halperin), Isser (1912–): Latvian born, Mapai member, senior SHAI officer, founder of Shin Beth, second head of Mossad (1952–1963).

Harel (Hamburger), Yossi (1917–): Lieutenant Colonel, Palestine born, veteran Haganah officer (commander of famed immigrant ship *Exodus*, 1947), MI, succeeded Ben-Zur as Unit 131 commander, retired from IDF 1960 to business.

Hareven, Aluf (1927–): Major, Palestine born, MI research section, Givly's aide de camp (1954–1955).

Harkabi, Yehoshafat (Fati) (1921–1994): Major General, Palestine born, MI senior officer, deputy head of Intelligence branch (February 1953–March 1954), head of intelligence branch (May 1955–April 1959), professor of political science, Hebrew University (1966–1994).

Hausner, Gideon (1915–1990): Major, Polish born, member of Haganah legal service, JAG Jerusalem (1948–1950), Israel's attorney general (1960–1963), prosecutor of Adolf Eichmann (1961), Knesset member (1965–1981).

Hayerushalmi, Levi Yitzhak (1927–): Palestine born, journalist, Mapai spokesman (1954–1955), spokesman for Lavon and Histadrut (1955–1961), *Maariv*'s deputy editor (1969–1985).

Herzog, Haim (Vivian) (1918–): Major General, Irish born, deputy head of MI (1948–1949), head of MI (1949–1950), military attaché to the United States and Canada (1950–1954), head of intelligence branch (1959–1961), Ambassador to the UN (1975–1978), sixth president of Israel (1983–1993).

Hoter-Ishai (Hoteritzky), Aharon (1905–): Lieutenant Colonel, Russian born, Mapai member, IDF's second JAG (1949–1951).

Kollek, Teddy (1911–): Austrian born, head of Haganah mission to United States (1946–1948), minister in Israel's Washington embassy (1950–1952), director general of prime minister's office (1952–1964), mayor of Jerusalem (1966–1993).

Laskov, Haim (1919–1982): Lieutenant General, Russian born, IDF's fifth chief of staff (February 1958-January 1961).

Lavon (Lubianiker), Pinhas (1904–1976): Polish born, founder of Gordonia youth movement, senior Histadrut official and prominent Mapai member, minister without portfolio (1950), minister of agriculture (1952–1953), acting minister of defense (August–October 1953), minister of defense (December 1953–February 1955), Secretary general of Histadrut (1956–1961).

Levi, Victor (1932–): Egyptian born, member of Unit 131 Alexandria, agronomist, sentenced in Cairo trial to life, freed 1968, businessman in Israel.

Manor (Mendelovitch), Amos (Arthur) (1918–): Hungarian born, second head of Shin Beth (1953–1963).

Marshov, Shoshana (Shosh) (1919–): Major, Palestine born, Haganah activist, served in British Army (1942–1945), secretary at SHAI HQ and to Givly (1948), administrator in MI and Mossad.

Marzuk, Moshe (1926–1955):   Egyptian born, M.D., first commander of Unit 131 Cairo, sentenced to death and executed January 1955. Disinterred and buried April 1977 in central military cemetery at Mount Herzl, Jerusalem.

Meir (Meyerson), Golda (1898–1978):   Born in Russia, raised in America, prominent Mapai leader, Israel's first ambassador to Moscow (1948–1949), minister of labor (1949–1956), minister for foreign affairs (1956–1965). Played dominant role in supporting both Lavon's dismissal in 1955 and his rehabilitation in 1960. Later Mapai secretary general (1965–1968), prime minister (1969–1974).

Meyuhas, Meir Samuel (1926–1994):   Egyptian born, member of Unit 131 Alexandria, sentenced in Cairo trial to seven years imprisonment, immigrated to Israel in 1961, became a businessman and honorary consul of Zaire in Israel (1982).

Natanson, Philip (1933–):   Egyptian born, member of Unit 131 Alexandria, cotton trader, sentenced in Cairo trial to life imprisonment, freed 1968, businessman in Israel.

Ninio, Victorine (Marcelle) (1929–):   Egyptian born, professional secretary, liaison officer between Unit 131 teams in Egypt and MI HQ, only individual in Egypt aware of Binnet's presence there and his identity as MI agent; sentenced in Cairo trial to fifteen years imprisonment, freed in 1968, living in Israel.

Olshan (Olshansky), Yitzhak (1895–1983):   Lithuanian born, prominent lawyer, Mapai member, Sharett's school friend, member of Israel's supreme court and its president (1954–1965).

Peres (Persky), Shimon (1923–):   Polish born, Mapai member and activist, Director General of ministry of defense (1952–1959), deputy minister of defense (1959–1965), minister of posts and transport (1969–1974), minister of defense (1974–1977), prime minister (1984–1986), minister of finance (1986–1988), foreign minister (1988–1990; 1992–1995), prime minister (1995–).

Rabin, Yitzhak (1922–1995):   Lieutenant General, Palestine born, Palmach senior officer (1940–1948), senior IDF commander (1948–1964), IDF's seventh chief of staff (1964–1968), Ambassador to the U.S. (1968–1972), minister of labor (1974–1974), prime minister (1974–1977), minister of defense (1984–1990) prime minister and minister of defense (1993–1995).

Salomon, Ya'akov (1905–1980):   Palestine born, studied law at Liverpool University, barrister (Gray's Inn), leading trial lawyer in Palestine and Israel.

Sapir (Koslovsky), Pinhas (1909–1975): Polish born, prominent Mapai leader, director general of ministry of defense (1949–1951), director general of ministry of finance (1952–1957), minister of trade and industry (1955–1963), minister of finance (1963–1968, 1969–1974), Israel's economic czar during the 1960s and 1970s.

Shalmon (Salomon), Katriel (1914–1967):   Colonel, Palestine born, British Army captain, 1941–1945, financial adviser to Chief of Staff Dori (1948–1949), Israel's first military attaché to the United Kingdom and Scandinavia (1951–1954), military attaché to the United States and Canada (1954–1957).

Shaltiel, David (1903–1969):   Major General, German born, senior Haganah officer, head of SHAI (1946–1948), General Officer Commanding Jerusalem (1948), military attaché to France (1950–1952), senior diplomat.

Shapira, Ya'akov Shimshon (1902–1993):   Russian born, studied law at Government of Palestine's Law Classes, Mapai member, Israel's first Attorney General (1948–1949), Member of Knesset (1951–1958), Minister of Justice (1969–1973).

Sharett (Shertok), Moshe (1894–1965):   Russian born, prominent Mapai leader, head of the political department of the Jewish Agency (1933–1948), Israel's first foreign minister (1948–1956), second prime minister (acting, August–October 1953; elected, December 1953–1955), and chairman of the Jewish Agency (1961–1965).

Shiloah (Zaslani), Reuven (1909–1959): Jurusalem born, Mapai member, member of the Jewish Agency's political department specializing in intelligence, adviser to prime minister Ben-Gurion and foreign minister Sharett (1948–1952), first head of intelligence services that became Mossad (1950–1952), senior diplomat.

Sinai (Grad), Dov (Frank) (Fritz) (1922–): Lieutenant Colonel, Polish born, SHAI counterintelligence officer for Jerusalem (1948), MI intelligence-gathering officer, IDF spokesman (1958–1963), Israel's consul general in South Africa (1963–1965) and Canada (1965–1969).

Tubiansky, Meir (1903–1948): Captain, Polish born, industrial engineer, longtime Haganah member, major with British Royal Corps of Engineers during World War II, consumer engineer of the [British] Jerusalem Electric Corporation, IDF's CO of the Jerusalem airstrip, accused by B. Givly of being a spy and traitor.

Yadin (Sukenik), Yigael (1917–1984): Lieutenant General, Jerusalem born, IDF's first director of operations and head of General Staff branch, acting chief of staff (1948–1949), IDF's second chief of staff (1949–1953), noted professor of archaeology, deputy prime minister (1977–1981).

Yaski, Dov (1926–): Lieutenant, Jerusalem born, SHAI counterintelligence officer, Jerusalem (1948), served in MI (1948–1950).

Zafran, Meir Yosef (1928–): Egyptian born, member of Unit 131, Marzuk's best friend, sentenced in Cairo trial to seven years imprisonment.

Notes

Abbreviations:

AHR: Aharoni's Report.

ASB: Isser Harel, *Anatomia Shel Begidah* (Anatomy of Treason): The "Third Man" and the Collapse of the Israeli Spy Network in Egypt, 1954), Edanim Publishers, Jerusalem, 1980.

ISA: Israel State Archive, Jerusalem.

BG: David Ben-Gurion.

BGHOD: Ben-Gurion Heritage Institute's Oral Documentation Department, Sdeh Boker.

CCR: Cohen Committee Hearings and Report.

CM: Cabinet meetings.

COS: Chief of General Staff, IDF.

DCCF: District Court Criminal File, ISA.

DVK: David Ben-Gurion, *Devarim Kahawyatam* (Things As They Are), Am Hasefer, Tel Aviv, 1965.

DMI: Director Military Intelligence.

EMR: Examining Magistrate Ramleh, ISA.

GS: General Staff of IDF.

JAGF: Judge Advocate General Files, ISA and IDFA.

IDF: Israel Defense Forces.

IDFA: Israel Defense Forces Archives, Givaataim.

IPF: Israel Police Files.

KFDC: Knesset's Foreign Affairs and Defense Committee.

MAPSC: Minutes of Mapai's Secretariat, Central Committee and Conferences.

MI: Military Intelligence Department, or Branch.

MNEH: Haggai Eshed, *Mi Natan Et HaHoraha* (Who Gave The Order), Edanim
           Publishers, Jerusalem, 1979.

MOD: Minister of Defense, Israel.

ODR: Olshan-Dori's Report.

SMCC: Records of The Seven Member Cabinet Committee.

YBG: BG's Diaries, BG's Heritage Institute, Sdeh Boker.

YOISH:,   Moshe Sharett, *Yoman Ishi* (Private Diary), 8 volumes, Sifriat *Maariv*,
           Tel Aviv 1978.

General Note on Sources for the Tubiansky Affair, Chapters 1–6

Documents

In large part, the Tubiansky narrative is based on documentation. The main sources are: minutes of the District Court in Tel Aviv that tried Isser Be'eri, Criminal File 147/149 in Israel State Archives (ISA) in Jerusalem, henceforth referred to as DCCF; Minutes of the Examining Magistrate's court in Ramleh, Criminal File 25/49, (ISA), henceforth referred to as EMR, and the testimonies and statements gathered and numbered by IDF's JAG Lieutenant Colonel Hotter-Ishai, who was assisted by Israel's police, also kept at ISA and referred to as JAGF. These files comprise statements and depositions given by:

1. Elisheva Tubiansky (Magen) to Hotter-Ishai, March 17, 1949.
2. Captain Arieh Tubiansky (Magen) to Hotter-Ishai, March 17, 1949.
3. Major Benyamin Givly to Hotter-Ishai, March 6, 1949, to Assistant Superintendent of Police R. Lustig, July 12, 1949 (unnumbered).
4. Captain David Karon to Hotter-Ishai, March 16, 1949.
5. Captain Avraham Kidron to Hotter-Ishai, March 7, 1949.
6. Lieutenant Colonel Isser Be'eri to Hotter-Ishai, March 23, 1949.
7. Hugo Wolf to police inspector S. Schwartz, July 29, 1948.
8. Aharon Cohen to police inspector A. Saltzman, July 25, 1948.
9. Alexander Singer to inspector Schwartz, July 28, 1948.
10. Major General David Shaltiel to Hotter-Ishai, March 10, 1949.
11. Yehiel Ben-Ze'ev to assistant district superintendent Yehudah Prag, August 3, 1948.
12. District superintendent of police Yeshurun Schiff to Hotter-Ishai (undated).
13. Major A. Gorali to Hotter-Ishai, April 26, 1949; (unnumbered) Major

Nehemia Argov to police inspector A. Bauer, July 12, 1949; (unnumbered) Lieutenant Colonel Hotter-Ishai's report to chief of staff Dori, June 26, 1949.

Other relevant documents, in DCCF and EMR include:

14n. Report by Dov Sinai (Fritz's Report), undated.

14. Dubby's Report to Yeruham, June 25, 1948, [which includes 14a: authorized list of electricity consumers; 14b: Report on Tubiansky (undated) and 14c:
Report on Bryant (undated)].

15. Benyamin's [Givly's] letter to Ittai [Be'eri] June 25, 1948.

16. List of essential electricity consumers (in English).

17. Short list of electricity consumers (in English).

18. A request for detention order, June 30, 1948.

19. Detention order, June 30, 1948.

20. Instruction by Yigal P. [General Yigal Alon] "To Mula or Itti" June 29,
1948.

21. Written note by Boaz (General Zvi Ayalon) to David Sh. (General David
Shaltiel) June 6, 1948.

22. "Report on the interrogation of Meir Tubiansky of Jerusalem, June 30,
1948" (in Givly's handwriting).

23. JAG's (Gorali's) Opinion, July 13, 1948.

24. "Report by head of criminal investigation division of Israel Police to
Chief Inspector of Police on interrogation of Michael Bryant" of July 25, 1948.

Other documents of importance are: Ben-Gurion's diaries (referred to as
YBG) and letters at Ben-Gurion's Heritage Institute at Sdeh Boker.

Major Interviews.
To fill gaps in the documented evidence and clarify background, I conducted interviews. With respect to the Tubiansky Affair, I was helped by Tubiansky's
son, Ya'akov Bentov, his niece Ms. Elisheva Magen, and Major (Res.) Shoshana
Marshov, Be'eri's devoted friend. Sadly, I was unable to interview the members
of the military tribunal that tried Tubiansky. Lieutenant Colonel Isser Be'eri and
Major Avraham Kidron were long dead, while Colonel (Res.) Benyamin Givly
and Major (Res.) David Karon (except for a brief telephone conversation)
refused any kind of cooperation, choosing to keep their lips sealed and preserve
their long silence. However, invaluable interviews were conducted with:

1. Mr. Dubby Yaski (January 13 and 15, and February 4, 1991).

2. Lieutenant Colonel (Res.) Dov (Fritz) Sinai, (January 15, 1991).

3. Major (Res.) Shoshana (Shosh) Marshov, (July 11, 1990 and January 20,
1991).

4. Lieutenant Colonel (Res.) Yitzhak (Levitze) Levi (January 22, 1991).

5. Lieutenant Colonel (Res.) Yossef Kariv (March 21, 1989).

6. Mr. Isser Harel (October 18, 1980, February 18, 1989, December 19,
1990, February 14, 1991, May 9, 1991, November 10, 1991, December 4, 1991).

7. Major General (Res.) Chaim (Vivian) Herzog (April 6 and 30, 1989; January 8 and 27, 1991).

8. Lieutenant Colonel (Res.) Daniel Magen (March 29, 1992).
9. Brigadier General (Res.) Zvi Inbar (March 3, 1992).
Other interviews and bibliography will be found in the chapter notes.

Chapter 1. Introducing: Givly and Friends

Documents: JAGF: #6. Be'eri.
Diaries: YBG: April 5, 1947.
Press: "The Tubiansky Affair," taped Israel Radio documentary program, produced by Yehudah Kaveh, July 3, 1973; "Meir Tubiansky," videotaped Israel TV documentary program, produced by Yehudah Kaveh, May 14, 1981; *Haaretz*, August 14 and October 17, 1949.
Interviews: Shoshana Marshov, Yitzhak Levi, Dubby Yaski; Dr. Eliahu Arel, July 17, 1990; Nehama Burstein, July 14, 1990; Aharon Ben-Ezer, July 18, 1990; Nahum Barnea, July 14, 1990; Esther Givly, July 11, 1990; Zvi Gilat, July 18, 1990; Major General (Res.) Meir Amit, January 10, 1991; Lieutenant General (Res.) Zvi Zur, September 25, 1990; Ahuvah Givly, July 7, 1990.
Bibliography: *Anshei HaAliya HaShniah*, Vol. 3, Hamerkaz LeTarbut Velehinuh, p. 131; Yitzhak Levi, *Tisha'a Kabin*, Hotsaat Maarahot, 1986, p. 398; Assa Lefen, *HaShai—Sherut HaYediot Shel HaHaganah*, Doctorate thesis in manuscript, unpresented due to author's death. Parts of this work were published in *Modiin VeBitahon Leumi*, ed. Zvi Ofer, Hotsaat Maarahot 1987.

Chapter 2. Givly the Spycatcher

Documents: DCCF; EMR; JAGF: #3 Givly, #5 Kidron, #7 Hugo Wolf.
Letters: Be'eri to Marshov, April 4, 1950.
Press: "The Tubiansky Affair"; "Meir Tubiansky"; *Haaretz*, August 14, October 18, 1949.
Interviews: Dubby Yaski, Dov Sinai, Levi Yitzhak; Eitan Ron (Reinitz), September 9, 1992.

Chapter 3. Without Mercy

Documents: DCCF and EMR: #22 "Report on the interrogation of Meir Tubiansky of Jerusalem, June 30, 1948"; JAGF: #3 Givly, #5 Kidron.
Letters: Be'eri to Marshov, April 4, 1950.
YBG: May 24, 1948.
Press: "The Tubiansky Affair"; "Meir Tubiansky."
Interviews: Dubby Yaski, Dov Sinai, Yehoshua Bloom, March 25, 1992; Levi Avrahami, March 31, 1992.
Bibliography: Isser Harel, *Bitahon VeDemokratia*, Edanim Publishers, Tel Aviv 1989, pp. 101, 113.

Chapter 4. Taking Responsibility

Documents: DCCF: October 16, 1949; EMR: Gorali's testimony; Alon's testimony, August 12, 1949; IDFA: IDF's Special Tribunal File M/1/49; Hotter-Ishai's Letter to COS March 9, 1949.

Knesset: Eshkol's remarks at the Knesset, October 21, 1964.

KFDC: Knesset Member Y. Harari at the Knesset's Foreign and Defense Committee, November 24, 1964, cited in Chaim Israeli's letter to Berl Repetur, January 11, 1976.

Letters: Gorali to BG July 13, 1948; BG's letters: to the GS July 12, 1948, to minister of justice Rosen, December 10, 1948; to COS Dori, December 16, 1948; Minutes Of The Five Minister Committee, July 3, 1948, ISA; D. Mushin's (BG's secretary) letter to Mrs. Tubiansky, January 2, 1949; Mrs. Tubiansky's letter to BG January 12, 1949; Reisner's letters to BG July 16, 1949, and November 6, 1964; Be'eri's handwritten note to Nehemia Argov, October 26, 1948; BG's Letters: to to Chaim Weizmann, December 13, 1949; to Mrs. Tubiansky, July 1, 1949; to Reisner, July 8, 1949; to Yehudah (Jule) Amster, March 20, 1964; Yadin's to MOD December 12, 1948.

Diaries: Nehemia Argov, *Min HaYoman* (Nehemia's Diary), published by friends, entry of, December 27, 1948; YBG: June 30, July 1, 5, 12, 15 and 17, August 29, September 6, 18, and 25, November 9 and 29, December 6, 9, 12, 16, 20, 23, and 31, 1948; March 16, July 1 and 8, October 26, December 20 and 31, 1949; October 20, November 3, 1964.

Press: Government Press Communique (Ministry of Defense announcement) July 3, 1949; Minutes of Israel press editorial board, July 4, 1949; *Yediot Aharonot*, October 14, 1964, February 16, 1979 (Shapira's Interview); *Ashmoret*, July 21, 1949; *Al HaMishmar*, October 14, 1964; *Lamerhav*, October 14 and 16, 1964; *Haaretz*, October 13 and 14, 1964; *Davar*, October 14, 23 and 30, November 3, 1964; *Kol HaAm*, October 18, 1964; *Herut*, October 21, 1964; *Haboker*, October 15, 1964; "The Tubiansky Affair"; "Meir Tubiansky."

Bibliography: Bitahon VeDemokratia, pp. 88–89, 104, 114 ff., 123–124, 138 ff., 152–140; Raphael Bashan, *Yesh Li Ra'ayon*, Am Oved 1965, p. 94 (interview with Israel Galili); Natan Alterman, "Almanat Haboged" (The Traitor's Widow), *Hatur HaShvei II*, Davar 1954; Berl Repetur, *Lelo Heref*, Hotsaat HaKibbutz HaMeuhad 1973, 3: 255–276; Ya'akov Salomon, *Bedarkhi Sheli* (*Salomon*), Edanim Publishers 1980, pp. 196, 208.

Chapter 5. Alone in the Dock

Documents: DCCF; JAGF: #3 Givly, #4 Karon, #5 Kidron, #6 Be'eri EMR: Givly's testimony, August 12, 1949.

Letters: Shapira to MOD Lavon, "personal and confidential" February 6, 1955; Mrs. Tubiansky's letter to BG November 18, 1947; BG's letter to Mrs. Tubiansky, July 1, 1949.

YBG: July 8, November 11, 1949.
Press: Yediot Aharonot, February 23, 1979; "Meir Tubiansky."
Interviews: Dov Sinai, Dubby Yaski, Shoshana Marshov; David Karon (by telephone) April 3, 1992.
Bibliography: Salomon, p. 196.

Chapter 6. The Lesson Not Learned

Letters: Mrs. Tubiansky to BG November 18, 1948; BG to Mrs. Tubiansky, July 1, 1949.
IDFA: BG's instruction to GS July 12, 1948.
YBG: July 8, October 26, November 14, 1949.
Press: Yediot Aharonot, February 16, 1979; "Meir Tubiansky."
Interviews: Marshov; Major General (Res.), Chaim Herzog, January 8, 1991.
Bibliography: Salomon, p. 149.

General Note on Sources for the Lavon Affair, Chapters 7—24

Documents: Essential to the understanding of "The Sorry Business" and the Lavon Affair are documents that are still classified in Israel: Cabinet minutes, records of the Knesset's Foreign Affairs and Defense Committee, and MI and Mossad files. Luckily, however—during an entirely unfortunate chapter in Israel's history—much of the forbidden material was brought out and publicized by the adversaries themselves, notably Ben-Gurion, Sharett, Lavon, and others then in positions of power. Most, if not all, cabinet and Knesset discussions of the Mishap and the Lavon Affair were leaked to the press. Many of the secret minutes and documents found their way to Mapai's secretariat and central committee, and from there to the press and into private hands. A large portion of the MI records came to light in various publications initiated or sponsored by the warring sides. With these and the help of private collections it became possible to put together a complete, reliable picture of events and developments.

Crucial to the narrative of the Mishap and the Lavon Affair are the following documents: Olshan-Dori's Report (ODR); Cohen Committee Hearings and Report (CCR); Minutes of Mapai's secretariat, central committee and conferences (MAPSC); Aharoni's Report (AHR), and records of the Seven-member Cabinet Committee (SMCC).

Major Interviews: Basic interviews were conducted with:

1. Mr. Zvi Aharoni (August 20, 1979; November 12, 1988).
2. Colonel (Res.) Mordechai Almog (May 8 and 16, 1991).
3. Colonel (Res.) Ariel Amiad (May 12, 1991).
4. Major General (Res.) Meir Amit (Novemeber 2, 1978; January 3, 1988).
5. Lieutenant Colonel (Res.) Mordechai Ben-Zur (February 12 and, July 9, 1990).

6. Mrs. Dalia Carmel-Goldstein (August 23, December 2 and 6, 1989; May 3, June 9, November 15 and 16, 1990; September 18, October 29, 1991; January 12, 1992).

7. Mr. Haim (Victor) Cohen (May 26, 1991).

8. Major (Res.) Avraham Dar (December 14 and 24, 1990; March 29, 1991).

9. Lieutenant General (Res.) Moshe Dayan (February 19, 1980).

10. Mr. Efraim Evron (August 20 and 30, 1987; February 27, 1988; June 10, November 5, 1990; March 9, May 5 and 13, September 30, and November 19, 1991).

11. Mr. Isser Harel (October 12, 1980, February 18, 1989, December 19, 1990, May 9, October 11 and December 4, 1991).

12. Lieutenant Colonel (Res.) Yossi Harel (May 19, 1970; January 1, May 9 and November 4, 1991).

13. Lieutenant Colonel (Res.) Aluf Hareven (November 8, 11 and December 9, 1990; May 6, July 21, and August 26, 1991).

14. Major General (Res.) Yehoshafat Harkabi (February 5, 1981; December 28, 1989; September 19 and 22, 1991).

15. Mr. Levi Yitzhak Hayerushalmi (August 16 and September 17, 1991; January 26, 1992).

16. Brigadier General (Res.) Ya'akov Hefetz (July 18, and September 2, 1990).

17. Major General (Res.) Chaim Herzog (April 6 and 30, 1989; January 8 and 27, 1991).

18. Mr. Amos Manor (March 18 and 25, April 3 and 15, and, July 15, 1988;, January 27, 1989; November 11, 1990, June 5, September 2 and 27, 1991).

19. Major (Res.) Shoshana Marshov (July 11, 1990 and January 20, 1991).

20. Knesset Member Shimon Peres (December 19, 1969; October 22, 23, 1971; October 24, 1987; August 9, 1991).

21. Brigadier General (Res.) Rehavia Vardi (February 26, 1990).

22. Lieutenant General (Res.) Zvi Zur (September 25, 1990).

Benyamin Givly remained silent about both the Mishap and the Lavon Affair, explaining—as he has done repeatedly during the last 40 years—that he was writiing his own version for publication.

Bibliography: The following works were based on official documents: YOISH; DVK; *Anatomia* and MNEH.

Other interviews and bibliography will be found in the chapter notes.

Chapter 7. Faces Old and New

Documents: ODR: Lavon's testimony, January 2, 1955; Peres's testimony, January 5, 1955; Dayan's testimony, January 6, 1955; Givly's testimony, January 3, 9, 1955; Avidar's testimony (undated); Evron's testimony, January 7, 1955; Ben-Zur's testimony, January 5, 9, 1955; Elad's testimony, January 6, 9, 1955.

CCR: Conclusions and Report, October 15, 1960.

MAPSC: Mapai's Tenth Conference, Session I, February 17, 1965.

Letters: Sharett's to Lavon, August 14, 1953, May 25, September 13 and December 4, 1954; Givly's to Carmel, November 16, 1960; to Nehemia Argov, April 1, 1953; BG's to Meir Argov, November 3, 1953.

YBG: September 23, 1953, November 9, 1961.

BGHOD: Avigur, December 28, 1975; October 25, 1977.

Press: Yediot Aharonot, April 7, 1988 (Amos Nevo); *Haaretz,* March 23, 1954; Israel TV, "This Is Your Life" (with Cairo Prisoners) December 28, 1989.

Interviews: Marshov, Hefetz, Dar, Vardi, Ben-Zur, Hareven; Major General (Res.) Aharon Yariv (January 19, 1991); Colonel (Res.) Avraham Elson (July 18, 1990); Lieutenant Colonel (Res.) Shmuel Toledano (March 27, 1991).

Bibliography: DVK, p. 23; Nehemia's Diary, February 12, 1955; YOISH, 3: 639, 641, 672.

Chapter 8. Unit 131 Strikes

Documents: ODR: Givly's Memorandum to COS and MOD "Renewal of negotiations on Withdrawal of Canal Zone" June 16, 1954; Harkabi's letter from Paris to Givly, December 3, 1955 [should be 1954]; Ben-Zur's report to Givly "On Operations in Egypt" August 1, 1954; Evron's note to Lavon, December 30, 1954.

AHR: much of this report was published in Harel's ASB, see pp. 61, 63–66, 69–71, 76, 78–79, 82, 84–85, 89, 92–93, 100, 205, 299.

GS *meetings:* November 1, 1954 (IDFA).

Reports: Givly's to COS November 1, 1954 (IDFA).

Letters: Evron's letter to Nehemia Argov, February 18, 1954 (IDFA); Dov Yosef's to Israel's president, April 26, 1964; COS Laskov's to BG June 27, 1958; Ben-Zur's to Almog, October 25, 1953 (AHR); Nehemia's Diary, October 18, 1954.

Press: Dvar Hashavua (Interview with Givly) August 1, 1969; *Haaretz,* July 7, 1954; Radio Cairo, July 9, 1954.

Interviews: Vardi, Ben-Zur, Evron, Hefetz.

Bibliography: MNEH, pp. 39–41, 64–68; Isser Harel, *Kam Ish Al Ahiv,* Hotsaat Keter, Jerusalem 1982, pp. 17, 18, 22, 24; YOISH 3: 734; Avri Elad, *HaAdam Hashlishi* (Elad), Hotsaha Meyuhedet, Tel Aviv, 1976.

Chapter 9. July 16

Documents: ODR: Lavon's testimony, January 2, 10, 1955; Isser Harel's testimony, January 5, 1955; Givly's testimony, January 3, 9, 1955; Elad's testimony, January 6, 1955; Ben-Zur's testimony, January 5, 9, 1955; Dayan's testimony, January 6, 1955; Evron's testimony, January 7, 1955.

MOD's weekly meetings with IDF: April 22, August 12, September 9, 1954.

GS *meetings:* July 27, November 1, 1954 (IDFA).
CCR: Ben-Zur's testimony.
Reports: Ben-Zur's: to Givly, August 1, 1954; to acting DMI October 5, 1954; Isser Harel's: to Sharett on Unit 131, August 1, 1954 (MNEH, p. 82); Givly's: to MOD Lavon "Activitiy in Egypt—July 1954" August 8, 1954 (ODR); Memorandum to MOD Lavon "Renewal of Psychological Warfare in Egypt" August 8, 1954 (ODR).
Letters: Ben-Zur's to Dar, September 13, 1954.
YBG: August 24, November 20, 1954.
Press: Haaretz, July 16, 19, 25, 26, September 23, 1954; *Yediot Aharonot,* July 26, 1954.
Interviews: Ben-Zur, Yossi Harel; Major General (Res.) Dan Tolkovsky, May 4, 1991; Lieutenant General (Res.) Yitzhak Rabin, February 23, 1990.
Bibliography: MNEH, pp. 56, 69–70, 78–79, 82–84, 86–89, 100, 104, 111; YOISH 2: 560–562, 585, 3: 623.

Chapter 10. Line of Defense

Documents: ODR: Conclusions, January 12, 1955; Givly's testimony; Lavon's testiminy; Avidar's tetimony (undated); Peres's testimony, January 5, 1955; Dayan's testimony; Dayan's notice, January 12, 1955; Evron's testimony; Affidavits collected by Evron from: Shalom Eshet (December 16, 1954), Evron (December 23, 1954), Avidar (December 24, 1954); Peres (December 24, 1954), Yuval Ne'eman (in COS ledger, December 28, 1954); Stenographic record of Lavon-Givly talks (December 28, 1954).
Diaries: Nehemia's Diary, September 12, 1954; COS's (Dayan's) diary, December 28 and 31, 1954.
Letters: Givly to MOD Lavon, December 27, 1954; Dayan to BG September 4, 1964; Evron to Dayan, December 30, 1954.
Interviews: Marshov, Vardi.

Chapter 11. Before the Commission

Documents: ODR: Conclusions; Isser Harel's testimony, January 5, 1955; Evron's testimony; Ben-Zur's testimony; Stenographic record of Lavon-Givly talks, December 28, 1954; CCR: Hareven's testimony, October 13, 1960; IPF: Hareven's statement to assistant superintendent Z. Margalit, December 21, 1960; Carmel's deposition to Margalit, December 15 and 18, 1960; MAPSC: Sharett at the secretariat, January 15, 1961.
Letters: Harkabi to Givly, December 3, 1954 [1955]; Lavon's to ODR January 13, 1955; Avigur's proposal for the composition of an Inquiry Committee, December 29, 1954; Ya'akov S. Shapira to MOD Lavon "personal and secret" February 2, 1955.

Reports: Dar's "Report on a Talk with MOD Lavon" December 29, 1954.
Diaries: COS's (Dayan's) Diary, December 28, 1954.
Press: Davar, October 21, 1960 (Sharett's "Beshulei Haparasha"); *Haaretz,*
July 7, 1989 (Segev's "Zihronoteha Shel Mazkira").
Interviews: Hareven, Carmel, Vardi, Dar.
Bibliography: YOISH 3: 617–666; DVK, pp. 36, 41; MNEH, p. 106.

Chapter 12. Almog's Mission

Documents: ODR: Report and Conclusions; Balance, con and pro (undated);
Elad's testimony;Lavon's testimony; Givly's testimony; Dayan's testimony.
CCR: Report and Conclusions.
Reports: AHR.
Diaries: COS (Dayan's) diary, January 5, 1955.
Interviews: Dayan, Harkabi; Major General (Res.) Elie Zeira, July 5, 1991;
Isser Harel; Vardi; Amiad; Aharoni; Victor Cohen.
Bibliography: Yitzhak Olshan, *Din Udvarim* (*Olshan*), Hotsaat Schocken,
Jerusalem and Tel Aviv 1978, pp. 266–270, 272–276, 278–289; Elad, pp. 176,
177–183; YOISH 3: 637–638, 640; ASB, pp. 34 ff., 98 ff.

Chapter 13. Sharett in Torment

Documents: MAPSC: Secreteriat, January 15, 1961.
Letters: BG to Haim Shurer, January 11, 1955; Sharett to Lavon, December
22, 1954.
Diaries: Nehemia's Diary, February 12, 15, 1955.
YBG: January 8, 9, 25, 27, 1955.
BGHOD: Avigur, December 28, 1975, October 25, 1977.
Press: Lamerhav, January 10, 11, 1955.
Interviews: Meir Ben-Gur, August 4, 1991.
Bibliography: YOISH 2: 606, 3: 617–621, 624, 627, 630, 632, 634, 637–638,
641, 644, 648–649, 652, 656–669, 670–671, 673, 676, 680, 683, 689, 692, 694,
697, 701, 714, 732, 736; *Divrei HaKnesset* (Official Knesset Records), Vol. 17, Ses-
sions, January 16, 25, 1955.

Chapter 14. Lavon Resigns

Documents: ODR: Peres's testimony.
CM: February 20, 1955.
KFDC: October 23, 1960.
Letters: Evron (on Lavon's behalf) to Laskov (undated) 1954; Lavon to
Sharett, February 2, 1955; BG's to Eshkol, September 9, 1964.
Diaries: Nehemia's Diary, June 5, September 7, 1954, February 12, 15, 1955;
COS (Dayan's) Diary, January 5, 6, February 16, 1955.

YBG: January 27, February 17, 1955; September 30, October 4, November 17, 1960.

Press: Haboker, February 2, 1955; *Davar*, February 2, 1955; *Lamerhav*, February 16, 1955; *Haaretz* (and Israeli Hebrew daily press) February 17, 1955; *Jerusalem Post*, February 18, 1955; Israeli Hebrew daily press, February 18, 1955.

Interviews: Evron, Hareven, Ben-Gur, Peres; Zalman Aran 1970.

Bibliography: YOISH 3: 683, 694, 699–700; 702, 704–706, 711, 716–717, 720, 726, 730–732, 738–739; *Olshan*, pp. 268; DVK, pp. 44–64, 50; Moshe Dayan, *Avneh Dereh* (Autobiography), Hotsaat Edanim-Dvir 1976, pp. 121, 124.

Chapter 15. Ben-Gurion Returns

Documents: ODR: Dayan's testimony.
CCR: Hareven's testimony, October 13, 1960.
CM: February 20, 1955.
MOD's weekly meetings with IDF: May 12, 1955.
Knesset: Divrei HaKnesset Vol. 16, meeting #554, p. 859–860.
MAPSC: 10th Conference First Session, February 17, 1961; BG to Mapai Jerusalem student group, March 6, 1961.
Letters: BG's: to Avigur, September 9, 1964; to Yehudah Gotthelf, October 18, 20, 1960; to Dr. Natan Rothenstreich, October 25, 1960; to COS Dayan, February 28, 1955; to Sharett, March 18, 1955; Lavon to BG October 3, 1960; Sharett to BG March 15, 1955; Harkabi's: to Hefetz, February 9, March 5, undated (probably April) 1955.
Diaries: COS (Dayan's) Diary: August 24, 27, 1954; January 18, February 10, 20, March 3, April 11, May 3, 11, 12, 13, 14, 1955.
YBG: February 6, June 14, 17, July 13, 28, December 12, 1954; January 25, 27, February 18, 21, 22, 1955.
BGHOD: Avigur, December 28, 1975; October 25, 1977; Ehud Avriel, November 27, 1979.
Press: Haaretz, February 20, May 17, 1955; *Herut*, February 20, 21, 1955; *Lamerhav*, February 20, 1955; *Maariv*, February 18, 20, 1955; *Al HaMishmar*, February 18, 20, 1955; *Bamahaneh*, May 28, 1956.
Interviews: Hareven, Carmel, Harkabi, Evron, Hefetz; Moshe Zak, August 18, 1991; Sara Karni, August 6, 1961; Colonel (Res.) Yuval Ne'eman, August 27, 1991; Jane Binnet, August 28, 1991; Dayan, February 19, 1980; Naora Bar-Noah (Matalon) March 21, 1980.
Bibliography: DVK, pp. 9–10, 16, 17–21, 28–29, 36, 44–48; YOISH 3: 624, 632, 717, 739; ASB, pp. 230, 248; MNEH, pp. 173–174.

Chapter 16. Fears of a Putsch

Knesset: BG's answer to Rokach's question (January 6, 1959), *Divrei HaKnesset* (January 7, 1959), meeting #572, p. 795.

MAPSC: Central Committee (Rehovot) September 16, 1954; November 27, 1958; Secretariat: December 31, 1960; January 11, 1961.

Letters: BG's: to MOD's departments, November 28, 1948; Exchange of notes with Yadin, May 27, 1952; to COS Yadin, May 27, 1952; to Shalmon, May 27, 1952 (not sent); To COS Yadin, May 28, 1952; to Aran, August 15, 1954; to Dayan, January 28, 1958; to Lavon, November 26, 1958; November 29, 1959; to Yadin, March 9, 1964; Correspondence with Tabenkin, September 1959; Sharett to BG July 9, 1954; Nehemia Argov to Yosef Izraeli, December 13, 1948; Dori's letter of appointment (of Shalmon) December 6, 1948; Shalmon to N. Argov: February 25, March 7, 1951, August 6, 1952 ("Notations After a Visit in Israel"); Urgent Cable to N. Argov, September 11, 1952; N. Argov's cable to Shalmon, September 12, 1952; N. Argov's "internal letter" to BG September 27, 1953.

Diaries: Nehemia's Diary: May 30, July 7, August 18, September 12, 1954; COS (Dayan's) Diary: December 14, 1954.

YBG: November 21, 1948; May 27, 1952; October 28, 1952; March 16, 26, May 23, July 1, 3, 11, August 20, 26, September 16, December 12, 1954; July 15, 1956; March 28, June 30, July 5; November 23, 26, December 6, 31, 1958; June 16, November 21, 1959; February 2, 1960.

BGHOD: Avriel, November 27, 1979.

Press: *Yediot Aharonot*, May 23, 1955; January 17, 1968 (Isser Harel joins Rafi); November 15, 1974 (Avriel's interview), March 20, 1981 (Yadin's interview); *Maariv*, December 20, 31, 1954; June 17, November 23, December 7, 1958; January 2, 1959; Septeber 21, 1983 (Kollek's interview); *HaOlam Hazeh*, January 22, 1953, November 18, 1954; *L'Express*, May 3, 1969 (Dayan's interview).

Interviews: Evron, Isser Harel, Peres, Amos Manor; Yigael Yadin, December 19, 1970; Avriel, January 26, 1970; Elhanan Yishai, June 8, 1979; Haim Israeli, November 16, 1991.

Bibliography: Shabtai Teveth, *Moshe Dayn* (Biography), Hotsaat Schocken, Jerusalem Tel Aviv, 1971, pp. 367–368, 406–407, 416–421, 481–501, 507; YOISH 2: 377, 488, 511, 539, 550, 553, 570, 579, 581, 3: 624, 632, 654, 747, 794–795, 4: 924, 938, 944, 975, 1037, 1048, 1054, 1120–1121, 1124, 1195; Ben-Gurion, *Nezah Israel*, Hotsaat Ayanot 1954, p. 133 (August 4, 1953); Ben-Gurion, *Hazon VaDereh*, 5 Vols., Hotsaat Ayanot 1958, 5: 140 ff., 206, 215, 540 ff., 5: 256; Yosef Weitz, *Yomani*, 5 Vols., Hotsaat Massada, 1965, 4: 292, 294; Asher Yadlin, *Edut*, Edanim Publishers, Jerusalem 1980, pp. 108, 111.

BG's library has the following works by Niccolo Machiavelli: *Adamotu (La Mandragola)*, in Turkish, Istanbul 1951; *The History of Florence, The Prince*, in English, London 1947; *Le Prince* (in French) Paris, late 19th century, *The Prince and the Discourses* (in English) New York 1940; Machiavelli's biography by Orestes Ferrara (in French) Paris 1928; Pasquale Villari's biography (in English), London 1878.

Chapter 17. Ups and Downs

Knesset: *Divrei HaKnesset*, Vol, 16, January 1962.

MAPSC: Ideological Forum, meeting of, June 7, 1958, at Beit Berl.

Letters: COS Laskov to BG June 27, 1958; Ada Golomb's: to BG February 2, March 17, 1957: BG's: to Ada Golomb, February 8, March 24, 1957; to Sharett, January 15, 17, 1962; to Lavon, January 19, 1956; to Josephtal, March 25, 1958; to Mapai members, May 21, 1959; Sharett's: to BG January 15, 17, 1962.

Reports: AHR (on Elad) June 10, 1959.

Diaries: COS (Dayan's) Diary: June 29, 1955.

YBG: December 12, 1954; August 15, 1956; March 28, December 6, 1958; January 6, 1964.

Press: *Maariv*, March 23, June 17, November 23, December 7, 12, 1958; *Davar*, May 16, June 17, December 5, 30, 31, 1958; May 24, 1959; *Haaretz*, May 30, June 6, 13, 15, 17, 22, November 1, 13, December 2, 28, 1958.

Interviews: Evron, Ben-Zur, Carmel, Manor, Peres, Avraham Ofer, BG, Aran, Gad Ya'akobi; Yossef Harmelin, January 28, 1992.

Bibliography: YOISH 6: 1632; 7: 1936, 2027, 2043; 8: 1947–1954, 2320; Abel Thomas, *Comment Israel fut sauvé*, Albin Michel, Paris, pp. 74–92; Mordechai Gazit, "Sharett, Ben-Gurion VeIskat HaNeshek HaGdolah im Tsarfat Be-1956" (Sharett, BG and the large Arms Transaction with France in 1956), Gesher, #1/108, spring 1983; Yossef Almogi, *BeOvi HaKora*, (*Almogi*), Edanim Publishers, Jerusalem, 1980, p. 175; *Edut*, p. 105 ff.; *Biography*, pp. 481–501.

Chapter 18. Under Fire from the Press

Documents: CCR: Letter of Appointment, September 12, 1960.

CM: Prime Minister's Press Communique, October 2, 1960.

SMCC: Meeting of December 19, 1960.

MAPSC: Secretariat, September 29, October 18, 1960; February 10, 1961; central committee, October 19, 1960; January 12, 1961.

Letters: H. Ben-David's: to BG May 10, July 15, 1960; Ben-Zur to Ben-David, July 29, 1960; Yitzhak Navon to Haggai Eshed, January 24, 1963 (Eshed's papers); COS Laskov to BG August 25, 1960; BG's: to Laskov, August 28, 1960; to Lavon, November 29, 1959.

Diaries: Peres's Diary: June 23, 26, 1960.

YBG: June 28, 1958; February 5, May 5, September 4, 9, 18, 26, 28, October 4, 1960.

Press: *Yediot Aharonot*, September 19, 25, 1960; *Maariv*, July 27, September 25–30, October 1, 9, 10, 1960; December 13, 1987; May 15, 17, 18, 19, 22, 29, June 2, 19, 26, July 3, October 2, 3, 4, 9, 10, 1960; *Haaretz*, *Haboker*, *Al HaMishmar*, *HaTzofe*, *Lamerhav*, September 26, 1960; *Hadashot*, August 14, 1991; *Davar*, October 5, 1960.

Interviews: Yossi Harel, Evron, Hayerushalmi; Haim Israeli, February 26, 1980; Shalom Rosenfeld, December 12, 1960; Moshe Zak, November 8, 1991; the author discussed the role played by the daily press in the Lavon Affair with: Yeshaiahu Ben-Porat, David Giladi, Uri Dan, Dov Yudkovski, Yehoshua Yustman, Moshe Meisels, Shalom Rosenfeld, Moshe Zak, Heyerushalmi, Yoel Marcus, and Shlomo Nakdimon.

Bibliography: Edut, p. 111; *Almogi,* pp. 187–188, 190–191; DVK, pp. 22, 26–27, 29–30; MNEH, pp. 202 ff.; YOISH 1: 217, 221, 225; 3: 750, 753; 5: 1343; 6: 1583.

Chapter 19. "Dreyfusiada"

Documents: CCR: Report and Conclusions, October 10, 1960.

CM: Cabinet meetings, Ocotber–December 1960.

KFDC: BG's remarks on Lavon's testimony, November 7, 1960.

MAPSC: Secretariat, October 15, 18 (BG's letter to KFDC's chairman), December 16, 1960; Central Committee, October 19, 1960.

Letters: BG's: to Sharret, September 29, October 1, 2, 1960; to Haim Schwartz, March 8, 1961; to Cabinet Legal Advisor Hausner, October 18, 1960; Sharett to BG October 2, 1961; Hausner's: To BG October 21, 1960; March 5, 1964.

Diaries: Nehemia's Diary: August 10, 1954; February 12, 1955.

YBG: December 13, 1956; March 28, December 30, 1958; September 28, October 10, 19, 1960.

Press: Maariv, January 14, 1955; September 26, October 3, 4, 5, 7, 9, 10, 11, 12, 14, 17, 18, 24, 25, 26, 1960; *Davar,* October 17 (Dayan's article), 18, 19, 25, 1960; Shlomo Nakdimon, "HaHadlafot Min HaMemshala HaRishonah VeAd HaYom" (Government Leaks), Army Radio (*Galei Zahal*) September 2, 1980; *Monitin,* #66, March 1984; *Lamerhav,* January 10, 1955; December 30, 1958; *Herut,* September 28, October 5, 14 (Bader's article) 1960; *Al HaMishmar,* January 30, 1953; *Yaad,* October 3, 1960; *HaOlam HaZeh,* October 11, 26, 1960.

Interviews: Shalom Rosenfeld, December 16, 1991; Pinhas Yurman, April 24, 1992; Yoel Marcus, October 11, 1991.

Bibliography: YOISH 3: 637, 640, 750 ff., 755–766; 4: 934; MNEH, p. 255; *Olshan,* p. 280; Yohanan Bader, *HaKnesset VeAni,* Edanim Publishers, Jerusalem, 1979, p. 130 ff.; DVK, pp. 22, 31.

Chapter 20. Eshkol the Healer

Documents: MAPSC: Secreteriat, October 18, 19, 20, December 31, 1960; Central Committee, October 18, 19, 1960; BG to Mapai Jerusalem student group, March 6, 1961.

Letters: Givly's: to Carmel, September 26, November 16, 1960; Eshkol's: to Carmel, November 5, 12/13, 24, 1960; Aharon Doron to Carmel, October 17,

1960; Pinhas Sapir to BG (in *Haaretz*, November 26, 1964); BG to Rosen, November 21, 1964.

YBG: October 13, 15, 21, November 7, 1960; July 18, 19, 1963; November 17, December 1, 1964; January 21, 1965; January 7, 1967.

Press: *Maariv*, October 10, 14, 17, 19, 23, 25, 26, 28, 30, 31, 1960; January 28, 1977; *Haaretz*, November 20 (Rosen's article), 26, 1964; *Haboker*, October 28, 1960; *Davar*, October 21, 1960; November 20 (Rosen's article), 1964.

Interviews: Carmel, Evron; Palmoni, January 7, 1991; Moshe Meisels, October 29, 1991; Miriam Eshkol, December 22, 1991; Dan Alon, December 24, 1991.

Bibliography: Almogi, pp. 193, 195; YOISH 3: 762, 766; *Salomon*, pp. 221 ff.

Chapter 21. Givly Demands an Inquiry

Documents: CM: October 31, 1960 and Review of all cabinet meetings which discussed Givly's demand for an inquiry and the setting up of SMCC in YBG July 18, 1963 and November 17, 1964.

SMCC: Meetings of November 3, 14, December 5, 1960.

MAPSC: Secretariat, October 18, 1960.

Letters: Givly's: to Hefetz, April 14, 1960; to Carmel, November 3, 6, 16, 1960; Hareven to Givly, October 18, 1960; BG to Gotthelf, October 18, 1960; Teddy Kollek to Carmel, October 24, 1960; Eshkol's: to Carmel, November 5, 12/13, 24, 1960.

YBG: January 1, February 25, March 3, October 21, 1960; July 18, 1963; April 14, November 17, 1964.

BGHOD: Mordechai Surkiss, July 10, 1975.

Press: *Haaretz*, January 13, 1960; November 20, 1964; *Maariv*, October 10, 24, 25, 30, 1960; November 2, 1960; *Davar*, November 17, 23, 1960; November 20, 1964.

Interviews: Hareven, Almog, Ben-Zur; Mordechai Surkiss, June 11, 1988; Givly to Eshed (Eshed's papers).

Bibliography: YOISH 3: 763; *Salomon*, pp. 221, 223, 244.

Chapter 22. Carmel's Confessions

Documents: SMCC: Records of all meetings.

MAPSC: December 13, 1964.

Letters: Givly to Carmel November 3, 1960; Avigdor Slutzky to Carmel (English) November 10, 1960; Hausner to Salomon, January 10, 1961.

Reports: Notes taken by Z. Margalit of reviews given by Attorney General Hausner and Minister of Justice Rosen, December 13, 1960; Major Shmuel Hollander's, of IDF's Military Police, Summation Report, December 26, 1960; Memorandum by Z. Margalit to Attorney General Hausner "Supplementary Investigations," January 10, 1961; Hausner's letter to Chief Inspector of Police, December 12, 1960; Margalit's Report to Minister of Justice containing Dalia Carmel's statements of December 15 and 18, 1960; Summation Report by Margalit, December 27, 1960; Police and Military Police reports in Eshed's papers.

YBG: February 19, 1964 (Hausner letter to Salomon, January 10, 1961).

Press: *Maariv*, December 16, 19, 20, 22, 23, 25, 1960.

Interviews: Carmel; Rachel Slutzky, January 28, 1992.

Chapter 23. Downhill

Documents: Eshkol's Office Appointment Calendar for 1961 (by kind permission of Mrs. Miriam Eshkol); Record of BG's meeting with *Haaretz* editorial board, February 13, 1961.

SMCC: Meetings of Decemner 5, 11, 13, 1960.

MAPSC: Secretariat, October 18, December 16, 31, 1960.

Letters: Givly to BG December 23, 1960; Eshkol to Shmuel Dayan (see Im Avot HaHityashvut); Eshkol's: to Carmel, February 26, 1961; (undated), April 21, May 24, June (undated), October 15, 25, November 4 (two letters), November 6, 1962; December 30, 1963; March 4, 1964; Carmel to Givly, February 17, 1965; Givly to Carmel, January 20, 1965; Salomon's: to Moshe Kashti, June 9, August 27, 1961; H. Ben-David to Hausner, November 15, 1961; Hausner to Ben-David, November 20, 1961; Yosef Kukia, of the Ministry of Justice, to Ben-David, November 30, 1961; Hausner to Salomon, January 10, 1961; Givly to Eshkol, November 22, 1964; Salomon's letter and memorandum to Eshkol, December 11, 1964; BG to Eshkol, December 27, 1960; Eshkol to BG December 28, 1960 (in *Igeret LaHaverim*, February 11, 1965, and in *Davar*, February 16, 1965); Moshe Dayan to BG September 4, 1964.

YBG: November 7, 1960.

Press: *Maariv*, November 4, December 7, 8, 9, 11, 13, 23, 26, 27, 28, 29, 1960; *Haaretz*, March 12, October 24, 1961; *Lamerhav*, December 27, 1960; *Davar*, February 16, 1965.

Interviews: Carmel; Efraim Ilin, January 16, 1991; Aharon Ben-Ezer, July 18, 19, 1990; Shalom Shasha of Israel's Land Administration, July 18, 1990; Yitzhak Navon, January 24, 1963 (Eshed's papers).

Bibliography: Salomon, pp. 226 ff.; Shmuel Dayan, *Im Avot HaHityashvut*, Hotsaat Masada, 1967, pp. 442, 446; DVK, pp. 92 ff.; *Salomon*, pp. 228–230, 235–236; Almogi, pp. 202 ff..

Chapter 24. The Banana Peel

Documents: Record of BG's meeting with *Haaretz* editorial board, February 13, 1961.

MAPSC: Secretariat, December 16, 31, 1960; January 12, 1961; Central Committee, January 11, February 4, 1961.

Letters: Givly's latters to Carmel: November 29, 30, 1964; Janury 20, 1965; Carmel's letters: to Givly (English), February 17, 1965; to Eshkol (English) March 26, 1967; Teddy Kollek to Carmel, September 10, 1963; Eshkol to Arieh Manor, March 8, November 3, 1962; Eshkol's letters to Carmel: February 12, March 7, undated (probably March 24), May 6, 11, 1963; Sharett to BG October 30, 1960 (see YOISH); Benyamin Eliav to Carmel, February 25, 1965.

YBG: October 22, November 2, 1964; May 31, 1965; October 17, 1966.

Press: *Davar,* December 30, 1960; December 8, 9, 1964; *Dvar Hashavua*h, August 1, 1969; *HaOlam HaZeh,* June 4, 1986; *Maariv* (SofShavuah) November 7, 1986.

Interviews: Zvi Zur; Yizhar Smilansky, March 18, 1992; Major General (Res.) Efraim Ben-Artzi, May 18, 1992; Asher Yadlin, September 13, 1991; Major General (Res.) Moshe Goren, January 11, 1991.

Bibliography: Asher Zidon, *Beth Hanivcharim,* Hotsaat Achiassaf, Jerusalem, 1964, p. 332; YOISH 3: 765

Index

Abdullah, King of Jordan, 183
Aharoni, Zvi, 275; Amiad Committee and, 185; Elad and, 128, 129, 131, 264
Ahituv, Elisheva, 265
Almog, Mordechai, 222, 275
—Cohen Committee on, 208, 221
—Dayan and, 93, 164
—Elad and: Ben-Zur and, 79, 80, 126–27, 206–7; Givly and, 126–27, 128, 132, 206–7; Hareven on, 221; Harkabi and, 165
Almogi, Yossef, 195, 198, 199, 218, 251
Alon, Yigal, 259, 275; Be'eri and, 19–20, 22, 23; Ganizi and, 21
Amiad Committee, xiii, 185
Amiad, Ariel, 185, 275
Amihai, Ittiel, 20
Amster, Jules, 36, 37, 38
Aran, Zalman: Dayan on, 255; education post and, 181; on Lavon, 143, 148, 159, 204, 246; Lavon resignation and, 151, 152; on Mapai veterans, 190; party tactics of, 187; prestige of, 182; putsch fears of, 176, 177; on secretariat meet-ings, 215; Sharett and, 135, 139, 141, 142, 146; "troika" and, 179
Argov, Nehemia, 162, 275–76; on Ben-Gurion, 35, 161; on electoral reform proposal, 173; Evron and, 68; on Lavon, 145–46; Shalmon and, 174; Sharett and, 157; on Tubiansky affair, 31–32, 35
Avidar, Yosef, 69, 276; Dayan and, 74, 92, 96; Givly on, 115; at July 31, 1954 meet-ing, 98; on Lavon-Givly consultations, 75; testimony of, 107
Avigur, Shaul, 276; Ben-Gurion and, 144–45, 148, 157, 266; I. Harel and, 140; on Lavon, 143, 144; Sharett and, 136, 141, 142
Avrahami, Levi, 21, 22
Avriel, Ehud, 276; I. Harel and, 139, 140, 171; at October 28, 1952 meeting, 170; Shalmon and, 174, 175–76, 178; Sharett and, 135
Ayalon, Zvi, 19
Azar, Shmuel, 276; arrest of, 89; execution of, 92, 131, 147; transmitter and, 130; unwarned, 88
Azazath, Suleiman, 82

—Cairo defendants on, 124
—confession of, 176, 185, 202
—debriefing of, 90, 131–32
—Egyptian intelligence and: Aharoni-Cohen investigation of, 128, 129, 131, 264; blame assigned to, 118; disinformation campaign of, 84; I. Harel and, 83, 184–85; radio transmitter and, 130
—German mission of, 163, 164–65, 184–85
—indiscretions of, 78–80
—interrogation of, 185, 192
—Olshan-Dori testimony of, *see under* Olshan-Dori Committee
—"On the episode of the teams," 90–91; Ben-Zur and, 118, 120; Givly on, 92, 114; on incendiary device, 93–94
—operational instructions to, 81–82, 207, 208, 243, 264
—professed ignorance of, 100
—reenlistment of, 77
—secret communications with, 85–86, 87–88
—trial of, 193, 194, 206, 261
Eliav, Benyamin, 266
Engel, Rolf (head of Egypt's missiles project), 129
Eshet, Shalom, 98, 99
Eshkol, Elisheva, 212
Eshkol, Levi, ix, 277–78; Ben-Gurion and (*see under* Ben-Gurion, David); Carmel and (*see under* Carmel, Dalia); Dayan and, 145, 151, 171; defense portfolio offer to, 140, 143; Givly and, 224–25, 262; inquiry commission proposal, 133, 134; Lavon and, 153, 154, 155, 242; party mediation by, 246; on Peres, 152; principles of, 254; putsch warning to, 176; Rosen and, 216–17, 219, 223, 225; Sapir and, 187; at Sdeh Boker, 148; Sharett and, 135, 139, 141, 142, 146; Surkiss and Givly meet with, 224, 225
Eshkol, Miriam, 215, 248, 263
Evron, Efraim, 278; affidavits of, 99, 104–5, 112; Argov and, 68; Ben-David and, 192–93; Dayan and, 93, 96, 97, 136, 162; Elad and, 127; Eshkol and, 211, 213, 214, 216; on Givly- Lavon consul-

tation, 74; Histadrut and, 183; at July 15, 1955 meeting, 75, 115; on Lavon-Dayan-Peres "troika," 70; *Maariv* and, 195, 196; Navon and, 194; on October 28, 1952 meeting, 170; Sharett and, 68, 98, 105, 135, 136; testimony of, 98, 99, 103, 106, 107; threats against, 218

Fahmi, Ragib, 130
Fawzi, Captain, 130
Frank, Paul, *see* Elad, Avraham

Galili, Israel, 188, 259
Ganizi, Shmuel, 19, 20–21, 60
Gaulle, Charles de, 190
Gavison, Judge, 43
Giladi, David, 252
Givly, Benyamin, 1–6, 278
—appointments of: Israeli military attaché to Great Britain, 184, 213; colonel, 57; Golani infantry OC, 183; Kaiser-Fraser, 248; MI acting head, 57; MI branch director, 58; MI deputy, 56; MI director, 64; MI division chief, 21; Northern Command chief of staff, 163, 166; SHAI Jerusalem commander, 5–6; SHAI South district officer, 3–4
—Egyptian mishap and, 168; Ben-Gurion and (*see under* Ben-Gurion, David); Ben-Zur and (*see* Ben-Zur, Mordechai); Cohen Committee and (*see under* Cohen Committee); Elad and (*see* Elad, Avraham); inquiry demand of, 221–32, 247, 248, 250, 259; July 19, 1954 letter of (*see* Carmel, Dalia: letter forgery of); June 6, 1954 memorandum of, 112; Lavon and (*see under* Lavon, Pinhas); ministerial discussion of, 156; Ne'eman and, 164; November 1, 1954 letter of, 94–95, 96, 97; "Operations in Egypt, July 1954," 87–88, 123; proposed state inquiry and, 259–60; testimony of (*see under* Olshan-Dori Committee)
—IDF personnel changes and, 67–68, 69
—policy proposals of, 73–74
—travels of, 63, 93, 94
—Tubiansky affair and, viii, ix, x, 30; Ayalon and, 19; Be'eri complicity with,